✓

IMPORTANT - PLEASE READ CAREFULLY BEFORE OPENING
By opening the sealed disk package, you indicate your acceptance of the following Wall Data License Agreement:
Wall Data Incorporated
Software License Agreement

1. Grant. Subject to the restrictions and other terms set forth in this Agreement Wall Data Incorporated ("Wall Data") grants you ("You"), the end user, a non-exclusive license to do the following with the enclosed software program (the "Software"): (a) use the Software solely for the non-commercial education and evaluation purposes at an accredited college or university in the United States or Canada; and (b) reproduce and distribute copies of the Software to faculty members and students of accredited colleges and universities in the United States or Canada who agree to comply with the terms of this Agreement. You shall ensure that any Software copy You make includes the notices of copyright, patent, trademark or other proprietary present on or in the original.

2. Restrictions. You shall not: (a) use the Software for any commercial purpose or for any purpose other than education and evaluation purposes at an accredited college or university in the United States or Canada; (b) transfer the Software to another person or entity other than a faculty member or student described in Section 1(b) above; (c) reverse engineer, disassemble, decompile, or otherwise attempt to discover the source code of the Software; (d) modify, translate or create derivative works based on the Software; (e) remove or obscure any notice of copyright, patent, trademark or other proprietary rights; or (f) transfer the Software to any person or entity in violation of the applicable United States export control laws. Wall Data may terminate your license if You violate any provisions of this Agreement. Upon termination of the License, You must cease use, reproduction and distribution of the Software and either destroy or return the Software and related items to Wall Data.

3. Proprietary Rights. Wall Data or its suppliers own the Software an all associated patent, copyright, trade secrets, trademarks and other proprietary rights in the Software. No title to or ownership of the Software or any associated proprietary rights are transferred to You by this Agreement.

4. Disclaimer. The Software is provided by Wall Data, and accepted by You and any person receiving a copy of the Software from You "AS IS" and "WITH ALL FAULTS, DEFECTS AND ERRORS." Accordingly, WALL DATA WILL NOT HAVE ANY OBLIGATION OR BE LIABLE FOR ANY: (A) FAILURE, ERROR, OMISSION, DEFICIENCY OR DEFECT IN ANY SOFTWARE OR OTHER ITEM FURNISHED UNDER THIS AGREEMENT; (B) IMPLIED WARRANTY OR CONDITION OF MERCHANTABILITY OR FITNESS FOR A PARTICULAR PURPOSE; OR (C) CLAIM IN TORT, WHETHER OR NOT ARISING IN WHOLE OR IN PART FROM WALL DATA'S FAULT, NEGLIGENCE, STRICT LIABILITY, OR PRODUCT LIABILITY (WHETHER ACTIVE, PASSIVE OR IMPUTED). Some states do not allow the exclusion or limitation of incidental or consequential damages, so the above limitation may not apply to you.

5. LIMITATION OF DAMAGES. IN NO EVENT WILL WALL DATA HAVE ANY OBLIGATION OR LIABILITY (WHETHER IN CONTRACT, WARRANTY, TORT (INCLUDING NEGLIGENCE, WHETHER ACTIVE, PASSIVE OR IMPUTED)) OR OTHERWISE FOR COVER OR ANY DAMAGES SUSTAINED BY YOU OR ANY OTHER PERSON ARISING FROM OR ATTRIBUTABLE TO USE OR ATTEMPTS TO USE THE SOFTWARE, INCLUDING WITHOUT LIMITATION ANY DIRECT, INDIRECT, INCIDENTAL, SPECIAL OR CONSEQUENTIAL DAMAGES (INCLUDING LOSS OF DATA, SAVINGS, OR PROFITS), EVEN IF WALL DATA HAS BEEN ADVISED OF THE POSSIBLY OF SUCH DAMAGES.

6. Limitation of Liability. Wall Data's liability (whether in tort, negligence, contract, warranty, product liability or otherwise; and notwithstanding any fault, negligence, strict liability, or product liability of Wall Data) with regard to the Software will not exceed $50.

7. U.S. Government Restricted Rights. If your acquisition and use of Software is subject to the procurement regulations of the U.S. Government, the Software and documentation are provided with RESTRICTED RIGHTS. Use, duplication or disclosure by You and the U.S. Government are subject to the restrictions set forth in subdivision (c)(1)(II) of the Rights in Technical Data and Computer Software clause at 48 CFR 252.227–7013, or in subdivisions (c)(1) and (2) of the Commercial Computer Software-Restricted Rights clause at 48 CFR 52.227–19, as applicable. The contractor/manufacturer is Wall Data Incorporated, 11332 N.E. 122nd Way, Kirkland, Washington 98034–6931.

8. Miscellaneous. This Agreement constitutes the entire agreement between You and Wall Data with regard to the Software. Statements or representations made by agents, employees, distributor and dealers of Wall Data which add to or vary this Agreement or the related documentation do not constitute warranties by Wall Data, do not bind Wall Data, and should not be relied upon. This Agreement will be fully binding upon, inure to the benefit of, and be enforceable by the parties and their respective successors and assigns. This Agreement may only be modified in a written amendment signed by an authorized Wall Data officer. If any provision of the Agreement is unenforceable, all others will remain in effect. This Agreement shall be governed by the laws of the State of Washington, without reference to its choice of law rules. The provision of the 1980 U.N. Convention of Contracts for the International Sale of Goods are waived and shall not apply. YOU ACKNOWLEDGE THAT YOU HAVE READ, UNDERSTOOD AND AGREE TO BE BOUND BY ALL OF THE PROVISIONS OF THIS AGREEMENT. If you have any questions concerning this Agreement, please contact in writing: Wall Data Incorporated, 11332 N.E. 122nd Way, Kirkland, Washington 98034–6931.

Localization Strategies for Global E-Business

The acceleration of globalization and the growth of emerging economies present significant opportunities for business expansion. One of the quickest ways to achieve effective international expansion is by leveraging the web, which allows for the technological connectivity of global markets and opportunities to compete on a global basis. To systematically engage and thrive in this networked global economy, professionals and students need a new skill set – one that can help them develop, manage, assess, and optimize efforts to successfully launch websites for tapping global markets. This book provides a comprehensive, non-technical guide to leveraging website localization strategies for global e-commerce success. It contains a wealth of information and advice, including strategic insights into how international business needs to evolve and adapt in light of the rapid proliferation of the "global internet economy." It also features step-by-step guidelines to developing, managing, and optimizing international multilingual websites and insights into cutting-edge web localization strategies.

NITISH SINGH is Associate Professor of International Business at the Boeing Institute of International Business at Saint Louis University, Missouri, where he is also Program Leader for the Executive Certificate in Web Globalization Management (www .globalizationexecutive.com). He has researched and taught extensively in the area of global e-commerce and has published more than thirty-five papers in peer-reviewed academic journals. He is co-author of *The Culturally Customized Web Site* (2005) and *Proliferation of the Internet Economy* (2009).

Localization Strategies for Global E-Business

Nitish Singh

CAMBRIDGE
UNIVERSITY PRESS

CAMBRIDGE UNIVERSITY PRESS
Cambridge, New York, Melbourne, Madrid, Cape Town,
Singapore, São Paulo, Delhi, Tokyo, Mexico City

Cambridge University Press
The Edinburgh Building, Cambridge CB2 8RU, UK

Published in the United States of America by Cambridge University Press, New York

www.cambridge.org
Information on this title: www.cambridge.org/9781107008892

First published 2012

Printed in the United Kingdom at the University Press, Cambridge

A catalogue record for this publication is available from the British Library

Library of Congress Cataloguing in Publication data
Singh, Nitish.
  Localization strategies for global e-business / Nitish Singh.
     p.   cm.
  Includes bibliographical references and index.
  ISBN 978-1-107-00889-2
  1. Electronic commerce.   2. International trade.   3. Business networks.
  4. Internet marketing.   I. Title.
  HF5548.32.S563   2012
  658.8'72–dc23
  2011040513

ISBN 978-1-107-00889-2 Hardback

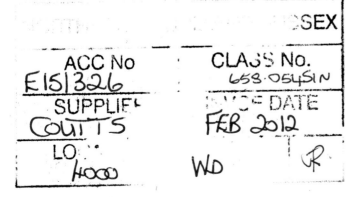

CONTENTS

FIGURES

TABLES

PREFACE

The acceleration of globalization and the growth of emerging economies present significant opportunities for global business expansion. One of the quickest and most effective ways to tap into global markets is to leverage the web. However, there is a dearth of books, courses, and training programs that can help companies understand the dynamics of conducting global e-business. Well-trained web globalization professionals are difficult to find, reflecting, at least in part, the lack of academic offerings and specialized training in this area.

In the broadest sense, web globalization requires an interdisciplinary potpourri of skills from areas such as international business and marketing, advertising, project management, IT and e-commerce, language technology, linguistics, intercultural communications, technical writing, and even human resource management. Thus it has been difficult for universities, organizations, and professional bodies to provide the kind of comprehensive web globalization training required for tapping global e-commerce markets.

The sheer lack of structured information on this topic was one of my primary motivations to undertake the daunting task of creating a text that can provide a comprehensive overview of the strategies, processes, and resources necessary to create an effective global online presence. I have leveraged my ten years of research, training, and consulting experience in this area to develop content for this book. During these years I have completed research and consulting projects, spanning several disciplines, to acquire a better understanding of various global e-commerce issues, such as knowing about international online business strategies, developing culturally customized websites, assessing web localization efforts, conducting global website usability testing, segmenting global online users, and developing global e-commerce profiles for various countries. This research and consulting experience, along with my experience in developing several academic courses in the field of web localization, has enabled me to offer readers a broad, interdisciplinary, and unique perspective for enabling global e-business. In addition, the help from industry experts in terms of examples, cases, and other materials – for which I am extraordinarily grateful – has allowed me to enrich the book with practical insights and other points of view.

My goal is to provide the reader with a truly comprehensive non-technical guide to web localization strategies for tapping global e-commerce markets. I hope such a non-technical treatment of this subject matter will enable a variety of professionals, students, and academics to understand the dynamics of this complex process. It is my sincere wish that knowledge of web localization issues should not remain restricted to specialized IT and translation professionals but, instead, be widely dispersed among various functional areas throughout organizations undertaking this important task. I also hope that more universities can train students with the cutting-edge skills necessary to thrive in our global and networked economy.

While this book is not a panacea for all global e-business challenges and the limited academic offerings in this area, it is a step toward a better understanding of how to develop, localize, manage, assess, and optimize international multilingual websites. The book presents a blend of strategies, models, checklists, tools, research insights, examples, and cases to help readers comprehend the complexities of global e-commerce and learn practical ways to facilitate the conduct of global e-commerce. Readers will gain insights into how to analyze the global e-business environment, manage global e-commerce expansion efforts, and implement the necessary infrastructure for an effective international and multilingual website presence. The book also provides an overview of various tools and emerging technologies to facilitate the conduct of global e-business.

The book leverages information from several sources, such as articles, academic databases, industry insights/reports, expert viewpoints, company websites, and other web resources. Descriptions of the content accessed from the web are based on the information available at the time of the access (2009 to 2011). I have also provided an extensive resource section that may prove helpful for additional research on various topics related to localization and global e-business. Examples mentioned in the book are based on my research and do not represent any conscious favoritism, bias, or endorsement from me to promote one specific tool or company over any other.

In conclusion, I would like to acknowledge the support and encouragement I have received from the John Cook School of Business, Saint Louis University, and dean Dr. Ellen Harshman. I would like to thank Cambridge University Press, and specifically Paula Parish and Philip Good, for assisting me with the publication process. My special thanks go to Megan Brenn-White and the Brenn-White Group for copy-editing, and to Kyle Coble and Yung-Hwal Park for research assistance. I would also like to acknowledge the help and advice received from various experts – Adam Asnes, Angelika Zerfaß, Anna Schlegel, Ariane Duddey, Carsten Kneip, Chris Raulf, Craig Van Slyke, Daniel Nackovski, David Lunatto, Donna Parish, Eric Neigher, Francis Tsang, Gary Muddyman, Kate Edwards, Kathleen Bostick, Kirti Vashee, Jennifer Hofer, Martin Guttinger, Martin Spethman, Michael Kriz, Michele Carlson, Olivier Libouban, Pierre Cadieux, Richard Sikes, Riteesh Singh, Seung Kim, Stephen Miller, Ulrich Henes, Willem Stoeller, Zia Wigder – and my friends.

ILLUSTRATION CREDITS AND ACKNOWLEDGEMENTS

1 Global e-commerce opportunities and challenges

Chapter objectives

- Present various opportunities and challenges posted by global e-commerce.
- Outline how companies can achieve enhanced economic performance and competitive advantage through global e-business expansion.
- Discuss several challenges facing global e-business as they relate to socio-cultural, geopolitical, legal, and economic issues.
- Present suggestions to enable companies to handle e-business challenges relating to the international e-business environment.

Global e-commerce opportunities

Global e-commerce is about leveraging electronic networks to tap global markets, and it includes the sum of all transactions taking place in the worldwide electronic market space. Transactions between global buyers and sellers can take the form of business-to-business (B2B), business-to-consumer (B2C), consumer-to-consumer (C2C), business-to-government (B2G), and other hybrid forms of transactions.

The market opportunity presented by global e-commerce is evident from projections that B2C sales will reach almost $1 trillion by 2012.[1] The global B2B market is expected to be even greater than the B2C market, and B2B revenues are expected to surpass B2C revenues many times over in the coming years. Companies now can reach almost 1.9 billion online consumers worldwide via their global web presence. The online user population is expected to increase by almost 42 percent by 2014 (Wigder *et al.*, 2010). Today, major e-commerce markets include the United States, the European Union, Japan, and China. Furthermore, there are signs that e-commerce activity and online population growth patterns now are shifting in favor of emerging economies such as China, India, Brazil, and others.

---

[1] http://ecommercearticles.co.uk/eCommerceFutureProjections.aspx.

Zazzle Inc. International expansion and localization

Zazzle has achieved international growth by offering unique customized products and leveraging local content creator communities to meet localized consumer needs. It uses the concept of micro-retailing to allow content owners to sell to Zazzle's consumer base without worrying about huge set-up costs or inventory issues – and they even get to name their own royalty amounts. Zazzle currently has fifteen international sites, in Australia, Austria, Belgium, Brazil, Canada, France, Germany, Japan, the Netherlands, New Zealand, Portugal, Spain, Sweden, Switzerland, and United Kingdom, in addition to the home site in the United States. For its international sites, it offers content translation and localization (e.g., local currency, local language customer support, local domain names). Each country site features sellers, content, and designs that are fairly idiosyncratic to each country market. The site provides a creative outlet for international users to create, design, and customize unique products to meet their individual tastes and preferences.

Source: Zazzle.com (accessed October, 2010).

If a US online business has facilities to service only domestic online users, then it could be missing out on the almost 85 percent of online users that reside outside the United States. Top companies that are leveraging the web for global e-commerce now generate the majority of their revenues from international markets (see Table 1.1). For example, Google boasts over 120 international sites, and its international markets accounted for 53 percent of total revenues in 2009.[2] Similarly, eBay's approximately twenty-nine international sites contributed almost 54 percent of its total revenues in the same year.[3] Estée Lauder hopes to generate more than 60 percent of its sales from outside the United States, and is already leveraging and launching international sites to achieve double-digit growth (Stambor, 2010). Amazon generated almost $11.68 billion in international sales online (2009) and is solidifying its position in various emerging markets such as China, which is supposed to generate about $1 billion in annual sales by 2011 (Brohan, 2010). Wal-Mart, which has been a late bloomer in global e-commerce, now has overhauled its online efforts to better leverage its multichannel capabilities in order to achieve efficiencies through global online expansion. Wal-Mart has created a new organization called Global.com to pursue global e-commerce opportunities and to drive sales and growth. A Forrester survey of 250 website decision makers in 2009 finds that almost two-thirds of them leverage their sites to tap global markets and will continue to invest in online global expansion (Wigder *et al.*, 2009).

Companies have a strategic choice either to leverage their investments in products/ services and online infrastructure within the confines of their domestic online markets or to gain economies of scale and scope through international online expansion.

---

[2] Datamonitor database.
[3] Ibid.

Table 1.1 Global e-commerce potential

Company	International sites, 2010	International revenues as a percentage of total revenues, 2009–10
Google	Google site search is available in several languages via more than 120 international sites	53 percent
Microsoft	Microsoft also boasts more than 120 international sites, available in multiple languages	42 percent
Amazon	In contrast, Amazon has only 7 international sites, for Austria, Canada, China, France, Germany, Japan, and the United Kingdom	47.7 percent
eBay	eBay has about 29 international sites	54 percent
Dell	Dell boasts more than 120 sites	48.3 percent
Cisco	Cisco has about 85 international sites	47 percent approx.

Source: Datamonitor database.

Economies of scale

Economies of scale can be achieved when increased production leads to a reduction in average per-unit cost, thus leading to cost advantages. Companies such as Amazon, eBay, and Expedia have gained economies of scale by leveraging their e-commerce capabilities and products to reach global markets. However, it must be understood that gaining economies of scale through online international expansion is a unique capability, and one that not all companies possess.

Companies that have achieved significant economies of scale using global online expansion have done so by uniquely leveraging their global web user interfaces, core capabilities, and modular product design to provide locale-specific solutions for international users. One such example is that of the largest online travel company, Expedia, Inc., which has more than ninety localized websites under various brands. Expedia gains economies of scale by globally leveraging its capabilities – such as a global booking engine, the global selection of properties and airlines, an online search facility, global marketing, and a global user interface – for creating multiple localized website offerings. By strategically leveraging core resources, the cost of launching every additional international website may go down as a company expands its online international operations.

Economies of scale and scope

Economies of scale can be achieved when increased production leads to a reduction in average per-unit cost, thus leading to cost advantages.

Economies of scope can be achieved by leveraging synergies from core resources and capabilities across multiple products and services.

Economies of scope

Economies of scope can be achieved by leveraging synergies from core resources and capabilities across multiple products and services. Thus economies of scope help companies to achieve product diversification by allowing them to leverage their core assets across multiple products or services. Economies of scope can help companies achieve efficiency gains and cost advantages. Amazon has been successful in achieving economies of scope by leveraging its core e-commerce capabilities to diversify into various product segments, such as toys, clothing, music, software, shoes, etc. Zazzle, which specializes in a variety of custom consumer products, is now leveraging content from its international users to aid its international expansion. For example, Zazzle has sites

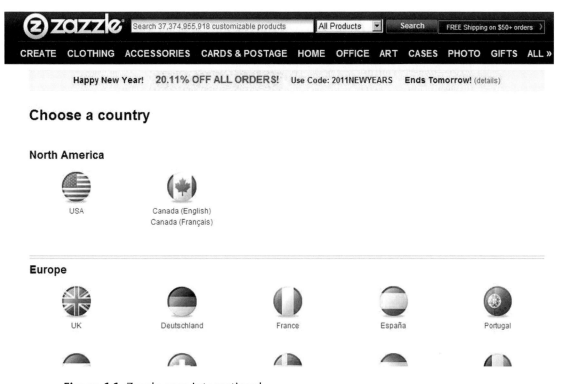

Figure 1.1 Zazzle.com International

in Australia, Brazil, Canada, France, Germany, Japan, Portugal, Spain, and the United Kingdom, wherein users from these countries create and sell unique localized products for these markets (see Figure 1.1).

Global commercial collaborative alliances

Other opportunities that global e-commerce provides include the ability to leverage virtual networks of global commercial collaborative alliances and to use the power of these global market forces to develop, manufacture, distribute, and support product/ service offerings. For example, Yahoo!, in a quest to integrate its offerings from the web with the mobile interface, has recently formed an alliance with Nokia. In this alliance, Nokia will be the sole global provider of Yahoo! maps and navigation services, and Yahoo! will be the exclusive provider of Nokia's Ovi mail and chat services.[4] Thus Nokia and Yahoo! have both been able to gain access to each other's complementary assets in order to enhance their own customer offerings. Luxembourg-based Skype, which provides free video and voice calls over the internet, is forming an alliance with

[4] http://news.thewherebusiness.com/content/nokia-and-yahoo-announce-global-alliance.

Facebook. This international alliance will allow each of these companies to provide complementary services to each other's half a billion users. Such synergistic alliances provide companies with access to complementary assets, such as technologies, content, user base, products, and services.

Electronic brokerage effect

Companies now are leveraging the web to reach not only their end consumers, which obviously represent a much larger market than their domestic audiences alone, but also their suppliers. B2B online marketplaces such as Ariba are creating an almost perfect market for finding suppliers around the world. Emerging forms of companies connecting various buyers and sellers are creating an electronic brokerage effect, increasing the number of alternatives or choices, and, in the process, helping buyers select the best quality at the best price. The Ariba network now provides firms with access to almost 300,000 suppliers from around the world, and its online platform supports cloud computing, e-procurement, and e-invoicing. eBay uses a similar concept to connect global buyers and sellers to each other on the web. In fact, eBay is exploring how to integrate its various international sites so that all its international users can browse products across countries, translate the content, and pay in their local currencies. Some of the direct effects of leveraging global network alliances and online marketplaces include the lowering of coordination costs, an enhancement of allocative efficiencies, access to complementary assets, the sharing of information and knowledge resources, and the development of cooperative norms. These are just some benefits by which global e-commerce can help companies scan the globe to acquire unique capabilities so as to enhance their customer offerings and gain competitive advantage.

Access to complementary assets: case of Visa and CyberSource

Visa Inc.'s acquisition of CyberSource in 2010 will enhance Visa's online payment management capabilities by giving it access to complementary assets provided by CyberSource, such as global payment processing, fraud management, payment security management and other web services. CyberSource will be able to achieve greater global expansion using Visa's vast network of institutional relationships and global web presence.

Source: http://corporate.visa.com/media-center/press-releases/press1010.jsp.

Global e-commerce challenges

An Internet Retailer survey of US companies found that almost three-fourths of them accept orders from international customers, but that few have succeeded in creating localized international websites (Siwicki, 2010). The same survey found that only

17 percent of the merchants surveyed have fully functioning international e-commerce sites. Major online challenges that companies face in terms of selling their products globally are issues related to international e-commerce capabilities such as managing multiple languages, the availability of local currency and transactional ability, local language customer support, shipping methods, documentation, legal issues, technical issues, and other issues related to localizing and optimizing international sites.

Website localization

The process of adapting websites in accordance with linguistic, cultural, technical, functional, legal, and other locale-specific requirements of the target market.

Companies need to create localized international sites so as to effectively communicate with and sell to an international online audience. Website localization is the process of adapting websites in accordance with the linguistic, cultural, technical, functional, legal, and other locale-specific requirements of the target market. Various studies show that consumers prefer localized sites over standardized websites, and tend to stay and interact longer with localized sites (Singh and Pereira, 2005). Online users also experience better ease of use and content usefulness when

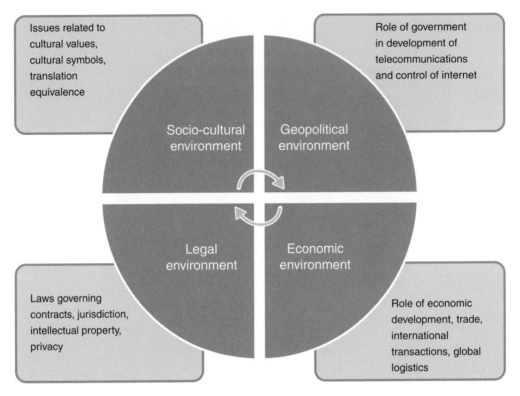

Figure 1.2 International e-environment

browsing web pages that are localized to their cultures. Studies documenting online preferences from various countries now show that a higher degree of localization, in the form of cultural customization, leads to better attitudes toward the site and higher purchase intention (Singh *et al.*, 2006; Baack and Singh, 2007). Web users from different countries prefer different website characteristics that meet their distinct needs in terms of navigation, security, product information, customer service, shopping tools, and other features (Fink and Laupase, 2000). A survey of multinational executives also found that 71 percent of these executives consider the localization of websites a strategic priority for successful international expansion (Petro *et al.*, 2007). The adaptation of web content to local market expectations is particularly important in view of the fact that global e-commerce provides international marketers with an exceptional channel to reach their potential customers worldwide. To be able to tap into these international markets, web marketers need to specifically adapt their content to the international e-environment. At a broad level, the international e-environment comprises the socio-cultural environment, the geopolitical environment, the legal environment, and the economic environment (see Figure 1.2). I discuss these four pillars of the international e-environment in greater depth in the following sections.

Socio-cultural environment

The socio-cultural environment plays an important role in web communications, as websites from different countries are a reflection of the culture and communication style prevalent in that country or locale (Singh and Pereira, 2005). Studies have shown that the web is not a culturally neutral medium; instead, websites from different countries are impregnated with the cultural markers of that country's culture.

There is now a vast body of research showing how important culture is in determining how we acquire, process, and interpret information. Culture prescribes broad guidelines for acceptable ways of behaving and acting in particular situations; it is also public in nature, as meaning is stored and transmitted through such cultural symbols of society as language, ritual, and custom (Geertz, 1973; Feather, 1995). From a consumer perspective, culture is a powerful force that shapes our motivations, lifestyles, and product choices (Tse, Belk, and Zhou, 1989). The most public aspect of any culture is its unique language. Linguistic theory offers various views on the effect of language on thought, and thus perception. A widely discussed view in this area is that of Edward Sapir and his student, Benjamin Lee Whorf. A commonly quoted passage representing this view is the following (Sapir, 1958 [1929]: 67):

> Human beings do not live in the objective world alone, nor alone in the world of social activity as ordinarily understood, but are very much at the mercy of the

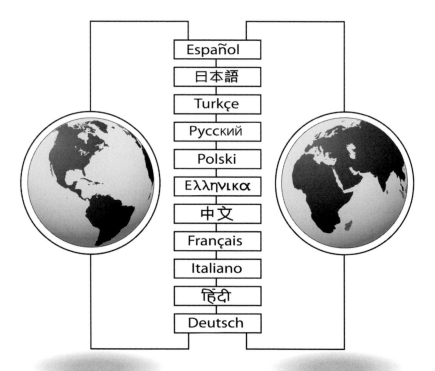

particular language which has become the medium of expression for their society. It is quite an illusion to imagine that one adjusts to reality essentially without the use of language … The fact of the matter is that the "real world" is to a large extent unconsciously built upon the language habits of the group. No two languages are ever sufficiently similar to be considered as representing the same social reality. The worlds in which different societies live are distinct worlds, not merely the same world with different labels attached.

Sapir's views are reflected in the Sapir–Whorf hypothesis, which proposes that language provides conceptual categories that influence how people encode and store knowledge. As such, to the extent that languages vary across the globe, individuals – and consumers – vary in their methods of coding and storing information.

There is substantial research on the effect of language on how people think; for example, it has been found that Chinese learn more quickly with visual inputs because of the pictographic nature of Chinese script (Turnage and McGinnies, 1973). Kaplan (1966) observes that English writing is correlated to linear thinking, Semitic writing facilitates parallel thinking, and much writing in Asia is marked by non-linear thinking. From a global e-commerce perspective, websites that are linguistically and culturally congruent to local consumer expectations decrease the cognitive effort to process information on the site, leading to easier navigation and favorable attitudes toward the websites (Luna, Peracchio, and de Juan, 2002). In the following section I explore the role of language on website design.

Impact of language and culture on website and content design

Spatial orientation

By "spatial orientation" we mean how the web content is structured. According to Barber and Badre (1998), spatial orientation has a direct effect on usability because it affects visual perception. For example, many of the Asian scripts (Japanese, Korean, and Chinese) are justified and read vertically. On the other hand, Arabic is read from right to left (in contrast to English, for example), so for Arabic readers a left-justified web page might not be visually appealing. When designing international sites it is important to consider how to spatially orient the content based on how the language is read. For example, Yahoo!'s international sites for various countries have content spatially oriented based on the language. In Yahoo! Japan and China, the content is more center-justified, while the Arabic language content for Yahoo! Middle East is all oriented from right to left.

Navigation

Variations in language readability (left to right [LTR], or right to left [RTL], or vertical) across cultures also impact how people navigate web pages. When designing

Figure 1.3 Yahoo! Maktoob right-to-left navigation

international sites, companies also need to consider the orientation of navigational elements, such as navigation bars, scroll bars, buttons, links, breadcrumb trails,[5] tabs, and other navigational aids. Figure 1.3 displays a screenshot of Yahoo! Maktoob (Yahoo! Middle East), in which the scroll bar and navigation bar are on the left, the navigation buttons, links, and icons are structured with right-to-left orientation, and the search button on the top is on the left of the search box.

Translation equivalence

When translating websites, special attention must be paid to how various concepts, words, and sentences are translated from one language to another. Several machine translation (MT) tools on the web today are still too simplistic and are prone to numerous translation errors in the style of their grammar, vocabulary equivalence, idiomatic equivalence, and conceptual equivalence. Several companies eager to reach international online customers tend to use tools such as Google Translate to allow users to view pages in their local language. However, many times these machine translation

---

[5] The breadcrumb trail is a navigation aid that shows users the path they took to get to the current page. For example, a breadcrumb trail may look like: Home>Product>Support>Checkout>.

tools actually produce incorrect, and sometimes quite humorous, translations. New developments in translation technology are making translations better, but we almost always still need good human translators to ensure translation equivalence. In a later chapter I provide a more in-depth discussion of the new advancements in machine translation technology. It is advisable, when launching multilingual content on the web, to ensure that the content has achieved true translation equivalence. When visitors encounter translation errors, it signals to them that their language or country was an "afterthought" or less significant to the business that produced the website. Mistakes in translation equivalence can lead to some serious miscommunications, and even embarrassments.

Translation errors on websites

Fanny Pack (Amazon.co.uk)
The Disney Classic Mickey Mouse Fanny Pack being sold at Amazon's website for the United Kingdom. In the United Kingdom, the word "fanny" refers to female genitalia and is considered vulgar.

Waterpik (Ekulf.com)
Ekulf AB, a Swedish oral care company, sells an oral care product called "Waterpik" via its websites for Sweden, Denmark, and Norway. The words *pik* and *pikk* refer to male genitalia in Danish and Norwegian, respectively.

Cat Dress (Petoffice.co.jp)
Petoffice is a Japanese site for pets that sells various pet products including clothes for cats. Their English translations on their website have some unique grammar and wording choices. One example: "You need to dress a cat. And you will say to a cat together with a family. 'It has changed just for a moment'. ['it being very dear' or] You will pass pleasant one time" (*sic*) (www.petoffice.co.jp/catprin/english).

Country-specific symbols

Culture acquires historic durability when people try to preserve their most cherished and motivation-laden cultural understandings through the representation of their private matters in public form, which can include symbols, icons, codes, and colors (Strauss and Quinn, 1997). Country-specific symbols include anything that portrays a way of life or a piece of culture-specific knowledge. For example, the use of visual metaphors from religions – such as the cross, the crescent, or a star (see Figure 1.4) – as well as animal figures, taboo words, hand gestures, or aesthetic codes, may require detailed research in a specific country prior to their use on websites. In India, the swastika is extensively used as a religious symbol, seen as a sign of good luck and fertility. It is not uncommon to see the swastika on Indian product labels, brands, packaging, and

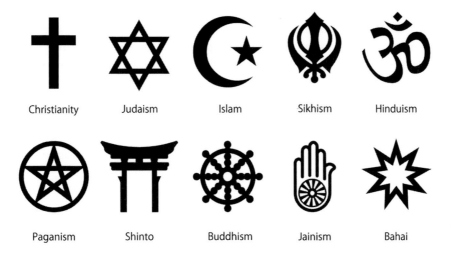

Figure 1.4 Religious symbols

websites, and even in advertisements. However, it was strange to see US retailer Zazzle .com having a line of "Swastika" T-shirts, mugs, hats, etc. on some of its international sites, although it does seem that the swastika symbols are based on Hindu or Buddhist context.[6] More in-depth discussion on the importance of values, colors, and symbols follows in subsequent chapters.

Geopolitical environment

For as long as there has been commerce, governments have been active in controlling and shaping the business environment and protecting national industries. With the emergence of e-commerce, governments are facing many challenges in terms of the free flow of information, national security, content and communications technology, the digital divide, and media convergence. These issues include the impact of the internet on national sovereignty, more demands from businesses and consumers to interact internationally, and continued pressure to be competitive in the e-business environment. However, governments in several countries still have strong control over telecommunications infrastructure, laws governing international money transfers over the web, foreign exchange controls, the kind of information their citizens are allowed to see, and a plethora of other issues.

Governments have a direct impact on the internet through laws, jurisdictions, economic policy, technology/infrastructure, investment, etc. Here are some examples of how governments' influence impacts e-commerce.

[6] Zazzle websites were accessed for this information on October 7, 2010.

- Many Asian governments deregulated their telecommunications sectors in the 1990s, which led to a telecommunications industry boom, and allowed these countries to catch up, in terms of telecommunications infrastructure, with their Western counterparts (Umali, 2002). For example, Indian villages that never saw a telephone have leapfrogged to using cellphones.

- A number of countries are developing key public infrastructure to facilitate the national development of electronic commerce. Today, South Korea is one of the most broad-band-connected countries in the world. More recently, the Obama administration, as part of the Economic Recovery Act, is pushing for the expansion of high-speed internet availability across the United States.

- With enough will and resources, governments can track who goes where and does what on the internet. For example, the Chinese government has been in the news in its attempts to monitor its citizens' internet searches. Google, in response to government censoring and accessing of internet search activities, has stopped censoring its Chinese-language search engine Google.cn and is directing its mainland Chinese users to an uncensored site in Hong Kong (Discovery News, 2010).

- "E-government" refers to governments' use of the internet to make information and services available to businesses and citizens. The government of Singapore now conducts most government functions – such as taxes, permits, and fines – via the internet. Singapore and Canada are leading countries in terms of e-government, followed by the United States. Some of the activities done through e-government initiatives include: registering to vote, getting different licenses, getting certain permits, paying fines, filing taxes, etc.

- Governments around the world are seeing the internet as a target for generating new taxes. For example, in early 2010 the French were considering a proposal to tax Google and other online advertising networks in order to compensate the creators of music and other works who lose out to digital piracy (Sayer, 2010).

- Across Latin America, governments are implementing internet-related policies to close the digital divide (Hawkins and Hawkins, 2003). Examples include:
  - increasing internet access by reducing or setting prices or tariffs, including establishing special dialing plans for dial-up access;
  - setting up public internet access centers (also known as telecenters);
  - reforming education by incorporating the internet and computers in schools; and
  - promoting the use of information technology (IT) in businesses and developing the local technology or software industry.

Governments do not just impact the internet in isolation. The geopolitics of countries and economic areas such as the European Union and North American Free Trade Agreement (NAFTA) also are having an impact on how e-commerce is conducted. For example, physical goods supplied to customers in the European Union are already subject to value added tax (VAT), even when they are ordered over the internet. Regional disputes might also impact how e-commerce is done on the web. According to Edwards (2005), marketers need to be careful when assigning flags or countries on their sites. Two areas that are especially problematic are China/Taiwan (whether or not to depict Taiwan as a separate nation or as part of China) and India/Pakistan (how to show the disputed borders in the region of Kashmir). In both cases, it is necessary to be sensitive to the reactions of both governments, as well as to the reactions of individual consumers. Simple map labels such as "Persian Gulf" can be a serious issue in Arab states, which use "Arabian Gulf," as well as using the term "Sea of Japan" in Korea, where the only acceptable term is "East Sea" (Edwards, 2005).

e-Citizen Portal: Singapore's e-government initiative

The "e-Citizen Portal" was initiated by the Singapore government in 1999 to migrate all public services that can be suitably delivered to the internet. Singaporeans can now carry out a wide range of transactions with government agencies online. In fact, the government has now gone one step forward and made most of these e-services available via mobile interface, and citizens now can get customized messages and alerts for their bills, taxes, renewals, etc. on mobile devices such as cellphones. The e-government initiatives not only have made it convenient for citizens to interact with government services, but also have led to system-wide efficiency gains and carbon footprint reductions. For example, transaction fees for ETS (electronic road pricing) using a mobile service are $4; using the internet, $8; and over the counter, $10. As of 2008 about 85 percent of Singaporeans transacted with the government electronically, and 90 percent of them were satisfied or extremely satisfied with the services.

Sources: www.ida.gov.sg/Publications/20090717150535.aspx; www.igov.gov.sg/Singapore_egov/?indexar=1.

Legal environment

Even if the company has headquarters in only one country, many decisions and actions can place it under another country's jurisdiction. Examples include hosting data on overseas databases, sending e-mail between global offices, and collecting personal information about current and potential overseas customers. The legal environment presents even more challenges when conducting global e-business. Companies need to be sensitive to evolving regional and national laws relating to e-commerce and internet use. Since the internet is a relatively new domain for governments and jurisdictions, the laws are evolving, and companies ideally should either be conversant/trained in national and international law, or else hire a law firm to meet national and international law requirements. Most of the laws related to contracts, advertising, copyrights, trademarks, domain names, information dissemination, data privacy, etc. are nationally governed. Companies therefore need to check the local laws of each country before setting up a website. The following paragraphs describe the impact of evolving laws on e-commerce and the internet.

Transactions

Conducting overseas transactions electronically presents several challenges relating to the enforcement of contracts, foreign exchange requirements, import/export regulations, data privacy and security issues, and fraud prevention. According to Smedinghoff (2005: 3), based on US and international law, there are seven important issues to keep in mind when conducting traditional transactions in the electronic environment.

(1) Is the transaction authorized in electronic form? Does existing law allow the parties to conduct the transaction in electronic form, or does it present legal barriers that make its enforceability uncertain?

(2) Will the online process result in an enforceable contract? Does the online process for entering into a contract support the creation of a valid contract?

(3) Has all required information been disclosed?

(4) Are the transaction records accessible to all parties? Are copies of the electronic records comprising the transaction available to and capable of being downloaded and printed by all parties?

(5) Has a valid electronic signature been used? Have the signature formalities required for this transaction (where applicable) been satisfied with a legally valid form of electronic signature?

(6) Is the transaction trustworthy? Has appropriate information security been built into the process to ensure the authenticity and integrity of the communications?

(7) Have appropriate electronic records been retained? Will the electronic records of this transaction satisfy applicable legal record-keeping requirements?

Another critical element of online transaction processing is security for online credit card payments. With the growth of e-commerce, the payment card industry (PCI) has implemented new standard security practices for handling consumer credit information. Companies that handle credit card data are required to comply with government regulations for protecting that data. The PCI Data Security Standard (PCI DSS) is a multifaceted security standard outlining requirements for security management, policies, procedures, network architecture, software design, and other critical protective measures. The goal of the PCI DSS is to help organizations proactively protect customer account data (www.pcisecuritystandards.org).

Action plan for international transactions: Work with your company's legal counsel, purchasing/sales subject matter experts, and lawyers to ensure that online transactions are valid and secure.

Contracts

According to DePalma (2002), some of the best practices for developing contracts for international online markets include the following.

- Make sure you translate the entire contract or click-through agreement on the website into the local language using the help of local counsel. For example, German laws will not enforce any click-through agreements that are not in German.
- If you have not created the agreements and contracts for each country, then at least create a generic agreement or international contract and take advice from legal counsel.
- Note in the contract that any disputes that arise will be resolved based on the laws of your country.

Action plan for contracts: Review all contractual agreements with your company's legal counsel in both the home country and in each foreign country where you conduct business.

Jurisdiction

When transactions take place in cyberspace, the question becomes: who has jurisdiction over the transaction? Is it the courts at the consumer's end or the seller's end? Internationally, this becomes even more complex, with the laws of different countries coming into the picture. For example, French courts have asked both Yahoo! and eBay not to sell items related to Adolf Hitler or the Nazis to French users. Identifying French users, not only those from France but from all across the world, would be an elaborate exercise, so eBay actually has stopped selling Hitler/Nazi items on all its sites. In other words, here the French ruling has had an overarching international impact on what eBay sells.

If you conduct e-business and have local and international customers, you have to take the jurisdiction issue into account. Out-of-state and out-of-country lawsuits could prove very expensive. So how do you protect yourself? The concept of "minimum contact" is crucial here. If a court can establish that a company had minimum contact with the defendant in a specific locale or country, then the defendant can sue the company in the defendant's own locale. A minimum contact can be established if a business maintains offices, subsidiaries, representatives, employees, or even direct advertising in the locale/country (Baumer, Iyengar, and Moffie, 2003). According to Harrison and Langford (2007), the US Federal Court concluded that Canadian courts have jurisdiction over foreign defendants operating websites that are accessed by Canadians only if the defendant either (i) has real and ongoing contacts to Canada, independent of the plaintiff's cause of action, or (ii) has "purposefully" directed activities toward Canada. In the following paragraphs, based on Baumer, Iyengar, and Moffie (2003: 23–5), recommendations and suggestions are outlined to protect a company from out-of-state courts. (Please note that these suggestions are intended to be used as discussion points when meeting with a lawyer, and are not intended to be used without additional legal consultation.)

The terms of agreement on websites can include sentences such as the following.

- Users of, and visitors to, the website agree that by visiting the website they are enjoying the benefit.
- In exchange for benefits users derive from visiting the website, they agree that, in any legal dispute, the courts designated by the website have jurisdiction, and the law to be applied by those courts is also specified by the website.

Alternatively, the terms of service agreement could call for the use of arbitration and specify the substantive law to be used by the arbitrator. For example, Amazon's website clearly states under the heading "Disputes": "Any dispute relating in any way to your visit to Amazon.com or to products or services sold or distributed by Amazon or through Amazon.com in which the aggregate total claim for relief sought on behalf of one or more parties exceeds $7,500 shall be adjudicated in any state or federal court in King County, Washington, and you consent to exclusive jurisdiction and venue in such courts" (www.amazon.com).

Action plan for jurisdiction: Obtain legal guidance on contract and mediation law for each country where you conduct business, and clearly specify legal jurisdiction in all customer agreements.

Privacy laws

The field of privacy law deals with how consumer and website users' information is used, stored, and disseminated. Privacy laws vary from country to country, and marketers need to pay close attention to them. The federal Electronic Communications Privacy Act (ECPA) in the United States, for example, makes it unlawful under certain circumstances for someone to read or disclose the contents of an electronic communication (United States Code title 18, section 2511). This law applies to e-mail messages. The US Federal Trade Commission (FTC) urges commercial website operators to spell out their information collection practices in privacy policies posted on their websites. Most commercial websites now post policies about their information collection practices. Look for a privacy "seal of approval," such as TRUSTe (www.truste.com), on the first page of the website. TRUSTe participants agree to post their privacy policies and to submit to audits of their privacy practices in order to display the logo.

TRUSTe

TRUSTe is one of the most popular online trust seal providers. It also provides seals for international sites. Below are some of TRUSTe's services on its website www.truste.com.

- TRUSTe certifies the privacy practices of international businesses, enabling the conduct of business-to-business and business-to-consumer exchange online.
- TRUSTe's turnkey international solutions certify foreign-language privacy policies, as well as administering foreign-language dispute resolution. These services are supported in thirty-five languages.
- With the EU Safe Harbor Seal, companies can conduct overseas business in alignment with the safe harbor framework created by the US Department of Commerce and European parties to avoid trade disruptions resulting from international privacy laws. For example, Monster.com uses the EU Safe Harbor Seal.
- Japan Privacy Seal, TRUSTe: The seal, developed in partnership with – and administered by – the Japan Engineers Federation (JEF), extends TRUSTe's certification, oversight, and dispute resolution services to Japanese-language websites. It also provides cross-border privacy support in accordance with Asian Pacific Economic Cooperation guidance (www .truste-jp.org).

Action plan for privacy law: Research individual country privacy laws, consider using trust seals and services. Review your plans and decisions with your company's legal and risk management experts.

Intellectual property: copyright, domain, trademarks, patents

Intellectual property law includes copyrights, trademarks, service marks, patents, etc. Various companies explicitly mention their copyright and intellectual property policies on their websites. These policies can be generally found at the bottom of the home page and govern issues related to content/image use, dissemination, copying, permissions, phishing, and trademarks. A great deal of information related to online rights pertaining to intellectual property can be found at www.chillingeffects .org, which is a collaboration between law school clinics and the Electronic Frontier Foundation. One of the most common violations of such laws on the web is cybersquatting. "Cybersquatting refers to the bad faith registration of a domain name containing another person's brand or trademark in a domain name" (http://cybersquatting.com). Examples are names of famous people, brands, etc. Trademark and domain name laws deal with how a name or term is legally protected against unauthorized use by a third party.

Typosquatting, which is a variation of cybersquatting, deals with acquiring domain names that might be a variation of an existing domain or trademark so as to trick people to come to the variant site rather than the site they originally intended. It is called typosquatting because it uses a misspelling or typographical error to create variants of existing domains. McAfee's Internet Security Suite software warns users about any site that triggers its typosquatting criteria. The Anticybersquatting Consumer Protection Act (ACPA) is a law passed in the United States in response to the growing trend of cybersquatting. In October 2010 the Bharatiya Janata Party (BJP) – a major political party in India – accused the ruling Indian National Congress of floating a site under the domain www.bjp.com to direct users to the All India Congress Committee website (Sharma, 2010). The original site for the BJP is www.bjp.org, while for Congress it is www.congress.org.in.

Action plan for protecting intellectual property: Research your new domain names globally to ensure that you are not violating others' property. In the United States, you can also visit www.uspto.gov to check if the name infringes on existing trademarks. Another resource that can help you evaluate the intellectual property (IP) environment in various countries is the International Property Rights Index (IPRI), which is available at www.internationalpropertyrightsindex.org.

NO SPAM!

Spamming (sending large volumes of unsolicited e-mail) is a common activity on the web, but there are laws and penalties against it. According to the US FTC's CAN-SPAM Act of 2003 (Controlling the Assault of Non-Solicited Pornography and Marketing Act), unsolicited commercial e-mail messages must be labeled (though not by a standard method), and must include opt-out instructions and the sender's physical address. Also prohibited is the use of deceptive subject lines and false headers in such messages. The FTC was authorized (but not required) to establish a "do-not-email" registry. Similarly, several countries have their own version of spam laws in place.

Action plan for direct marketing via e-mail: If you plan to use e-mail as part of your marketing campaign(s), ensure that you are compliant with US and other anti-spam regulations (e.g., EU data protection directives). Establish business processes to check "do-not-email" registries before sending unsolicited e-mail to potential customers.

EU regulations

There are several EU rules and regulations that are different from those in the United States. EU privacy laws are much stricter than US privacy laws. The European Union also has more extensive tax laws, such as value added tax, and other jurisdiction issues. Examples of EU privacy directives include: the EU Directives on Distance Selling and Privacy, the EU E-Commerce Directive, the EU Data Protection Directive, and the EU Privacy Directive.

Action plan for EU compliance

Wijnholds and Little (2001) provide a precautionary checklist for US e-business marketing to the European Union.

- Choose web server hosting, warehousing, locations, and representatives carefully, and weigh the pros and cons of having these contacts and incur the "minimal contact."
- Choose countries with zero or low VAT rates if your products or services are liable to be taxed this way.
- Pay attention to your privacy policy and get the EU-law-compliant privacy seals.
- Clearly state the terms and conditions upon which business is trading, and place the contractual offer in a visible location on the website.
- Clearly state in your e-contracts on the website which country's courts and laws will be applicable in case of a legal dispute.
- Make the content of your website compliant with country rules.

Economic environment

In terms of the economic environment, companies need to understand various issues related to the economic development of any country and its tax structure, income distribution, growth rates, patterns of foreign direct investment (FDI), and trade barriers. Other economic factors to take into consideration include: inflation, purchasing power, market size, market potential, exchange rates, tariffs and customs, and demand and supply trends. It is important to analyze how such economic factors may impact e-business expansion, and how current economic trends are impacting e-commerce in a particular country. Factors specific to the e-business environment, such as internet penetration rates, telecommunication and logistics infrastructure, e-business-related taxes and duties, and the impact of regional economic agreements on trade and e-commerce, also should be considered. For example, VAT rates vary across EU countries and may have an impact on country-specific pricing.

International online customers need to see their own local currency on the website, as well as clear information about the availability and cost of shipping. Websites selling internationally need to take into account multiple currencies to facilitate international transactions, security and fraud protection for international customers, international shipments and returns, and customer service options in different languages.

Logistics

In order to sell and ship internationally, a company may need to work with freight forwarders, brokers, and integrated carriers with fully scalable solutions for managing import and export programs as well as trade agreements, regulatory controls, documentation needs, information on Harmonized System (HS) six-digit number codes assigned to internationally traded items, and customs and homeland security initiatives. For example, Management Dynamics provides Global Trade Management (GTM) solutions for importers, exporters, and logistics service providers (www.managementdynamics .com). Freight forwarders such as DHL, FedEx, etc. can help companies with product shipping. In the United States, the International Trade Administration (www.trade.gov) and Small Business Administration (www.sba.gov) have various resources to enable US companies to conduct international business.

Import/export resources

Following are some US-based resources on import restrictions, documentation, and tariffs.

- Shipping and customs documentation and other helpful import/export tips are available from the US Customs and Border Protection website: www.cbp.gov/xp/cgov/trade/ basic_trade.
- Incoterms (www.iccwbo.org/incoterms) has standards, rules, and reference guides for international trade. Example: Under the FOB (free on board) agreement, the buyer has more control after shipment occurs, but also assumes most of the post-shipment cost and risk.
- Harmonized Tariff Schedules (www.usitc.gov/tata/index.htm). These define how much extra you will have to pay in tariffs and fees to import certain goods.
- Denied Persons List (www.bis.doc.gov/dpl/default.shtm). This is a list of people who are prohibited from importing goods into the United States.

Another issue with regard to logistics is that of handling international customer returns. Various companies now offer comprehensive international shipment solutions that include covering all international documentation, calculating landed costs and taxes, information on import/export compliance, and even reverse logistics. Examples: Returninc.com specializes in return services, UPS offers international returns services in ninety-eight countries and territories, and FedEx's returns system facilitates international returns.

Payment methods

So as to facilitate international transactions, it is important to offer prices in local currencies and also to account for total landed costs and other taxes and duties that may apply. Fraud and security issues become even more important and complex internationally. Companies also need to offer a variety of payment methods to their international customers. Online payment methods that are internationally popular include: credit cards (e.g., Visa, MasterCard), bank transfers, cash on delivery, e-wallets (e.g., PayPal, WebMoney), direct debits, and prepaid cards (e.g., Ukash, Walliecard). Online payment methods tend to differ from country to country. For example, the direct debit method is popular in Germany and credit cards are popular in the United States, while in China money transfers are the preferred online payment method (Leggatt, 2010). Various companies can assist in terms of multicurrency conversions, international transactions and payments, and fraud protection. Some examples of full-service international transaction services include Global Collect, CyberSource, and FiftyOne.

FiftyOne, Inc.: multicurrency global transactions

FiftyOne is in a class of companies that offer third-party managed global e-commerce capabilities for businesses eager to carry out international transactions. The global e-commerce services that FiftyOne provides include automated multicurrency merchandising, international payment processing, fraud and risk management, landed cost calculation, logistics and customs clearance facilitation, and international returns management.

FiftyOne's global e-commerce solution seamlessly integrates with a merchant's existing website so that online shoppers never leave the merchant's site. This is a key differentiator for FiftyOne, enabling the retailer to retain complete control of its brand and the customer experience. As a first step, FiftyOne screens the online merchant's entire product catalog to assign codes that will help in future determination of what import/export/shipping restrictions or rules may apply.

Anthropologie, an Urban Outfitters' brand, uses FiftyOne's global e-commerce solution. By detecting a visitor's IP address, FiftyOne determines the country of origin for international shoppers at Anthropologie.com. Thus an Australian customer sees the Australian flag and an Australian welcome message on the home page of Anthropologie .com. Thereafter, only those products that are available for sale in Australia are shown, and the shopper can pay in Australian dollars (or in any of the forty-three currencies listed), and get the order shipped to any Australian address. The shopper does not have to worry about exchange rates, customs/duties, or hidden shipping costs. FiftyOne's order fulfillment and international logistics service ensures that the customer from Australia experiences the process no differently from buying at a local Australian online store. The benefit for Anthropologie is that it is able to sell globally without creating an internal infrastructure for international transactions and logistics. FiftyOne's US hub manages all global logistics issues for Anthropologie, such as landed cost calculations, customs clearance, end delivery, and international trade compliance.

Source: www.fiftyone.com.

Conclusion

The Economist Intelligence Unit (EIU) publishes annual rankings of the e-readiness of the world's sixty-nine largest economies. These rankings are insightful, because they evaluate the technological, economic, political, and social assets of these countries through an e-business lens. E-readiness is the "state of play" of a country's information and communications technology (ICT) infrastructure, and the ability of its consumers, businesses, and governments to use ICT to their benefit. The six main factors considered by the EIU in calculating the e-readiness ratings of a country are as follows.

(1) Connectivity and technology infrastructure. This factor measures the extent to which individuals in the country can access and afford mobile networks, the internet, broadband, personal computers (PCs), and wi-fi and other networks. The EIU gives this factor a weight of 20 percent in the overall e-readiness ranking of a nation.

(2) Business environment. The EIU calculates the overall business climate of a country on factors such as the strength of the economy, political stability, taxation, competition policy, the labor market, FDI, and openness to trade and investment. The EIU gives this factor a weight of 15 percent in the overall e-readiness ranking of a nation.

(3) Socio-cultural environment. When calculating this factor, the EIU takes into account the level of education, the level of internet literacy, the degree of entrepreneurship, the technical skills of the workforce, and the degree of innovation in the country. The EIU gives this factor a weight of 15 percent in the overall e-readiness ranking of a nation.

(4) Legal environment. The EIU takes into account factors such as the effectiveness of the legal framework in the country, laws covering the internet, the level of censorship, and the ease of registering a new business. The EIU gives this factor a weight of 10 percent in the overall e-readiness ranking of a nation.

(5) Government policy and vision. The EIU calculates this factor on the basis of how proactive the government is in terms of investing in ICT as a proportion of gross domestic product (GDP), the overall digital development strategy of the

government, e-government initiatives, and online procurement. The EIU gives this factor a weight of 15 percent in the overall e-readiness ranking.

(6) Consumer and business adoption. The EIU calculates this factor on the basis of variables such as consumer spending on ICT per capita, the level of e-business development in the country, the level of e-commerce in the country, and the availability of online public services for citizens and businesses. The EIU gives this factor a weight of 25 percent in the overall e-readiness ranking.

Updated e-readiness rankings can be found at the EIU site: globaltechforum.eiu.com.

Besides taking into consideration the geopolitical, socio-cultural, legal, and economic environments, companies also struggle with technological issues to facilitate the conduct of global e-business. There are several technical and functional issues that need to be considered when designing international websites and user interfaces. In later chapters I explore these technical challenges, so that technical and non-technical readers of this text alike can better understand the issues involved in designing and maintaining localized and multilingual international websites.

Chapter summary

- This chapter provides an overview of various opportunities and challenges facing global e-commerce.
- Global e-business expansion can help companies gain competitive advantage by leveraging economies of scale and scope.
- The global web also provides companies the ability to leverage virtual networks of global commercial collaborative alliances and to use the power of these global market forces to develop, manufacture, distribute, and support product/service offerings
- When designing international sites, companies need to consider socio-cultural factors such as spatial orientation, navigation, translation equivalence, and country-specific symbols.
- From a geocultural perspective, companies need to consider challenges in terms of the free flow of information, national security issues, the digital divide, the convergence of media, content, and communication technology, issues involving the internet and national sovereignty, and content that can be geopolitically sensitive.
- The legal environment impacts global e-business in such areas as jurisdiction, transactions, contracts, privacy, intellectual property, spamming, and other issues related to the conduct of e-business.
- When selling internationally, the economic environment presents two very tangible challenges, related to international logistics and international payments (e.g., multicurrency conversions, processing, management, and fraud protection).

REFERENCES

Baack, Daniel W., and Singh, Nitish 2007. "Culture and web communications," *Journal of Business Research* 60: 181–8.

Barber, Wendy, and Badre, Albert 1998. "Culturability: the merging of culture and usability," paper presented at the 4th conference on "Human factors and the web," Basking Ridge, NJ, June 5; available at zing.ncsl.nist.gov/hfweb/att4/proceedings/barber (accessed April 5, 2009).

Baumer, David L., Iyengar, Raghvan, and Moffie, Robert P. 2003. "Legal liabilities of web site operation and internet privacy issues," *Internal Auditing* 18: 22–46.

Brohan, Mark 2010. "Amazon expands in China," Internet Retailer, www.internetretailer.com.

DePalma, Donald A. 2002. *Business without Borders: A Strategic Guide to Global Marketing.* Global Vista Press.

Discovery News 2010. "Google stops censoring search results in China," March 22, http://news.discovery.com/tech/google-china-censorship.html.

Edwards, Tom 2005. "The geopolitics of content development," *MultiLingual* 16: 46–50.

Feather, N. 1995. "Values, valences, and choice," *Journal of Personality and Social Psychology* 68: 1135–51.

Fink, Dieter, and Laupase, Ricky 2000. "Perceptions of web site design characteristics: a Malaysian/Australian comparison," *Internet Research* 10: 44–55.

Geertz, Clifford 1973. *The Interpretation of Cultures.* Basic Books.

Harrison, Brett, and Langford, Matthew 2007. "Internet jurisdiction a 'minimum contact' sport for foreign defendants," *Cross Border Litigation Bulletin*, Spring; available at www.mcmillan.ca/Upload/Publication/InternetJurisdiction_0407.pdf.

Hawkins, E., and Hawkins, K. 2003. "Bridging Latin America's digital divide: government policies and internet access," *Journalism and Mass Communication Quarterly* 80: 646–65.

Kaplan, R. B. 1966. "Cultural thought and patterns in inter-cultural education," *Language Learning* 16: 1–20.

Leggatt, Helen 2010. "yStats: global preferred online payment methods revealed," BizReport, May 19, www.bizreport.com/2010/05/ystats-global-preferred-online-payment-methods-revealed.html.

Luna, David, Peracchio, Laura A., and de Juan, Maria D. 2002. "Cross-cultural and cognitive aspects of web site navigation," *Journal of the Academy of Marketing Science* 30: 397–410.

Petro, Bryan, Muddyman, Gary, Prichard, Jared, Schweigerdt, Katy, and Singh, Nitish 2007. "Strategic role of localization in MNE," paper presented at Applied Business Research conference, Honolulu, January 5.

Sapir, Edward 1958 [1929]. "The status of linguistics as a science," in Mandelbaum, David G. (ed.), *Culture, Language and Personality: Selected Essays.* University of California Press: 65–77.

Sayer, Peter 2010. "President Sarkozy adds his support to French Google tax plan," PCWorld, January 8, www.pcworld.com/article/186356/president_sarkozy_adds_his_support_to_french_google_tax_plan.html.

Sharma, Anil 2010. "BJP accuses Congress of '.com job', casts legal net," Daily News and Analysis, October 4, www.dnaindia.com.

Singh, Nitish, Fassott, Georg, Chao, Mike C. H., and Hoffmann, Jonas A. 2006. "Understanding international web site usage: a cross-national study of German, Brazilian, and Taiwanese online consumers," *International Marketing Review* 23: 83–97.

Singh, Nitish, and Pereira, Arun 2005. *The Culturally Customized Web Site: Customizing Web Sites for the Global Marketplace*. Elsevier Butterworth-Heinemann.

Siwicki, Bill 2010. "Internet Retailer survey: international e-commerce," Internet Retailer, March 31, www.internetretailer.com.

Smedinghoff, Thomas J. 2005. "Seven key legal requirements for creating enforceable electronic transactions," *Journal of Internet Law* 9: 3–11.

Stambor, Zak 2010. "Estée Lauder focuses on international e-commerce," Internet Retailer, September 1, www.internetretailer.com.

Strauss, Claudia, and Quinn, Naomi 1997. *A Cognitive Theory of Cultural Meaning*. Cambridge University Press.

Tse, D. K., Belk, R. W., and Zhou, N. 1989. "Becoming a consumer society: a longitudinal and cross-cultural content analysis of print ads from Hong Kong, the People's Republic of China, and Taiwan," *Journal of Consumer Research* 15: 457–72.

Turnage, T. W., and McGinnies, E. 1973. "A cross-cultural comparison of the effects of presentation mode and meaningfulness on short-term recall," *American Journal of Psychology* 86: 369–81.

Umali, Celia Lopez 2002. "Asian telecommunications: market deregulation and competition," *International Journal of Management and Decision Making* 3: 256–79.

Wigder, Zia Daniell, Evans, Patti Freeman, Walker, Brian K., Lovett, John, and McGowan, Brendan 2009. *Global Web Site Spending: Benchmarking Spending on International Offerings*. Forrester Research; available at www.forrester.com.

Wigder, Zia Daniell, Johnson, Carrie, Sehgal, Vikram, and McGowan, Brendan 2010. *Global Online Population Forecast, 2009 to 2014: An Overview of Global Adoption to Help Plan for International Initiatives*. Forrester Research; available at www.forrester.com.

Wijnholds, H., and Little, M. W. 2001. "Regulatory issues for global e-tailers: marketing implications," *Academy of Marketing Science Review* 9: 1–15.

2 International e-business expansion and market entry strategies

Chapter objectives

- Provide insights into how the web has lowered the barriers to market entry.
- Show the new forms of international companies emerging on the web.
- Introduce the importance of strategic factor markets for international e-business.
- Highlight internationalization challenges faced by both brick-and-mortar and online companies.
- Provide insights into internationalization approaches used by various forms of online companies.
- Describe various international market entry modes for enabling global e-business expansion.

The new multinationals

The emergence of the web has created a unique situation, in that a company launching its e-business is global from day one. Before the emergence of the web, international business was the prerogative of big business. Now a company has access to consumers from around the world as soon as it launches its website. Companies can therefore be "born global" when they leverage the web to tap into global markets.[1]

Nero AG: international expansion

Nero, a creator of liquid media technology, started as a small software company in Germany in 1995. It has achieved international expansion over the past sixteen years by leveraging its website (www.nero.com) in combination with a few international offices and international partners. The web has allowed this relatively small company to sell in several countries in South America, North America, Europe, Asia, the Middle East, Africa, and Oceania. It has web pages in more than twenty-eight languages and allows customers from various countries to price products in their local currencies. Nero is just one example of a company that has achieved international growth by leveraging the web.

Source: www.nero.com.

---

[1] The term "born global" is used by Knight and Cavusgil (1996) to explain small firms that within a short period start exporting their products globally.

Global reach is the biggest entry barrier that the web has surmounted for many companies, largely leveling the playing field for firms of all sizes. The unique characteristics of the web have also resulted in the lowering of traditional international market entry barriers associated with intermediaries, transportation costs, information asymmetry, physical infrastructure, bureaucratic hurdles, and transaction costs.

Elimination of intermediaries

The internet has led to companies being able to sell directly to consumers all over the world. Now companies no longer have to rely solely on distributer agreements or access to local distribution channel networks in order to gain market access. Various online retailers have made intermediaries obsolete and are now selling directly to consumers worldwide. For example, neither Amazon nor Dell uses direct intermediaries to achieve their sales; instead, they use their online presence and e-commerce capabilities.

Transportation costs

Issues related to logistics and distribution have traditionally posed a major entry barrier to international expansion. The web has helped ease this entry barrier by allowing the digitization of several kinds of products and services (music, books, films, and IT, financial, and media services). For example, movie rental stores such as Blockbuster are now becoming obsolete, as movies can be digitally delivered right onto consumers' TV screens. Technologies such as enterprise resource planning software have helped companies manage their supply chains more effectively through efficient routing, scheduling, and real-time inventory management and delivery. Moreover, the software as a service (SaaS) model, which started primarily as a means to deliver customer relationship management (CRM) solutions, has now been used to deliver various software applications over the web as needed by clients. Consumers no longer have to buy and install software on their personal computers; instead, they can subscribe to the software over the internet as a service.

Information asymmetry

Before the advent of the web, companies and consumers were separated by a large information gap. The web has made it possible to bridge this gap between the various stakeholders involved in the business environment. New forms of web-based organizations – such as infomediaries (or online information brokers), social media sites, and comparison search engines – are reducing information asymmetry. Infomediaries, such as online marketplaces (eCrater.com and eBay.com) and comparison shopping tools (PriceGrabber.com and Nextag.com), are allowing businesses and consumers to scan the market for the best offers and make informed choices. Online collaboration and information sharing via various community sites also facilitate the reduction of information asymmetry worldwide. Most importantly, the web provides a central platform for aggregating information from worldwide sources, making it easily and quickly accessible via its hyperlink structure.

Less reliance on physical infrastructure

Traditionally, most multinationals needed physical infrastructure for international marketing and distribution. The web has enabled the virtualization of various facets of this physical infrastructure. For example, companies do not need to have a physical office in each country if they can support the local business with a country-specific website. Even customer service and products/services can now be delivered online. Online banks, as one example, do not need physical infrastructure, and can pass these savings along to their customers. Online banks thus not only overcome a major barrier to international market entry but also are able to compete effectively with well-established banks. Companies are now also overcoming cost barriers by migrating several business functions – such as IT, data storage, and payroll – by using the scalable potential of cloud computing.[2]

Bureaucratic hurdles

The web has enabled companies to conduct international business without necessarily investing in country-specific labor, infrastructure, and other location-specific assets. This means that companies can circumvent some of the local laws and bureaucratic hurdles related to labor hiring, building permits, licenses, certain tax filings, environmental clearance, and the usage of water and other local resources. However, companies still have to deal with various regulations and requirements (taxation, consumer protection, intellectual property) relating to the conduct of business, as well as pertinent import and export requirements.

Lowering of transaction costs

Traditionally, impersonal relations, self-interest, profit maximization considerations, and opportunism have led to an increase in the transaction costs[3] of doing business. Multinationals tend to internalize markets to shield themselves from these costs, which has been one of the major barriers for firms when internationalizing. The

---

[2] "Cloud computing" refers to internet-based computing wherein resources/information/data/ knowledge are virtually hosted, shared, and accessed via a web browser or web-based applications. For example, instead of having to store software or data on a disk or on your computer, the software can be stored, accessed, and delivered via the internet.

[3] Transaction costs are costs related to conducting a market exchange, such as buying or selling.

internet has now changed the dynamics of traditional business. The internet is characterized by extensive connectedness, and firms leverage this network to acquire information and forge relationships to reduce threats arising out of impersonal relations and opportunism.[4] The web makes it possible for people to connect with each other easily and forge relationships globally. The links or ties, and the strength of these ties between interconnected firms on the web, lead to the development of relationship-specific investments[5] based on trust, which become critical to the performance of web-based firms. Finally, the interconnectedness on the internet also encourages frequent interactions, further leading to the development of relationship-specific investments. Such frequent interactions, characterized by intermediate-level asset specificity, lead to the development of two-way ties and the emergence of norms of reciprocity and mutual trust (Williamson, 1985). Thus the web enables the "network" form of governance, based on norms of reciprocity and trust, to emerge and reduce transaction costs.

E-commerce corporations

ECCs are organizations that, from inception, are engaged in electronic commerce and derive significant competitive advantage from the use of the network resources in virtual networks of commercial and collaborative alliances.

ECC internationalization: the case of AllPosters.com

AllPosters.com is one of the world's largest online retailers of wall décor. It is a sub-brand of Art.com Inc. AllPosters.com is an example of how an ECC can take advantage of its "born global" status and leverage the web to internationalize. The company was started in 1998 in a small room near Berkeley, California. Within twelve years it has used its websites to sell products in 120 countries. Today AllPosters.com boasts about twenty-five international sites, which have multilingual content and give international customers the ability to purchase in their own local currencies. Its most recent additions include sites for Argentina, the Czech Republic, and Turkey in September 2010.

Sources: Allposters.com and corporate.art.com.

Now we see a new breed of multinationals, which tend to be smaller and usually technology-focused, that leverage the web and associated technologies to surmount

---

[4] Opportunism is an important transaction cost consideration for multinationals. There is always a possibility during arm's-length transactions that one of the parties may act opportunistically and take advantage of the other party. For example, a licensee may copy the technology and, after the licensing contract is over, may start its own line of products based on the copied technology.

[5] Relationship-specific investments relate to personal, interpersonal, and physical assets and relations that facilitate the development of interdependence, mutual reciprocity, and trust between the parties.

entry barriers and achieve international expansion. Singh and Kundu (2002) define such web-based multinationals as e-commerce corporations (ECCs). ECCs[6] are organizations that, from their inception, are engaged in electronic commerce and that derive significant competitive advantage from the use of the network resources resident in virtual networks of commercial and collaborative alliances. This inherent global scope is a result of three definitional components of ECCs from inception: (1) they have multinational accessibility; (2) they can compete internationally; and (3) they access a global network of alliances and resources (Singh and Kundu, 2002). The four main types of emerging e-commerce corporations are

- portals (e.g., MSN.com, AOL.com, Yahoo.com);
- market makers (e.g., eBay.com, Ariba.com, Alibaba.com);
- social/networking organizations (e.g., Facebook.com, MySpace.com, LinkedIn.com); and
- product and service providers (e.g., ETrade.com, LandsEnd.com, Amazon.com).

International e-business strategic factor markets

As we have seen, the web has enabled the lowering of international market entry barriers and provided firms of various sizes an opportunity to compete globally. Beyond the lowering of entry barriers, the web is also a rich source of resources that can enhance a firm's global competitive advantage. Firms can access these resources via international e-business strategic factor markets. Strategic factor markets are an important concept in international business literature, and they can generally be defined as markets in which firms can acquire the resources necessary to implement their strategies (Barney, 1991). The international e-business strategic factor markets are global in scope because the web allows for access to resources on a global scale. Companies can leverage the international e-business strategic factor markets to access global resources, in the form of information and knowledge, for e-procurement, e-marketplace information, e-auctions, e-payments, data mining, market segmentation information, customer relationship management, market intelligence, and other functions. The resources available from e-business strategic factor markets are distinct from other business markets in that they tend to be information-rich, knowledge-oriented (Achrol and Kotler, 1999), relationship-specific, and intangible in nature. These unique e-business strategic factor markets can be classified into three types: (1) internet-based strategic factor markets; (2) alliance- or network-based strategic factor markets; and (3) location-based strategic factor markets.

---

[6] These ECCs are, by definition, international, and they resemble Knight and Cavusgil's (1996) "born global" firms and Oviatt and McDougall's (1994) "international new ventures."

Internet-based strategic factor markets

Internet-based strategic factor markets provide access to strategic assets and resources that are created, dispersed, and reside in electronic networks. Much like ECCs, the internet-based strategic factor market is international by nature, with global suppliers and buyers creating and vying for resources. These resources include web applications and web services, such as electronic customer relationship management (E-CRM) tools, enterprise resource planning (ERP) tools, log file data, and meta-softwares. Other internet-based resources include real-time interactivity, feedback mechanisms, digital convergence, trust-generating features, intranet applications, unhindered connectivity, cloud computing, and virtual value chains. All these internet-based strategic resources and tools inherent to the web help companies to leverage important competitor, customer, supplier, and technological information on a global scale.

Alliance- or network-based e-business strategic factor markets

Network-based strategic factor markets help ECCs assemble complementary strategic capabilities. This includes access to complementary assets (Zhu and Kraemer, 2002), technological know-how (Amit and Zott, 2001), virtual industry value chains, and co-opetitors[7] (Afuah, 2000). Online strategic alliances, affiliate programs, viral marketing programs, infomediaries, online communities, portal agreements, and promotion agreements are a rich source of strategic network resources and market information. Such inter-firm linkages and networks result in the quick and widespread dispersal of consumer data and tacit knowledge (Uzzi, 1997), the lowering of coordination costs, and the enhancement of allocative efficiency. They also span national boundaries, allowing global alliances and networks to flourish. For example, DoubleClick.com serves as an infomediary that collects the clickstream data of millions of web users; it then sells the data to companies to deliver targeted ads. Network-based strategic factor markets on the web enable the full potential of network externalities to become manifest.

Network externalities

The open nature of the internet implies that it can bring a number of buyers and sellers together, leading to positive network externalities. For example, on the internet, B2B and B2C exchanges are flourishing because they thrive on network externalities, which create incentives to include ever more suppliers and buyers. The Ariba supplier network is a perfect example, in that, due to its network externalities, it now conducts transactions worth over $100 billion annually in eighty currencies.

> **Network externalities**
>
> According to Metcalfe's law (Hanson, 2000), the value of the network to each of its members is directly proportional to the number of other users of the network. Thus the value of a company website increases as the number of web users accessing the internet increases. Network externalities and value clustering are two primary benefits of network economics.

Location-based e-business strategic factor markets

A company can gain a significant competitive advantage from both its regional location and its location on the web. Regional location serves as a significant source of social capital for companies. For example, a study by Cohen and Fields (1999) indicates that new "start-ups" and high-tech firms in Silicon Valley used local networks to gain innovative ideas and technological competencies. Additionally, as ECCs are inherently international, they often have access to multiple regional clusters from which to leverage local knowledge. For example, the Indian city of Bangalore and the Zhong Guan Cun section of Beijing have both been referred to as the "Silicon Valleys" of their respective countries, and represent additional regional clusters that firms can access. Moreover, the knowledge that firms access from these clusters can be exchanged

---

[7] The term "co-opetitors" refers to a situation in which competitors, suppliers, or customers collaborate. NUMMI, for example, was a joint venture between two competitors, GM and Toyota.

formally (with explicit compensation) or informally (without any compensation) but in either case it is a source of competitive advantage (Tallman *et al.*, 2004). The location of a company's website on the web also determines the type of resources that can be accessed from the site (Singh, 2001). The centrality and network position of the website determine the number of links accessible from the site, which in turn determines the website traffic and network connectivity to web-based resources.[8]

Location-based e-business strategic factor markets also provide companies access to two types of infrastructure: media infrastructure and network infrastructure. With the wider adoption of broadband and the digitization of information, we are seeing the convergence of media and networks. Convergence relates to the merger of data, content, audio, and video. This digital convergence synergistically combines the power of the media with the accessibility of the network, leading to gains in the form of highly interactive web content with graphics, video, and audio. These are the web-location-based strategic factor markets that firms can gain on account of their ability to leverage the internet. For example, Netflix.com is leveraging the digital convergence resource of e-business strategic factor markets to deliver movies digitally via the Xbox360 and PS3 platforms.

Internationalization challenges

Internationalization, in the context of this chapter, is defined as the propensity of a firm to move beyond domestic markets and tap international markets. Challenges related to socio-cultural, geopolitical, legal, and economic factors were discussed in the previous chapter. In this chapter, I explore the challenges related to the process of internationalization. The "liability of newness,"[9] for example, may arise because of the age of the firm, experience, size, or other factors that ultimately lead to firm closure. Younger firms usually have less experience plus fewer networks and resources, and thus face a higher liability of newness. When companies internationalize, they also face the liability of newness because they are exposed to new rules, new methods of doing business (e.g., transactions, advertising, etc.), and different consumer expectations. Thus, regardless of whether a company is brick-and-mortar, internet-based, or some hybrid, it will be exposed to the liability of newness when it enters international markets. The web, to some extent, reduces this liability, because companies can minimize their physical international presence by leveraging the web, limiting their direct exposure to country-specific market risks.

However, success on the web is, to a great extent, determined by how effectively firms leverage commercial and non-commercial collaborative alliances. Two concepts that are explored in more depth in this chapter include the "liability of outsidership" and the "liability of foreignness" (see Figure 2.1). Beyond these liabilities, newly

---

[8] Singh (2001) provides an extended discussion on network centrality, network density, network connectivity, and relationship-specific investments.

[9] For a more in-depth review of the liability of newness, refer to Freeman, Carroll, and Hannan (1983).

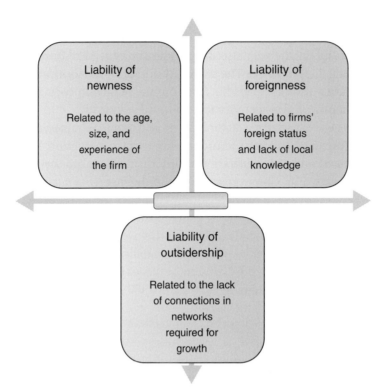

Figure 2.1 Internationalization process challenges

internationalizing firms also face cultural, psychic, and institutional distance when they expand in foreign markets. The following paragraphs explore these ideas further.

Liability of foreignness

The liability of foreignness is the well-documented struggle that firms face when embarking on internationalization efforts. Their foreign status, lack of local knowledge and rules, relatively low level of government and local contacts, and decreased control over operations make it challenging to succeed in foreign countries. Moreover, local consumers see them as foreign firms, and prefer to stick with locally known brands. In China, for example, the global giant Google lags behind Baidu, the Chinese search engine. Similarly, eBay and Amazon also lag behind their local competitors in China, Taoboa and Dang Dang, respectively. One of the strategies used by companies to overcome the liability of foreignness is to form strategic alliances with local companies or to acquire local companies in order to gain marketing, economic, cultural, and institutional knowledge. For example, when eBay saw its market share in China dwindling, it decided to adopt a growth strategy based on partnering with local Chinese companies, and it is currently exploring an alliance with China's largest auction company, Alibaba. Furthermore, as companies become more successful in their internationalization efforts, they tend to accumulate knowledge that helps them ease their liability of foreignness in future internationalization efforts. AllPosters.com facilitated its initial international expansion by acquiring the German site poster.de, and launched international sites for Germany, Italy, Spain, and the United Kingdom in 2005. AllPosters.com's next major international expansion took place in 2010 with the launch of seventeen additional international sites.[10] The initial internationalization efforts by AllPosters.com, between 2005 and 2010, helped it gain a better understanding of the factors involved in international e-business expansion, and likely facilitated its launch of the additional seventeen international sites in 2010.

Liability of outsidership

As emphasized above, firms conducting international e-business expansion often attempt to leverage strategic alliances and partnerships to overcome the liability of foreignness. The combined forces of globalization and technology make the development of cross-national, cross-industry, and multilateral networks possible. In fact, according to Johanson and Vahlne (2009), country-specific factors related to the liability of foreignness are becoming less important compared to the role played by multilateral networks and network relationships. For example, in China the role of informal networks, also called "guanxi," is important for decreasing the liability of outsidership. If a company is not well connected in the networks that can provide it with resources and capabilities for international expansion, then the company will suffer from the liability of outsidership. One way to view this issue is that the rise of globalization and technology not only has made it easy to form global relationships, but also has created valuable networks and network positions that, if not leveraged, can pose a liability of outsidership.

Cultural distance

The term "cultural distance" implies that there are significant differences in ways of acting and behaving in two different cultures. Studies have shown that, when companies internationalize, they tend to go first to countries that are more culturally similar to their own. For example, a US firm may first internationalize to culturally close markets, such as the United Kingdom or Canada, and then go to more culturally distant markets, such as Mexico or Japan. However, global e-commerce is narrowing this cultural divide with the help of web technologies, the greater dispersal of information, and social networking. Furthermore, as mentioned before, the web allows companies to do business without heavily investing in country-/locale-specific factors, and thus

---

[10] Based on art.com Timeline: corporate.art.com.

to some extent the web mitigates the effect of cultural distance. Managers have various resources available to help them determine the cultural distance between countries. One of the most prevalent approaches is the cultural value framework proposed by Hofstede (1980). This cultural framework ranks various countries on four main cultural values – individualism versus collectivism, uncertainty avoidance, power distance, and masculinity versus femininity – providing countries with scores on these values. Hofstede has also proposed a value related to long-term versus short-term orientation, which is now considered the fifth cultural value.

Psychic distance

Unlike the cultural distance, which measures differences between nations, the psychic distance concept is a measure of the gap that individuals perceive in relation to differences between their home country and a foreign country (Sousa and Bradley, 2008). Thus psychic distance relates to how an individual perceives cross-national differences. This concept is useful when exploring how an individual responds to internationalization pressures. In the context of global e-commerce, the psychic distance may be narrowing for individuals who are more technology-savvy and internationally oriented, and who leverage technology and other resources to bridge the knowledge gap between nations.

Institutional distance

The institutional distance determines how different the foreign institutions are in terms of laws, regulations, taxes, and rules, as well as in terms of norms and ethics (Scott, 1995). On the web, companies have to consider a plethora of international institutional issues related to:

- tax structures in various countries;
- import/export restrictions;
- security and privacy issues;
- foreign jurisdiction, laws about advertising and web content, domain law, antidumping, the FCPA (Foreign Corrupt Practices Act, United States);
- trade agreement compliance, such as NAFTA and EU regulations;
- import tariff rates;
- insurance and risk mitigation;
- intellectual property rights (IPR) protection regarding patents, copyrights, trademarks, and domains; and
- the infrastructure, especially technology-infrastructure-related regulation.

Research shows that, the larger the institutional distance, the more difficulty the firm has in establishing itself or even entering a foreign market (Kostova and Zaheer,

1999). In the context of global e-business, institutional norms related to regulation are still evolving. For example, countries are still exploring how best to tax web-based purchases, curtail international web-based arbitrage opportunities, and achieve better IPR protection, and even how to enforce international contracts. Global e-commerce is also leading to the development of new institutions, such as the Internet Corporation for Assigned Names and Numbers (ICANN), which is responsible for managing Internet Protocol (IP) addresses, and the Internet Network Information Center (InterNIC), which is responsible for governing domain names and IP addresses. A Pew Center study has found that technology experts see the role of the internet gaining momentum in terms of institutional evolution, and that, "[by] 2020, innovative forms of online cooperation will result in significantly more efficient and responsive governments, business, non-profits, and other mainstream institutions" (Anderson and Rainie, 2010: 2).

Internationalization approaches

The international business literature has devoted considerable efforts to understanding how companies internationalize and what internationalization path they take. Several internationalization approaches have been put forward by researchers, and some of these approaches are discussed in the following sections.

The Uppsala internationalization model

Traditionally, firms have expanded in stages, such that, once they gain enough experience to reduce their liability of newness, they explore further growth and investment opportunities. As a firm gains more international experience, it also commits more resources and extends its international commitments. This gradual increase in international commitments is based on psychic distance and cultural distance. As has been stated above, expansion normally happens first in the countries that are much closer culturally and/or geographically, and then broadens to other countries. This stage-oriented path of internationalization was first proposed by Johanson and Vahlne (1977), and it is also called the "Uppsala model," as it is based on research conducted at the University of Uppsala in Sweden. However, in the new networked economy, the cultural, psychic, and even institutional distances are getting smaller, reflecting the forces of globalization and also the interconnectedness and reach of the internet. Companies now are making their internationalization decisions based on much better information than beforehand. The internet allows them to have a significant global presence with minimal country-specific location-based investment. For example, Amazon – one of the earliest internationalizers on the web – actually entered both France and Japan in the same year, even though, traditionally speaking, Japan would be considered more culturally distant from the United States than France. Amazon entered the Canadian market all the way in 2002, after it had already entered more culturally distant countries such as Germany, France, and Japan. However, recent evidence by Forrester Research shows that, in general, US e-retailers are, in fact, following the Uppsala model, wherein they expand first to Canada, a country lower in cultural and institutional distance, and then to more culturally distant countries (Wigder *et al.*, 2009).

The internationalization path of Amazon.com

(1) 1998: Amazon acquires British seller Bookpages Ltd. and uses this acquisition to launch Amazon.co.uk.
(2) 1998: Amazon acquires Telebook of Germany to help establish Amazon.de. Telebook's longtime local expertise in online bookselling in Germany combined with Amazon.com's worldwide brand and powerful technology is seen as a great synergy.
(3) 2000: Amazon opens Amazon.fr for French consumers.
(4) 2000: Amazon opens Amazon.co.jp for Japanese consumers.
(5) 2002: Amazon.ca is formed to enter the Canadian market
(6) 2004: Amazon acquires Chinese bookseller Joyo.com to enter the Chinese market. Initially, it keeps the site under Joyo.com, then slowly moves toward Joyo-Amazon.cn.
(7) 2010: Amazon reaches an agreement to acquire BuyVIP.com, which has 6 million members in countries including Spain, Germany, and Italy. This allows Amazon to grow further in Europe.

The "born global" concept

A "born global" is defined as "[a] firm that is heavily involved in exporting at inception or shortly after establishment" (Knight and Cavusgil, 1996). Born globals are becoming more common, on account of their global nature and the connectivity of internet-based mediums. Since its inception, Amazon has been shipping goods internationally; so do many other e-retailers (e.g., Bluefly.com, Gap.com), even without having international sites or any physical presence abroad. The inherently global nature of the internet not only allows well-financed or capital-rich companies to start selling internationally from their inception but also permits companies with limited resources to take their businesses global from the day they launch their websites. Amazon, Google, and Yahoo! all started as small companies that later expanded and grew globally. Internet-based companies have the advantage of tapping global online markets and being able to seek out almost 1.8 billion online users worldwide. However, for an American born global internet firm to have only an English website catering to the US market is not the most effective way to attract international visitors. This also applies to companies from other countries with a web presence in their local languages only. A company must create localized content for different country markets to be able to truly tap them effectively. This is not a simple decision. Should the company then roll out hundreds of websites for countries, worldwide? How should

a company decide which international market to cater to and localize for? I explore these issues in the following sections.

The network model of internationalization

The network model of international expansion is based on network theory. The basic premise of network theory is that economic action is embedded in a network of relations (Granovetter, 1992). According to this view, firms are embedded in networks of social, professional, and economic relations. Neglecting the strategic networks in which firms are embedded can lead to an incomplete understanding of firm behavior and performance (Gulati, 1999; Singh and Kundu, 2002). The network model of internationalization proposes that firms internationalize with the help of their own business networks, the external business networks, and the relevant network structure in foreign markets.[11] In fact, internationalization is a process of multilateral network development and growth (Johanson and Vahlne, 1990). ECCs, from their inception, have multinational accessibility, but real global competitive advantage accrues only to those

---

[11] For a more in-depth explanation, refer to Johanson and Mattsson (1988) and Johanson and Vahlne (1990 and 2009).

firms that can effectively and strategically scan global markets for partnerships, assets, resources, and consumer segments. It is the creation of such relationships that gives ECCs access to valuable global resources – and a competitive edge. As mentioned earlier, for any company involved in global e-commerce, the international e-business strategic factor markets provide a rich source of partnerships, network-specific resources, and other relationship-specific assets. For example, Google acquired YouTube in 2006 for almost $1.65 billion. This acquisition provides Google with network resources that combine the online video entertainment community with Google's expertise in organizing information and creating new models for advertising on the internet.[12] Expedia announced in 2010 that it would partner with the WPP Group, a major global marketing and communications group. The WPP Group will provide global strategy and public relations (PR) services to Expedia's brand, Hotels.com, to achieve further expansion in the South American market. Craigslist, Facebook, and Zazzle.com are examples of companies that have leveraged their international customer networks and relationships to achieve international presence. These three companies rely on their customer networks to create content, community, and services across regions. Facebook has even leveraged its community of international users to create translations of its English content to its development of multilingual websites for its international markets.

Firms can acquire important data and information from their unique network position (Gnyawali and Madhavan, 2001). The network connectivity, network density, and network portfolio diversity (Singh, 2001) of an ECC's website determines its access to diverse information sources on the web, including web traffic data, customer usability data, and web linkage data. For example, Alexa.com has built a vast database of information about sites that includes site statistics, related links, and more. This information related to network connectivity, network density, etc. can be used by companies for search engine optimization, finding competitor sites, understanding cross-national and cross-industry traffic patterns, and answering many more strategic questions to drive international growth.

Achieving international e-business expansion

Till now I have discussed general approaches to achieving international expansion. Now is the time to discuss some specific ways that companies leverage their online presence to aid their international expansion efforts.

International shipping

Shipping internationally tends to be one of the easiest ways to tap the potential of international markets without having to make major investments in e-business

---

[12] www.businesswire.com/news/home/20101020006608/en/Expedia-WPP-Group-Form-Strategic
-Alliance-Latin.

infrastructure or other foreign market entry requirements. Since international shipping requires the least level of commitment, it is a favored mode for serving international markets when a company does not have much experience with global commerce. A survey of e-retailers by Forrester Research finds that almost a half of mid-size retailers used shipping as a tool for tapping international markets (Wigder *et al.*, 2009).

Once companies gain experience with international customers and/or see the potential for revenue growth, they may make more investments in terms of fully localized sites for different countries. As mentioned in the previous chapter, there are several companies that provide full-service shipping and international transaction facilitation. Thus an e-retailer has only to coordinate with one of these integrated logistics solution providers to be able to ship globally. For example, iShopUSA logistics solution takes care of all logistics issues related to shipping, returns, taxes, duties, and international payments. A unique aspect of iShopUSA is that it aggregates all the retailers that use its solution and provides them with additional marketing and reach via its website. Shoppers from around the world can come to iShopUSA and buy merchandise from retailers listed on its website or any US online retailers.

Country market/language

Under this approach, companies tend to first create additional localized websites to serve a large bilingual or multilingual population that already resides in their home country. For example, Hispanics in the United States number more than 40 million, which constitutes a population that is larger than that of the whole of Scandinavia put together. So US companies may first think of adding some web pages in Spanish, or even create localized Spanish sites for Hispanics in the country. Once the company gains experience in terms of localizing its content and website for the local Hispanic population, it can then leverage this knowledge to create more extensive sites for other Spanish-speaking countries. For example, BestBuy.com started BestBuy.com/espanol in 2007, as a site to enable the Spanish-speaking US population to be able to access its catalog and make purchases. Best Buy now also has a site for Mexico in which the content is translated into Spanish, but online ordering is not available. Home Depot experimented with a Spanish site for Hispanic consumers in the United States and learned that the site did not get enough traffic or sales, while the costs of maintaining the site were high. This experiment with a Spanish-language site led Home Depot to cut down most of the functionality related to online ordering and the online catalog, routing customers to the English pages for online purchases. Thus companies may learn a great deal about their competencies and consumer segments by first targeting specific populations in their home countries.

Incremental approach

The incremental approach is a strategy of making incremental investments toward taking the e-business global via website localization (Yunker, 2003). Companies with limited resources, knowledge, experience, or willingness to create fully localized international websites tend to invest resources in first localizing certain web pages or site content. For example, companies can localize just their help section, or shipping or contact sections, to help international consumers interact with the site. Sites may also experiment with first providing limited language support before delving into creating fully scaled multilingual sites. Urban Outfitters has not undertaken any localization of its sites for different countries, but customers from Europe can go to its regional site, urbanoutfitters.co.uk, to shop in pounds and euros (see Figure 2.2). Zara International is an example of a company that is using limited translation to develop country-specific sites. The international sites of Zara use very limited translation, but include a lot of images in a catalog style. This enables Zara achieve a meaningful connection with international users despite not investing heavily in localization and translation.

Beyond providing multilingual translations on their websites, companies also need to think about their multilingual customer service capabilities. In terms of multilingual customer service options, companies can either develop limited capacity to answer queries in certain languages, outsource multilingual customer service, or, with even greater investment and experience, develop extensive in-house multilingual support.

Examples of multilingual customer service support include the following.

- Companies such as Nveevo and TechTeam Global are just two examples of multilingual customer service support providers. They provide services such as chat support, technical support, and twenty-four-hour helplines to service consumers in various parts of the world.
- Yahoo! has announced that customer care services in Spanish, German, French, Italian, Turkish, Polish, Romanian, and Russian – plus those for future Arabic versions of its products – will be provided on the company's behalf by IBM.

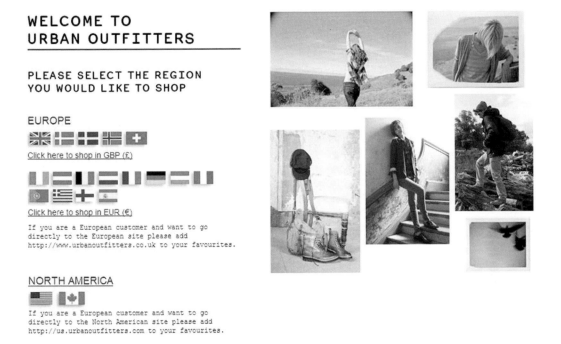

WELCOME TO URBAN OUTFITTERS

PLEASE SELECT THE REGION YOU WOULD LIKE TO SHOP

EUROPE

Click here to shop in GBP (£)

Click here to shop in EUR (€)

If you are a European customer and want to go directly to the European site please add http://www.urbanoutfitters.co.uk to your favourites.

NORTH AMERICA

If you are a European customer and want to go directly to the North American site please add http://us.urbanoutfitters.com to your favourites.

Figure 2.2 Incremental approach: Urban Outfitters

Web analytics

Web-based companies can gain useful information about visitors to their websites. Several web analytic softwares (Webtrends, Google Analytics, Clicktracks, etc.) are available to help companies understand all sorts of aspects of user demographics and behaviors on their sites. They can also see where the visitors come from and what languages they use. Companies can correlate this information with data about where orders, e-mails, and other forms of communications are coming from. Using this information, companies can then decide which country or countries may represent significant opportunities and decide to create a localized website. Information using web analytics can also be beneficial to appropriately target international search engine optimization efforts to countries or international search engines that send the most traffic – or countries where a company wants to achieve higher traffic (see Figure 2.3). International search engine optimization can allow international users to find international sites more easily and companies to gauge the interest of users in international markets. Such international targeting efforts require minimal localization investment and could serve as a preliminary phase of international expansion.

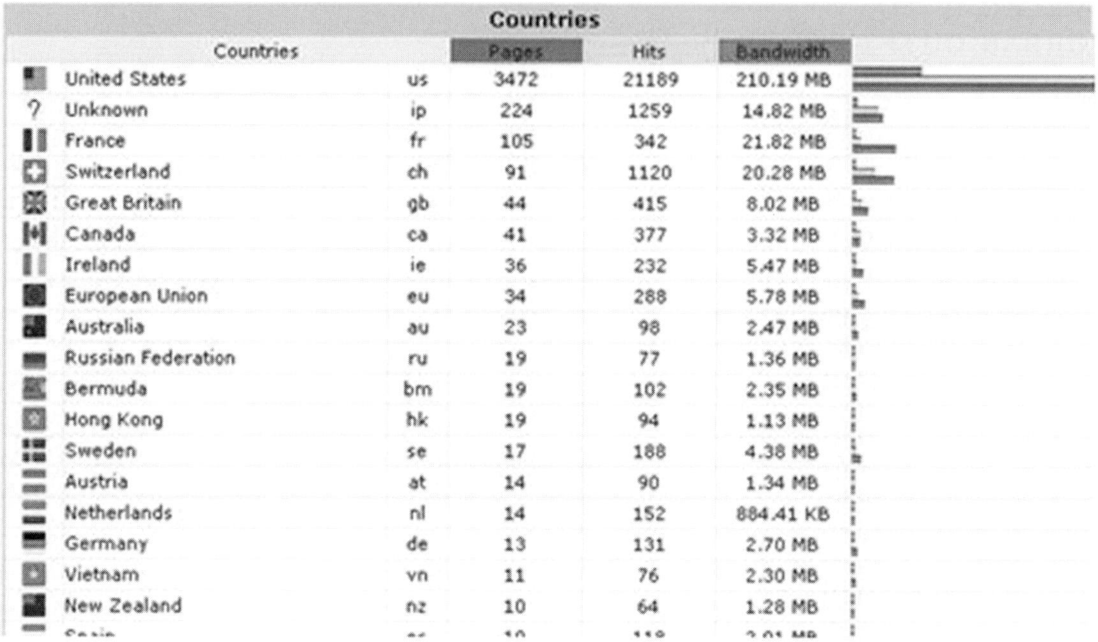

Countries				
Countries		Pages	Hits	Bandwidth
United States	us	3472	21189	210.19 MB
Unknown	ip	224	1259	14.82 MB
France	fr	105	342	21.82 MB
Switzerland	ch	91	1120	20.28 MB
Great Britain	gb	44	415	8.02 MB
Canada	ca	41	377	3.32 MB
Ireland	ie	36	232	5.47 MB
European Union	eu	34	288	5.78 MB
Australia	au	23	98	2.47 MB
Russian Federation	ru	19	77	1.36 MB
Bermuda	bm	19	102	2.35 MB
Hong Kong	hk	19	94	1.13 MB
Sweden	se	17	188	4.38 MB
Austria	at	14	90	1.34 MB
Netherlands	nl	14	152	884.41 KB
Germany	de	13	131	2.70 MB
Vietnam	vn	11	76	2.30 MB
New Zealand	nz	10	64	1.28 MB
Spain	es	10	118	3.01 MB

Figure 2.3 Web analytics data

Social media and social network websites such as Facebook, Twitter, Flickr, and YouTube can also serve as a rich source of international consumer market intelligence, in addition to being an important tool for interacting with international customers. Companies can, in fact, test international waters using social media to get a read on how consumers in a particular country feel about the company's offerings. I discuss the growth and role of social media in global e-business further in Chapter 10.

Country market assessment

Before investing in the creation of international sites, it is important for a company to determine if the country market is lucrative enough to justify its investment. Companies need to analyze the following information:

(1) the internet penetration rate/online population;
(2) the market potential of the country for their products;
(3) the purchasing power of consumers;
(4) whether logistical and sales support is available;
(5) regulations, taxes, and duties; and
(6) the expense of designing and maintaining the site.

It is also important to do a thorough product, competition, and market review. The following are some pointers to help focus efforts.

(1) Product factors
    (a) Consumer product expectations.
    (b) Consumer receptivity to product receptivity.
    (c) The level of product complexity the general consumer can accept.
    (d) Product resistance.
    (e) Product and country-of-origin effects.
    (f) Product specifications and product requirements based on country laws.
(2) Competitive factors
    (a) The competitive intensity.
    (b) Competition from foreign and domestic companies.
    (c) Competitive practices related to pricing, promotion, branding, packaging, distribution, and manufacturing.
    (d) The competitive structure and presence of oligopolies, cartels, etc.
    (e) Competitive political influence.
(3) Market factors
    (a) Consumer buying habits.
    (b) The distribution structure and logistics in the country.
    (c) The demand and supply gap in the country market for the product in question.
    (d) The industry size and sales.
    (e) Regulations in the existing industry under consideration.
    (f) The price elasticity of the product under consideration.

Foreign market entry modes

To enter foreign markets, companies have a choice from among several market entry modes. These can be broadly categorized into equity-based and non-equity-based entry modes.

When a firm makes a foreign direct investment, it uses the equity-based market entry mode. In equity-based modes, a company actually owns equity in its foreign venture and has control over its activities. Some of the equity modes for entering foreign markets include joint ventures, mergers and acquisitions, and green-fields (a company creates a wholly owned subsidiary by extending its full control into a country market).

Non-equity modes of entry do not require any equity participation, and thus also come with less control over the activities. Non-equity modes of foreign market entry include exporting, licensing, franchising, co-marketing, and others. In the following paragraphs I delve into these market entry approaches. Additional information can also be found on export/import regulations, market entry, documentation, etc. at www.export.gov, which serves as the US government's export portal.

Indirect exporting

For companies with a major domestic focus, local markets are of prime importance, and international operations are seen merely as an extension of domestic marketing. These companies use intermediaries in international markets to reach consumers in that locale. Companies that have less international experience or knowledge of international markets can use a foreign intermediary with good knowledge of distribution channels to facilitate market entry. The principal advantage of indirect marketing for a smaller company is that it provides a way to penetrate foreign markets without the complexities and risks of direct exporting. The two kinds of intermediaries that can be used are as follows.

Export management company (EMC)

An EMC is an independent company that may or may not take title of goods while managing all operations related to successfully taking products to an international market. EMCs are experienced in all facets of exporting, including foreign travel, export marketing, etc. They have expertise in:

- answering inquiries, preparing quotations, entering orders, handling shipping details, and receiving payments;
- market research, patent protection, shipping, and logistics; and
- establishing a strong foreign distribution system; they have the know-how to select agents and distributors, and to manage their distribution network.

Some third-party logistics firms, such as OHL, Bongo International, and iShopUSA, play the role of the traditional EMC by helping many internet retailers and other companies not just to achieve international logistics and customs clearance but also to facilitate international transactions. In fact, companies such as Digital River go beyond providing just logistics services to providing full global, multichannel e-commerce solutions, ranging from site development and hosting, order management, fraud protection, export controls, tax management, physical and digital product fulfillment, to even multilingual customer service and strategic marketing services.

Export agent

Unlike large EMCs, export agents tend to specialize in one market and provide limited services. Like an EMC, an export agent has all the necessary knowledge to handle export documentation, but it may not be able to conduct extensive market analysis and research.

Direct exporting

When a company directly exports or uses its own foreign intermediaries to export to foreign markets, this is called "direct exporting." Companies find independent distributors in foreign markets, and these distributors then sell the company's products. The independent foreign distributor gets a margin on the selling price of the product.

Several companies on the internet use this approach to sell worldwide. The web provides direct access to international markets, so companies do not have to rely on finding foreign distributors and sales agents. Thus the web, in fact, disintermediates, which helps companies lower their transaction costs and reach the worldwide consumer directly. For example, L. L. Bean's website sells directly to its customers worldwide via direct exports, with no actual country-specific presence, except for Japan. However, companies – even in this networked economy – sometimes need local agents, partners, and distributors to help them manage aspects of their international expansion. For example, even Amazon, when it entered Canada, selected Assured Logistics, a part of the Canada Post group of companies, to handle fulfillment services for Amazon.ca.

Fig Leaves tapping international markets via exports

- 1998: Figleaves.com starts as Easyshop.co.uk, selling perfume and lingerie, primarily for the UK market.
- 2000: Rebrands itself as Figleaves.com, selling in the United Kingdom.
- 2003: Launches its US site, and learns that products need to be translated from British English to American English; for example, "panties" is a term not commonly used in the United Kingdom. Later in the year it opens its office in New York.
- 2004: Reaches the million-dollar mark for worldwide sales.
- 2005: Opens warehouses in Detroit, United States, and Ontario, Canada, to meet demand in North America and easily handle the logistics.
- 2011: Expands into France and Germany, but still takes international orders via its UK site, offers product catalog in various currencies, and exports all over the world.

Licensing and franchising

In licensing, a company – instead of selling its products and technology – loans or gives its technology and access to patents or copyrights for a fee or royalty. These licensing agreements can be extensive, outlining the terms of use and the number of years the agreement is valid. Although licensing can be an easy way to leverage technology and services, and to reach international markets with no direct investment, it can also be risky. When the technology or software product has proprietary knowledge, there is a built-in risk that the partner may learn it, and once the agreement expires it may build its own product or technology using the appropriated proprietary knowledge rather than renew the agreement. Thus a company faces the risk of losing its proprietary knowledge. In the fall of 2010 Netflix signed Canadian license agreements with major motion picture studios and distributors (e.g., Lions Gate Entertainment Corp., MGM Studios, Paramount Pictures) so as to facilitate the streaming of movies and content to the Canadian market.

In the case of franchising agreements, the company has even more rigid terms and conditions of use for the franchisee. Here the franchisee has to follow restrictions related to the use of brand logo, products, and even methods of operation. KFC and McDonald's are good examples of companies that have expanded internationally using franchising agreements. A McDonald's franchisee is required to adhere to strict color, logo, delivery, and marketing specifications. iSold It is an eBay drop-off chain that has expanded all over the United States using the franchise model.

International licensing agreement

In 2005 AdStar, an application service provider for the advertising and publishing industries, entered an international licensing agreement with Associados, one of Brazil's largest media organizations.

Associados uses AdStar's technology to reverse-publish its web ads back into print, and also uses AdStar's XML Gateway to build the leading advertising and e-commerce system in Brazil.

To AdStar, Associados offers the opportunity to expand its technology deployment outside the United States into South America's largest media market.

Joint ventures (JVs)

JVs are partnership agreements between two or more companies to create a separate legal entity in which the partners share joint management and equity. Several countries – especially emerging markets such as India, China, etc. – require some degree of local participation for operations in their country, necessitating the formation of joint ventures for companies seeking to expand into these markets beyond a simple exporting or licensing model. Mergers with distribution companies or with companies that already have well-established local distribution may provide rapid market access and distribution to foreign companies entering a country. Sometimes companies also join forces in order to broaden the merchandise they have available, thereby gaining marketing efficiency and a better public image. Joint ventures can also help companies gain in-depth local understanding of distribution and marketing in a country. When Pepsi and Coca-Cola entered India, they used JVs to gain a better understanding of the distribution and logistics network in India. This helped them realize marketing efficiencies. Another major benefit of joint ventures is that they spread the risk of international expansion among the partners. In an online context, a JV can help companies expand their subscriber base, enhance website traffic, increase marketing opportunities, gain international credibility, and acquire complementary assets such as e-commerce capabilities.

Joint venture: eBay and PChome

In 2006 eBay and PChome joined hands to form a joint venture for an online co-branded auction site, www.ruten.com.tw, to serve the Taiwanese market. This JV brings in the complementary strengths of both parties to create a unique brand that provides enhanced online auction-style trading that is localized to the tastes and preferences of the Taiwanese market. eBay's global branding, international experience, and technological expertise complements PChome's unique local knowledge and strong market presence in the Taiwanese e-commerce market.

Source: www.ebayinc.com.

Mergers and acquisitions

As mentioned above, mergers and acquisitions can help companies tap international markets at a rapid pace by acquiring local companies. A merger is a combination of two companies to combine their complementary assets. Mergers occur in a consensual setting in which both parties agree to implement a due diligence process to ensure that the deal is beneficial to both parties. An acquisition is when a company takes over another company for rapid growth. In a friendly takeover, companies cooperate and have lengthy negotiations, but the dominant partner still ultimately takes over the acquired company. Acquisition is considered hostile when the takeover target is unwilling to be bought or the target's board has no prior knowledge of the offer. In either case, the acquiring company often offers a premium on the market price of the target company's shares in order to entice shareholders to sell.[13]

Acquisition-led growth of Rakuten Inc.

The Rakuten group is a major e-commerce player in Japan and has various business line-ups in e-business, credit card business, portals, travel, security, and telecommunications. For example, its company Rakuten Ichiba is the largest internet shopping mall in Japan, offering more than 50 million products by more than 33,000 merchants. Rakuten was founded in 1997 and achieved its diverse and global portfolio via mergers and acquisitions. For example, to enhance its portal and travel offerings, it acquired Infoseek Japan and MyTrip.net. Its global expansion was facilitated by various acquisitions, such as:

- the acquisition of LinkShare for global internet marketing expertise;
- the acquisition of Buy.com, a major US global internet shopping portal with presence in Canada, France, Germany, Italy, Spain, the United Kingdom and the United States; and
- the acquisition of PriceMinister, a major French e-commerce site.

In addition to these acquisitions, Rakuten has formed joint ventures with local companies to expand into China, Thailand, Indonesia, and Taiwan.

Source: http://corp.rakuten.co.jp.

---

[13] www.investopedia.com, www.sec.gov.

Strategic alliances

In this form of international expansion, two or more companies work together to leverage each other's strengths. These complementary relationships help companies take advantage of their partners' technology, distribution, production, or similar strengths, and share the risk of foreign expansion. While JVs involve significant inputs of both capital and management, strategic alliances are just business relationships that capitalize on the complementary business strengths of each partner. For example, American Airlines, Cathay Pacific, British Airlines, Canadian Airlines, Aer Lingus, and Qantas are partners in the Oneworld alliance, which integrates schedules and mileage programs. In the context of the internet, an example of a strategic alliance would be Proformative, which is a free online community for finance, accounting, and treasury professionals, leveraging a strategic alliance with the Weiland Financial Group to gain complementary assets in bank fee analysis and bank account management.[14]

Strategic alliance

Chinese auction site eBay EachNet and Chinese internet search leader Baidu (BIDU) have a partnership in which Baidu promotes PayPal Beibao in exchange for becoming the exclusive provider of text-based search advertising on the eBay EachNet site.

Wholly owned subsidiaries

Here, a company directly invests and owns an entire operation in the host country, and takes full charge of capital, management, and other investments. Thus its parent owns 100 percent of its common stock. These wholly owned subsidiaries are a way for a company to enter the market, take advantage of local labor and local tax incentives, and gain access to raw materials while maintaining full control over its foreign operations. At the same time, the company runs the full risk of operating in the foreign market.

Wholly owned subsidiary

Expedia has grown internationally primarily by launching wholly owned international websites in several countries. Expedia operates internationally with localized sites in Canada, the United Kingdom, Germany, France, Italy, Spain, the Netherlands, Norway, Sweden, Denmark, Australia, Japan, India, New Zealand, and China, through an investment in eLong™, which is the second largest online travel company in China.

[14] proformative.com/press-releases.

> **Chapter summary**
>
> - The goal of this chapter is to help readers understand how the nature of the internet is changing the dynamics of conducting international business and allowing companies, both large and small, to achieve international expansion.
> - Insights are provided as to how the internet mitigates several market entry barriers associated with intermediaries, transportation costs, information asymmetry, the physical infrastructure, bureaucratic hurdles, and transaction costs.
> - The concept of international e-business strategic factor markets is introduced as a source for acquiring and leveraging tradable assets to achieve international e-business success.
> - The chapter extends the concepts of the liability of newness, the liability of foreignness, and the liability of outsidership, as well as those of cultural, psychic, and institutional distance, to help explain the challenges companies may face during their international e-business expansion.
> - Various approaches to internationalization are discussed as they relate to international e-business expansion.
> - The chapter shows how companies can internationalize by leveraging different market entry modes, such as exporting, joint ventures, mergers, acquisitions, strategic partnerships, and wholly owned subsidiaries.
> - In conclusion, the chapter provides a broad perspective to help managers understand the dynamics of international e-business expansion.

REFERENCES

Achrol, Ravi S., and Kotler, Philip 1999. "Marketing in the network economy," *Journal of Marketing* 63: 146–63.

Afuah, Allan 2000. "How much do your co-competitors' capabilities matter in the face of technological uncertainty?" *Strategic Management Journal* 21: 387–404.

Amit, Raphael, and Zott, Christoph, 2001. "Value creation in e-business," *Strategic Management Journal* 22: 493–520.

Anderson, Janna Quitney, and Rainie, Lee 2010. *The Impact of the Internet on Institutions in the Future*. Pew Research Center; available at www.pewinternet.org.

Barney, Jay B. 1991. "Firm resources and sustainable competitive advantage," *Journal of Management* 17: 99–120.

Cohen, Stephen S., and Fields, Gary 1999. "Social capital and capital gains in Silicon Valley," *California Management Review* 41: 108–30.

Freeman, J., Carroll, G. R., and Hannan, M. T. 1983. "The liability of newness: age deference in organizational death rates," *American Sociological Review* 48: 692–710.

Gnyawali, Devi R., and Madhavan, Ravindranath 2001. "Cooperative networks and competitive dynamics: a structural embeddedness perspective," *Academy of Management Review* 26: 431–45.

Granovetter, Mark S. 1992. "Problems of explanation in economic sociology," in Nohria, Nitin, and Eccles, Robert G. (eds.), *Networks and Organization: Structure, Form, and Action*. Harvard Business School Press: 25–56.

Gulati, Ranjay 1999. "Network location and learning: the influence of network resources and firms' capabilities on alliance formation," *Strategic Management Journal* 20: 397–420.

Hanson, Ward 2000. *Principles of Online Marketing.* Southern Western College Publishers.

Hofstede, Geert 1980. *Culture's Consequences: International Differences in Work-Related Values.* Sage.

Johanson, Jan, and Mattsson, Lars-Göran 1988. "Internationalisation in industrial systems: a network approach," in Hood, Neil, and Vahlne, Jan-Erik (eds.), *Strategies in Global Competition: Selected Papers from the Prince Bertil Symposium at the Institute of International Business, Stockholm School of Economics.* Croom Helm: 287–314.

Johanson, Jan, and Vahlne, Jan-Erik 1977. "The internationalization process of the firm: a model of knowledge development and increasing foreign market commitments," *Journal of International Business Studies* 8: 23–32.

1990. "The mechanism of internationalization," *International Marketing Review* 7: 11–24.

2009. "The Uppsala internationalization process model revisited: from liability of foreignness to liability of outsidership," *Journal of International Business Studies* 40: 1411–31.

Knight, Gary A., and Cavusgil, S. Tamer 1996. "The born global firm: a challenge to traditional internationalization theory," in Cavusgil, S. Tamer, and Madsen, Tage K. (eds.), *Advances in International Marketing.* JAI Press: 11–26.

Kostova, Tatiana, and Zaheer, Srilata 1999. "Organizational legitimacy under conditions of complexity: the case of the multi-national enterprise," *Academy of Management Review* 24: 64–81.

Oviatt, Benjamin M., and McDougall, Patricia Phillips 1994. "Toward a theory of international new ventures," *Journal of International Business Studies*: 45–64.

Scott, W. Richard 1995. *Institutions and Organizations.* Sage.

Singh, Nitish 2001. "Economic action on the internet: a network organization approach," *Journal of E-Business* 1: 65–88.

Singh, Nitish, and Kundu, Sumit 2002. "Explaining the growth of e-commerce corporations (ECCs): an extension of the eclectic paradigm," *Journal of International Business Studies* 33: 679–97.

Sousa, Carlos M. P., and Bradley, Frank 2008. "Cultural distance and psychic distance: refinements in conceptualisation and measurement," *Journal of Marketing Management* 24: 467–88.

Tallman, S., Jenkins, M., Henry, N., and Pinch, S. 2004. "Knowledge clusters and competitive advantage," *Academy of Management Review* 29: 258–71.

Uzzi, Brian 1997. "Social structure and competition in interfirm networks: the paradox of embeddedness," *Administrative Science Quarterly* 42: 35–67.

Wigder, Zia Daniell, Evans, Patti Freeman, Camus, Lauriane, and McGowan, Brendan 2009. *Global Expansion through International Shipping: Serving Customers in International Markets from a Domestic Base.* Forrester Research; available at www.forrester.com.

Williamson, Oliver E. 1985. *The Economic Institutions of Capitalism: Firms, Markets, Relational Contracting.* Free Press.

Yunker, John 2003. *Beyond Borders: Web Globalization Strategies.* New Riders.

Zhu, K., and Kraemer, K. L. 2002. "E-commerce metrics for net-enhanced organizations: assessing the value of e-commerce to firm performance in the manufacturing sector," *Information Systems Research* 13: 275–96.

3 Global online consumer segmentation

Chapter objectives

- Introduce readers to various market segmentation approaches.
- Discuss how traditional market segmentation approaches can be used to facilitate online segmentation.
- Present a model for global online consumer segmentation.
- Discuss how global customer relationship management can be facilitated by the help of CRM software tools.
- Explore various global online consumer segments.
- Present a selection of key emerging global consumer trends.

Segmentation approaches

Global e-commerce opens a world of more than 2 billion consumers worldwide, but it is challenging for companies to effectively reach a significant number of these global consumers without an appropriate market segmentation strategy. Market segmentation is the process of dividing the overall market into subsets of buyers who share similar needs and wants under certain segmentation criteria. To be viable to a marketer, these market segments have to be identifiable, reachable, and measurable, and they must be big enough to justify targeting. Market segmentation helps companies effectively target their customer base and then develop product or brand positioning that relates to the needs of that particular market segment. Segmentation also helps companies differentiate their offerings from their competitors'.

In the context of global e-commerce, market segmentation relates not only to the products and services being sold on the website but also to how the website is localized on the basis of international consumer expectations. In the first half of the chapter I explore ways of segmenting traditional markets, and in the latter half I explore strategies related to segmenting international online consumers to better position company offerings, including international websites.

Traditionally, businesses have segmented consumers on the following criteria.

- *Geographic segmentation* Consumers are classified on the basis of the region where they are located: country, city, zip code, etc. For example, marketers use geographic information systems (GISs),[1] which integrate hardware, software, and data for capturing, managing, analyzing, and displaying all forms of geographically referenced information. ESRI (www.esri.com) is one of the major GIS companies that develop GIS solutions for businesses, governments, education, natural resources management, and other industries. The information captured via GISs can help locate populations of people on the world map to target, with route planning, logistics, demographic trends, etc. On the internet, web users' geographic information can be captured by tracking their IP addresses, the unique number that identifies each computer connected via the internet. Geolocation technology can identify each visitor's geographical location, including geographic markets such as country, region, city, and internet service provider (ISP). Using geolocation, companies can effectively present localized offerings for their international customers. Today, a variety of devices, such as Global Positioning System (GPS) devices in cars and mobile phones, also use geolocation to deliver more relevant content. The topic of geolocation is discussed further in later chapters.

Geolocation

Yunker (2008) defines geolocation as a process of automatically identifying a web user's location without the web user knowing it or providing any location information. Geolocation uses the user's IP address to identify the user's location; it does not use cookies or other web plug-ins. According to Yunker, almost 12 percent of large multinational companies use geolocation to improve global navigation and serve their global online consumers customized content. By using geolocation, companies can provide their consumers with country-specific websites in their local language. They can also create targeted promotions for different countries so that people from specific countries may be able to see only specific promotions. This can raise some ethical issues, while at the same time it can solve other legal or ethical issues. For example, if certain material might be considered offensive in one country or is even illegal, companies could give their customers in that country different material that is more appropriate.

- *Demographic segmentation* Consumers are segmented on the basis of variables such as age, gender, family size, income, generational level, nationality, ethnicity, religion, education, and occupation. Companies can combine demographic information with geographic information to get powerful insights into their consumers' wants and needs. Geo-demographic segmentation tools can help companies interpret data from demographic databases, digitized maps, and GIS applications. Some popular geo-demographic segmentation tools are Prizm (US), Tapestry (US), CAMEO (UK),

---

[1] www.gis.com/content/what-gis.

ACORN (UK), and MOSAIC (UK). Companies can also capture demographic data on the internet via web forms, registration profiles, and other customer data entry mechanisms.

- *Behavioral segmentation* This is the process of segmenting the market on the basis of actual user behavior. Such behaviors include the benefit that the customer is seeking, how the consumer uses the product (for example, baking soda has several uses and thus can be marketed based on usage segmentation), consumers' brand loyalty, or even usage occasion. Online user behavior can be observed using online user tracking and web analytics software tools available in the market, such as Webtrends, Clickstream, or the free Google Analytics service.

- *Psychographic segmentation* Also called lifestyle segmentation, this strategy is used to create extensive consumer profiles based on their lifestyles or their activities, interests, and opinions (also called the AIO). One example of a lifestyle-based consumer segment is "soccer moms," representing middle-class, suburban mothers who are actively involved in their children's sporting events. SRI Consulting has created one of the most sophisticated methods of identifying segments on the basis of values and lifestyles. VALS™ (value and lifestyle survey) places US adult consumers into one of eight segments based on their responses to the VALS questionnaire. According to SRI, the eight segments are innovators, thinkers, achievers, experiencers, believers, strivers, makers, and survivors.[2] SRI Consulting has also created GeoVALS™, which estimates the proportion of the eight VALS segments across all residential zip codes and block groups. This is like combining the power of all three major segmentation parameters: demographics, geographics, and psychographics.

Various classifications of global online consumer segments, based on information gathered online, are now emerging. In the following sections some of the global online consumer segments are discussed.

Importance of segmentation

Segmentation can help companies focus their marketing efforts and market more efficiently. Addressing the needs of smaller groups of customers sharing similar needs is easier than marketing to a large, heterogeneous consumer group that might have varying expectations. Market segmentation also helps companies identify niche markets, as well as approaches to target them. For example, www.singlemom.com is a place for single mothers in the United States to meet online and find information, products, and services related to education, parenting, legal questions, housing, health, and other issues. Thus singlemom.com is using market segmentation to market to the single mother segment. Marketers now use various community sites, blogs, fan pages,

---

[2] www.strategicbusinessinsights.com.

and other social media applications to micro-target their consumers and deliver them niche messages and offers.

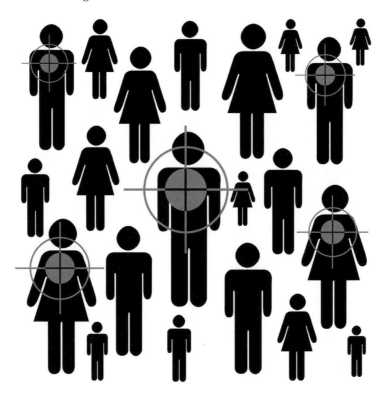

By identifying customers on the basis of segmentation criteria, companies can better tailor the content of their sites to the specific segments, improving the customer experience and, ultimately, sales. For example, companies use geolocation technology to identify which country the web user is in, and then decide accordingly which country page this web user will see. In this way, Dell uses market segmentation to create different web sections for home computer users, for small and medium businesses, for the public sector, and for large enterprises. Each segment receives content specific to its needs as well as purchasing potential. Likewise, American Express's site has sections for merchants, small businesses, large corporations, and regular customers.

Websites also use information about consumer behavior and demographics to create unique offers and online experiences. For example, Americanexpress.com, Drugstore .com, and Amazon.com use past purchase data, browsing data, and even demographic data to customize web pages for their users. These companies use such information to present customers with customized offerings. Amazon's recommendation system is well known for tracking users' purchasing and browsing behavior to come up with product recommendations, and Drugstore.com gathers similar information to suggest cosmetics or other products its online consumers might like.

Global online user segments

Companies can use several data sources to effectively segment their consumers in the online context. One of the most important questions to ask is if these online consumers are different in general from offline consumers. Are they better educated and better off? Is there a digital divide?

Digital divide

Basically, the digital divide is the gap between people who have access to digital technologies and people who don't. In an international context, people in countries where access to the internet via a computer is limited for some of the reasons below may also be more likely to go online via mobile devices. Causes of the digital divide include the following.

- Income gaps: people with low incomes are less likely to be able to access the internet on a regular basis.
- Educational gaps: less educated people might have difficulty properly accessing and using the digital content.
- Geographic gaps: certain geographic areas might not be connected to the internet.
- Connectivity speed gaps: certain communities might not be able to access digital content properly due to slow connection speeds.

A large-scale study by McKinsey & Company (Hartung, 2001) finds six behavior-based categories of online users.

(1) *Simplifiers* account for 29 percent of internet users and seek convenience and ease of use when browsing sites.
(2) *Surfers*, 8 percent of active users, leverage the web to find information and shop.
(3) *Bargainers*, 8 percent of active users, are online bargain hunters and browse the web for shopping and entertainment.
(4) *Connectors*, 36 percent of active users, generally use the web to stay in touch with people.

(5) *Routiners*, 15 percent of active users, generally use the web to obtain information and revisit their informational sites of interest.

(6) *Sportsters*, 4 percent of active users, generally spend most of their time on sports and entertainment sites.

Another way to look at customer segmentation is by motivation-based preferences. A study by Kau, Tang, and Ghose (2003) analyzed 3,700 internet users to understand their information-seeking patterns as well as their motivations for shopping online. Their study finds six online consumer segments (Kau, Tang, and Ghose, 2003: 149–50).

(1) *On-off shoppers* are those who like to surf the internet and collect online information but prefer to shop offline. They enjoy looking for advertisements, are frequent users of bookmarks, and use the same search engine on a regular basis. They are experienced in surfing and often look out for the best deals. Demographically, a person in this segment is likely to be single and in the younger age group of fifteen to twenty-four years. An offline on-off shopper is equally likely to be a male or a female.

(2) *Comparison shoppers* are those who compare product features, prices, and brands before making purchase decisions. They also actively look out for promotional offers. In terms of age, this group has a slightly higher percentage of respondents in the age group of twenty-five to twenty-nine years, although the gender distribution is very similar to the overall sample.

(3) *Traditional shoppers* are those who typically buy from brick-and-mortar stores. They do not surf the internet for comparative information, neither do they look for bargains on the internet. Although they may come from all different age groups, a higher proportion of this group of shoppers is around forty to forty-nine years old (11 percent, compared to 7 percent of the total sample).

(4) *Dual shoppers* are more likely to be single, male, and in the younger age group of fifteen to twenty-four years. They like to compare brands and product features. They also rely on the internet for information gathering. However, they are not particularly likely to look for or act on special offers.

(5) *e-laggards* are slightly more likely to be a female (37 percent, versus 34 percent for the whole sample) and in the older age group of thirty-five years and above (20 percent, versus 16 percent for the whole sample). He or she has lower interest in seeking information from the internet. Only 7 percent of the e-laggards can be considered to possess a high level of navigation expertise, the second lowest group after the traditional shoppers (4.5 percent).

(6) *Information surfers* are more likely to be married (43 percent compared to 30 percent for the whole sample). Only about 31 percent of them are between fifteen and twenty-four years old, compared to 41 percent for the whole sample. They love banner ads and click on them often. An information surfer also looks out for promotional offers. He or she has good navigation expertise and online purchase experience.

Another online consumer segmentation study of British online consumers finds that the majority of consumers online are motivated by economic orientation and clustered under the segment "price sensitives," making up almost 27 percent of the total sample (Jayawardhena, Wright, and Dennis, 2007). In this study, the second most prevalent online consumer segment was "convenience shoppers" (23 percent), who are attracted to the internet for the convenience and ease of use that it provides. The other three consumer segments found in the survey are "brand loyal," comprising 20 percent of the sample, followed by "discerning shoppers" (17 percent) and "active shoppers" (13 percent).

Each of the segmentation models described above provides a useful framework that companies can use to understand target markets and to predict their likely behavior when using the internet to purchase products and services. Of course, companies also have to take into account the unique socio-cultural and other international e-environmental factors that may impact online consumer behavior in various countries.

One of the most significant efforts in the area of creating global online consumer profiles has been undertaken by the "Digital Life" research project. Under this project, more than 50,000 consumers across forty-six countries are being surveyed, and click-stream data is also being collected. The data from this project will help companies understand the global heterogeneity in consumers' online activities. Such information may help marketers gain insights into how consumers access the internet, their online behaviors, and their usage of a variety of online formats such as social media and online shopping sites.

BRIC online consumers

Today, the emerging economies of Brazil, Russia, India, and China are collectively called the "BRIC" countries. The BRICs represent significant online populations. The highest growth in internet usage is anticipated in these countries and countries like them. According to Internet World Stats, as of 2010 North America accounted for only 14 percent of global internet users. Asia had the largest number of internet users, accounting for almost 42 percent of the global online population, followed by Europe, with about 24 percent (www.internetworldstats.com/stats.htm). Furthermore, the purchasing power of BRIC online consumers is also increasing as these economies strengthen and expand their middle class. KPMG's (2009) fourth survey on the use of convergence technology and global consumers reveals that BRIC consumers are more willing to pay for online and mobile content than consumers in G7 countries (Canada, France, Germany, Italy, Japan, the United Kingdom, and the United States). Some of the characteristics of BRIC consumers are highlighted in the following sections.

Brazil: online consumers

- Internet users in Latin America, including Brazil, tend to be younger than the population as a whole and are more likely to be from the middle or upper socio-economic segments (Belcher, 2006).
- Online consumers in Brazil spend even more time online than their European counterparts in terms of using audio-visual content, e-banking, and e-commerce. In fact, Brazilian teenagers spend more time browsing the web, almost fourteen hours more per month, than they spend on reading or going to the movies (Raso, 2006).
- Brazilians primarily access the internet from home and their workplace.
- According to D'Alessio and Pradas (2002), Brazilian users have a strong nationalist attitude regarding content on the web.
- Brazilian online consumers tend to be some of the most prolific shoppers. According to the Nielsen Company (2010a), 84 percent of Brazilian online consumers plan to make an online purchase in the next six months. The items most popular among online Brazilian consumers are books, electronic equipment, computer hardware, and DVDs/games.
- Social networking sites are also popular in Brazil, which is no surprise considering the collectivist nature of its culture. According to Michael *et al.* (2010), 69 percent of Brazilian consumers are active in social networking sites. Google's Orkut social networking site, for example, is hugely popular.
- In general, Latin American consumers prefer to pay mostly by credit card, followed by PayPal, bank transfer, debit card, and cash on delivery (COD), in that order (nielsen .com). PayPal is especially popular in Brazil.
- The government of Brazil seems to have embraced the internet wholeheartedly. Almost 12 million tax filers, or 95 percent of tax filers in Brazil, file their taxes electronically (Raso, 2006).

Russia: online consumers

- According to a Consumer Commerce Barometer survey of almost 2,000 Russian internet users, the internet is now a well-established tool to research online purchases.

Most Russian users commonly use online search engines for online shopping research (consumerbarometer.eu).

- A large-scale survey of Russian online consumers by PricewaterhouseCoopers (2009) indicates the high readiness of Russian consumers to make online purchases. Almost 80 percent of respondents reported that they had made at least one purchase over the internet. However, according to the report, most Russians still lack confidence in online retailing, and the preferred method of payment still tends to be COD. Books and consumer electronics are the most popular types of goods for online shopping in Russia.

- The Consumer Commerce Barometer survey also shows that online consumers in Russia have major concerns with security and trust. The survey finds that almost 54 percent of the users read the "terms and conditions" before buying products online. Further, just 9 percent of Russians are comfortable buying products from foreign websites (consumerbarometer.eu).

- The PricewaterhouseCoopers (2009) study also finds that 73 percent of the respondents usually go online to use social networking sites. Based on this report, it also seems that Russian consumers seek to overcome their lack of trust and confidence in internet businesses by leveraging social networks and recommendations from friends to guide their online shopping choices.

- Broadband and mobile use for internet access is growing rapidly in Russia. According to Michael *et al.*, 2010), almost 12 percent of Russians access the internet via their mobile devices.

India: online consumers

- In India, urban and rural users of the internet have been separated by a digital divide. This gap has narrowed in recent years, with more rural Indian users interacting with web-based activities. According to the Internet and Mobile Association of India (IAMAI, 2010), the amount of internet use among people in lower socio-economic groups is steadily increasing; however, young people are the most active users of the internet in India.

- According to the IAMAI (2010) report, the most common online activity among Indian internet users is e-mail, followed by "general information search," "educational information search," music/video over the internet, text chat, online job search, and gaming.

- Indians tend to be value- and price-conscious consumers, and thus actively search for information to ascertain product value. According to a recent Nielsen Company survey (2010b), Indian consumers also actively seek online product reviews, especially when purchasing consumer durables and electronics. The network of family and friends is also an important source of information to facilitate online shopping.[3]

[3] www.indiantelevision.com/headlines/y2k10/sep/sep66.php.

- Indians are also active social media users, and Orkut.com has traditionally had a strong hold on the online social networking market in India. However, on the basis of the study by Nielsen Company (2010b), 50 percent of online users now use Facebook and are also switching from Orkut to Facebook. Twitter has also seen exponential growth in India recently; 57 percent of Twitter users in India signed up in the past year.

- Internet matchmaking is now complementing the age-old "arranged marriage" tradition in India. Various internet matchmaking sites, such as Shaadi.com, BhararMatrimony.com, and Jeevansathi.com, are making it possible for Indians to find their life mates online.

China: online consumers

- In China, bulletin boards are the most popular form of social media. According to the Nielsen Company survey (2010b), more than 80 percent of social media content is delivered via bulletin boards.

- One of the distinct characteristics of Chinese online users (Michael *et al.*, 2010) is that almost 87 percent of Chinese consumers preferred to communicate via instant messaging compared to 53 percent via e-mail.

- Another unique characteristic of Chinese online users is that they are more likely to post and share negative product reviews. Based on Nielsen Company (2010b), almost 62 percent of Chinese online users tend to share negative product reviews, compared to 41 percent globally.

- Chinese consumers perceive online shopping to be riskier than their US counterparts do, which is due to a lack of online shopping experience and an insufficient e-commerce infrastructure (Liao, Proctor, and Salvendy 2009).

- Chinese and Korean online consumers tend to be the most prolific online shoppers in the Asia-Pacific region, with 95 percent of internet users intending to make a web purchase in the next six months (Nielsen Company, 2010a).

- Among Chinese online users, common online purchases include books, clothes, and electronics (Nielsen Company, 2010a).

Identifying global customers using global CRM

The foundation of customer relationship management is the concept of "relationship marketing," which deals with establishing one-to-one relationships with customers on an ongoing basis. Relationship marketing transcends the concept of interacting with customers on a piecemeal basis; instead, this marketing strategy is a long-term process to develop relationship capital. The aim here is to get the "mind share," and the market share will follow. The end result is an ongoing dialog between the customer and the company. Relationship marketing therefore forms the core or foundation of any CRM effort.

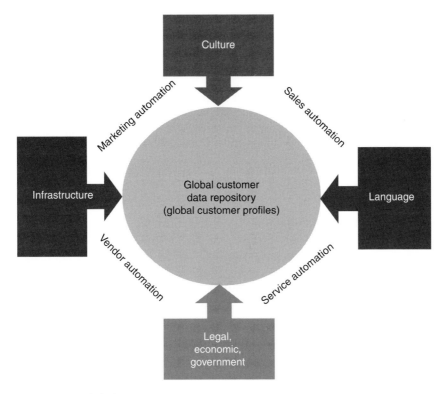

Figure 3.1 Global CRM

CRM can be defined as a company-wide effort to align corporate strategy to customer needs, in turn generating customer value and customer loyalty (Shumanov and Ewing, 2007). At its core, CRM is a combination of strategy and database marketing, which together facilitate implementation of the relationship marketing philosophy. CRM involves a variety of applications and processes that help a company develop one-on-one relationships with its customers, leading to enhanced customer value. Common CRM applications include sales force automation, marketing automation, customer support, inventory management, customer analytics, workflow management, e-mail management, and social media campaigns.

CRM becomes global CRM when firms or their customers are located in multiple countries. When dealing with multiple countries, companies have to account not only for diversity of languages but also for customer preferences, cultural issues, legal issues, corporate headquarters and local subsidiary control issues, content consistency issues, and many other country-specific issues (see Figure 3.1). *Thus global CRM represents a company-wide orientation toward integrating customer information on a global basis, while letting the local execution of CRM vary from country to country.* The global CRM philosophy can be best captured in the phrase "Think globally and act locally."

The primary application of CRM software is to manage customer data effectively and use it to make customer-centric decisions. However, when going global, the task of identifying and segmenting customers from various countries poses new challenges. CRM software helps answer questions in a global context, such as the following.

- How do we identify which customer is coming from which country?
- What are the cultural value orientations of prospective global customers?
- Do Spanish-speaking customers visiting Spanish-translated web pages come from Spain, Central America, and/or Latin America?
- Are the Spanish customers visiting the Spanish pages comfortable with the language, or do they need modification in dialects such as Castilian or some other region-specific dialect?
- Which products are more popular in which country?
- What kind of product/service information do consumers from various countries seek?
- Which search engines and referral sites do visitors from various countries use?

Therefore, when going global, companies need CRM applications that can successfully identify, segment, and target customers from different countries. CRM systems take different approaches to tracking international online customers. One approach is to take into account the search engine type used by a visitor to know the country of origin – for example, uk.yahoo.com (United Kingdom), es.Yahoo.com (Spain), or in.yahoo.com (India). CRM software can also identify global visitors through the URL used by the visitor, as in .uk, or .ca, or .jp. Another approach is to simply count the number of unique IP addresses, and then further fine-tune search data by utilizing user agents and external referrals to distinguish among different users with the same IP address by recording the browser version of the visitor and/or the IP number of the referring site. Cookies are also used for identifying unique visitors. However, these measures may not tell the full story. We want to know not only the country of origin of each unique visitor, but also his or her browsing behavior, purchasing habits, and desired products, and a plethora of other information to develop correct and complete customer profiles.

Thus it is important to have a clear-cut segmentation strategy that uniquely identifies global visitors and develops visitor profiles. It is critical to capture all customer information at each customer contact point. To achieve this, CRM applications must connect seamlessly with a company's various consumer communication platforms, including local and international websites. It is also important that the back-end systems of the company are able to accommodate the complexities of the international e-environment, such as the diversity of languages, formats, currencies, files, symbols, etc. Customers come in contact with the company in different locations and in a variety of ways; the company should be able to capture customer information at each of these customer contact points. A partial list of customer contact points is included in Table 3.1.

Table 3.1 Customer contact points

- e-mail
- wireless
- message boards
- escorted browsing
- web form processing
- web log files
- page tagging
- IP address
- online customer service chat
- offline customer service calls
- automated voice response
- telephone
- instant messaging
- face to face, sales reps, etc.
- regular mail
- retail stores
- kiosk, digital TV
- other interactive technologies

Segmenting global customers

The evolution of global e-commerce raises new issues about the standardization versus the localization of web content. There has been an ongoing debate over whether to localize websites to meet unique cultural needs or to expect consumers to adapt to standardized content. Although some people predict the emergence of a global internet culture and a transnational web style, a growing body of literature supports a localized-specialized approach to web advertising and web content development. However, both the academic literature and the business press indicate a lack of guidance and a lack of cross-cultural models and frameworks to support localization efforts on the web. The first step toward customizing products and messages for specific consumer segments is to develop unique customer profiles based on common interests, cultural value orientations, and language usage. Log file analysis is the most commonly used application to understand aspects of visitor browsing behavior, such as the number of pages visited and the time spent on each web page. Web user data can also be collected via files based on the Common Gateway Interface (CGI) (in which a client computer runs a program known as a CGI script on the web server to collect and save user information). This protocol is used to communicate between web forms and a program, and provides information on users' access patterns, user requests, and the time users spend with each service (Wiedmann, Buxel, and Walsh, 2002).

Packet sniffer

A packet sniffer is a program that monitors network traffic between networked computers. This information is generally used by network administrators to troubleshoot problems with network traffic, but in malicious hands this technology can be used to find sensitive personal information on the network. *Word of advice: encryption!*

> **Web bugs**
>
> A web bug is an invisible object that is embedded in a web page or e-mail and allows a check to be made as to whether a user has viewed the page or e-mail. One common use is in e-mail tracking. There are *great privacy concerns* with using them; phishing e-mails use them to verify if the e-mail address is legitimate.

Through these log files and CGI-based files, the companies can acquire valuable web metrics about browsing behavior, purchases made, and return visits. More extended discussion on web metrics follows in later chapters. Such data-mining CRM applications help companies build customer profiles that can help them predict particular behavior, such as purchasing, upgrading, or not coming back (the customer attrition rate). Furthermore, such applications may also be useful in developing, managing, controlling, and personalizing country-specific marketing campaigns; doing localized search engine optimization; and customizing and tracking social media usage.

Customizing for global customers

Another major application of CRM software is to leverage the customer data collected at various contact points and to personalize the web-browsing experience for visitors as they navigate the site. However, when CRM applications are implemented globally major modifications are needed.

For example, it is not yet clear what type of global user interface structure will emerge on the internet. Other complicating factors are translation procedures and the use of roman and non-roman scripts. Many web users have difficulty viewing Chinese or Japanese websites because special add-on software or plug-ins are required, though these problems are becoming less frequent. Moreover, translating web pages is only the tip of the cultural iceberg facing global marketers. Language styles, dialects, typography, colors, icons, symbols, metaphors, and values differ vastly across the globe. In later chapters I discuss these issues in depth and provide more guidance for culturally customizing websites.

Ideally, CRM applications should not only identify visitors from different countries but also use this information to guide visitors to country-specific pages to give them a personalized, culturally congruent experience. For example, people from Arabic countries read from right to left and would like web pages with content and navigation in a right-to-left manner, rather than the Western left-to-right orientation.

Managing global customers

Finally, at the global CRM implementation level, companies must pay special attention to how the CRM application can be locally modified and globally integrated. The chosen CRM application should be able to handle country-specific differences in work style and customer behavior. It is not enough just to have multilingual software and a local customer service center. To implement CRM globally, companies also need to take into account how sales and customer service decisions are made in different countries, and simultaneously integrate and localize their marketing automation systems, sales force automation applications, customer databases, vendor databases, and customer service records. This would not only help to create a centralized country-centered e-CRM application but also help to share and access the country-specific records globally on a real-time basis.

Different countries will place different emphases on marketing automation, sales force automation, call center sales, call center service, and field service. A standardized CRM solution may not suffice. Even using a single CRM application for managing different functions ranging from marketing automation to field service automation may not be efficient. Many varieties of CRM software are available; thus it is important to match the CRM software competency with the type of automation the company is looking for. For example, TRACKWeb Mobile by Soffront Software, Inc. is a good CRM application for collecting field data and sales force automation, while Hyperion's (Oracle) CRM analysis works well for the integration of data systems and log file analysis. Moreover, companies should pay careful attention to the scalability (incremental advancement of computing power), openness, ability to be delivered as web service, and user friendliness of the CRM solution sought for global implementation.

The CRM application should also be able to virtually process any log file format, or, for that matter, any file format from any kind of server, and ensure support for new formats as they are introduced in different countries. In fact, a global CRM system should provide global visibility to various aspects of CRM, such as multicurrency transactions, customer types, country/regional sales data, quotas, leads, marketing campaign data, etc. For example, NetSuite OneWorld rolls up multicurrency forecasts within and across multinational sales entities, allowing sales reps to manage orders and forecast against their quota in local currency.[4] Another CRM vendor, Salesforce.com, seems to be at the forefront of leveraging a cloud computing and web services model to deliver its CRM solutions globally. Salesforce.com customers now do not have to worry about hosting the CRM packages or periodic updates and can share all kinds of market information across various platforms among varied parties in real time. For example, Software AG, a client of Salesforce.com, was able to integrate marketing information across seventy countries in fourteen languages by leveraging the Salesforce.com's CRM system, which is delivered via a flexible web interface that permits easy and real-time connectivity.[5]

The biggest challenge for the evolution of global CRM is to acknowledge the diverse needs of global customers and at the same time integrate country-specific applications

---

[4] www.netsuite.com/portal/products/oneworld/global-crm.shtml.
[5] www.salesforce.com/customers/hi-tech-software/software_ag.jsp.

in a centralized hub. The cloud computing model, which thrives on scalability and provides enough flexibility for application customization, is to a great extent alleviating these challenges and allowing for real-time connectivity via the web. The next two sections describe cultural differences in CRM practices and provide some critical success factors for CRM implementation.

International CRM practices

Ramaseshan *et al.* (2006) identify several differences in CRM practices by culture.

(1) US companies see global markets as more homogeneous and tend to have more standardized CRM practices than European companies.
(2) The studies by Ramaseshan *et al.* (2006) and others in this area have found that US firms are more focused on the technological aspects of CRM and are mainly led by IT departments. In Nordic countries, companies are more likely to view CRM as a customer relationship tool that is managed by marketing and sales departments (Schultz, 2000).
(3) Firms from emerging markets with limited training in CRM philosophy and techniques/tools generally are less sophisticated in CRM implementation.
(4) US firms in general like to collect a lot of customer data compared to non-US firms.
(5) In Europe there is more concern for customer data privacy than in the United States.

CRM success factors

(1) Acquire the right customer. Companies need to calculate the lifetime value of the customer and then prioritize their CRM efforts.
(2) Craft the right value proposition. The value proposition must be appealing to the customer but must also reflect the amount of money the enterprise can afford to spend on that customer.
(3) Learn from the best practices of other companies that have implemented CRM successfully.
(4) Ensure that top management is committed to the implementation of the CRM system. Management buy-in is crucial to instilling a sense of confidence throughout the enterprise that the company is committed to the technology.
(5) Institute coordinative routines to facilitate the global implementation of CRM. Organization-wide, collaborative efforts can be facilitated with the help of cross-functional and cross-national teams of CRM champions.
(6) Align coordinative routines with existing organizational and departmental routines. This is vital, as many CRM efforts fail due to a lack of alignment between CRM goals and company culture and routines.

(7) Have a global, holistic view of worldwide customer data and integrate all customer-related systems into a global customer data repository. All the data and information should be available in a universal, user-friendly format, which can then be easily translated, formatted, or localized by the international offices.

(8) Engage employees. Employee motivation and training is the key to turning silent bystanders into active champions of CRM implementation and maintenance. If employees are unconvinced by the CRM system or do not know how to use it properly, critical inputs to the system can be compromised. Employees are, in fact, the main interface between the company and its external customers.

(9) Ensure that the all-important customer contact points are being leveraged to compile customer and market information in the CRM system.

(10) Be selective when choosing a CRM vendor. The CRM vendor should be treated as a business partner that can work with the company to achieve the global scalability of the CRM system and enhance CRM customization to specific local and global needs.

(11) Implement the CRM system in stages in order to better align the system with the existing infrastructure and routines and enable a smoother transition.

(12) Involve CRM experts, outside consultants, integrators, and, most importantly, people with expertise in both CRM and international business operations to facilitate implementation of the CRM system.

(13) Measure the effectiveness of the CRM implementation in terms of customer retention and customer satisfaction, revenue growth, employee productivity gains, cost reductions, and CRM adoption and usage by employees.

(14) Make continuous improvements to the CRM system. The implementation of CRM systems is a continuous process loop.

Customer relationship management processes and tools can help companies achieve one-to-one marketing with their customers, thereby increasing customer loyalty, satisfaction, and retention. By leveraging CRM operational and analytical capabilities, companies can perform more effective targeting, personalization, and customization of their websites to meet unique consumer needs.

Segmentation for optimizing web localization efforts

When a company launches a website, it is "born global" from day one, whether or not it is prepared to be. By the simple nature of the web, consumers worldwide can access its content immediately. The tremendous global reach provided by the internet has been a source of opportunities and threats alike for companies. For companies prepared to conduct global e-commerce, global access via the web presents a unique opportunity. However, the majority of companies still see the global reach provided by the web as a challenge. One of the most fundamental decisions companies have to make is whether to leverage the same home-country site for multiple markets or to develop new international sites to meet the linguistic, cultural, and functional expectations of their international consumers. Some studies in the academic literature point to the emergence of a transcultural web style, while others have documented that websites of different countries tend to be culturally unique and require content adaptation based on locale-specific requirements (Singh and Pereira, 2005).

This issue of standardization versus adaptation/localization was first discussed by Buzzell (1968), and since then the choice between a standardized or adapted marketing mix has been one of the core issues in international marketing. The balance is between the cost savings from the use of a standard marketing mix in all markets, and the increased sales and stronger consumer relationships from customizing the marketing mix to meet the needs and wants of each consumer (Jain, 1989). Several companies have now realized that complete standardization is not always an effective approach to reaching international markets. The contemporary viewpoint is that "total standardization is unthinkable" (Jain, 1989: 17). As such, the "contingency approach" (Lemak and Arunthanes, 1997) has emerged, which favors a combination of both standardization and localization of the marketing mix. By taking the contingency approach, marketers are able to form relationships effectively with local consumers while still garnering the cost savings from some level of global standardization. The contingency approach to using a mix of standardization and localization is becoming more acceptable, as the globalization process continues to unleash forces of both homogenization and fragmentation.

On the one hand, the globalization process has led to homogenization in consumption and the emergence of a global consumer segment (Keillor, D'Amico, and Hortan, 2001). Emerging research shows that this global segment appears to share a global consumer culture transcending the need for the localization of products, services, and media to meet specific cultural demands. Consider the MTV generation or global communities around certain video games. On the other hand, the globalization process has also led to fragmentation or heterogenization, as individuals sense a loss of control, national identity, and local traditions. For example, Arnould, Price, and Zinkhan (2004) note that global "earthscaping," or accelerated trends in globalization, are resulting in the "creolization" of global consumer patterns, which, in turn, leads to the blending of local and foreign consumption traditions.[6] Thus a challenge for international online marketers is to understand how these forces of cultural homogenization and fragmentation interact to form unique online consumer segments and how these segments can be targeted.

Before we jump into the global online consumer segmentation model, it is important to understand what makes the online consumer globally or nationally oriented.

---

[6] "Earthscaping" is the accelerated movement of people, ideas, and factors of production. "Creolization" is the adoption and adaptation of commodities to local needs and consumption patterns.

Figure 3.2 Harajuku Girl

Global and national identity

The concept of global identity is related to world-mindedness, or a sense of togetherness or sharing with the rest of humanity. Individuals exhibit a global orientation when they identify themselves with humankind and issues that affect humankind broadly.[7] The concept of national identity, on the other hand, is seen as an amalgamation of nationalistic tendencies such as patriotism, ethnocentrism, nationalism, national character, and national heritage (Cui and Adams, 2002). However, in the current context of globalization, global and national identities are not two rigid and mutually exclusive concepts, but hold in combination a complexity, richness, and intrinsic tension. According to Appadurai (1990), the processes of cultural homogenization and cultural heterogenization have created a system of global interactions that are "triumphantly universal and resiliently particular." The orthogonal cultural identification theory explains how an individual can experience multiple cultural identities simultaneously (Oetting and Beauvais, 1991). According to this model, an individual's identification with any one culture is essentially independent of his or her identification with any other culture. Thus a person can be high on national identity at the same time as being high on global identity, or low on global identity at the same time as high on national identity (or inversely), or even low on both. For example, Mr. Joe may be very patriotic but still have a well-developed global identity that manifests itself in the form of his concern for global issues such as poverty, climate change, and education.

Around the world we see new and interesting segments of consumers that epitomize the existence of hybrid identities incorporating both local and global identities. The Harajuku fashion style is popular among a certain segment of Japanese youth; these Japanese youths dress in flamboyant colors, fashions, and styles (Lolita or Gothic, for

[7] The concept of global identity can be traced back to the work of Sampson and Smith (1957), who conceptualize global- or world-mindedness as a value orientation that emphasizes a sense of belongingness, empathy, and sharing with humankind as a whole.

example) that combine aspects of various world cultures (see Figure 3.2). This style screams out the high sense of individualism and distinctiveness in a Japanese national culture that takes pride both in its traditional cultural ways and in a high degree of collectivism.

Global online consumer segmentation model

As mentioned in the last section, globalization has exposed consumers worldwide to a variety of cultural influences from around the world in addition to their experience of their home culture. These global cultural experiences are facilitated by the global reach of the internet and the mass media, and the exchange of ideas via personal contact made possible by global travel. The result is that consumers worldwide subscribe to multiple identities on the basis of their national culture and global influences. In this section I explore four different global online consumer segments in terms of the level of their identification with national and global identities.

Patriots

Patriots are online consumers who identify very strongly with their national culture. Their global orientation is less developed, and they tend to be driven either by consumer ethnocentrism or by some other nationalistic beliefs. They are driven by the urge to patronize local culture and products and shun foreign labels in the form of products, services, and websites. One site that might attract patriots who tend to patronize their national products, companies, and websites is BuyAmerican.com, which is dedicated to selling and providing information on products that are only "Made in America." The website says, "BuyAmerican.com makes every effort to verify that the manufacturers and products represented on this site are 'Made in USA'... If the country of origin is not clearly stated on the manufacturer's site, we contact them directly to ensure that we are presenting the most accurate information."[8]

[8] Cited from www.buyamerican.com/aboutus.html.

How, therefore, should online marketers target this segment of global consumers? Some strategies for targeting patriots are as follows.

- Online marketers promoting global brands, products, and services will find it hard to reach this segment, so, at the broadest level, companies should make a concerted effort to localize their websites culturally.
- These consumers tend to emphasize the positive aspects of domestic products and discount the virtues of foreign products and services. Companies therefore need to sell products and services that are locally manufactured or can be locally sourced. Companies also need to ensure on their website that products and services clearly show their local origins.
- Marketers need to use "local consumer culture positioning" (Alden, Steenkamp, and Batra, 1999) to reach these customers. In the web context, this means that companies should emphasize that the website is locally produced for local consumers, and diminish the global or foreign origins of the site by imbuing it with local cultural meanings.

World citizens

World citizens are at the opposite end of the spectrum compared to patriots, because they have an expanded global identity and a low sense of nationalism. This is the segment of online consumers that is most amenable to standardized global marketing and standardized websites. This could be your dream segment if you are not planning on localizing, and these consumers understand the language used on your website. World citizens generally have a higher affiliation with global issues, global trends, global media, and global institutions. They also seem to share a sense of community with others around the world and are not restricted by their national identity. In fact, their nationalism could be very low, as they identify themselves more as the citizens of the world than of any specific country. Several factors have led to the emergence of this consumer segment worldwide. One of the main reasons is the pace of globalization and

the interconnectedness of the world, which is made possible by the internet and mass transportation. Another reason for the rise of world citizens is the increasing number of consumers in various countries who identify themselves with multiple cultures. In countries such as the United States, the United Kingdom, South Africa, Australia, and France, increasing numbers of people are biracial or multiracial.

From a marketing perspective, individuals in this segment show greater similarities in terms of lifestyle, product, and brand choices with the same groups across the border than within their own countries (Mooij, 2004). Individuals in this segment have an expanded identity that gravitates toward broader global values, and they tend to distance themselves from their national home culture. Here are two strategies for companies to consider when targeting world citizens.

- This segment embraces international websites and global brands and products, and it has lower expectations for cultural adaptation. Thus, if this is your consumer segment, extensive localization and cultural adaptation might not be necessary.
- Marketers who have recently embarked on the path of global e-commerce and have minimal experience or resources for website localization can target this international segment. However, they still may need to translate their web content into the local language.

Glocals

Glocals, as the name suggests, are both global and local in their mindset. They do not tend to exclude or discount their national culture or heritage in lieu of the global culture, or vice versa. Glocals are open to global influences, products, and websites but also have an expectation that they will be addressed in their own language and culture. The rise of glocals may be attributed to globalization as well as to the threat that the homogenization of consumption may pose to local culture. Thus glocals, while open to global culture, also actively seek to maintain and support their national culture.

Some implications for web marketers include the following.

- Consumers in this segment are more open to using international websites, reflecting their openness to global products, but at the same time glocals demand a high level of website localization, reflecting their strong patronage of and attachment to their national culture.
- These consumers can be a lucrative consumer segment provided marketers develop localized websites that are in the local language and culturally customized.
- To meet these ends, marketers may need to actively involve their foreign subsidiaries or local partners in their website localization efforts.

Mini-I

Mini-I, as the name suggests, tend not to identify with any national or global influences but have an idiosyncratic sense of identification. They are unique in that their identity is driven by a specific ideology, lifestyle, or subculture. They may even have a fragmented sense of self in which they construct and reconstruct their identities. Thus, for web marketers, they are a difficult segment to target and assess. Marketers have to customize their communication to such consumers by understanding their peculiar identification. For example, Mecca Cola was launched back in 2002 as an alternative to major US beverage brands. The positioning of Mecca Cola seems to be driven less by any specific national or global culture but more by religious ideology. Another example of mini-I could be postmodern consumers who are described as having multiple and transitional identities. Postmodern consumers focus more on products and experiences that enhance their individuality and recognize them as unique and not a part of a traditional market segment.

Some implications for web marketers when dealing with mini-I consumers include the following.

- They consitute an elusive segment that needs to be investigated further in order to ascertain their preferred type of lifestyle. This lifestyle information can then be used as a basis for targeting them on the web.

• Consumers in this segment may be open-minded toward foreign brands, but when targeting them it is important to use rational appeals emphasizing self-interest rather than localized marketing messages that are based on national culture or global consumption.

In conclusion, achieving a balance between the localization and the standardization of web content is critical for global e-business success. Companies do not need to invest heavily in localizing and culturally customizing their websites if most of their consumers do not actually have any expectation of localization. On the other hand, if a company's target market comprises consumers who value their national identity (e.g., patriots or glocals), then the company will need to invest in localization and cultural customization to achieve success. Thus companies should thoroughly understand their global online consumers before really deciding the level of localization on international websites. This initial investment in understanding global online consumer segments can lead to significant cost savings in the long term and help optimize web localization efforts.

Global consumer trends

This last section of the chapter outlines some emerging global consumer trends. These trends are general in nature and applicable to all kinds of businesses.

Alternatives to Barbie

In response to Barbie, which looks very Western and embodies Western values, companies in Islamic countries have adapted the doll to Islamic values.
Fulla Doll: with a head scarf and embodying Islamic values; sold in China, Brazil, the Middle East, Indonesia, and elsewhere.
Sara Doll: for children in Iran.
Razanne: meant to build Islamic identity and self-esteem among Muslim children.
Jamila: another Muslim doll sold across the Middle East.
Saghira: a Muslim Barbie sold in Morocco.

As the pace of globalization accelerates, consumers are facing cultural flows unimaginable a decade ago. This trend will continue and be complemented by rising consumerism, ethical consumption, and even nationalistic and religious consumption. Already products such as Mecca Cola, as mentioned in the previous section, and versions of Muslim adaptations of Barbie are a reaction against the global homogenization of consumption and values. A resurgence of nationalistic and religious values to counteract the trends of global consumerism is happening. Some more global consumer trends that will shape the consumer world of tomorrow include the following.

- *Individualization* This trend takes its meaning from individualistic cultural values. Countries such as the United States, the United Kingdom, Germany, and others value individual freedom, choice, and expression. This value is spreading worldwide, piggybacking on the rise of global consumerism. Consumers around the world now expect, and are being given, the products and services they demand. Consumers equipped with technology can now customize their music, media, advertising, web pages, and cellphone ringtones. In the future, marketers will work more closely with consumers to create customized offerings that express a customer's taste and individuality.

- *Premiumization* According to trendwatching.com, luxury is no longer associated only with a few industries and products, but is becoming increasingly widespread. Florin *et al.* (2007) call this trend "the democratization of luxury," as more consumers are able to afford what were once considered true luxuries. China and Russia are among the top ten countries with the highest growth in "high net worth individuals" or millionaires. There is a growing trend toward creating high-end and luxurious products in every product and service category possible. Examples include Bling h_2O bottled water, which is embellished with Swarovski crystals, and fancy *kimchi* refrigerators by Samsung. Renova, a leading European brand, markets the "sexiest paper in the world," including toilet tissue, paper towels, and napkins. Their voluptuous, soft, and glamorous toilet paper comes in several colors, including red, black, orange, red, green, azure, and fuchsia.

- *Gender complexity* The blurring of gender roles is happening around the world, as more women become part of the global workforce and more men feel comfortable stepping beyond traditional masculine roles. Florin *et al.* (2007) observe that men are also becoming more "feminized" in that they place higher value on beauty and fashion. The cosmetics industry is taking advantage of this emerging trend by marketing skin care lines and beauty products for men. In a traditionally masculine society such as India, men are embracing beauty products exclusively reserved for women just a decade ago. For example, fairness creams, which are common among Indian women, are now also being adopted by Indian men.

- *Threenagers* A survey by MTV of 25,000 people in eighteen countries revealed that people well into their mid-thirties want the youthful look and orientation of teenagers. Marketers who ignore this trend may lose out on significant opportunities to create products that can make people in their thirties feel younger. Forever 21 is one fashion apparel company that markets trendy fashion garments to men and women who are "young at heart" regardless of their biological age.

- *Eco-iconic* This emerging trend is related to the growing demand for eco-friendly products with bold and iconic designs that customers can visibly show off (trend watching.com).

- *Other trends* Products and services are becoming more short-lived, intended to be used and thrown away. This includes the growing popularity of 100-calorie snack packs and wear-only-a-few-times fashions (trendwatching.com). "Hiving" is another growing trend, as more generation Xers embrace a homebody's lifestyle (Florin *et al.*, 2007).

Conclusion

Recognizing various global online segments on the basis of their identification with global, national, or postmodern culture is a useful way for companies to effectively target their global online users and optimize their web globalization budgets. Academic survey instruments are available to measure global and national identity; the usage and deployment of these tools will depend on the context of analysis and a company's type of business. Describing the methods and instruments to measure various constructs for generating global online consumer profiles is beyond the scope of this book.

Chapter summary

- The chapter starts with an explanation of market segmentation and the traditional approaches to market segmentation. Four main segmentation approaches are geographic segmentation, demographic segmentation, behavioral segmentation, and psychographic segmentation.
- The various ways that technology is being applied to market segmentation are highlighted. Examples include the use of geolocation technology, web tracking, and web analytics.
- Various typologies defining online consumers are discussed. For example, online consumers can be broadly divided into surfers, simplifiers, bargainers, connectors, routiners, and sportsters. The chapter also discusses unique aspects of online consumers from BRIC nations on the basis of their web usage and purchasing patterns.
- An extended discussion focuses on how CRM technology can help web marketers collect customer information on a global basis and then leverage this information globally to develop customized marketing campaigns.
- The last topics covered in this chapter are the four segments of online global consumers based on their identification with global and national identity. Marketers can use the global online segmentation model to decide on the optimal level of web localization needed for specific country markets.

REFERENCES

Alden, Dana L., Steenkamp, Jan-Benedict E. M., and Batra, Rajeev 1999. "Brand positioning through advertising in Asia, North America, and Europe: the role of global consumer culture," *Journal of Marketing* 63: 75–87.

Appadurai, Arjun 1990. "Disjuncture and difference in the global cultural economy," *Public Culture* 2: 1–23.

Arnould, Eric J., Price, Linda, and Zinkhan, George 2004. *Consumers*. McGraw-Hill.

Belcher, James 2006. *Latin America Online*. eMarketer; available at www.emarketer.com.

Buzzell, Robert. 1968. "Can you standardize multinational marketing?" *Harvard Business Review* 46: 102–13.

Cui, Charles C., and Adams, Edward I. 2002. "National identity and NATID: an assessment in Yemen," *International Marketing Review* 19: 637–62.

D'Alessio, Nora de, and Pradas, Carola 2002. "Internet users in Argentina, Brazil, and Mexico," paper presented at the 7th ESOMAR Latin American conference, São Paulo, May 14.

Florin, Dave, Callen, Barry, Mullen, Sean, and Kropp, Jeane 2007. "Profiting from mega-trends," *Journal of Product and Brand Management* 16: 220–5.

Hartung, Steve 2001. "All visitors are not created equal: knowing online consumer segments and how to attract them are key." McKinsey & Company; available at www.mckinsey.com/practices/marketing/ourknowledge/pdf/Solutions_AllVisitorsAreNotCreatedEqual_consumer.pdf.

IAMAI 2010. *I-Cube 2009–2010: Internet in India*. IAMAI; available at www.iamai.in/reports1.aspx.

Jain, Subhash C. 1989. "Standardization of international marketing strategy: some research hypotheses," *Journal of Marketing* 53: 70–9.

Jayawardhena, Chanaka, Wright, Len Tiu, and Dennis, Charles 2007. "Consumers online: intentions, orientations and segmentation," *International Journal of Retail and Distribution Management* 35: 515–99.

Kau, Ah Keng, Tang, Yingchan E., and Ghose, Sanjoy 2003. "Typology of online shoppers," *Journal of Consumer Marketing* 20: 139–56.

Keillor, Bruce D., D'Amico, Michael, and Hortan, Veronica 2001. "Global consumer tendencies," *Psychology and Marketing* 18: 1–19.

KPMG 2009. *Consumers and Convergence IV: Convergence Goes Mainstream: Convenience Edges out Consumer Concerns over Privacy and Security*. KPMG International; available at www.kpmg.com.

Lemak, David J., and Arunthanes, Wiboon 1997. "Global business strategy: a contingency approach," *Multinational Business Review* 5: 26–37.

Liao, Huafei, Proctor, Robert W., and Salvendy, Gavriel 2009. "Chinese and US online consumer preferences for content of e-commerce websites: a survey," *Theoretical Issues in Ergonomics Science* 10: 19–42.

Michael, David, Aguiar, Marcos, Boutenko, Vladislav, Rastogi, Vaishali, Subramanian, Arvind, and Zhou, Yvonne 2010. *The Internet's New Billion: Digital Consumers in Brazil, Russia, India, China, and Indonesia*. Boston Consulting Group; available at www.bcg.com/documents/file58645.pdf.

Mooij, Marieke D. 2004. *Consumer Behavior and Culture: Consequences for Global Marketing and Advertising*. Sage.

Nielsen Company 2010a. "Global trends in online shopping: a Nielsen global consumer report: June 2010." Nielsen Company; available at www.nielsen.com.

2010b. "Social media dominates Asia Pacific internet usage," http://blognielsen.com/nielsenwire/global/social-media-dominates-asia-pacific-internet-usage.

Oetting, E. R., and Beauvais, F. 1991. "Orthogonal cultural identification theory: the cultural identification of minority adolescents," *International Journal of Addictions* 25: 655–85.

PricewaterhouseCoopers 2009. *Online Retailing in Russia: Social Media Marketing*. PrincewaterhouseCoopers; available at www.seribd.com/doc/46437139/Online-retail-March2010-Eng.

Ramaseshan, B., Bejou, David, Jain, Subhash C., Mason, Charlotte, and Pancras, Joseph 2006. "Issues and perspectives in global customer relationship management," *Journal of Service Research* 9: 195–208.

Raso, Ebe 2006. "E-commerce in Brazil." US Commercial Service; available at www.buyusa.gov.

Sampson, D. L., and Smith, H. P. 1957. "A scale to measure world-minded attitudes," *Journal of Social Psychology* 45: 99–106.

Schultz, Don E. 2000. "Learn to differentiate CRM's two faces," *Marketing News* 34: 11.

Shumanov, Michael, and Ewing, Michael 2007. "Developing a global CRM strategy," *International Journal of E-Business Research* 3: 70–82.

Singh, Nitish, and Pereira, Arun 2005. *The Culturally Customized Web Site: Customizing Web Sites for the Global Marketplace*. Elsevier Butterworth-Heinemann.

Wiedmann, Klaus P., Buxel, Holger, and Walsh, Gianfranco 2002. "Customer profiling in e-commerce: methodological aspects and challenges," *Journal of Database Marketing* 9: 170–84.

Yunker, John 2008. "Going global with geolocation: how companies are using geolocation to improve navigation for web users around the world." Byte Level Research; available at www.quova.com/downloads/wp-going-global-eng.pdf.

4 Web globalization strategies

Chapter objectives

- Identify the major strategic concerns that organizations have when implementing their web globalization efforts.
- Provide insights into how to address concerns about web globalization.
- Identify six web globalization dilemmas and present specific recommendations.
- Present examples and cases of how companies are managing their web globalization efforts.

Web globalization challenges

As companies leverage the web to expand globally, they also experience various challenges involved in successful international e-business expansion. A number of challenges associated with the international e-environment have been outlined in the previous chapters. In this chapter the goal is to outline some challenges related to the organizational and technological capabilities required for international e-business expansion, particularly challenges related to the development of international web-sites. Companies that understand these challenges are more likely to have a successful web globalization effort.

Web globalization

Web globalization addresses all enterprise-wide issues that are involved in successfully launching and maintaining international websites and achieving international e-business expansion.

When companies launch international sites for various countries, ideally they should be adapted to various country-specific requirements. To facilitate the localization of the content for multiple locales, companies need skills, knowledge, vision, and a clear sense of direction in order to steer their web globalization efforts successfully. The concept of "web globalization" addresses all company-wide issues that are involved in successfully launching and maintaining international websites and achieving international e-business expansion. Thus "web globalization" is a broad term that takes into

83

account not only the technical processes involved in the design of international sites but also the strategic decisions and processes that facilitate the development, management, and implementation of international websites.

Several companies cited the following reasons that have prevented them from taking the plunge into web globalization (Yunker, 2005: 8).

- "We lack the skills for successful web globalization."
- "Lack of knowledge and application of tools to achieve web globalization."
- "We're not big enough to partner with the CMS and GMS[1] vendors."
- "Geopolitical and regulatory uncertainties."
- "There are not enough words on those web pages."

To help companies globalize their web presence, this chapter presents tools and approaches to help companies identify and solve challenges associated with web globalization issues. One of the first decisions, in the context of web globalization, to be made is the level of standardization versus localization of the web content and functionalities. Companies also must decide the extent to which they want to centralize their web globalization processes and how much control over the content they want their local subsidiaries to have.

Another issue is whether the company wants to develop all its multilingual content internally or whether outsourcing these requirements to localization vendors or translators is preferred. Most companies do not have the resources or consider it necessary to localize websites in hundreds of languages. Thus companies need to decide which languages should be used and how much localization should be implemented in terms of translating the content and adapting various web functionalities.

Beyond these challenges, many companies do not possess the skills and knowledge associated with web globalization issues. Job descriptions for web globalization expertise are still developing, and most organizations lack a dedicated department to facilitate web globalization efforts. Today many people find themselves working in the web globalization area on the basis of not specific training in web globalization but on their expertise in languages or technical skills, or just their international experience. The following sections in this chapter cover these outlined challenges and provide insights to handle these challenges.

Web globalization dilemma 1: standardization or localization?

Finding the balance between standardization and localization in terms of the web content is one of the preeminent dilemmas that companies face when developing web

---

[1] Companies partner with content management system (CMS) vendors and even localization vendors to implement globalization management systems (GMSs) to help them in their web globalization efforts.

content for international markets. Companies struggle to make a decision about the extent to which they should localize. The web is a global communication medium, in which technology makes mass customization or adaptation possible, while forces of global integration and the emergence of transnational web style (Sackmary and Scalia, 1999) seem to justify the use of a standardized web marketing and communication strategy. It is important to begin any discussion with a clear sense of what standardization and localization mean in the business context.

> ### Standardization strategy
>
> In standardization strategy, marketers assume that global markets are homogeneous and, in response, offer standardized products and services using a standardized marketing mix.

Standardization is commonly defined in the literature as a strategy in which marketers assume global markets to be homogeneous and, accordingly, offer standardized products and services using a standardized marketing mix (Jain, 1989.) Advocates of the standardization approach argue that as technology develops and is globally dispersed, cultural distance will be minimized, leading to the convergence of national cultures into a homogeneous global culture.

Advantages of standardization

- Researchers such as Levitt (1983) argue that the forces of technology and globalization are creating homogenized consumer markets, and marketers should use standardized marketing to tap these global consumers. For example the MTV generation spans various countries and shares similar tastes and preferences in terms of the general music style.
- Standardization appears to be a cost-driven strategy for marketers, as it leads to leveraging the same template/product/service configuration globally, creating economies of scale and cost savings. If companies could leverage their home-country site for multiple international markets, this would significantly reduce localization expenses in terms of translation and other local content adaptation.
- Standardization can also lead to the development of single and unified brand and corporate identity worldwide. This can lead to better global recognition and provide a global competitive advantage over competitors.
- Standardization can lead to having a rationalized product line that includes only a few core global brands instead of multiple localized brands and brand extensions. This could lead to a better allocation of resources, higher efficiencies, consistent marketing, and higher profits. For example, the costs and effort of maintaining a single global website can be significantly less than having several different multilingual sites on account of lower resource allocation and marketing requirements.

- When implementing a standardization strategy, companies assume homogenized consumer needs. Thus investments in international market research related to modifying the marketing mix are minimal. The marketing mix includes company efforts related to four basic "Ps" of marketing: product, price, place (distribution), and promotion.
- Firms following a standardized approach to marketing tend to have a centralized global marketing program, and thus the need for coordinating, managing, and controlling local subsidiaries for local marketing strategy is minimized.

However, emerging research studies are showing that standardization as a strategy does not really impact the financial performance of firms (Samiee and Roth, 1992; O'Donnell and Jeong, 2000). Furthermore, the complex nature of the international marketing environment promotes diversity in terms of the physical environment, political and legal systems, cultures, product usage conditions, and economic development. Several international marketing researchers (Hill and Still, 1984; Boddewyn, Soehl, and Picard, 1986; Wind, 1986) argue that, because of fundamental differences between markets, it is neither desirable nor feasible for firms in several industries to achieve standardization in terms of their marketing activities. However, in certain industries, such as industrial or very high-end technology products, global standardization is more feasible than in industries such as consumer non-durables (Boddewyn, Soehl, and Picard, 1986). Even when dealing with industries or product categories that do not seem to need localization, though, there is a chance that a certain element of the marketing mix may need adaptation for the product(s) to be marketed internationally. Could companies really standardize customer service, distribution, pricing, and products when global variations in institutions, cultures, and other peculiarities are considered? For example, Intel ads promoting a microprocessor experienced severe backlash in the United States for showing black men bowing in front of a white man; this imagery evoked feelings of the dark practice of slavery. Thus it is preferable for firms to localize or adapt their marketing programs to the specific conditions prevalent in each market, bringing us to the concept of localization.

Localization, or "adaptation strategy," takes into account the inherent diversity that exists in international markets, and treats individuals as "cultural beings" whose values and behaviors are shaped by the unique culture in which they live. Localization strategy is geared toward understanding local consumer preferences and other locale-specific requirements and then adapting the marketing mix and other business strategies to best satisfy consumer needs and wants. Several companies have created standardized products and communications that have offended people in international markets. There is a long list of companies, including Pepsi, Electrolux, Chevrolet, Colgate, and Gerber, whose non-localized messages were misinterpreted in various countries. Although several of the publicized marketing blunders came from US or other developed-country multinationals, we are now seeing multinationals from China, India, Brazil, and other countries making the same mistakes. The Chinese automobile industry is growing rapidly and is poised for global expansion, but the industry faces international barriers related to the poor quality perceptions of Chinese cars. Even the name of Chinese car brands seem to be less global. I asked my students what they thought of Chinese car brands such as Geely or Cherry; they responded that they sound too feminine. Another brand name that received a lot of giggles in my class was "Bimbo bread," for obvious reasons. Bimbo bread is being marketed in the United States by Bimbo Bakeries, which is a part of Grupo Bimbo, a Mexican company. The lack of localization strategy can mean missing the consumer sweet spot or, even worse, making costly errors that result in sanctions, product recalls, or even consumer boycotts.

> **Localization strategy**
>
> Localization strategy is geared toward understanding local consumer preferences and then adapting the marketing mix (product, price, place, and promotion strategies) to best satisfy consumer needs and wants.

Here are some blunders that highlight why implementing a localization strategy is important.

Importance of localization strategy

(1) Proper localization can save a company millions, because the cost of offending a group of consumers by insensitive marketing messages can be very expensive and in some cases permanent, leading to costly efforts in terms of repositioning. In 2002 Abercrombie & Fitch's T-shirts with Asian stereotypes led to consumer protests in the United States, especially among the Asian-American community. T-shirt slogans such as "Two Wong's can Make it White" or "Get your Buddha on the Floor" were widely condemned and led to petitions for consumer boycotts.[2]

(2) Losing money from a lack of local sensitivity is bad enough, but local insensitivity can also lead to legal and regulatory troubles. Below are two examples.
- When coloring in 800,000 pixels on a map of India, Microsoft colored eight of them a different shade of green to represent the disputed Kashmiri territory. The difference in greens meant Kashmir was shown as non-Indian, and the product was promptly banned in India. According to geopolitical expert Kate Edwards, Microsoft was left to recall all 200,000 copies of the offending Windows 95 operating system software to try to heal the diplomatic wounds. "It cost millions" (Best, 2004a).
- Following protests by the Taiwanese government and Taiwanese American organizations, Google removed the "Province of China" label from its map of Taiwan on the Google Maps site.

[2] One of the petitions was still available as of November 1, 2010, at http://boycott-af.com.

(3) Less than careful translation and proofreading can also cause major issues. For example, a Spanish-language version of Windows XP, destined for Latin American markets, asked users to select their gender between "not specified," "male," or "bitch," because of an unfortunate error in translation (Best, 2004b).

(4) Localizing brand names into other languages without compromising brand identity is a crucial international marketing challenge for many companies. This becomes more of a problem when brand names need to be localized for languages in which phonetic and semantic issues pose a challenge. The most common example is when companies use transliteration strategies to localize their English brand name to a completely different writing system, as in the case of Chinese script. For example, Carrefour chose its Chinese brand name (*Jia-le-fu*) on the basis of how it sounds (phonetic appeal), and its positive meaning in Chinese: it means "home/family-happy-fortunate" (Labbrand, 2009). The famous example of a bad brand name translation into Chinese is that of Coca-Cola: the translation of *ko-kä-kö-la* means something like "bite a wax tadpole."

(5) Disregarding local history and traditions can also land companies in trouble. The case of the Nike commercial "Chamber of fear," which was released in several countries, is illustrative. It showed the American NBA hero LeBron James competing against Chinese historical and legendary characters and defeating the Chinese martial art master. The Chinese government found this ad to be offensive. In December 2004 China's State Administration for Radio, Film, and Television banned the ad, explaining that it was disrespectful toward Chinese culture and offended Chinese national dignity (Li and Shooshtari, 2007).

(6) Lack of sensitivity to cultural practices can also land a company in hot water. Take, for example, Avon's entry into Japan. Avon wanted Japanese women to follow the same "Avon Lady" business model it had perfected in the United States. However, it failed to consider Japanese cultural characteristics, since Japanese housewives generally are reluctant to sell products to total strangers. Japanese also consider their home as a refuge from the crowded streets and high population density in Japanese cities and thus are hesitant to entertain total strangers. Finally, Avon's strategy for Japan failed to consider that saving face is very important for Japanese, and direct sales techniques may at times result in situations that could be embarrassing for buyer or seller, if the expectations are not met. Based on these mistakes, Avon localized its strategy in Japan by having saleswomen represent territory that included some kind of in-group such as her own neighborhood or her extended family or friends (Knight, 1995).

(7) Even something as primal as how people bathe differs between countries. For example, Americans frequently use washcloths, while the practice of using washcloths in India is relatively uncommon. Avon bath additives misfired in Japan because the company failed to understand that, in Japan, the bath tub is used for relaxing and not for bathing. Family members in Japan always clean themselves before taking a plunge in the bath tub because the same bath water is used

by other family members to soak. Thus the same water is shared by all, and it is considered unacceptable to use soap or bath additives in the tub (Knight, 1995).

(8) In August 2002 the British sportswear manufacturer Umbro was denounced as "appallingly insensitive" for naming a running shoe the Zyklon. This is the same name as the lethal gas used in Nazi extermination camps during the Second World War. Umbro dropped the name after complaints from various quarters, including the Board of Deputies of British Jews (Petre, 2002).

(9) IKEA's initial failure in Japan can be attributed to the lack of localization of its retailing strategy; its lack of product customization to Japanese preferences; and, most importantly, its promotion of its self-assembly furniture line, which was not popular in Japan during that time (Sanchanta, 2004).

(10) Leaders of India's Jewish community expressed outrage over a line of bedspreads called "the Nazi Collection" from a Mumbai-based home furnishing company that used swastikas in its promotional material (*Times*, 2007).

(11) Even a simple thing such as the use of a number in a culturally inappropriate way can derail product sales. A golf ball manufacturing company packaged golf balls in packs of four for convenient purchase in Japan. Unfortunately, the pronunciation of the word "four" in Japanese sounds like the word "death," and items packaged in fours are unpopular. Similarly, in the United States, the number 420 is associated with the cannabis culture, and in India 420 spoken in Hindi refers to a conman or conwoman and has negative connotations.

These are just a few examples of how a lack of consideration for local culture, norms, practices, etc. can lead to major business blunders.

Localization best practices

To better target their international audiences, many companies have proactively adapted or localized their products and marketing mix. Some examples are Nabisco, McDonald's, and KFC.

Product localization

Since Japanese consumers prefer less sugar, Nabisco attempted to make its Oreo cookies less sweet for the Japanese market. Japanese consumers still considered them too sweet and wanted them without the cream, so Nabisco introduced smaller "Oreo non-cream cookies" in Japan. Similarly, Oreo did not do well in China for years until Nabisco also introduced less sweet versions of its traditional cookie. Nabisco also changed the design of Oreo from round to a long, narrow, layered stack of crispy wafers and vanilla and chocolate cream, all coated with chocolate. In Germany, Kraft, the parent company of the Oreo brand, is introducing dark chocolate under its Milka brand to satisfy the German liking for dark chocolate (Jargon, 2008).

Yum! Brands, the parent company of KFC, Taco Bell, Pizza Hut, and Long John Silver's, has become a success story in China by adapting its menus and food retailing strategies. Now Yum! Brands is experimenting with the idea of East Dawning, a quick-service restaurant brand, providing authentic Chinese food to the Chinese customer that leverages the successful KFC business model.

Price localization

A company's products and communication are not the only areas that need adaptation; prices may also need to be adjusted to meet local market needs. For example, McDonald's and KFC might be considered inexpensive fast food outlets in the United States but in India and China they are considered suppliers of higher-priced alternatives to local cuisine. For example, in India, the menu items for KFC and McDonald's range from Rs 20 to more than Rs 300, which is still more money than Indians pay for food from street vendors.[3] Some of the food alternatives available from street vendors and local shops in India cost less than a half of these prices. Thus these American brands have localized their pricing effectively to match the Indian consumers' perception of relatively high-end family dining. (In the photograph is an image of McDonald's in India being promoted as a family dining restaurant.) On the other hand, in an attempt to reach rural markets in countries such as India, Indonesia, Philippines, and other emerging markets, various multinationals are creating product packaging and product sizes that can be sold at cheaper prices. The goal is to enable populations with low monthly incomes to afford their products. For example, Colgate sells economically priced small "sachets" of toothpaste and small

[3] An American dollar is worth around 40 to 45 Indian rupees.

containers of tooth powder to appeal to the price-sensitive rural population of India and other south Asian countries.

Place localization

Companies need to localize their distribution, logistics, retailing infrastructure, and even merchandising on the basis of local consumer preferences. Logistics and distribution infrastructure vary globally. In India, major multinationals such as Coca-Cola, Colgate, Nestlé, and others use non-traditional channels of distribution to reach the vast majority of the Indian population, which resides in small towns and villages. Some of the distribution and retailing methods used to reach consumers in rural India include rickshaws, bullock carts, boats, cycles, trucks, and *dukandaars* (small "mom and pop" stores). In Japan, companies leverage the extensive network of corner stores to achieve maximum market penetration. "*Konbini* commerce" represents the merger of Japanese convenience store and e-commerce. There are more than 50,000 *konbini* or Japanese convenience stores across Japan. *Konbini* are an integral part of Japanese shopping culture and daily life. They are also an integral part of Japanese e-commerce, as they allow the consumer to order online and pick up and pay for the merchandise at the store. 7-Eleven is the largest chain, followed by Lawson and FamilyMart. 7-Eleven Co. Ltd has set up a shopping site, 7dream.com, on which Japanese shoppers can purchase from more than 100,000 items and then pay and collect the orders at the nearest twenty-four-hour 7-Eleven store. Similarly, Amazon Japan (amazon.co.jp) allows its Japanese customers to shop online and pay at their local convenience stores, such as 7-Eleven, Sunkus, FamilyMart, Daily Yamazaki, and others. McDonald's in India has localized its delivery service with the introduction of a "McDelivery" option in some cities: Indian consumers can order online or call 6600666 for home delivery.

Localizing translations

When localizing websites, companies need to pay special attention to how various concepts, words, and sentences are translated from one language to another. The multilingual software translation packages that are in vogue today are susceptible to various translation errors in idiomatic equivalence, vocabulary equivalence, and conceptual equivalence.

Idiomatic equivalence

Each language has unique idioms, and translating them appropriately is challenging. For example, how does one translate English idioms such as "cross your fingers" or "fighting tooth and nail"? The box contains examples of idioms from various languages that might or might not make sense to someone from a different cultural background.

Idioms

Melon field, under the plums: a Chinese idiom that implies suspicious situations.
Mexican standoff: an English idiom meaning a strategic deadlock or impasse.
Tear of a sparrow: a Japanese idiom that is close in meaning to what in English is called "a drop in the ocean."
Goma-suri, **which means to grind up sesame seeds**: a Japanese idiom that means something similar to brown-nosing or flattering.

Vocabulary equivalence

How does one translate a word that has many meanings, or that has no equivalent? For example, Shenkar and von Glinow (1994) note that a word such as "autonomy" cannot be adequately translated into Chinese, and that alternative Chinese terms such as "right of self-determination" (*zi zhu quan*) convey a quite different meaning. In Hindi, which reflects the culture of India, there is no equivalent for the word "divorce." The closest word used in India is an Urdu word, "*talak*"; alternatively, Hindi speakers just use the English word "divorce." The absence of a word for divorce in Hindi also reflects the fact that "divorce" is not considered an important concept in relation to marriage in the Indian culture. Hindus generally see marriage as a life-long commitment, and thus divorce rates in India are quite low compared to other countries in the world.

Another example, provided by Levine (1988), talks about the challenges of translating into Portuguese a questionnaire containing the verb "to wait": "Several of our questions were concerned with how long the respondent would wait for someone to arrive versus when they hoped the person would arrive versus when they actually expected the person would come. Unfortunately for us, it turns out that the term to wait, to hope and to expect are all typically translated as the single verb esperar in Portuguese" (Levine, 1988: 48–9).

Conceptual equivalence

How does one translate so as to ensure that exact conceptual meaning is retained in translation? Unless one has a conceptual understanding of a word's use, errors will result. An interesting example that explains the complexity of conceptual equivalence is the concept of "trust." According to Usunier (1999), the concept of trust is conceived of differently in English, French, German, and Japanese. In discussing the various meanings, Usunier goes on to say that, in English, the word "trust" relates to ideas of reliance, worth, and reliability. In German, the concept of trust is based on two verbs, *trauen* and *vertrauen*, which translate to trust. *Trauen* has a negative connotation of "I don't trust you," while *vertrauen* is used in a positive sense that implies "I trust you." The French idea of trust is based on the notion of sharing common beliefs, identity, or similarity, somewhat akin to conveying confidence in someone or something; thus the French have only one word for both "trust" and "confidence." Finally, the Japanese concept of the word trust is *shin-yô*, meaning literally "sincere business." Thus the Japanese conceive of trust as being more about sincere expectations on the part of the parties involved in an exchange (Singh and Pereira, 2005).

Dialects

Language differs not only between cultures but also between various subcultures, in the form of different dialects. Even though the United States and the United Kingdom are considered culturally similar, English usage and spelling differ significantly. Similarly, there are various Spanish dialects in use in various parts of the world. It is important for companies to ensure that the dialects are used correctly. For example, Amazon seems not only to have created an international site for the United Kingdom but also to have ensured that all content on the site is written in British English. A British user searching for a "jumper" can find what he or she needs; an American consumer can search under "sweater" to find similar products.

Different words, same meaning	
American English	**British English**
Truck	Lorry
Eraser	Rubber
Chips	Crisps
Fries	Chips
Hood (car)	Bonnet
Trunk (car)	Boot
Mudguard	Fender
Trash can	Dustbin
Cookie	Biscuit

To standardize or to localize?

A simple way to help solve part of this dilemma is to analyze to what extent the end user uses the products and services on offer for self-expression. The higher the degree of self-expression associated with a product, the more product, price, promotion, web, and logistical localization the product will need – especially cultural customization. B2C companies that sell products used by individuals for self-expression (e.g., beauty, automobiles, home décor, travel, and other lifestyle-oriented products, services, and cultural industry products) may need a higher level of localization than companies that sell products low on self-expression (e.g., Caterpillar, DuPont, Shell, and other companies involved in B2B commerce). Products that are purchased, at least in part, to help the consumer express his or her identity need to be positioned in consumers' minds in relation to their identities, and thus companies need to understand both the culture and the psyche of the people to whom it is marketing.

The "Indianization" of Spiderman is a good example of how global brands can be imbued with local meaning and marketed and integrated in the local psyche. In the Indian adaptation, Pavitr Prabhakar (a phonetic distortion of Peter Parker) roams the streets of Mumbai instead of Manhattan. Moreover, now Spiderman is even being integrated with Indian myths and religion. Indian culture is very eclectic in terms of the numerous forms of gods that are worshipped; during one religious celebration there were reports and blog posts of Indians celebrating and worshipping "Spiderman-Ganesh," in which Spiderman is infused into Lord Ganesh, the Indian god of good luck and prosperity. (The illustration depicts the real Indian god Ganesha.)

By infusing iconic brands with cultural myths and symbols, "cultural icons" are born. Cultural icons can be both global and local. Brands such as Marlboro cigarettes, Harley Davidson motorcycles, and the Volkswagen Beetle car have succeeded in gaining the status of global cultural icons because they are closely related to culture and its relationship to self-expression. Thus companies selling products linked closely to self-expression need more localization than most. Localization efforts will need to take into account extensive cultural customization (see Figure 4.1). These companies have an opportunity to turn their brands into "cultural icons."

B2C companies that sell to a cross-section of international customers, serving their day-to-day needs in the fast-moving consumer goods area (Coca-Cola, P&G, Unilever), also need to localize (and culturally customize) their products, but not as extensively as products that are a clear reflection of self-image. On the other end of the spectrum are products in the B2B segment, such as earth-moving equipment, which is not used at all by consumers for self-expression. For these companies, the need for localization in certain areas may be low, but they still need to localize their communications, and even their products, to account for functional, language, and other variations found cross-nationally. Thus even Caterpillar localizes its international websites and has around twenty-eight country-specific sites in more than twelve languages.

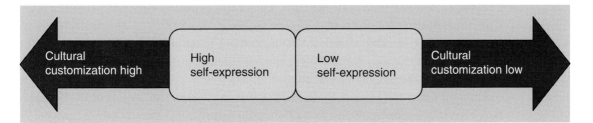

Figure 4.1 Level of cultural customization

Sometimes companies localize by emphasizing the country of origin rather than the country of sale. For example, Marlboro is seen as an iconic American brand, and Levi's jeans are seen as synonymous with an image of the American West. However, even such companies do not ignore functional aspects of localization; for example, Levi's may have to create different sizes for different body shapes around the world. (In a recent twist of events, Levi's is experimenting with advertising standardization by launching its first global marketing campaign in which print and television ads contain the same theme, content, and slogan – "Live unbuttoned" – the world over; only the models will resemble the local populace [Smith, 2008].) Beyond this, iconic brands associated with a specific country sell well not only because of their association with the country of origin but also because they have learned the art of "serving" global or cultural iconic brands on a local "platter." For example, MTV is a uniquely American invention and is marketed as such, but it is presented in a variety of ways to appeal to the local consumer in different markets. MTV localizes to national or regional tastes by promoting local DJs, VJs, and artists. MTV India is selling American-style entertainment with a local twist: the MTV India website is populated not just with Western-style music and videos but also with Bollywood videos, Indian celebs, English written in the form of "Hinglish" (which is a unique amalgamation of English and Hindi), and commentaries on Indian popular culture.

Web globalization dilemma 2: to centralize or to decentralize?

Companies can achieve significant costs savings by minimizing inefficiencies in human capital use, as well as redundancies in systems and processes. When developing international websites, companies can achieve significant productivity gains and cost reductions if they are able to centralize important core processes. Examples include the following.

- *A centralized global content management system* that enables a company to create, manage, publish, and archive information in various formats and languages for use in multiple countries. I explore the use of content management systems in more depth in future chapters.

- *Centralized common hosting* (sometimes, because of regulatory or governmental pressure, local hosting solutions may also be required).
- *A centralized localization workflow* that automates collaboration between important stakeholders in the web globalization process, such as project managers, localization engineers, translators, reviewers, etc.
- *Centralized CRM applications* to capture global customer data in a centralized database that is accessible globally to authorized users.
- *A centralized localization vendor selection process.* Various vendors that provide services related to web globalization efforts tend to use different formats, tools, and standards. Thus the centralization of vendor selection will ensure that the organization is using consistent tools for technology, translation, workflow, and content management. It can help get better deals from vendors when making bulk decisions for all locales, and also will help avoid usage of multiple tools, standards, formats, and deliveries that can cause inconsistencies. Such an approach is useful for achieving scalable technology architecture.
- *Centralized translation memory (TM), which can be leveraged for future multilingual projects.* TM software stores previously translated sentences or parts of sentences for reuse in the future, helping to lower translation costs and keep translations consistent.
- *Centralized management of terminology among multiple users.* Terminology data relating to one or more projects in an organization is received from one or more users and stored in a central memory area associated with these users. The central memory area can be made accessible to other authorized users. Several products on the market can help companies achieve significant productivity gains, including MultiTrans Expert, which provides comprehensive tools to capture, manage, update, share, and use multilingual terminology effectively and consistently. It enables multi-user, real-time access to centralized terminology assets.
- *Centralized global brand management processes* that support a consistent global marketing message, while allowing local offices to localize the content to suit national needs. This also applies to websites in terms of creating a standard global web template – an important step to achieving consistent global branding. A successful template will ensure that each international site has a look and feel that is consistent with the global brand but also accommodates local variations. IKEA and HP both have international templates that successfully straddle the need for a global brand with local customization. HP has created extensive terminology and style sheets so that important details such as the HP logo font and color are used consistently worldwide.

Style guide and terminology glossary

A **style guide** contains broad guidelines on how to present content on the web or other communication mediums. Style guides provide translators with a source of reference to understand corporate stylistic requirements relating to the tone of the voice, formatting instructions, the rules of capitalization, the usage of abbreviations, the format for numbers, etc.

> The **terminology glossary** contains definitions of the important terms or technical words used in either the source or local language, so that they can be consistently translated into multiple languages.

- *A centralized web globalization team* that is empowered, responsible, and accountable for the seamless integration of web globalization workflows and coordination with regional offices. This central team will serve as a key resource for local teams in terms of training, tools, technological support, maintenance, quality assurance, and other workflow functions. Most companies at present do not have well-defined or centralized web globalization teams.
- *Centralized security and validation.* Localization teams modify software resources to make products suitable for local markets. By including poorly localized resources, localization vendors may introduce security threats into products. The application may crash if, for example, the string resources do not adhere to certain guidelines (Elgazzar, 2008). Thus appropriate localization verification procedures should be centralized to monitor all localized resources. Security should also be built in so that intellectual property rights can be tightly controlled. Centralized security for payment transactions could also lead to significant savings if leveraged across all global websites.

On the other hand, it is also important to decentralize certain web-globalization-related activities, especially the process of local content adaptation. Allow local offices to provide local content to the centralized global content management system – but lay down the parameters that will remain constant, such as brand identity, specific icons and fonts, the use of graphics and Flash, etc. Having a carefully crafted style guide and terminology glossary is very important, but, beyond that, it is also important to have a centralized global web template that works as a core shell within which local offices can provide localized content. Various content management systems allow for this kind of flexibility. Some important aspects that need to be decentralized include:

- adaptation related to country-specific website content, products and services;
- local advertising and promotion;
- search engine optimization – especially in terms of creating local content that is optimized for local language and user search preferences; and
- the collection of local market intelligence, which can then be input into a centralized database.

A balanced approach, therefore, could be to centralize the core processes that are scalable, are integral to the seamless functioning of a multitude of global processes, and are capable of generating economies of scope and scale, while decentralizing processes that benefit from local input and local ingenuity.

Wikipedia, for example, is one of the better designed global websites. According to Brad Patrick, the former interim executive director and general counsel for Wikipedia, Wikipedia was built from the ground up, and in order to rely on its content contributors it relinquished a high degree of control over content from the start. Content stays close to the user because it is written or translated by the very people who consume the content. Although it is rarely practical to entirely hand the content reins to customers, local employees and partners can and should play an active role in content creation and management (Yunker, 2006a).

Another good example of a company implementing a decentralized approach to web globalization without compromising the centralization of core processes is the United Nations Children's Fund (UNICEF.) UNICEF has some forty-six international sites in multiple languages. According to Yunker (2006b), UNICEF's web globalization strategy was to leverage its central content management platform to create centralized parameters for its local offices. However, UNICEF allowed its local offices to develop local content within these parameters, and even gave them control to help them quickly produce and deploy the content as the need arose. UNICEF's central office still provides technical and customer support and training to its local offices so that they can remain adept at handling the local content adaptation while still adhering to centralized systems and guidelines. For example, all the UNICEF sites from various countries such as the United States, Japan, Turkey, and Spain have a unifying theme around the logo and the design of template that keep them looking consistent, but with different content, issues, colors, models, etc.

Web globalization dilemma 3: in-house versus outsourcing

The next dilemma that organizations face is whether to do translations and other localization processes in-house or to outsource them. Organizations must ask themselves whether localization and translation should be included in their core competencies and whether doing translation and other localization processes in-house contributes to their value-generating activities. Another way to view this dilemma is to ask questions such as the following.

- Will doing this activity enhance the firm's competitive advantage?
- Is doing localization in-house central to the revenue stream?
- Will doing this activity create firm-specific assets that are difficult to imitate by competitors? In other words, are there specialized skills and innovative approaches to localization that are unique to the firm?
- Can localization be performed significantly better in-house than with outside vendors?
- Will it be more productive and less expensive to perform localization in-house? Is the total cost of ownership (TCO) lower than the cost of outsourcing?

- Is localization something the business should develop as a core competency in the long term, or will it dilute the organization's focus?
- Can the company scale sufficiently to meet unexpected peaks in demand for translation and localization, as in the case of simultaneous international product launches?

When doing this introspective exercise, most firms realize that having hundreds of in-house translators, several localization engineers, and project managers, etc. is cost-prohibitive. However, in some cases the translation and other processes have to be kept in-house, for example if there is high degree of asset specificity or risk of corporate espionage, or in cases in which the information is very sensitive or the client desires high-security protection. Intelligence agencies constitute one example of a group that hires in-house translators because of the sensitive nature of their information. For most large, multinational companies, the tendency is to have some in-house translators or reviewers while outsourcing most of the work to external vendors. Additionally, most multinationals invest in a team of web globalization professionals who facilitate the web globalization process and coordinate with localization vendors and translators. Some multinationals naturally tend to be more invested in in-house localization if they have some core competencies they can leverage. For example, Microsoft, IBM, and HP are all technology companies; Microsoft, with its expertise in creating software for local and international markets, sees localization as one of its core competencies and thus invests heavily in in-house localization processes and products. Microsoft has vast resources and high standards, and, in its .NET framework,[4] it has a large library of pre-coded solutions to common programming problems. These unique and, to some

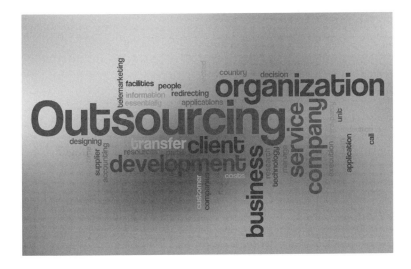

---

[4] The .NET framework is programming infrastructure or framework developed by Microsoft to enable the development of applications supported by .NET technologies.

extent, inimitable assets provide relatively ideal conditions for Microsoft to undertake various internationalization and localization tasks in-house.[5]

Thus organizations adopt some sort of mix between in-house solutions and the outsourcing of various parts of localization and translation processes. According to Bergmann (2007), different permutations of in-house/outsource include the following.

- *Full outsourcing* All the localization and internationalization work is handled by external vendors. Generally, small and medium enterprises tend to use a full outsourcing model if the total cost of owning localization processes exceeds the cost of outsourcing.
- *Full insourcing* Companies with constant streams of translation work and special requirements may handle all translation work in-house. Government organizations such as the Central Intellegence Agency or National Security Agency in the United States are extreme examples of groups that cannot outsource their translation work for security reasons. According to the Localization Industry Standards Association (LISA), a strictly in-house model was adopted by large multinationals in the 1980s and 1990s, but now the in-house model is extremely rare for most companies since localization is not seen as a core process and the TCO is much higher than outsourcing.
- *Insourcing plus outsourced peak coverage* Full insourcing is plagued by resource utilization problems, which is one of the reasons LISA has identified a trend moving away from in-house localization. Companies frequently, at a minimum, purchase external services to cover utilization peaks. A company may maintain a small team of in-house translators to cover recurring internal communications needs while outsourcing product localization to external vendors.
- *Outsourcing plus internal project management* A frequent variant of "full outsourcing" is the maintenance of a small in-house team dedicated to managing providers of full localization services.
- *Outsourcing plus internal project management plus internal quality control* Large localization buyers frequently seem to go a further step toward insourcing by maintaining an internal quality control team to evaluate providers and to provide "language lead" services for projects.

Furthermore, according to LISA,[6] some companies outsource to single-language vendors (SLVs) and some outsource to multiple-language vendors (MLVs).

---

[5] The term "internationalization" here means technical processes necessary to make the website or software "world-ready" or amenable to future localization efforts. I discuss internationalization as a technical process in greater depth in future chapters. The term "localization" here means the adapting of web or software content to meet locale-specific requirements. There are companies called localization service providers, language service providers, or localization vendors that generally provide localization and internationalization services to clients.

[6] The reference is to LISA, "Business models," www.lisa.org/Business-Models.506.0.html, last accessed in January 2011. However, as of February 28, 2011, LISA was declared insolvent and dissolved, and its website was closed down.

- *Outsourcing to SLVs* Outsourcing to several single-language vendors is one of the two dominant localization business models, according to LISA. These SLVs specialize in a particular language and sometimes even in a particular industry. Normally, companies have an internal localization staff comprised primarily of project managers (PMs) who then coordinate with the SLVs. One advantage of this model is that, if there is a surge in the need for translation and localization, the PM can find more SLVs or send more work to the same SLV. Thus, by outsourcing, the increased workload can be seamlessly accommodated. However, if the workload is not enough, then companies incur the risk of having a full-time PM on their payroll with insufficient work.
- *Outsourcing to MLVs* Another dominant localization business model, according to LISA, is to outsource most aspects of localization processes (translation, desktop publishing, localization engineering, questions and answers, testing, etc.) to a multiple-language vendor. The MLV has a large network of in-house and external localization professionals and translators to help with fully scalable localization/globalization projects. MLVs have the latest localization tools and technologies to manage the whole localization process, and clients can rely on the MLV for full project management and localization workflow automation.

Web globalization dilemma 4: level of localization

Companies struggle with the issue of the extent to which they should localize their international sites. It is almost a certainty that, if more web pages are localized, the higher the cost will be. Is the level of localization therefore just a function of cost? There are several variables to consider when deciding the level of desired localization. Some of these variables are as follows.

- Are all home-country website pages sufficiently relevant to require translation and localization for location-specific sites or international sites? For example, translating the complete bios and hierarchy structure of the head office in the United States is probably not necessary for the French site; that information could be summarized, and more attention could be given to content related to organizational structure in France. A two-level approach can help solve this problem.
  - One effective strategy could be to classify the content that needs to be kept standardized across locales and the content that needs to be localized. Content that generally transcends locale-specific characteristics or is applicable only to one specific locale can be kept standardized. Such standardized content could include press releases that are relevant to specific countries, internal corporate policy documents that do not need localization, content developed for locale-specific social media, company hierarchy information that is country-specific, and metadata[7]

[7] Metadata is used for classifying and labeling web content. For more information, check the Dublin Core Metadata Initiative: www.dublincore.org.

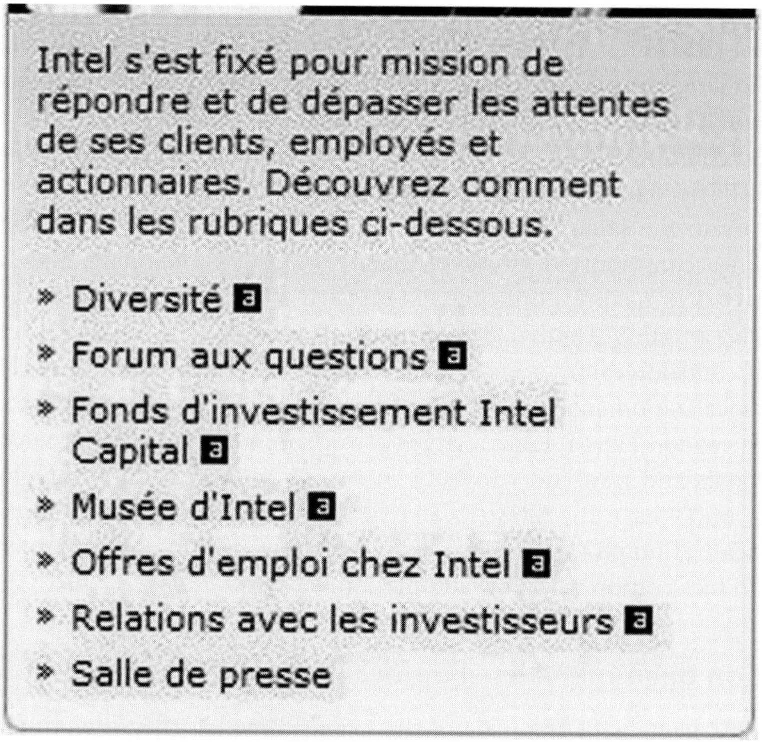

Intel s'est fixé pour mission de
répondre et de dépasser les attentes
de ses clients, employés et
actionnaires. Découvrez comment
dans les rubriques ci-dessous.

» Diversité 🅰
» Forum aux questions 🅰
» Fonds d'investissement Intel
  Capital 🅰
» Musée d'Intel 🅰
» Offres d'emploi chez Intel 🅰
» Relations avec les investisseurs 🅰
» Salle de presse

Figure 4.2 How to alert users of non-translated content

that is used to define other digital content and is not visible to front-end web users. For example, if you look at HP locale-specific sites (HP has sites organized not only by countries but also by locales, such as Flanders and Wallonia in Belgium), a user will feel that the French site, for example, is no less comprehensive than the German or US site, yet HP does not offer all its home-country pages translated into other languages. Moreover, in some cases, HP has additional pages for specific issues in some countries and not for others. For example, HP Germany has a dedicated web page titled *"Impressum,"* which is required by law for websites in Germany. In another example, on Intel's site for France, most of the content is translated into French, but links that direct users to untranslated or English content are marked as such (Yunker, 2007). This strategy of alerting the user to the fact that the content is not translated helps provide some degree of transparency to the customer. See Figure 4.2, the screenshot of the Intel site from France, and see how some hyperlinks have the symbol 🅰 to alert customers that the content for this hyperlink is in English.

- Content can be further classified into content needing extensive localization or content that just needs to be translated. Generally, companies can classify content needing extensive localization based on how locale-specific the content may be. So, for example, content relating to privacy may need not only translation but also localization on the basis of country-specific legal requirements. On the other hand, content such as general information about the corporation may be translated without requiring any more localization. Companies with limited budgets can decide on which content absolutely must be localized extensively and prioritize their budget accordingly. For example, a company can extensively localize its international help, country-specific compliance information (e.g., complying with legal standards), shipping, and order fulfillment aspects and just translate the pages that do not provide customers with the strategic information needed to facilitate their purchase or other required behavior.

- Are there certain web pages that are not very important to the international audience(s) that could rely more on machine translation or some blend of machine and human translation? Machine translation is getting more sophisticated and reliable, but it still is not perfect and may yield poor translation quality. In the last chapter of this book I elaborate various emerging machine translation solutions. If a company wants its international users to access comments and resources from various country blogs or other social media forms, then a machine translation tool can be an inexpensive approach to taking up the behemoth task of translating all social media content worldwide. (Be cautious if you use this approach, as the risks of producing incorrect translations often outweigh the potential rewards.)

- Does the country or language locale justify significant translation-related investment? This can be determined on the basis of an international market assessment and a strategic analysis of market potential. If the country is not a strategic source of revenues or is not likely to provide future customers, then extensive localization investments may not be needed. Even in this case, companies must still pay attention to the localization of regulations, taxes, legal text such as licensing agreements, etc.

- Does the country or locale demand extensive translation, or can localized content be provided with minimal translation? For example, in countries such as South Africa, India, and Australia a significant portion of the population is conversant in English. In such cases, the content managers may just need to ensure translation equivalence (conceptual, idiomatic, vocabulary, and dialect), functional localization, and a cultural adaptation for the internationalized country-specific website.

- Using the knowledge gained by carefully implementing online global consumer segmentation can help a company determine what kind of global or national mindset their customers have and then, accordingly, decide the level of localization investment needed.

- Companies use their websites for e-commerce, advertising, and communication. In some countries a company may use its site for all three purposes, and in others it may not. Issues related to infrastructure, consumer behavior, and regulations may prevent a company from doing e-commerce in a country. For example, several companies, such as HP, have fully functional e-commerce sites for certain countries and not for others.

Web globalization dilemma 5: in which languages to localize?

This is another question that companies face when making decisions about multilingual web content. Studies have shown that language is an important variable that impacts online consumers' willingness to interact with, and even purchase from, a website. For example, a study by DePalma, Sargent, and Beninatto (2006) of almost 2,400 online consumers from eight countries finds that consumers show a significant preference for content in their local language. The study shows that almost a half of the sample make purchases only at websites on which the information is presented in their local language. More than 60 percent of consumers in France and Japan prefer to buy from sites in the local language. The study also finds that people with no or low English skills were six times more likely not to buy from English sites compared to their counterparts. These findings become even more pertinent when paired with the fact that more than 70 percent of global online users are now non-English-speaking (www. internetworldstats.com/stats7.htm). Besides English, users who speak other languages including Chinese, Spanish, Japanese, and French represent a large proportion of global online users. Thus it becomes crucial for companies to provide their international online audience with content in their local language. The decision to add languages to international websites can be based on several factors, including the following.

- Which country or language locale sends the most traffic to the company website?
- Which country or language locale would be most profitable to target?
- What is the market potential and market growth of the country or the language locale?
- Does the country have several languages to target, such as Belgium or Switzerland?
- What are the most popular languages on the web? Which languages have the highest online population?
- Does the company have the capacity to provide customer support and other services in a particular language? If in-house capacity is not available, then can the company find an outside vendor to provide support in a specific language?
- Can the company justify the incremental cost of adding more languages?
- Will the investment in creating a multilingual site pay off?
- Does the international audience demand the content in a local language, or will they be satisfied by English content? For example, for most companies targeting the majority of online Indian users, having the content in English will suffice.

Table 4.1 Most commonly translated languages, 2007

(1) Canadian French
(2) Spanish
(3) French
(4) German
(5) Italian
(6) Chinese
(7) Japanese
(8) Dutch
(9) English
(10) Russian

Source: SDL "World language league table 2007," www.sdl.com/
enevents/news-PR/2007/Eastern-Europe-and-China-dominate
-2007-translation-trends.asp.

Top ten languages on the internet

(1) English
(2) Chinese
(3) Spanish
(4) Japanese
(5) Portuguese
(6) German
(7) Arabic
(8) French
(9) Russian
(10) Korean

Source: Internet World Stats, www.internetworldstats.com/stats7.htm.

The box shows the rankings of the ten most popular languages used on the internet, while Table 4.1 shows the most commonly translated languages through the systems of SDL, a major provider of software for translation and localization.

A study of the "best" global websites for 2008 by Yunker (2008) finds that the average number of languages supported by the 225 sites reviewed is twenty. German and French seem to be the two most popular languages other than English for companies trying to reach global online consumers. A survey of sixty-five multinationals by Singh, Baack, and Bott (2010) finds German, French, and Spanish to be the top languages into which websites are translated. This reflects the companies' desire to enter these strong online markets. Spanish, French, and German are also some of the easiest languages to translate content into, making it a quick and cost-effective entry strategy. Wikipedia supports the most languages on the web, offering content in more than 250 languages (Yunker, 2007), by leveraging a community of motivated and multilingual volunteers from around the world to create the content. Google is at the top of the list of websites providing the best multilingual web support. Google's search engine supports more than 100 languages. Today companies vying to compete in BRIC countries are creating multilingual web content to tap these online markets, so there has been a major upswing in, in particular, translating web pages into Chinese (simplified) for mainland China.

Web globalization dilemma 6: what skill set is needed for web globalization?

Since web globalization is still a relatively new functional area, web globalization job descriptions, job requirements, and educational qualifications have yet to be clearly outlined. In the broadest sense, web globalization requires an interdisciplinary potpourri of skills from areas such as international business and marketing, advertising, project management, IT and e-commerce, language technology, linguistics, intercultural communications, technical writing, and even human resource management. Thus it can be difficult to locate employees with such vast interdisciplinary backgrounds. In fact, no single university program in the past known to the author has really provided a blend of training with such an interdisciplinary focus to create a holistic understanding of what truly is needed to successfully implement web globalization efforts. There are some programs given by universities or localization vendors related to translation and translation/localization tools and technologies. However, a broader focus on training personnel to lead enterprise-wide web globalization efforts has been lacking. A summary of various programs in localization is provided in the box. In 2009 one of the first programs in web globalization was launched by the John Cook School of Business, Saint Louis University (www.globalizationexecutive.com); the program specifically deals with broad skills for managing organization-wide web globalization strategy.[8]

Educational programs in the field of localization

- *Saint Louis University, John Cook School of Business*: Executive Certificate in Web Globalization Management. Broad, self-paced, and comprehensive online 110-hour training program.
- *Monterey Institute of International Studies*: M.A. programs in translation and localization management. A full-time master's degree and other programs in translation and interpretation.

---

[8] In the interests of full disclosure, the author is closely associated with the Executive Certificate in Web Globalization Management at Saint Louis University and localization certification programs at California State University, Chico.

- *California State University, Chico*: the Regional and Continuing Education department provides a blended format (online and onsite workshop) training in localization and localization project management.
- *University of Washington*: the Professional and Continuing Education department offers a nine-month Certificate in Localization.
- *Kent State University*: M.A. in translation (French, German, Japanese, Russian, or Spanish) in addition to doctorate-level courses in translation technology.
- *University of Limerick, Localization Research Centre*: offers a full-time M.Sc. in global computing and localization and certificate courses.
- *Tecnológico de Monterrey (ITESM)*: global e-management MBA with technology and business focus.

Normally, an in-house web globalization team includes a web globalization manager who coordinates web globalization activities, leveraging the expertise of translators, editors/reviewers, web designers, developers and localization engineers, and individuals responsible for testing and quality control. People seeking future job prospects in the web globalization/localization industry can explore the following roles depending on their level of education, experience, and interest:

(1) project management;
(2) vendor management;
(3) business development;
(4) sales and marketing;
(5) localization engineering;
(6) translation/reviewer/linguist;
(7) technical writing and documentation;
(8) global content management;
(9) marketing and sales of localization products and services;
(10) global website strategy and design;
(11) quality assurance and testing;
(12) graphic localization;
(13) international e-marketing; and
(14) international e-business.

Global strategies for successful web globalization efforts

Many scholars have provided insights into the strategies used by companies to tap global markets through the use of web globalization. In this section some of these global business strategies are reviewed, and, on the basis of them, some insights are provided as to how to seek a balanced global online strategy to achieve success in web globalization efforts.

- Hout, Porter, and Rudden (1982) see global strategy from the perspective of the standardization approach, but also emphasize that global business strategy is not just a single approach but is, instead, a bag of many tricks. These include not just product standardization but also leveraging economies of scale to achieve global volume, gaining the first-mover advantage, and managing interdependencies between global markets in order to achieve synergy across different activities.
- Well-known strategists Hamel and Prahalad (1985) lean more toward the localization end of the spectrum. They propose setting global strategy on the basis of product varieties, so that investments in technologies, brand names, and distribution channels can be shared. According to them, economies of scope can be leveraged across product lines and markets, via well-recognized global brands and strong worldwide distribution systems. They see proprietary technology and the use of proprietary distribution channels as a way for companies to create strong global brands and gain competitive advantage.
- Kogut (1985), another well-known strategic thinker, recommends that companies exploit multiple sourcing, shift production to seek cheap labor and cost advantages, and look for arbitrage opportunities to take advantage of imperfections in financial and information markets. Kogut in fact recommends that companies should localize their global strategies in response to changing global economic needs and factors of production.
- Bartlett and Ghoshal (1987) and Ghoshal and Nohria (1993) propose four different strategies that companies should use, depending on the kind of industry environment in which they operate and the extent to which the industry environment demands standardization (global integration) or localization (local responsiveness). The four strategies are as follows.
  - *Global* The global strategy is more prevalent among companies in industries in which the forces of global integration are strong and the demand for local responsiveness is weak. Thus companies have a more centralized management operation, with all decisions being made at headquarters and subsidiaries taking orders and following central direction. Since in such industries the need for local responsiveness is minimal, the focus is on standardization of the marketing mix and economies of scale. Industries such as mining, heavy equipment, and construction fall into this category.
  - *Multinational* The multinational strategy is more prevalent in industries in which the forces of global integration are weak and demands for local responsiveness are strong. Companies in such industry sectors tend to have regional operations that are relatively autonomous and almost decentralized so as to increase the sensitivity to differences between the countries in which these organizations operate. Examples of such industries include beverages, food, and household goods.
  - *International* The international strategy is prevalent in industries in which the forces of global integration and local responsiveness are both weak. In such industries, companies have regional operations that are relatively autonomous (and thus decentralized). With such companies, successful internationalization depends

on transferring knowledge and expertise among its overseas subsidiaries so as to increase their sensitivity to differences between the countries in which these organizations operate. Industries following this strategy include textiles, paper, printing, and publishing.

- *Transnational* This strategy is prevalent in industries in which the forces of global integration and local responsiveness are both strong. For companies in such dynamic and global industries, it is difficult to succeed with a relatively uniform strategy that emphasizes only efficiency, responsiveness, or learning. Rather, a successful strategy must achieve all three goals simultaneously. Such companies therefore use a combination of standardization and localization to best leverage global opportunities. They leverage global information and organizational capabilities and store it centrally for global deployment. Thus the role of centralization is not to control or give orders to subsidiaries but to streamline organizational processes to "think globally and act locally." Examples of such industries include pharmaceuticals, automobiles, and computers.

Most companies face environments that simultaneously demand local responsiveness and global integration to fully leverage global opportunities and maintain a competitive edge. When possible, the "transnational strategy" is the most effective for competing in highly dynamic global markets. In the following examples we see how transnational strategy is being used in the context of web globalization efforts.

Case study: 3M

This case is based on the study by Boudreau and Watson (2006), in which they provide an analysis of 3M's implementation of transnational strategy online to tap global markets. Their analysis of the global and country-specific websites of 3M finds that 3M is following a transnational internet advertising strategy. The signs of this transnational strategy are apparent in the high degree of global integration and local responsiveness in the 3M websites.

Local responsiveness
Local responsiveness is shown on the website in several ways. First, visitors who attempt to reach the global domain of 3M (www.3m.com) are directed to a global gateway page. This global gateway page is meant to help global online visitors to find country-specific content. The global gateway page also links to a non-political world map so that users can easily locate their region. If a visitor does not understand English, 3M has provided country names in the local language and script.

Each country-specific website is well translated into the region's most used language. "Country sites exhibit good translation equivalence. For example, the 3M Chinese site has no literal translation. The brand names are all translated by using local words that reflect the meaning and are also easier to remember: *bao shi tie* for Post-it, *shi jue li* for Scotchlite, *xing xue li* for Thinsulate, etc. The content is very well edited to reflect the current and idiomatic usage of language. There are some changes in the way the sentences are worded. The mission statement, for example, is not translated word by word into Chinese. The linguistic changes better reflect the cultural and social customs of the nation. There are also some proverbs and fashionable words being used in the web site" (Boudreau and Watson, 2006: 30–1). This clearly shows that the 3M country sites did not just simply translate the pages but in fact took into account the importance of translation equivalence. A closer look at 3M country sites also shows that they have adapted the content, graphics, customer support, and other functional aspects of the international sites to meet locale-specific requirements.

3M also seems to be practicing some geolocation. If a potential customer types "3M" on Google Germany, the first few results are the 3M German site. The same is true when searching for 3M on Google Brazil or Google Japan.

Global integration

"Global integration on 3M sites is apparent because they seem to be using a standardized global web template. For most part, each local web site has a 3M 'look and feel,' embracing a common logo, colors, and functionality. The terms tend to be also used consistently across the sites. This shows that the company adheres to some kind of style guide and terminology glossary. Most international websites need to be accessed from the main corporate website. In other words, there is a need to go through the corporate web site prior to accessing an international website, as www.3m.de, for an example, is not valid. Finally, although each country-specific website is translated, some functionality, such as the search function, is solely in English. This also hints at 3M's desire to maintain some integration in its Internet strategy. Overall, 3M's web globalization strategy does strike a balance between integration and responsiveness, and is thus classified similarly as its corporate strategy, that is, as being transnational" (Boudreau and Watson, 2006: 30–1). Yunker (2011) also ranks 3M's website among the top sites in terms of best practices in web globalization.

Figures 4.3 to 4.5 show screenshots of 3M South Korea, United States, and Brazil.[9] The screenshots of the home page show that 3M is leveraging its global web template and also responding to national cultures by adapting in terms of translation, colors, structure, images, content, promotions, and other country-specific features.

Case study: Kodak

Kodak is an example of a company that has used both internationalization and localization to achieve its international web presence. Initially, Kodak adopted the strategy

---

[9] The sites for 3M were last accessed in January 2011.

Figure 4.3 3M South Korea

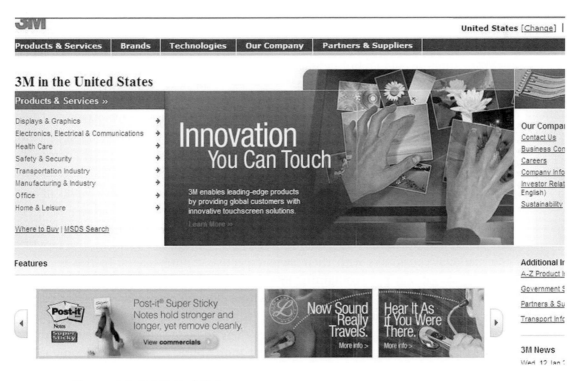

Figure 4.4 3M United States

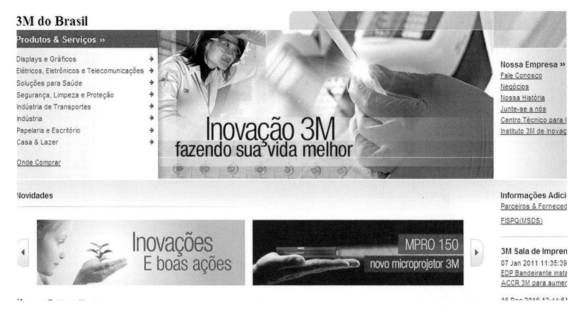

Figure 4.5 3M Brazil

of merely translating its English web pages into different languages, but it soon realized that plain translation was not enough to target and reach out to international users. For example, Terry Lund of Kodak explains that they translated their section on "Guide to better pictures" (a popular link at Kodak.com) into German and found that, even though the translation was accurate, Germans did not find it appealing and did not like the writing style (Blankenhorn, 1999). Thus Kodak consulted companies in the web globalization business and modeled its globalization efforts on the web into two parts: first they invested in developing global web templates (a part of the internationalization process), and then they sought local-country input to customize the content in a way appropriate for the country in question (the localization process). For example, the Kodak trademark phrase "Share moments, share life" has been carefully phrased in different languages, as its literal translation is not always suitable (Singh and Pereira, 2005).

Now Kodak's site is extremely well organized and is ranked as one of the top twenty-five global websites in the web globalization report (Yunker, 2011). Kodak also provides international consumers with their own respective country pages. In this regard, it has a global gateway page containing links to more than thirty-five different country-specific websites. Each country-specific website link on the global gateway page is recognizable by the name of the country, in the local language where appropriate. Kodak also seems to be using geolocation strategy to be locally responsive. The international sites of Kodak are well localized for most countries, though in some places translations are lacking. Kodak also has done a good job of reflecting local cultural

Figure 4.6 Kodak China

values, graphics, and models on its sites. For example, the Chinese site for Kodak uses unique China-centric images, colors, and human models, and also emphasizes Chinese cultural values such as family and groups via images and content. However, Kodak has still some way to go to achieve high-quality web globalization. Figures 4.6 to 4.8 show some screenshots of Kodak international sites, reflecting its commitment to create brand consistency but also to achieve some local adaptation. The screenshots, from Kodak China, Brazil, and Sweden, show the local content and graphic adaptation, and also the consistent branding of the Kodak brand name.[10]

Conclusion

To succeed in global e-business expansion, companies need to develop the capability to consolidate, understand, and replicate the processes that are needed for successful website globalization management. Global dynamic capabilities help companies integrate, build, and reconfigure their internal organization processes so that they can respond dynamically to the global environment.[11] Companies need to nurture these capabilities in order

[10] The sites for Kodak were last accessed in January 2011.
[11] Teece, Pisano, and Shuen (1997), Eisenhardt and Martin (2000), and Griffith and Harvey (2001) all provide extensive discussions of dynamic capabilities.

Figure 4.7 Kodak Brazil

Figure 4.8 Kodak Sweden

to formalize their web globalization process and document the workflow involved in the process. Once companies have created formalized routines that take into account the details of the various localization workflow steps, they are ready to respond dynamically to the global e-business environment and leverage these capabilities to tap new business opportunities. Some of the steps companies can take to initiate the development of organization routines related to web globalization activities are listed below.

(1) Have a clearly defined web globalization department and clear job descriptions.
(2) Formalize the functions and the role of the web globalization department.
(3) Develop actionable and measurable goals for the web globalization department and personnel.
(4) Outline the technology requirements for the successful implementation of web globalization efforts.
(5) Identify the standards and frameworks being used in the localization field.
(6) Develop a centralized process for core localization activities, such as vendor selection, technology and tools procurement, and hiring.
(7) Create a detailed localization workflow plan outlining each web globalization value-creating activity.
(8) Adopt a global management system to integrate various web globalization activities and generate workflow efficiencies.

Adopting a formalized web globalization structure is necessary to successfully develop, maintain, and disperse multilingual content and at the same time tap global e-business opportunities.

Chapter summary

- The chapter highlights important web globalization challenges that companies face arising from a lack of web globalization skills, tools, technologies, and web globalization frameworks.
- Six web globalization dilemmas that are explored are:
  (1) how to decide the extent of standardization versus localization;
  (2) determining the right balance between the centralization and the decentralization of web globalization efforts;
  (3) the extent to which to outsource and insource web-globalization-related tasks and processes;
  (4) the level of localization that needs to be implemented;
  (5) deciding the languages in which to translate international sites; and
  (6) determining the skill set needed to manage web globalization efforts.
- Depending on the industry, multinationals tend to follow one of the four international business strategies: global, multinational, international, or transnational.
- The chapter illustrates how companies such as 3M and Kodak are implementing a transnational strategy in their web globalization efforts by achieving a balance of global web design and local responsiveness.

REFERENCES

Bartlett, Christopher A., and Ghoshal, Sumantra 1987. "Managing across borders: new strategic requirements," *Sloan Management Review* 29: 43–53.

Bergmann, Frank 2007. "Localization department best practices," Project Open, www.project-open.com/whitepapers/loc_dept.

Best, Jo 2004a. "How eight pixels cost Microsoft millions," CNET News, August 19, http://news.cnet.com/How-eight-pixels-cost-Microsoft-millions/2100–1014_3–5316664.html.

2004b. "Microsoft's multicultural missteps: company offends foreign countries with software gaffes," CNET News, August 24, www.sfgate.com.

Blankenhorn, Dana 1999. "It's not such a small world after all," Datamation, March 1, http://itmanagement.earthweb.com/entdev/article.php/609301/its-not-such-a-small-world-after-all.htm.

Boddewyn, J. J., Soehl, Robin, and Picard, Jacques 1986. "Standardization in international marketing: is Ted Levitt in fact right?" *Business Horizons* 29: 69–75.

Boudreau, Marie-Claude, and Watson, Richard T. 2006. "Internet advertising strategy alignment," *Internet Research* 16: 23–37.

DePalma, Donald A., Sargent, Benjamin B., and Beninatto, Renato S. 2006. *Can't Read, Won't Buy: Why Language Matters on Global Websites*. Common Sense Advisory.

Eisenhardt, Kathleen M., and Martin, Jeffrey A. 2000. "Dynamic capabilities: what are they?" *Strategic Management Journal* 21: 1105–21.

Elgazzar, Mohamed 2008. "Security in software localization," Microsoft, http://msdn.microsoft.com/en-gb/goglobal/bb688162.aspx.

Ghoshal, Sumantra, and Nohria, Nitin 1993. "Horses for courses: organizational forms for multinational corporations," *Sloan Management Review* 34: 23–36.

Griffith, David A., and Harvey, Michael G. 2001. "A resource perspective of global dynamic capabilities," *Journal of International Business Studies* 32: 597–606.

Hamel, Gary, and Prahalad, Coimbatore K. 1985. "Do you really have a global strategy?" *Harvard Business Review* 63: 139–48.

Hill, John S., and Still, Richard R. 1984. "Adapting products to LDC tastes," *Harvard Business Review* 62: 92–101.

Hout, Thomas, Porter, Michael E., and Rudden, Eileen 1982. "How global companies win out," *Harvard Business Review* 60: 98–105.

Jain, Subhash C. 1989. "Standardization of international marketing strategy: some research hypotheses," *Journal of Marketing* 53: 70–9.

Jargon, Julie 2008. "Kraft reformulates Oreo, scores in China," *Wall Street Journal*, May 1; available at http://online.wsj.com/article/SB120958152962857053.html.

Knight, Gary A. 1995. "Educator insights: international marketing blunders by American firms in Japan – some lessons for management," *Journal of International Marketing* 3: 107–29.

Kogut, Bruce 1985. "Designing global strategies: comparative and competitive value added chains", *Sloan Management Review* 27: 27–38.

Labbrand 2009. "Chinese transliteration strategies for foreign brand names," November 2, www.labbrand.com/brand-source/chinese-transliteration-strategies-foreign-brand-names (accessed January 28, 2011).

Levine, Robert V. 1988. "The pace of life across cultures," in McGrath, Joseph E. (ed.), *The Social Psychology of Time*. Sage: 39–60.

Levitt, Michael 1983. "The globalization of markets," *Harvard Business Review* 61: 92–103.

Li, Fengru, and Shooshtari, Nader H. 2007. "Multinational corporations' controversial ad campaigns in China: lessons from Nike and Toyota," *Advertising and Society Review* 8: article 2.

O'Donnell, Sharon, and Jeong, Insik 2000. "Marketing standardization within global industries: an empirical study of performance implications," *International Marketing Review* 17: 19–33.

Petre, Jonathan 2002. "Umbro drops its Zyklon shoe after Jewish protests," *Daily Telegraph*, August 29; available at www.telegraph.co.uk/news/uknews/1405692/Umbro-drops -its-Zyklon-shoe-after-Jewish-protests.html.

Sackmary, B., and Scalia, L. M. 1999. "Cultural patterns of world wide web business sites: a comparison of Mexican and US companies," paper presented at the 7th Cross-Cultural Consumer and Business Studies research conference, Cancún, December 12.

Samiee, Saieed, and Roth, Kendall 1992. "The influence of global marketing standardization on performance," *Journal of Marketing* 56: 1–17.

Sanchanta, Mariko 2004. "Ikea's second try at Japan," *Financial Times*, August 5; available at ABI/INFORM Global (document ID: 570379381) (accessed November 2, 2010).

Shenkar, Oded, and von Glinow, Mary A. 1994. "Paradoxes of organizational theory and research: using the case of China to illustrate national contingency," *Management Science* 40: 56–71.

Singh, Nitish, Baack, Daniel W., and Bott, Jennifer P. 2010. "Are multinationals localizing their web sites? The link between managerial attitudes and MNE web content," *International Journal of Commerce and Management* 20: 258–67.

Singh, Nitish, and Pereira, Arun 2005. *The Culturally Customized Web Site: Customizing Web Sites for the Global Marketplace*. Elsevier Butterworth-Heinemann.

Smith, Ray A. 2008. "Levi's marketers hope one size fits all; jeans and ads will get only minimal tailoring in Global 501 campaign," *Wall Street Journal* (Eastern edn.) July 18: B7.

Teece, David J., Pisano, Gary, and Shuen, Amy 1997. "Dynamic capabilities and strategic management," *Strategic Management Journal* 18: 509–33.

Times 2007. "'Nazi bedspreads' taken off shelves," *Times*, October 2; available at www .timesonline.co.uk/tol/news/world/asia/article2570559.ece (accessed January 8, 2011).

Usunier, Jean-Claude 1999. "The use of language in investigating conceptual equivalence in cross-cultural research," paper presented at the 7th Cross-Cultural Consumer and Business Conference Studies research conference, Cancún, December 15.

Wind, Yoram 1986. "The myth of globalization," *Journal of Consumer Marketing* 3: 23–6.

Yunker, John 2005. "The web globalization opportunity (and threat)," presentation at the Association for Language Companies annual meeting, Pasadena, June 18.

2006a. "Web globalization intelligence," Global by Design, September 28, www.global bydesign.com.

2006b. "UNICEF's global web site: decentralized by design," *Global by Design* December: 2–7.

2007. "The best global sites (and why)," Global by Design, June 19, www.globalbydesign .com.

2008. "The best global web sites of 2008," Global by Design, February 28, www .globalbydesign.com.

2011. *The Web Globalization Report Card 2011.* Byte Level Research; available at www .bytelevel.com/reportcard2011.

5 Developing international websites: internationalization

Chapter objectives

- Introduce the concepts of globalization (g11n), localization (l10n), and internationalization (i18n).[1]
- Discuss technical concepts related to the development of international websites in a way that is accessible to readers without technical backgrounds.
- Discuss the basics of Unicode, a computing industry standard that is crucial to the creation of multilingual websites.
- Discuss various challenges related to international website development.
- Present an internationalization checklist as a quick reference guide.
- Discuss best practices for writing for international audiences.
- Present an industry insight into visual localization.

Developing international websites

Developing international websites without a well-laid-out plan can make the web globalization process disruptive, complex, and expensive. If a company lacks a systematic policy for its international web development and instead creates international sites only as needed, a number of problems can arise.

- *Brand inconsistency* Creating international sites on an ad hoc basis makes it difficult to maintain a consistent brand identity and at the same time meet locale-specific requirements. Replicating past efforts and ensuring that past standards are met adds to the project's time, coordination tasks, and cost.
- *Technical difficulties* Adapting program code and modifying user interface elements and customer input fields (e.g., if the format for addresses, time, and date differs in different locations) is more difficult and less efficient if a company lacks an organization-wide process to ensure a modular website design or if back-end processes are inflexible or incapable of being leveraged across multiple locales.

---

[1] The abbreviations "g11n," "l10n," and "i18n" are commonly used numeronyms in which the number in the middle stands for the number of letters between the first and last letters (i.e., "globalization" is written in shorter form as "g11n," as eleven letters are omitted between the "g" and the "n").

- *Functional difficulties* Without a proper plan for developing international sites, companies can run into issues such as how to depict and support various languages and writing systems on their websites, how to account for the text expansion and contraction that results from translating from one language to another, how to account for bidirectional text,[2] etc.
- *Cultural challenges* Symbols, icons, colors, cultural values, language, and other cultural markers can complicate the process of international website design. Thus companies need to have a framework and process in place to streamline the process of culturally customizing websites.
- *"Sim-ship" challenges* Companies face these challenges when they want to release their international websites or products worldwide simultaneously (e.g., "simultaneous shipment," or "sim-ship"). Without a proper internationalization (i18n) effort, the product will not be generalized enough or flexible enough to be quickly localized for several international markets.

Companies need a framework for their international website development processes that lays out a standardized policy for efficiently rolling out international sites. To be clear, this standardized policy relates to the processes and functions that need to be codified for successful international web development; it does not mean creating standardized websites for all countries.

For successful and efficient web globalization efforts, a framework should be based on three critical stages: globalization, internationalization, and localization. Through these three stages, international websites can be developed without the excessive replication of processes, resources are used more efficiently, errors are reduced, and quality control is better. The net result is a more efficient, streamlined, cost-effective, and successful implementation of international web development efforts. The next few sections describe these key concepts for successful international website development.

Website globalization, internationalization, localization, and translation

Globalization (g11n)

Before we jump into what globalization means in the context of web globalization, it is important to consider the broad usage of the term "globalization." A specific meaning for the term is elusive, as the concept of globalization is complex and ever-evolving. In the broadest perspective, globalization is the global integration or synthesis of economies, cultures, technologies, and systems of governance. Globalization is therefore a complex phenomenon, incorporating economic, technological, political, and geographic issues. Canton (2006) proposes a new globalization index to measure global

---

[2] Bidirectional text includes both right-to-left and left-to-right text. For example, while English is read left to right, Arabic reads right to left.

Table 5.1 Globalization index measure	
Globalization index measure	Relates to:
Economic integration	Trade and capital flows.
Political engagement	The strengthening and emergence of international institutions to facilitate and govern the process of globalization.
Technological connectivity	The ability of communication technologies such as the web to connect consumers worldwide.
Personal contact	The growing number of contacts that an individual makes with other people and world cultures due to international travel and the ease of connectivity through other means, such as the phone and the internet.
Quality of life	The increase in life expectancy due to better and more accessible healthcare, education, and nutrition.

interconnectedness. The globalization index comprises five sub-trends: economic integration, political engagement, technological connectivity, personal contact, and quality of life (see Table 5.1).

Traditionally, in the business context, globalization has meant operating with resolute constancy across the world, selling the same thing in the same way everywhere (Levitt, 1983). Furthermore, in a business context, the term "globalization" is used to describe the broad variety of processes that make the development of truly global products possible. According to the Localization Industry Standards Association (LISA), globalization is more than a technical process: "Globalization addresses all of the enterprise issues associated with making a product truly global." Globalization broadly includes organization-wide processes and functions associated with the development, integration, and deployment of globalized products. Globalization specifically involves integrating localization throughout a company after the proper implementation of internationalization and product design, as well as marketing, sales, and support in the world market.[3] Thus a multinational that is leveraging a product globally (e.g., a CRM system, a website, or some other software) needs the product to be globalized, namely globally integrated and neutral enough to be easily localized for multiple locales.

In an online context, for a company to successfully sell worldwide, it has to adapt its website linguistically, culturally, and in all other ways to be accessible to global consumers. Web globalization is a combination of website internationalization (developing a general website template) and website localization (adapting that template to create

---

[3] The term "globalization" has been defined by the Localization Industry Standards Association, and the definition was available at www.lisa.org/What-Is-Globalization.48.0.html?&no_cache=1&sword _list[]=globalization. However, LISA was declared insolvent and dissolved as of February 28, 2011, and its website was closed down.

web pages that conform to locale-specific requirements). However, web globalization also includes "organization-wide processes and capabilities," such as:

- researching global web design requirements;
- creating the technical and organizational infrastructure necessary for the internationalization and localization of the websites;
- integrating various internationalized applications and platforms around much larger globalization management systems; and
- implementing processes to manage the quality control, support, and marketing of internationalized and localized websites and related applications.

> **Website globalization**
>
> Web globalization encompasses all processes and functions involved in creating websites and related applications that are flexible and generalized enough to seamlessly accommodate multilingual computing while simultaneously supporting desired locale-specific conventions or requirements.

Before the websites or other applications are internationalized, companies need to consider multiple issues: the end user's experience, encoding for multiple languages, website deployment issues, and managing the various platforms that are used to deliver the web content. For example, multilingual websites must have the capability to compute in more than one language so that sites in multiple languages and with multiple locale-specific requirements can be supported simultaneously.

Multilingual computing is made possible by Unicode, the character-encoding industry standard designed to allow text and symbols from various languages to be consistently represented and manipulated by computers. Unicode allows users to process data and present user interfaces in almost any language without having to switch from one encoding standard to another (Gillam, 2005). Unicode enables cross-platform data interoperability. Unicode by itself does not make website internationalization possible, but it does make it easier. Thus character encoding via Unicode furthers website internationalization and is part of the larger process of website globalization. I delve more into Unicode in the next section. For the purposes of this book, web globalization is defined as *all processes and functions involved in creating websites and related applications that are flexible and generalized enough to seamlessly accommodate multilingual computing while simultaneously supporting desired locale-specific conventions or requirements.*

Internationalization (i18n)

Broadly speaking, "internationalization" is the process of generalizing a product so that it can handle multiple languages and cultural conventions. Website internationalization takes place at the level of software engineering and content development. It is a subset of website globalization, as it involves the creation of a locale-neutral platform that later can be localized and globally integrated.

> **Website internationalization**
>
> Website internationalization is the process through which back-end technologies are used to create modular, extendable, and accessible global website infrastructure for implementing future localization efforts.

Once web requirements have been researched, end user expectations have been clarified, and the globalization of the website has been made possible through the use of Unicode character encoding, the next step is to internationalize the website so that the back-end processes can efficiently and effectively support the future front-end localization efforts. For example, Zinc, a media agency, designed Saab's global website. The agency designed a global web template to standardize the back-end process and designed localized templates (based on the global template) for Sweden, France, Germany, and the United Kingdom. It also synchronized back-end processes and databases and designed intranet sites for each UK dealer so as to enhance coordination and localization (Gray, 2000). Thus the process through which back-end technologies are used to create modular, extendable, and accessible global website infrastructure is called "website internationalization." According to LISA, the internationalization process is as culturally and technically "neutral" as possible, so that it can most easily produce results that can be localized for a specific country or locale. Internationalization helps companies develop global platforms for future localization and reduces nonconformance costs by addressing global website design issues before they are released globally. However, many companies, acting either in haste or with insufficient resources or knowledge, ignore this important back-end process and either develop separate templates for different countries or just use machine-translated versions of the parent home page. Idiom Technologies conducted a global quotient survey and found that 36 percent of e-business executives interviewed had done nothing to prepare their website's back-end processes to meet the needs of international users, while an additional third had adjusted only a minority of their site capabilities.[4]

Localization (l10n)

Localization involves taking a product and making it linguistically and culturally appropriate to the locale where it will be used and sold. More specifically, localization is the process of adapting products and services (e.g., websites, manuals, and software applications) to the linguistic, cultural, technical, functional, and other locale-specific requirements of the target market.

> **Website localization**
>
> Website localization is the process of adapting various aspects of a website to meet the language, cultural, and other locale-specific requirements of the target market.

More specifically, according to LISA, website localization is the process of adapting various aspects of a website to meet the language, cultural, and other requirements of a specific target environment. When localizing a website to a specific country or culture, companies must pay special attention to local conventions, time, date, currency and number formats, units of measurements, addresses and phone numbers, layout and orientation, icons and symbols, language and verbal style, colors, aesthetics, and legal and other institutional issues. The next chapter takes a more in-depth look at website localization.

Localization is also a subset of globalization. The word "locale" is used here instead of "country" because a country may have more than one set of language and cultural requirements. For example, in Canada, companies might need to localize their sites for French- or English-speaking locales.

Translation

Translation is the linguistic aspect of localization. The goal of translation is to achieve meaning equivalence by ensuring idiomatic, vocabulary, and conceptual equivalence. Translation constitutes a subset of activities performed during the localization of a product.

Thus effective website globalization depends on internationalizing and localizing synergistically to create websites than can support and satisfy locale-specific requirements. These processes are complementary: internationalization prepares the website so that effective localization can take place.

---

[4] www.idiominc.com/worldwise/interview.asp.

Figure 5.1 Binary code

Unicode

Simply defined, Unicode is a character-encoding standard. However, before describing Unicode in more depth, it is important to explain what encoding entails.

Computers do not have any innate knowledge of text or characters; all computers really understand are numbers. To translate the thousands of characters of the world's many languages into the one language that computers do understand, programmers use various combinations of zero and one, or the binary code (see Figure 5.1). Encoding is the process of assigning a unique combination of numbers (zeros and ones) to each character. Integral to encoding is the concept of "bits" and "bytes."

- *Bits* Computers respond only to two kinds of electrical states: "on" or "off," like a light switch. Thus 0 = off, 1 = on. A bit is a binary digit and represents the smallest unit of data – either zero or one.
- *Bytes* By grouping bits we can make a more complex piece of information, called a byte. A byte is a sequence of eight bits. So 1 byte = 8 bits and therefore has 256 possible values: 2 x 2 x 2 x 2 x 2 x 2 x 2 x 2 = 256.

Broadly speaking, there are two main types of writing systems: ideographic and phonetic. Ideographic writing systems use symbols to communicate concepts and ideas. Phonetic writing systems are more abstract; a character represents a sound. Examples of ideographic systems include characters in languages such as Chinese (*hanzi*), Japanese (*kanji*; see Figure 5.2), and Korean (*hanja*). Examples of phonetic-character-based languages include Arabic, Cyrillic, Greek, and Latin. When the early encoding standards were developed, they were specific to English and did not take into account thousands of characters in other languages. For example, Chinese has more than 3,000 characters compared to the limited set of characters used in the English language. Thus, during the early years, encoding primarily used the English character set.

The following is based closely on Gillam (2005) and is reproduced with permission from MultiLingual Computing:

> The organization now called the American National Standards Institute (ANSI) published the ASCII encoding standard, one of the first standards to be published, in the 1960s. It uses the values from 32 to 126 to represent the 26 uppercase and lowercase letters of the English alphabet, the 10 digits, and various punctuation marks and symbols. The values from 0 to 31 and the value 127 were reserved for various signals that controlled the communication protocol, and byte values from 128 to 255 weren't used. ASCII only includes codes for the letters in the English alphabet, which presented a problem for speakers of other languages who didn't have codes for the letters of their alphabets. Since the byte values from 128 to 255 weren't standardized by ASCII, various other standards sprung up that used these code values for the letters of other alphabets. Computer vendors, national governments, and others put forth a variety of standards. A plethora of character encoding standards now exist, each of them defining code values for a single language or a small group of related languages. This created a "Tower of Babble" scenario in which systems using different standards couldn't communicate with each other.

Several problems emerged from the use of multiple encoding standards:

(1) The standards are mutually incompatible. While the value "65" almost always represents the capital letter "A," the value "215" can represent many different characters, depending on the encoding standard.
(2) Encoded text often travels across media without any external indication of the encoding standard it follows. Software receiving a message of unknown encoding has to guess or simply assume, which in many cases results in mangled characters. The sending software intends for a particular numeric value to represent a certain character, and the receiving software interprets it as something totally different, leading to garbage.
(3) Mixing languages in a single document often requires changing from one encoding standard to another in the middle of the document, and there are often no mechanisms in the software for doing that.

Unicode was designed to solve these problems. Unicode is an industry standard that allows text and symbols from all languages to be consistently represented and

Figure 5.2 *Kanji* symbols

manipulated by computers. Unicode characters can be encoded using any of several schemes termed Unicode transformation formats (UTFs). "The idea was to use a larger data type than a byte for each character and then give every character in every language its own unique numeric representation. This means you can mix languages freely in a document without special software to support mixed encodings, and you can send text from one system to another without worrying about it getting mangled on the other end (as long as the sending and receiving systems both support Unicode)" (Gillam, 2005). The Unicode standard is now adopted by most prominent software-developing companies, including Apple, HP, IBM, JustSystems, Microsoft, Oracle, SAP, Sun, Sybase, and many others. Unicode is required by modern standards such as XML, Java, ECMA Script (JavaScript), LDAP, CORBA 3.0, WML, etc., and it is the official way to implement ISO/IEC 10646 (Unicode.org). It is supported by many operating systems, all modern browsers, and many other products. According to the Unicode consortium, the emergence of the Unicode standard, and the availability of tools supporting it, is among the most significant recent global software technology trends.[5] A variety of methods are used to encode Unicode: UTF-EBCDIC (unpopular), UTF-8, UTF-16, UTF-32, etc. UTF-8, probably the most popular Unicode transformation format, allows the length of codes to vary from one byte to four bytes, to account for millions of characters in all world languages. UTF-8 also has plenty of room left for encoding undiscovered and little-known languages. UTF-8 is also compatible with ASCII. Its usage is recommended as a best practice for encoding by various professional bodies and it is especially common on the web (Gillam, 2005).

Common Locale Data Repository (CLDR) project[6]

International software applications and international websites must be translated into different languages, but they must also be customized to locale-specific requirements. Some examples of locale-specific requirements include:

- formatting (and parsing) numbers, dates, times, currency values, etc.;
- displaying names for language, script, region, currency, time zones, etc.;
- the collation order (used in sorting, searching, and matching text); and
- identifying measurement systems, weekend conventions, currencies, etc.

Most operating systems and many application programs currently maintain their own repositories of locale data[7] to support these conventions. However, such data is often incomplete, idiosyncratic, or gratuitously different from program to program. The purpose of the Common Locale Data Repository project is to provide a general XML format for the exchange of locale information for use in application and system development, and to gather, store, and make available a common set of locale data generated in that format. More information on this valuable open-source project can be found at www.unicode.org/cldr. The CLDR project can help companies create a platform to support multicultural requirements based on locale-specific conventions. Professionals involved in internationalization should ensure that all applications and websites are Unicode-compliant, and they should also use the CLDR's information in defining multicultural requirements.

---

[5] www.unicode.org/standard/WhatIsUnicode.html.

[6] Material based on information from www.unicode.org/cldr.

[7] "Locale data" defines the user language and other country-specific settings, such as number formatting, date setting, time setting, paper size, etc.

International Components for Unicode (ICU) by IBM

The International Components for Unicode by IBM comprise a portable set of the C/C++ and Java libraries for Unicode support and software internationalization (i18n) and globalization (g11n), providing consistency to applications across various platforms. It is an open-source standard that is sponsored, supported, and used by IBM. ICU provides robust, full-featured, commercial-quality, Unicode-based technologies. Some important support functions of ICU include the following.[8]

- *Code page conversion* Converting text data to or from Unicode and nearly any other character set or encoding.
- *Collation* Comparing strings[9] according to the conventions and standards of a particular language, region, or country. ICU's collation is based on the Unicode collation algorithm plus locale-specific comparison rules from the Common Locale Data Repository, a comprehensive source for this type of data.
- *Formatting* Formatting numbers, dates, times, and currency amounts according to the conventions of a chosen locale. This includes translating month and day names into the selected language, choosing appropriate abbreviations, ordering fields correctly, etc. These data also come from the CLDR.
- *Time calculations* Multiple types of calendars are provided beyond the traditional Gregorian calendar. A comprehensive set of time zone calculation application programming interfaces (APIs) is provided.
- *Unicode support* ICU closely tracks the Unicode standard, providing easy access to all the many Unicode character properties and other fundamental operations as specified by the Unicode standard.

Even non-technical members of a web globalization team should understand the importance of Unicode, CLDR, and ICU so that they can at least guide the software engineers to explore or follow these conventions for successful web globalization efforts.

Why internationalize (i18n)?

As mentioned before, internationalization (i18n) is integral to creating websites and applications that can be seamlessly adapted to various settings and then be efficiently developed and deployed. Internationalization (i18n) ensures that the core of the website or the back-end processes have a flexible architecture to operate without any problem with external modules. The core of the application or website must be entirely Unicode-encoded prior to further internationalization efforts. Internationalization should not be seen as an afterthought; if it is, the process can become very expensive.

---

[8] Adapted from http://site.icu-project.org/#TOC-What-is-ICU.
[9] A string is a finite sequence of data values.

In several examples that follow, handling the challenges of internationalization on a piecemeal basis resulted in massive inefficiencies and heavy expenses.

Internationalization should be seen as an integral part of the international product or international website development process and should be undertaken before the website or application is localized. In fact, internationalization makes the product "world-ready."

Good internationalization allows all the information on the site or software to be depicted seamlessly in all languages. Internationalization can enhance the delivery and deployment of multilingual versions of products or websites. Since the base platform is uniform and based on a single code, the internationalization process does not need to be repeated for every new language or country launch.

At Sun Microsystems, the international product development cycle starts with outlining the internationalization requirements. Designers and architects evaluate areas in the product offering that will require internationalization; then the team of engineers evaluates the internationalization considerations in the implementation of the global product. Next, the manager allocates resources and sets a map or time frame for internationalization activities. Finally, technical product reviewers and software quality assurance professionals evaluate the product's internationalization status and test for the proper performance of internationalization functionality, respectively.[10] By having a clear internationalization process, Sun is able to efficiently manage internationalization of its products.

Most companies do not have similarly well-structured internationalization plans or teams and may outsource such work to localization vendors/localization service providers. In such cases, the localization vendor should be involved from the beginning to save time and money and to improve the delivery and deployment of the products. Localization vendors complain that companies often come to them once they have put half-hearted efforts into internationalization or have run into problems. Correcting past mistakes in internationalization can be time-consuming, laborious, and expensive. For example, Ian Henderson, the CEO of a localization company, provides an instance in which one of its clients had updated its multilingual resource code files by adding an English string. Henderson's company had to extract the English strings from each section, translate them, and then integrate them back into the multilingual resource code files. According to Henderson, the client's partial effort complicated the internationalization effort and led to laborious engineering tasks to translate and patch each string (Henderson, 2010).

The internationalization step ensures that design work is done using a modular approach in which the software or website supports and is able to incorporate international characters, date and time formats, number formats, address fields, and other locale-specific elements.

The next section explores the various processes involved in internationalization in more depth.

---

[10] http://developers.sun.com/global/technology/arch.

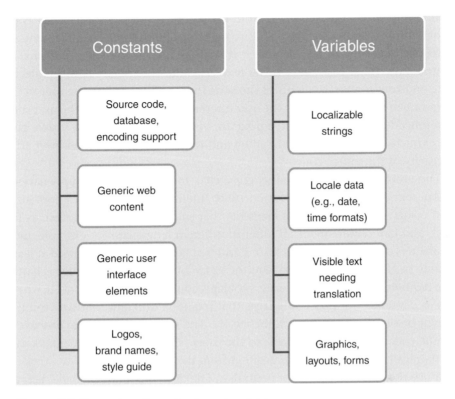

Figure 5.3 Examples of constants and variables

What does internationalization (i18n) entail?

The internationalization of software, online documentation, websites, etc. helps to isolate the "constants" from the "variables." According to Yunker (2003), a "constant" is anything that remains the same across locales and markets; "variables" include all the elements that need to be modified for each locale (see Figure 5.3). This process of separating the constants from the variables makes future localization jobs faster and more and cost-effective, as the localizable elements (i.e., the variables) can then be easily identified, extracted, and adapted to a specific locale. Thus separating the constants from the variables is truly the first step in the internationalization process. In technical terms, this means extracting all the localizable elements from the main code, which should be kept generic and neutral.

Extracting text and other localizable elements from the source code

The first step in the process of internationalizing a website is to identify and extract all the localizable items and strings into external resource files; the end user visible strings and resources must be separated from the source code. The source code is part of the programming language but also has strings that end users can see. Elements of the user interface (UI) contain translatable text such as various messages, buttons, and menu commands. Translatable text is the text visible to the users. Engineers need to delineate and later modify elements of the code that are displayed to the user in the form of interface or messages. Parts of the user interface that are visible to the user should never be embedded or hard-coded in a program's executable code. These visible parts should be extracted (stored in a resource file) and translated separately without affecting the integrity of the source code.

The visible UI text (print, paste, copy, etc.), formatting styles (hyphenation, punctuation, text delimiters, capitalization rules, line-wrapping rules, etc.), font sizes, names, and colors are all examples of elements that should not be hard-coded, as formatting, text, and font requirements all differ in different languages. For example, most English characters can be displayed on a 5 x 7 grid, but Japanese characters need at least a 16 x 16 grid to be clearly seen; Chinese requires a 24 × 24 grid.[11] If the font size is hard-coded for the requirements for one language, problems could develop in the future when the website is developed for other languages that require a different font size; some characters might be displayed too small to be legible. The solution is to create message identifiers in the code for text that is visible to the users. The message identifier should be able to dynamically retrieve the translated text from the resource file.

Since the source code is kept neutral and flexible and all translatable text and visible text is stored in resource files, this generalized code now can be adapted for almost any locale without needing much adaptation. Thus, when new websites are created for other languages, the source code will remain the same and only the localizable elements from the resource file will need to be translated and modified. Separating the strings and other resources from the source code also prevents translators from tampering with the program code, as all the localizable resources and strings are now contained in a separate resource file. Just imagine the problems that could occur if even one word of the code is translated and results in the program crashing. It is a good practice to write clearly and use consistent terminology in the resource file so that translators can easily understand the text to be translated. If the text in the resource file is not clear or needs special treatment, then adding comments for the translator's consideration is a good practice.

Another related issue is ensuring that all the text inside images and graphics that are visible to users is easily extractable and not embedded in the graphic itself. The text can be added to the graphic with layers or frames that can be later extracted for translation as needed. Computer-assisted translation tools can extract source text from the graphic and help replace it with the translated text. Costs increase if text is embedded in graphics, as it is more difficult to extract the text when translation is needed in order

---

[11] http://msdn.microsoft.com/en-us/library/aa292134(VS.71).aspx.

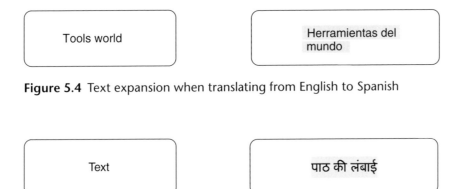

Figure 5.4 Text expansion when translating from English to Spanish

Figure 5.5 Character width, length, and height for letters in English and Hindi

to use the same graphic for other locales. Creating a whole new set of graphics for each country may be required. (However, sometimes it is necessary to create new graphics and use localized icons, depending on the cultural expectations of a specific locale.)

Another important consideration is to use the same resource identifiers throughout the life of the project. Changing identifiers makes it difficult to update localized resources from one software build version to another. It is also helpful to use standard language and country codes based on International Organization for Standardization (ISO) standards for naming various locale-specific files.

Creating text buffers

Creating text buffers is part of ensuring that the design of the UI elements (menus, website layouts, dialog boxes, etc.) is flexible and neutral. Allocating dynamic text buffers is necessary because text length can expand in translation. Some languages require up to 70 percent more space to express particular statements, and words can expand almost 300 percent. German and Danish tend to have lengthy words, and text can expand almost 20–30 percent when translating from English to German (see also Figure 5.4). The text can also contract during translation; for example, when translating from Japanese to English, text can contract anywhere from 10 percent to 50 percent and leave awkward empty spaces. Moreover, character width, height, and length all vary between languages and can further contribute to text contraction or expansion (see Figure 5.5). Thus, when translating, text expansion or text contraction can make it difficult to fit all the content in the given user interface. This can make the user interface look crowded, perhaps enough to make it difficult to read. The problem can become more acute when translated words expand in navigation bars or graphics. Furthermore, with mobile devices the UI and text display is limited to a smaller screen, further complicating the matter.

At the internationalization stage, therefore, companies need to anticipate the languages the software or website will be translated into in the future and make some standard adjustment in the UI and graphics to accommodate text expansion when it happens. If the source language is English, a safe approach is to allow a text buffer of at least 35 percent for future translation and probable text expansions. Text buffers can be made by manipulating column widths and font sizes. It is good practice to leave enough space for text expansion and allow for text wrapping; absolute positions and fixed-width items should not be used. Using the maximum allowable space for frames, especially around name and address text fields, may also help. Icons, cursors, or bitmaps that have text in them should be avoided. The best practice is generally to adopt bitmaps that are part of an international standard and not specific to a country. Visual localization and pseudo-localization are addressed in a later section as they are instrumental in correcting text expansion and contraction issues.

Text-processing functions

All visible text should be processed in a manner that is clear and easily interpreted across multiple locales. Issues related to string concatenation, punctuation, sorting, capitalization, hyphenation, etc. may make the visible strings complicated and illegible. Some important tips include the following.

- *Avoid text concatenation* "Concatenation" essentially means binding two strings together to form a new string. During programming, strings can be constructed from parts at run-time. This is acceptable if the compound string is not going to be localized, but if it is to be localized then the process can cause a lot of problems. This is because the languages use different sentence structure, and thus the order of words (adjectives and nouns, subject and verb) changes from language to language. The source code should be carefully combed for concatenated messages that may need to be localized.
- *Perform locale-sensitive sorting* Locale-sensitive linguistic sorting should be used to sort text strings in a culturally appropriate way. Text sorting needs to abide by the conventions and rules of a language, and these rules tend to vary from language to language. For example, the alphabetical sort order will change when translating from English to another language. Line-breaking, hyphenation, and word-wrapping rules also differ by language. The W3C[12] guidelines state that software that sorts or searches text for users should take into consideration appropriate collation units and ordering rules for the relevant language and/or application. The W3C also recommends that, when searching or sorting is done dynamically, the "relevant language"

---

[12] The World Wide Web Consortium (W3C) is the main international body involved with the development of standards pertinent to the growth of the World Wide Web.

should be determined to be that of the current user, and may thus differ from user to user.[13]

- *Casing* "Case folding" is the term used when a text string is converted from upper case to lower case or vice versa. According to Dr. International (2002), some applications automatically convert the first character in a word into upper case, but in some countries this might not work. Some languages, such as Hindi and Arabic, do not even have an upper case. In Russian, the names of the days of the week are never capitalized; capitalizing the word for "Wednesday" changes the meaning to "environment," and capitalizing the word for "Sunday" changes the meaning to "resurrection."[14]

- *Text input methods* Ideograph-based writing systems have thousands of characters, and computer keyboards have limited space. As a result, input method editors (IMEs) are used to map multiple keystrokes into single ideographic and phonetic characters. Applications should have built-in support for IMEs so that various characters that cannot be captured in limited keys of the keyboard can be easily entered.

- *Treating bidirectional text* The direction of the text and its position differ by language. English, like other Latin-based languages, is read from left to right, while Arabic and Hebrew are read from right to left. Thus most user interface elements, such as menus, dialogs, labels, and scroll bars, should be positioned on the basis of the direction in which the language is read. For Arabic, this would mean that most UI elements and text flows from right to left rather than left to right. The program being used should provide RTL support to address this issue. Engineers are advised to take this into consideration when developing websites for languages such as Arabic and Hebrew. For example, Yahoo! Maktoob and IKEA's websites for certain Arabic countries show the right-to-left orientation. HTML and CSS are designed to work with RTL languages.

Support locale-sensitive formats

Conventions for calendars, date, time, currencies, addresses, etc. all differ by country. Thus, at the internationalization stage, applications or websites should be enabled to depict correct locale-specific conventions for each locale. International Components for Unicode and the Unicode Common Locale Data Repository will both be of great help to software programmers and internationalization engineers in determining various types of locale-formats. CLDR has an extensive standard repository of locale data that is open source and can be easily accessed. ICU can help in formatting numbers, dates, times, and currency amounts according to the conventions of a chosen locale.[15]

---

[13] Excerpt from http://www.w3.org/International/techniques/developing-specs.

[14] Excerpt from http://msdn.microsoft.com/en-us/goglobal/bb688133.aspx.

[15] Refer to http://msdn.microsoft.com/en-us/goglobal/bb688110.aspx for a detailed explanation of various globalization issues.

Table 5.2 Different time formats

Country	Time format
United States	2:45 p.m.
Brazil	14:45
Russia	14:45
Germany	14:45 Uhr (sometimes "Uhr" is abbreviated "h")
Japanese	Pm2hour45min

- *Date formatting* Dates are formatted differently in different countries. Code should therefore be developed independent of locale-specific date and calendar formats. ISO 8601 specifies various date formats but uses the following standard for dates: YYYY-MM-DD. The W3C consortium recommends that a four-digit number is always used for the year, because this clearly distinguishes the year from the date or the month. Consider how December 20, 2010, is formatted in different countries:
  (1) Spanish (Mexico) is written as 20/12/10;
  (2) English (US) is written as 12/20/10; and
  (3) Japanese is written as 10/12/20.
- *Time formats* The order in which hours, minutes, and seconds are displayed also varies between locales. For example, in Europe and Asia a twenty-four-hour clock is used, while in the United States a twelve-hour a.m/p.m. clock is used (see Table 5.2). Normally a colon is used to demarcate hours, minutes, and seconds, but some Asian countries use ideographic characters. Moreover, other issues related to time also differ, including time zone names and time zone abbreviations. In some countries, such as China, India, and Japan, daylight saving time is not used. ISO 8601 specifies various time formats and uses the twenty-four-hour clock system.
- *Currency formatting* Currency symbols and even the way negative amounts are displayed vary between locales. In some countries the negative sign comes after the currency symbol and the number, and in others vice versa. Currency presentation also varies in the use of a comma, a period, or just a space. Since presentation formats for currencies differ, the presentation field should be flexible and have extra space. ISO 4217 is the international standard that assigns three-letter codes to various world currencies.
- *Number formatting* The formatting of numbers also differs between locales; Table 5.3 gives some examples of different formats. According to Dr. International (2002), some items to pay attention to include the following.
  (1) *The thousand separator* In the United States, a comma is used (2,500); in Germany, a period (2.500); and in Sweden, a space (2 500).
  (2) *The decimal separator* In the United States, a period is used, so we have 2,500.7; in Germany, the decimal separator is a comma (2.500,7).

Table 5.3 Number formatting		
Percentage format	Thousand separator	Decimal separator
90%	2,500	250.20
%90	2.500	250,20
90 pct	2 500	250'20
.90		

(3) *Digit grouping* Digits are most often grouped in sets of three (e.g., 202,123,345.00), but they also differ by languages. For example, in Hindi, the digits are grouped in pairs – except for the hundreds, which use three digits (e.g., 12,13,45,500.00).

(4) *Percentage sign* This is also difficult to hard-code, as it can be written as 45%, or %45, or 45 pct, or 45 %.

- *Addresses* Address formats are very different from locale to locale and should not be hard-coded. The best approach is to have multiple fields for flat/apartment/building number, street, postal code, city, country, etc. Moreover, postal codes vary in length and use both numbers and letters. Thus it is prudent not to specify a particular format or length for such fields. The Japanese use an address system that is the opposite of what is used in the United States: addresses in Japan start with the postal code and end with the recipient's name. The way names and titles are presented also varies by locale and thus should be not formatted on the basis of one specific convention. Users should be able to select the name format that can depict their name and title in the culturally appropriate way.

- *Telephone numbers* Similarly to address formats, phone number formats can be quite diverse. The input fields should therefore be able to handle a variety of formats. Phone numbers in different locales use different separators and different groupings and have a differen total number of digits. Thus at the design stage it is important to keep country codes, area codes, and phone numbers in separate fields, and also to avoid having any fixed number of digits for them. The digit count in country codes or area codes and phone numbers will vary. For example, the United States has a single-digit country code, Australia has a double-digit country code, and Saudi Arabia has a triple-digit country code.

- *Units of measurement* Although most countries have now adopted the metric system, some countries, such as the United States, continue to use the imperial system. Measurements can relate to weight, length, volume, area, temperatures, etc. Paper sizes also follow either the metric or the imperial system and vary between countries. Accordingly, it is important to ensure that the product is flexible enough to accommodate the varying units depending on the locale.

Finally, if a site or application for multiple locales uses third-party products, then it must support Unicode, and some internationalization may be needed. Adam Asnes, the

CEO of a localization company, gives an example of an instance in which the client's product used a third-party product for displaying animations in a children's game. "At first glance, you wouldn't think it would be an issue, as there was no text being processed or displayed. But when we looked at things more closely, the user name and file path info was being passed into the animation tool, which in this case could very well involve wide characters (e.g., Chinese). But the particular version of the animation product could not support this and so it would always crash." According to Asnes (2007), "This fix took time and some inventiveness."

Internationalization checklist

An attempt is made here to provide a comprehensive checklist of various things that may need to be checked and implemented at the internationalization stage. Software engineers and localizers need to consider these issues when internationalizing software or websites. Managers should also go over this list and give it to their engineers to help them guide their internationalization efforts.[16]

(1) Start the internationalization process right at the development stage. It should never be an afterthought. Internationalization support should be built in from the inception of the product.

(2) Ensure that web pages are Unicode-enabled and, ideally, in UTF-8 character encoding. Unicode is also essential for internationalized domain names (IDNs), which could be an important part of your global web strategy.

(3) Isolate and modify any software functionality that will require localization.

(4) Make sure all the translatable text is stored and centralized in one or two resource files.

(5) Strings or characters that should not be localized must be clearly marked so as to avoid confusion.

(6) Avoid run-time composite strings and concatenating strings (i.e., chaining the strings together to form new strings). Even if the individual text strings are translated correctly, the final concatenated text string may be meaningless or incorrect in other languages.

(7) In the code, avoid using the same string variable in more than one context.

(8) Minimize the use of variables and provide enough information to translators so that they adequately understand the context of what needs to be translated.

(9) Keep sentences in a single string, as the meaning is much better preserved during translation (human or machine).

---

[16] This is a general checklist based on the author's knowledge and insights from several sources, including books, software, documents, and websites (Esselink, 2000; Yunker, 2003; Hall, 2005; http://msdn .microsoft.com/en-us/goglobal/bb688110.aspx; http://www-01.ibm.com/software/globalization).

(10) Use clear, standardized, and unambiguous terminology.

(11) Ideally, place button text on the button, not linked to a string variable.

(12) Unused strings and boxes should be removed from the source to avoid any confusion for localizers.

(13) Avoid overlapping user interface controls; this makes it difficult for localizers to find them.

(14) Avoid using placeholders or variables such as "s" or "%," etc. (remember, the rule for placing "%" varies between locales). Instead, write a comment for the localizer about what to insert at run-time. Be especially careful to avoid adding "s" to pluralizing text.

(15) Weekend and holiday designations should be considered using locale-specific conventions; for example, Thursday and Friday are considered the weekend in certain Middle Eastern countries.

(16) Make sure your product's UI supports the use of input method editors, especially for vertical text and line-breaking rules. (MEs allow the entry of non-alphanumeric characters, using an alphanumeric keyboard or tablet interface.)

(17) Ensure that the input validation rules for internationalized software or websites and other applications allow the input of multilingual characters and multiple formats. Thus, if the postal code entry does not conform to the US standard, it should not generate an error message that will frustrate an international user.

(18) Try to keep icons, cursors, and bitmaps generic, culturally neutral, and without text.

(19) Anticipate text expansion and contraction and size the tables, dialog boxes, menus, and web layouts accordingly. In the case of websites, allow tables to resize dynamically. If the UI string contains a variable, then allow for some extra space, as it may expand during translation.

(20) For software products, ensure that the program code is designed to enable the input, display, and editing of bidirectional or east Asian languages.

(21) Ensure that code does not have hard-coded font names, numeric constants, file names, or, for that matter, any localizable string.

(22) Avoid using tabs and spaces when formatting the text.

(23) Ensure that the product supports a variety of punctuation formats, as they tend to vary by language.

(24) Ensure that the product is independent of text delimiters. Delimiters are one or more characters that separate parts of the text. Text delimiters vary from language to language.

(25) When designing multilingual websites, make sure that the database or folder structure clearly separates generic content from language-specific content.

(26) Create a naming system for all localized web files and an organizational system for new localized directories.

(27) Follow standard guidelines for specifying locale data. Languages are identified with two-letter codes specified by the ISO 639 standard. Country codes identify a country and are two-letter codes as specified by the ISO 3166 standard.

(28) Ensure that your website is sensitive to date, time, address, currency, phone, and other types of locale-specific conventions. W3C recommends that data should contain an explicit zone offset.

(29) For multilingual websites, consider having a global gateway page with a language selection menu.

(30) Modify back-end databases to support multi-byte languages and to provide language-specific search engines if required. Data repositories should be world-ready during their development stage.

(31) Spell-checking rules differ between languages and need to be localized.

(32) Never translate file names or file extensions.

(33) Select development and hosting tools that can support characters and locale-specific conventions for your target locales. Ideally, these tools should be able to handle multilingual data.

(34) Ensure that the application code is capable of identifying language selections or the user's locale.

(35) Create graphics with text using a separate text layer, so that it can be easily extracted. In addition, write captions in the document text, not inside the graphic.

(36) When creating text or writing for future localization, make sure to:
   (a) create a glossary of all terms that are company-, product-, or industry-specific and will apply consistently across all locales;
   (b) use simple, concise, and culture-neutral phrases and words, such as "Click on," "Click," "Select," etc.; and
   (c) create an extensive terminology glossary and style sheet for future localization.

(37) When synchronizing web content for mobile devices, interoperability and usability are the biggest issues, due to the platform, the browsers, and the actual size of the device. To avoid these problems:
   (a) keep UI elements simple and minimum as the screen space is limited;
   (b) design dynamic web pages so that they resize on the basis of the device;
   (c) keep the Uniform Resource Identifier (URI) short and simple;
   (d) utilize UTF-8 encoding;
   (e) ensure that web pages are tested on mobile browsers;
   (f) minimize the use of externally linked resources such as images, as they increase the load time;
   (g) size web pages correctly in order to achieve a balance between pagination and scrolling on the mobile device; and
   (h) avoid font-related styling and limit the use of tables – especially nested tables.[17]

---

[17] The tips are based on "Best practices for delivering web content to mobile devices," at www.w3.org/TR/mobile-bp. Refer also to http://mobiforge.com.

Some software tools automate the detection internationalization issues by scanning the software source code and then reconfiguring software applications.[18]

Writing for an international audience

To this point, the chapter has outlined issues related to internationalizing websites and applications to create a generalized and flexible platform for locale-specific adaptations. It is also important to internationalize the translatable text so that it can be translated easily into multiple languages while preserving its translation equivalence. Controlled languages have evolved in an attempt to create simple language structures that are flexible and use limited vocabulary. Controlled language is obtained by restricting the grammar and vocabulary in order to reduce ambiguity and complexity.

> ### Controlled languages
>
> Controlled languages enable authors to create simple language structures that are flexible and use limited vocabulary. Controlled language is obtained by restricting the grammar and vocabulary in order to reduce ambiguity and complexity.

The evolution of controlled language can be traced back to the work of Charles Ogden who outlined his ideas about basic English in 1930. Ogden proposed the use of English as a global language because it had far fewer arcane word endings to learn than any other language. However, he found that English suffers from several drawbacks, including varied spelling practices and a vast vocabulary (Weiss, 2005). Ogden therefore proposed a reduced vocabulary of 850 English words to capture the full richness of English and at the same time make it simple for global adoption.

Various companies, including Caterpillar, GM, IBM, and Kodak, have adopted some sort of controlled language. There are several advantages to using controlled language. Controlled language:

- is easy to learn and understand;
- increases terminological consistency;
- leads to simplified sentence structuring;
- is more amenable to translation equivalence;
- increases the quality of translation output;
- reduces editing and translation costs;
- reduces ambiguity;

---

[18] An example of such a tool is Lingoport's Globalyzer: www.lingoport.com/software-internationalization-products/globalyzer-3.

- is easy for post-processing work and future reuse;
- facilitates machine translation, because it reduces lexical ambiguity;
- increases the quality of technical documentation (Caterpillar Technical English and IBM's Easy English are two examples);
- is being used in web publishing and international websites – especially for global support pages and documentation and online help; and
- is good for creating translation memory.

Darwin Information Typing Architecture (DITA)

While on the topic of controlled languages, it is good to know about Darwin Information Typing Architecture, which is used for authoring and reusing already existing content. Companies that struggle with creating new content and successfully leveraging content across multiple formats can achieve efficiency gains if they develop a process of simplifying and storing information. This is where content management systems (CMSs) and DITA-type applications come into the picture. DITA encourages structured authoring for better reuse in the future. People involved with information architecture issues may already be familiar with DITA, but a brief background is nonetheless provided here.

DITA is an XML-based, end-to-end architecture for authoring, producing, and delivering readable information in discrete, typed topics. DITA is therefore an architecture for creating topic-oriented, information-typed content that can be reused and single-sourced in a variety of ways.[19] DITA enables organizations to deliver content as closely as possible to the point of use, making it ideal for applications such as integrated help systems, websites, and "How to" instruction pages. In layperson's terms, DITA allows authors to create content that is classified into clearly defined and labeled "chunks" of information that can be then reassembled into many different forms. For example, the content for online help can be written in the DITA format, and then published simultaneously across multiple deliverable formats – for example, printed manuals or mobile platforms such as iPhone, BlackBerry, or Android – to meet users' specific contextual needs.

Thus, according to Oasis, DITA has the following uses:

(1) managing readable information;
(2) reusing information in many different combinations and deliverables;
(3) creating online information systems, such as user assistance (help) or web resources; and
(4) creating minimalist books for easier authoring and use.

---

[19] www.oasis-open.org.

Preparing documents for translation

Translation equivalence is the goal of document translation. This means that the translation should give heed to idiomatic equivalence, vocabulary equivalence, conceptual equivalence, and even grammatical equivalence. A document that is simple, clear, consistent, and specific, and that uses unambiguous terms, culturally neutral concepts (avoiding slang and idioms), and a reduced-traditional vocabulary, is more likely to be well translated. Translation also greatly benefits from the use of a terminology glossary, style sheets, and, as mentioned, the use of controlled language. Below are some tips most frequently recommended by experts and translation companies to prepare a document for translation.[20]

(1) Keep sentences short and simple.

(2) Define all new and familiar terms in the terminology glossary.

(3) Avoid the use of abbreviations; especially avoid culture-specific abbreviations (for example, PB&J or ASAP).

(4) Have a corporate style guide and enforce it.

(5) Use words with their first or most common definition.

(6) Avoid the use of jargon, idioms, slang, humor, sarcasm, analogies, metaphors, etc.

(7) Avoid the use of homographic words (same in spelling but different in meaning or pronunciation). For example, "bow" could mean a bow on the top of a gift, a bow and arrow, or the act of bending at the waist.

(8) Avoid the use of "phrasal verbs" that combine a verb with one or two particles. For example, the verb "run" can be used in numerous phrasal verbs: to run around, to run down, to run into, etc.

(9) Use the simplest forms of verbs to make reading easier. For example, instead of "we will be arriving," use "we will arrive."

(10) Avoid word redundancy. For example, instead of "delve deeper," use "delve." Other examples include "variety of different," "safe haven," etc.

(11) Use the active voice instead of the passive voice when possible. Example of active: "The committee decided to postpone the vote." Example of passive: "A decision was reached to postpone the vote."

(12) Avoid nominalizations. A nominalization is a noun that has been constructed by adding grammatical inflections to a verb. For example, instead of saying "The principal conducted an investigation into the matter," say "The principal investigated the matter." Equally, instead of saying "Our discussion concerned a wage increase," say "We discussed a wage increase."

(13) Use modal auxiliary verbs sparingly. A modal auxiliary verb is an auxiliary verb (or helping verb) that can modify the grammatical mood (or mode) of a verb, such as will/would, shall/should, can/could. These tend to have multiple interpretations for non-native English speakers.

---

[20] References used include Yunker (2003); Weiss (2005); IBM (2006); Wylie (1998).

Table 5.4 Gender-neutral language	
Sexist	Gender-neutral
Cameraman	Camera operator
Foreman	Supervisor
Salesman	Salesperson/salespeople
Fireman	Firefighter
Fatherland	Homeland
Craftsman	Artisan
Layman	Laity/layperson
Milkman	Milk vendor

(14) Ensure that elements in the sentence are parallel. The parallel structure of a sentence refers to the extent to which different parts of the sentence match each other in form. When more than one phrase or description is used in a sentence, these phrases or descriptions should be consistent with one another in their form and wording. Parallel structure is important because it enhances the ease with which the reader can follow the writer's idea.[21]

(15) Try not to string nouns together one after the other, because a series of nouns is difficult to understand. One way to revise a string of nouns is to change one noun to a verb. For example, instead of "This report explains our investment growth stimulation projects," write "This report explains our projects to stimulate growth in investments."[22]

(16) Use affirmative forms rather than several negatives, because multiple negatives are difficult to understand. For example, this is unclear (multiple negatives, passive): "Less attention is paid to commercials that lack human interest stories than to other kinds of commercials." This is a better way to phrase it: "People pay more attention to commercials with human interest stories than to other kinds of commercials."[23]

(17) Do not use a dash for signifying parenthesis ("It is at this point – the starting point – that designers and writers meet"). However, translators accept the dash when used to show an extension of a sentence (IBM, 2006).

(18) Do not use a slash to mean "and/or." Rewrite the sentence to indicate the exact meaning. For example: "You can choose the green one, the blue one, or both."[24]

(19) Do not use an ampersand to mean "and."[25]

(20) Avoid gender-specific words (see Table 5.4). For example, when the pronoun "he" is used to refer to a specific male person, then its use is, obviously, correct. When

---

[21] http://faculty.washington.edu/ezent/imsc.htm.
[22] Purdue University Online Writing Lab: http://owl.english.purdue.edu/owl/resource/600/0.1.
[23] Ibid.
[24] Ibid.
[25] Ibid.

the pronoun is not used in this way, though, its use can be avoided, replaced, or defused in a number of ways.

Industry insight: visual localization[26]

Introduction

In this industry insight, localization expert Martin Guttinger discusses the concept of *visual localization*. The term "visual localization" refers to the process of translating and localizing the graphical user interfaces (GUIs), including things such as dialog boxes, menus, and other visual elements in software products and websites, using commercially available software translation/localization tools. Examples of such visual localization tools are SDL Passolo and Alchemy Catalyst. These are some of the common tools, and many more are available.

Unlike standard translation memory tools – in which translators localize text strings "blindly" (i.e., without knowing what they will look like at run-time) – visual localization tools offer WYSIWYG (what you see is what you get) environments that make localizing applications and web pages much simpler. They tend to be easy to use, with a customizable interface, and they support a variety of file formats.

The illustration below shows how text is presented in a visual localization environment. Note how text is presented in WYSIWYG as well as in text mode. As you can imagine, this simplifies translators' and localization engineers' tasks significantly.

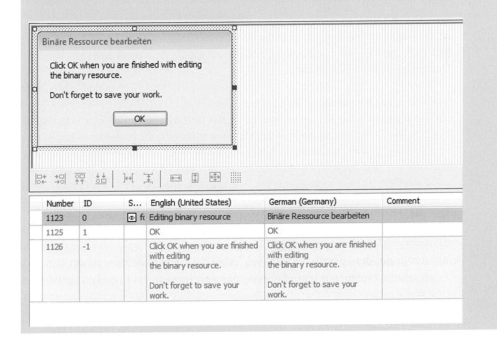

Number	ID	S...	English (United States)	German (Germany)	Comment
1123	0	▣ f(	Editing binary resource	Binäre Ressource bearbeiten	
1125	1		OK	OK	
1126	-1		Click OK when you are finished with editing the binary resource. Don't forget to save your work.	Click OK when you are finished with editing the binary resource. Don't forget to save your work.	

[26] This industry insight has been written and contributed by Martin Guttinger, manager Translation and Localization, Voice Technology Group, Cisco Systems, Inc.

Visual localization versus standard localization

Let us take a moment to compare visual localization to standard (non-visual) localization. Standard localization implies that products are localized using standard translation memory tools. An example of a standard translation memory tool is SDL Trados. The translator works in a simple text editor that offers the source text – typically in English – and the target text – one of the many languages spoken in the world. The translator is unable to see how the translated text will appear in the localized product, as he or she has no contextual information. The illustration below shows an example of a simple translation editor.

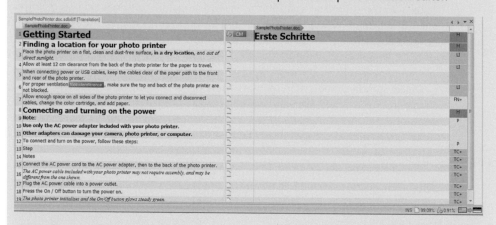

Visual localization, on the other hand, offers the translator visual clues (hence the name) and allows for more accurate translation of web pages, dialogs, menus, and other visual elements. Besides the visualization, both visual localization tools and standard localization tools offer similar functionalities.

Why is visual localization important?

Visual localization has a positive impact on the localization workflow and on the business bottom line. To cover the positive impact on workflow first: as the term implies, visual localization *visualizes* localizable elements. This means that translators can produce more accurate translations, and localization engineers require less time to produce the final product. Before visual localization became popular, translators had no way of knowing if their translations were accurate. Visual localization provides them with much-needed context. Translators used to be expected only to provide translations. Today they are also expected to perform basic localization tasks, such as resizing, spell-checking, alignment, leveraging, and the like. To be able to perform these tasks, they need visual localization tools. A standard localization tool (visual or non-visual) supports features such as *pseudo-localization* to test for internationalization problems, *error checks* to test for common mistakes such as clipped text, typos, and inconsistent translations, *translation alignment* to create translation memories from files that were previously translated, but are not stored in existing TMs, and *leveraging* to reuse existing translations across product lines.

Finally, visual localization has a very positive impact on a business's bottom line, because it allows the business to market web pages and products much more quickly. In fact, a product can be localized in half the time than it used to. This means that a business can achieve revenue from overseas sales much more rapidly than it used to be able to in the past.

Chapter summary

- Internationalization and localization are complementary processes. The internationalization process provides the essential foundation upon which to perform rapid, cost-effective localization.
- Unicode is essential for enabling proper internationalization for multilingual sites, as it provides character encoding in almost all world languages.
- When planning and executing internationalization efforts, refer to the internationalization checklist provided in this chapter.
- Web content needs to be internationalized, as well as code and other functionalities. Thus it is important to write content in a culturally neutral way so that it can be easily translated into multiple languages.
- Visual localization refers to the process of translating and localizing the graphical user interfaces.
- The remaining chapters in this book provide additional guidelines and tools for planning, executing, and measuring localization efforts.

REFERENCES

Asnes, Adam 2007. "Internationalization tips for successful globalization," Lingoport, www.lingoport.com/december-2007-internationalization-tips (accessed November, 2010).

Canton, James 2006. *The Extreme Future*: *The Top Trends that will Reshape the World for the Next 5, 10, and 20 Years*. Penguin Books.

Dr. International 2002. *Developing International Software*, 2nd edn. Microsoft Press.

Esselink, Bert 2000. *A Practical Guide to Localization*. John Benjamins.

Gillam, Richard 2005. "Unicode from 50,000 feet," in *Internationalization: Getting Started Guide*. MultiLingual Computing: 8–9.

Gray, Robert 2000. "Make the most of local differences," *Marketing* 13: 27–8.

Hall, Bill 2005. *Globalization Hardbook for the Microsoft .NET Platform*. MultiLingual Press; available at www.multilingual.com/books/welcomeOtherResources.php.

Henderson, Ian 2010. "Streamlining internationalization and localization," in *Language Technology: Getting Started Guide*. MultiLingual Computing: 4–7.

IBM 2006. "Globalize your on demand business," IBM, www-01.ibm.com/software/globalization/topics/writing/consider.jsp (accessed November, 2010).

Levitt, Michael 1983. "The globalization of markets," *Harvard Business Review* 61: 92–103.

Ogden, Charles K. 1930. *Basic English: A General Introduction with Rules and Grammar*. Paul Treber.

Weiss, Edmond H. 2005. *The Elements of International English Style*. M. E. Sharpe.

Wylie, Dovie 1998. "Tips for writing globally," *MultiLingual Computing and Technology* December: 40–1.

Yunker, John 2003. *Beyond Borders: Web Globalization Strategies*. New Riders.

6 Effectively localizing international websites

Chapter objectives

- Present important localization issues to consider when developing international websites.
- Outline techniques to make international websites more accessible to global online users.
- Present important considerations regarding the cultural customization of websites.
- Provide tips on incorporating cultural signs, colors, and values when designing international sites.
- Provide insights on culturally customizing writing styles when translating content for international markets.

Importance of website localization

As outlined in the previous chapter, localization in a broad sense involves adapting products, services, communications, and other assets involved in customer interactions so that they meet local consumer expectations. More specifically, localization is the process of adapting products and services (e.g., websites, manuals, and software applications) in accordance with linguistic, cultural, technical, functional, and other locale-specific requirements of the target market.

Various experts now agree that the web is like an advertising or communication document that mimics society's culture, values, and aspirations (Cyr and Trevor-Smith, 2004; Singh and Matsuo, 2004; Hermeking, 2005). Thus the web allows people to express themselves in a culturally meaningful manner, but also poses a challenge to companies, as they have to create content that their consumers find interesting and that meets their expectations.

Why localize?

Companies that can technically, linguistically, culturally, and functionally leverage the interactive properties of the web can deliver content that meets online consumer needs and results in desired consumer behavior.

Studies find that website localization and cultural customization can lead to better website navigation, web usage, and attitudes toward the site; it can even yield higher purchase intentions.

Miscommunication, in the international context, generally takes place when the message is mismatched with the local culture and therefore does not produce the expected response. A website that uses foreign language, signs or symbols, and web content that is different from what the user is accustomed to can confuse, frustrate, and sometimes even offend customers, which in the long run results in a loss of business (Luna, Peracchio, and de Juan, 2002). If the true meaning of the web content is not properly conveyed to consumers, the potential for miscommunication and consumer apathy is high.

For proactive companies, the web provides opportunities to create meaningful dialog with consumers worldwide. The web is inherently interactive, and companies that can technically, linguistically, culturally, and functionally leverage the interactive properties of the web can deliver content that meets online consumer needs and results in desired consumer behavior.

Emerging research in the web localization field has already linked localization activities to increased company performance and to stronger ties between a business and its consumers. Studies find that website localization and cultural customization can lead to improved navigation, increased usage, and better consumer attitudes toward the site; it can even yield higher purchase intentions (Baack and Singh, 2007). Higher purchase intentions have been shown to be a good proxy for consumer willingness to eventually make a purchase. Research also confirms that online customers stay twice as long on websites that have been localized. Online business users are almost three times more likely to make purchases online when websites are localized (Singh and Pereira, 2005). A survey of 2,400 worldwide internet users found that more than half the sample buys only from websites that present information in their local language (DePalma, Sargent, and Beninatto, 2006). All these studies point to the importance of localizing websites for an effective international web presence.

Website localization challenges

However, localizing websites is not a simple task. Many companies still think that, once they have translated the web content, their site is localized. Translation is one part of website localization, but website localization involves much more than this (see Figure 6.1). In this book I delve into more specific localization challenges and solutions, including the following.

(1) Localization of the user interface, which involves localizing various UI elements associated with data presentation. Some of the UI elements include menus, tabs, forms, tables, captions, icons, controls, and other elements that are not globally standardized. The navigation and spatial orientation of the content must also be localized, on the basis of how the target language is read.

(2) Implementation of global gateway pages/landing pages to direct global users to country-specific sites. Various other methods for delivering country-specific content are now often used in favor of gateway or landing pages (e.g., geolocation and language negotiation), and will be discussed later in the chapter.

(3) Localization of search engine optimization (SEO). This is necessary to enable international sites to be easily found on local search engines.

(4) Translation of the web content to meet local consumer linguistic expectations. The translation quality (translation equivalence) and writing style are critical issues during the translation process.

(5) Cultural customization of the content (text, images, graphics, etc.) so as to depict local cultural values, colors, symbols, and other cultural markers on international websites.

(6) Effective management of terminology, so that all localized content uses terms, concepts, and ideas consistently across multiple locales.

(7) Localization of various policies, procedures, instructions, and other documents to meet country-specific economic, cultural, functional, and legal requirements. This includes documents such as the privacy policy, security policy, terms and conditions of use, tax rates, and legal policy.

(8) Localization of various functional elements that enable the conduct of global e-commerce, such as shipping methods, payment methods, and currency conversions.

(9) Implementation of various methods and tools for providing local customer support, such as multilingual customer support, real-time chat, local contact numbers, and support documents.

(10) Consideration of various technologies and processes that facilitate website localization, including technologies such as translation management systems, translation memory software, project management, etc. These technologies are discussed in more depth in forthcoming chapters.

(11) Decisions about the extent to which the company wants to promote global brands versus creating localized brands. For example, Unilever sells a wide range of consumer products globally but localizes most of its brands and products into local languages, meeting cultural and functional requirements.

Although the localization of websites is not a simple task, it can be simplified if a company follows a systematic approach to handling the various facets of localization in an organized manner. Beyond website localization, companies also need to consider localization related to their products and services. The following sections outline various important localization-specific issues, including global navigation, the cultural customization of websites, the localization of writing style, and the management of terminology.

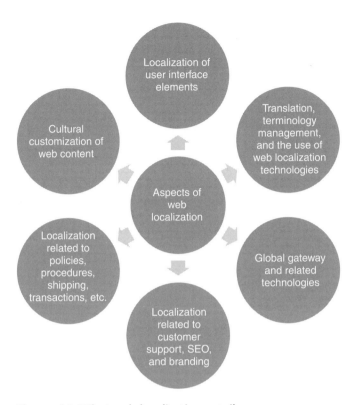

Figure 6.1 What web localization entails

Locating international websites

Having multiple, well-localized international sites is an important part of any global online strategy. However, if a company's international users cannot find these sites on the web, then all this web globalization effort goes to waste. Companies face several challenges in terms of matching the right locale-specific site to the right target audience. Some of these challenges may be as follows.

(1) The country-specific site a company has developed may not rank high on local search engines, making it unlikely that local users will find it.
(2) Local users may be unable to type a domain name in English (most sites still have English domain names).
(3) The home-country website may not have clear navigation to guide its international users to their respective locale-specific sites.
(4) The choice of country-specific sites listed on a company page is in the home country's language, and the international user cannot read this language to locate the relevant site.

Figure 6.2 Improving the accessibility of international websites

To address these challenges, companies need a two-tier approach.

Tier 1

First, companies need to conduct extensive multilingual and country-specific search engine optimization to raise their rankings on local search engines. As part of this search engine optimization effort, they need to acquire country-specific domains for international multilingual sites. Country-specific domains are also called county-code top-level domains (ccTLDs; for example, ".de" for Germany and ".fr" for France). Another consideration is to use multilingual domains or internationalized domain names as well. International search engine optimization and domain name issues are discussed in a later chapter.

Tier 2

Second, companies need to develop a system to deliver the correct international content to the target user. For example, an American company with multiple international sites should be able to help its French users to find the French site – or the company can use certain technologies to target its French users and automatically deliver them to the French site. This ability to connect the international user to the right country-specific site is made possible by various global navigation techniques and complementary technologies. Some of the techniques and technologies that facilitate global website navigation include global gateway pages, language negotiation, and geolocation.

Global gateway pages

Global gateway pages are web pages that help users find the localized content that meets their specific needs. Technically speaking, the global gateway page serves as a landing page for all online users; they select their locale-specific site from this page and are taken directly to that site. Several companies, including 3M, IKEA, and Nike, have implemented extensive global gateway pages.

The use of splash[1] global gateway pages is a recent trend, but developers need to make sure they avoid large, slow-loading graphics that may make it difficult for some international users to access the gateway page.

Using a global gateway page is a good idea for several reasons.

(1) It serves as a dedicated gateway page for all global online users. To achieve a truly "global feel" for the website, the global gateway page should serve as the entry page for all locales.

(2) Users select the country/language locale most suited to them; this eliminates potential machine errors that are possible with language negotiation, which is discussed in the next section.

(3) Once users have made a choice of country or locale, the next time they do not have to go to the gateway page; instead, they are routed directly to the relevant country page. Cookies can keep track of users' preferences during repeat visits. For example, the Kodak global gateway page remembers the country selection of the user.

(4) A nicely prepared global gateway page may quickly "differentiate" a company from other smaller competitors or start-up companies that are trying to establish themselves in the international arena.

(5) If a company has a global presence and websites for multiple countries, then the company should not hide it. The company should proudly display its vast international outreach via a global gateway page.

When creating global gateway pages, developers must remember not to let their assumptions dictate the design. These assumptions are a result of an ethnocentric attitude called the "SRC effect" (self-reference criteria), in which a person has an unconscious tendency to interpret the world on the basis of his or her cultural conditioning and value systems. The SRC effect (see Figure 6.3) can lead to many issues that make a global gateway page not so global in practice.[2]

- Several US-based companies have country-specific sites listed only in English. What if the user does not read English? For example, the gateway pages of UPS and Visa list all countries in English.[3] As a result, users who cannot read English

---

[1] Splash pages tend to use extensive graphics, animation, and flash.

[2] Global gateway pages for the companies listed were accessed December 18 to 20, 2010.

[3] These sites were accessed in December 2010 and reflect the company practice at that time.

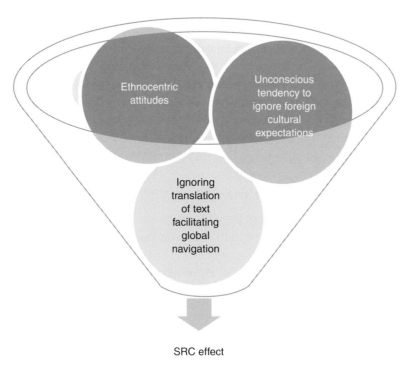

SRC effect

Figure 6.3 The SRC effect

cannot find their country-specific sites. Starbucks does not have a global gateway page, but a user can click on "Select location" at the top of the page, which opens a drop-down menu listing the names of the countries for which Starbucks has international sites. However, if you cannot read English, how will you locate the "Select location" link?

- Sometimes company sites use language selection instead of country selection. For example, the website of the United Nations has various language options in Spanish, French, Russian, etc. This may be appropriate for the United Nations, but, if a company or organization uses language as a proxy for a country, this might not provide the right information for the user's locale. For example, French is spoken not only in France but also in parts of Canada, Africa, and the Middle East.
- Some companies do not have dedicated global gateway pages and just include links for country selection on their home pages, which take users to their country sites. This is not the best strategy to make international sites visible. Moreover, several companies have placed these international site links so discreetly in the home page content that they are difficult to even locate. For example, the site for BestBuy.com has a link for some of its international sites hidden all the way at the bottom of the home page. The text of the link does not even say international sites; it just says, in English, "More Best Buy sites."

Figure 6.4 3M global gateway page

Some of the best global gateway pages give international users a variety of clues and clear instructions to easily locate their respective country-specific sites. For example, the IKEA global gateway page (www.ikea.com) is simple and well organized, and, most importantly, offers clear instructions for finding country-specific sites. The IKEA global gateway page clearly lists the name of country-specific sites in English and local languages. Thus non-English speakers can easily read the name of their country-specific sites. Similarly, the 3M global gateway page (www.3m.com) lets users know if their country content is available in their local language, and also provides a visual in the form of a highlighted map of the region to further facilitate navigation (see Figure 6.4).

Language negotiation

Language negotiation is a function of the HyperText Transfer Protocol (HTTP) that lets a server choose between several language versions of a page, on the basis of the Universal Resource Locator (URL) and on preference information sent by the browser (specifically in the "Accept language" header). This is distinct from page selection based on the IP address of the browser or from a manual selection by the user on a language selection page (www.w3.org). In other words, language negotiation helps companies automatically identify the language preferences on the web browser of a global online user. Web servers can be configured to respond to these preferences with language-specific web pages. Thus, if you use Microsoft's Internet Explorer browser and have set US English as a language preference, the web server will identify this and serve you web pages in US English when available.

Content negotiation requires that both the web browser and server participate. This involves setting user preferences on the browser and configuring the server to handle content language requests. You can provide multilingual, localized pages from a single Apache web server by enabling MultiViews support.[4] With this feature enabled, the server will negotiate the localized content with the client browser and provide the preferred browser-supplied preferences for things such as media type, languages, character set, and encoding. More information on this can be found at http://httpd.apache.org/docs/current/content-negotiation.html#about.

The following post, by Jesse Skinner (2008) on the blog thefutureoftheweb.com, showcases one of the major problems with using language negotiation technology to guide global navigation:

> *I'm an English-speaking Canadian living in Germany. Quite often I go to a website like Google or Kayak and find myself looking at a German version of the site. Okay, I do live in Germany, but why assume that everyone within Germany speaks German? What about visitors from other countries, or even people living here that would prefer to use another language?*

To illustrate some of the problems with language negotiation technology, a post by François Yergeau (2004) at www.w3.org gives an example of a hypothetical site, www.example.be, that offers its content in Flemish, French, and German, and implements language negotiation and defaults to Flemish for all pages. According to this example, Sylvia, an Italian-speaking woman who is able to deal with German, can face several challenges arising from language negotiation technology. Several situations that may arise include the following.[5]

- *Example 1* Sylvia's browser is correctly configured, expressing preferences for Italian first, German second. Italian is not available at www.example.be, the pages are returned in German, the visitor is fairly happy, all is well. This is what language negotiation is for!
- *Example 2* Sylvia is a non-technical person who has never heard of HTTP language negotiation and has never felt a need to alter the settings of her browser. Her web browser is an Italian version which (correctly) defaults to expressing a preference for Italian. Hitting www.example.be, Italian is not available and the site-default Flemish is returned, even though German is available. Bad.
- *Example 3* Sylvia is not using her own browser, she's sitting in an Internet café in Moscow. The browser there was configured for (or defaulted to) Russian. She gets Flemish again. Bad.

---

[4] http://developers.sun.com/dev/gadc/technicalpublications/articles/apache.html.
[5] This is an excerpt from Yergeau (2004); copyright © 2004–2006 W3C (MIT, ERCIM, Keio).

Geolocation

Geolocation is a broad concept that relates to identifying the real-world geographic location of users by tracking them via satellite navigation systems, IP addresses, media access control (MAC) addresses, or even radio frequency identification (RFID). Most people are familiar with geolocation through using the Global Positioning System, and GPS-enabled mobile devices can now easily locate a geographic position.

Geolocation in the web context mostly relates to using an IP address to locate the web user and then deliver content meant for that specific geographic location. Companies such as Yahoo!, Adidas, Google, Hertz, Samsung, and Amazon use geolocation to deliver country-specific content without the user having to actively select his or her country or language.

Companies can use this to deliver targeted region-/country-specific content to their users and block users from getting content they do not wish them to see. For example, a site about baseball may use geolocation techniques to highlight the Cardinals baseball team to its vast fan base in St Louis. Thus geolocation technology can be very beneficial for targeted advertising and marketing. Geolocation can also be used for a wide range of other purposes, such as fraud detection, authentication, security, and network efficiency.

Currently, the most relevant form of geolocation technology is based on translating IP addresses into geographical locations, by using information stored by the provider of the geolocation service (www.svantesson.org). The provider of geolocation services can not only give the geographic location of the user but can also provide information such as region, state, city, zip code, time zone, latitude/longitude, network connection type and speed, and domain name and type (Yunker, 2010).

Company websites can implement geolocation with the help of a geolocation application programming interface (API), which provides the best estimate of the user's position using a number of sources (called location providers). These providers may be "onboard" (GPS, for example, is located on the user's device) or server-based (a network location provider) (code.google.com). According to Yunker (2008), almost 12 percent of multinationals use geolocation to enhance their global navigation.

Amazon.com's geolocator system selects the Amazon website of the visitor's country if that country has an Amazon website with an Associates program; otherwise, the geolocator selects Amazon UK for visitors in Europe and Amazon USA for visitors in all other countries (jeffreyjmorgan.com, 2008). Quova, Inc. is one provider of internet geolocation data and services. The primary source for IP address data is the regional internet registries, which allocate and distribute IP addresses among organizations located in their respective service regions (Wikipedia.org):[6]

- American Registry for Internet Numbers (ARIN);
- RIPE Network Coordination Centre (RIPE NCC);

[6] Content from Wikipedia is further verified by additional research.

- Asia-Pacific Network Information Centre (APNIC);
- Latin American and Caribbean Internet Address Registry (LACNIC); and
- African Network Information Centre (AfriNIC).

Like language negotiation, geolocation is an automated process, and it may not accurately predict the language expectations of an individual. It is therefore better to use some combination of these technologies with global gateway pages or links to international sites.

What is culture?

Culture has been defined as software of the mind (Hofstede, 1980), as it influences how we think, behave, and interact with society. In fact, cultural conditioning starts as soon as we are born and start to interact with people. It mediates our communications and provides context and meaning to help interpret the world around us. To better grasp how this cultural wiring of our mind actually happens, the underlying structures that serve as building blocks of the cultural mindset must first be understood.[7]

Culture

Culture can be been defined as software of the mind (Hofstede, 1980), as it influences how we think, behave, and interact with society. It mediates our communications and provides context and meaning to help interpret the world around us.

According to Bourdieu (1977), the knowledge acquired from everyday practices and experiences is stored in its most primitive form in "habitus."[8] Knowledge in the habitus is organized into schemas, or simplified mental structures, which are collections of elements that work together to process information (Strauss and Quinn, 1997). In other words, schemas are simple elements or conceptual structures that serve as prototypes for underlying real-world experiences (Quinn and Holland, 1987; D'Andrade, 1992; Singh, 2004). When a set of complex schemas are shared by a group of people, they represent the cultural models of a society (D'Andrade, 1987).

These cultural models help individuals learn culture and communicate it. D'Andrade (1992) gives an example of a cultural model of achievement among Americans: according to him, this achievement model not only helps Americans to interpret achievements in a society but also acts as a goal with a capacity to instigate action.

---

[7] The following sentences are adapted from Singh (2004).

[8] According to Bourdieu (1977), habitus is a system of durable, transposable dispositions learned from everyday practices and experiences. This habitus forms the basic stratum of simplified world knowledge acquired by an individual through everyday practices in the society.

Cultural models differ from society to society. For example, cultural models for marriage are quite different for Americans from what they are for Indians in India. The underlying cultural models around marriage for Hindus in India include:

- the formalized arrangement of marriage (an arranged marriage or some combination of arranged and unarranged elements in a marriage);
- a general reliance on astrology for matchmaking;
- the importance of the exchange of gifts during marriages (the practice of giving a dowry is still prevalent in India);
- a heavy reliance on informal and formal sources such as relatives, priests, and newspaper and online matrimonial ads for arranging marriages;
- marriage as a social duty for the family and society;
- cohabitation and child-bearing prior to marriage being considered taboo;
- caste and social status as important determinants for seeking marriage partners; and
- divorce being regarded as taboo; the divorce rate in India is among the lowest in the world.

These underlying cultural models of marriage in India are unique to Indian society and may seem different or even strange to people from other cultures.

A typical Indian matrimonial ad[9]

"We are a Brahmin family from Bengal, looking for a suitable bride for our son. Our son is a doctor and a green card holder, 28 years, located in Seattle. The son is tall, dark, and handsome. Bride must be from Brahmin caste and Bengali, with fair or wheatish skin complexion, convent educated, old fashioned values, and be from well-to-do family."

It is clear that culture is an element that defines societies. Culture needs to be considered when communicating across different societies or nations. The web is a communication medium, and the importance of culture cannot be ignored by anyone who wants to use it to communicate effectively. Companies need to take into account various cultural parameters, such as values, colors, symbols, icons, language, etc., when developing web communications for different cultures.

Culturally customizing websites: importance of semiotics

When designing any form of communications materials, the role of cultural symbols, colors, etc. must be considered so that the material is culturally consistent with the

---

[9] This is just a hypothetical ad, reflecting some common criteria used by Indians when matchmaking. The word "Brahmin" used in the ad reflects the caste of the person and the word "Bengali" denotes the state from which the Indian family hails.

Figure 6.5 Metaphysical representation of the god Shiva in the form of a lingam

expectations of the end user. Websites and software are no different in this respect from other means of communication. Well-established research in advertising supports the use of culturally appropriate colors and symbols when targeting different locales. Emerging evidence also suggests that the web is not a culturally neutral medium; instead, websites for various countries and locales are imbued with local cultural symbols, colors, icons, and values.

Semiotics is the study of the signs used in society. According to Charles Sanders Peirce (see Hartshorne and Weiss, 1932), in semiotic or symbolic analysis there are three categories of signs. The signs can be studied in the form of:

- icons, signs that resemble the object they represent;
- index signs, signs that are a direct link between the sign and its object; and
- symbols, which stand for what people believe them to mean.

Symbols are the most subtle and powerful representations of cultural thought (Singh, 2004). According to Barthes (1977), an object becomes a symbol when it acquires by convention and practice a meaning that makes it stand for something else that it represents in people's minds.

Geertz (1973: 89) emphasizes that "culture is a historically transmitted pattern of meanings embodied in symbols, a system of inherited conception." The external world, of objects, events, and structures, acquires meaning in a cultural context because they serve as a conduit for cultural information from one generation to another. Similarly, according to another social scientist, Edmund Leach (1976), culture acquires public forms so as to give abstract ideas, mentifacts,[10] and values a permanent material form, so that they can be subject to analysis and interpretation (Singh, 2004).

---

[10] Mentifacts are representations of cultural beliefs and ideas.

Leach (1976) gives the example of how abstract ideas about God are externalized by telling stories (myths) and by creating metaphysical representations in the form of objects. For example, in India the god of divine potency, Shiva, is represented in form of a stone "lingam-yoni," which represents the union of the male and female principles (see Figure 6.5). Thus signs give cultural values, abstract ideas, and cultural tasks a concrete form, which endorses them and makes them public (Fiske, 1990).

Icons

Icons resemble the object they represent. In other words, an icon is a sign (word or graphic symbol) whose form suggests its meaning. An icon could be illustrative or diagrammatic, as in a "No smoking" sign with a red circle and a line through a lit cigarette. Icons play an important role in the design of software and websites. For example, there is a whole set of toolbar icons used in various software and web applications.

When creating international websites, careful attention needs to be paid to the use of icons, as they may have different cross-cultural meanings. For example, a toolbar image that includes a "magic wand" to represent access to a wizard interface in MS Windows will not be meaningful in many countries/regions. Other examples include the icons of a yellow school bus, a red hexagonal sign, an American mailbox with a flag, a trash can, and a shopping cart, which may not be well understood outside the United States.

Icon misunderstanding

Customers in the United Kingdom found the trash can icon in the Apple Macintosh "Trash can" very confusing, because it was a cylindrical bin, shaped exactly like mailboxes in Britain. In this case it was particularly difficult, because mail was mistakenly being sent to the trash can.

Nike used a logo meant to look like flames on a line of basketball shoes to be sold as Air Bakin', Air Melt, Air Grill, and Air B-Que. Some Muslims claimed that the logo resembled the word "Allah" written in Arabic script; Nike had to remove these lines and apologize.

Figure 6.6 shows a screenshot used by Yahoo! France with various icons being used to symbolize different kinds of services. Yahoo! seems to be customizing these icons for various countries such as China, Japan, and Taiwan.

Index signs

Index signs are direct links between other signs and their objects. For example, most traffic signs are index signs, as they represent information that relates to a location. Other examples include smoke as an index of fire or a thermometer as an index of

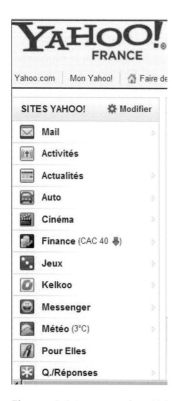

Figure 6.6 Icons used on Yahoo! France site

temperature. Index signs tend to vary from country to country, because they represent a link with an object, and objects are products of their particular cultural context. For example, various traffic signs tend to differ between countries, as they use different forms, language, and even colors. However, certain index signs are universal, such as the sign for nuclear waste.

Symbols

Symbols are the most subtle and powerful representations of cultural thought, as they stand for whatever people believe them to mean. Some symbolic variables that can be studied at this level of cultural analysis include the following.

- *Codes of society* Systems into which signs of the society are organized; for example, aesthetic codes, codes of conduct, and non-verbal codes.
- *Metonyms* Linguistic structures that make a part stand for the whole.
- *Myths* Myths stimulate us to construct the rest of the chain of concepts that constitute the myth (Fiske and Hartley, 1978). For example, a cosmetic company marketing in Japan used the theme of Nero coming to life when he sees a girl wearing the

company's brand of lipstick, but the theme was not well understood in Japan, as the myth of Nero was not a part of Japanese culture (Ricks, Arpan, and Fu, 1974).

- *Color* Cultures ascribe symbolic meaning to different colors (Leach, 1976).

Other variables include socio-culturally determined symbols, mores, taboos, rules, rituals, ceremonies, and different forms of semiotic structures.

Pocari Sweat

Pocari Sweat is a common sports drink from Japan, and it is also distributed in several southeast Asian countries. To an American the word "sweat" on a drink label might be offensive, but to Japanese it does not have such connotations; to them it is meant to imply diligence.

As mentioned in the international e-environment section in chapter 1, companies need to be very careful when using icons, index signs, and symbols on their websites and in other communication media. Some symbols should be avoided, such as symbols that have religious or political connotations. Knowledge of cultural signs can also yield positive results: natural symbolism, for example, is particularly potent in eastern cultures such as those of Japan and China, where it is used extensively as an aesthetic expression. Mountains, rivers, birds, trees, etc. are commonly used there in advertising, on packaging, and on websites.

Symbols have a very high potential for being misinterpreted and can cause grave concern for international marketing efforts. Here are some examples of misunderstandings related to the meanings and values that symbols and images carry.

- In China the dragon is considered auspicious, and dragon images should not be used for frivolous things.
- Cow images should not be used in frivolous ways in India, where the cow is sacred. In India even elephants and monkeys are revered in Hindu religious texts.
- The word "pansy" is (in one definition) a slang word for a coward in the United States – and "pansy" is also a Chinese brand of underwear.
- An advertisement for Toyota in China showed a stone lion raising its right front paw and saluting to a passing Toyota Prado. In China a stone lion is a symbol of dignity, solemnity, and power; this advertisement thus caused an outrage there (Han and Liu, 2006).
- Leo Burnett Shanghai Advertising, a Sino-US joint venture, published an advertisement design for Nippon Paint showing a freshly painted pillar whose twining dragon, unable to keep its grip because Nippon Paint is so smooth and silky, ends up in a coil at the bottom (Han and Liu, 2006).
- Worldwide, the swastika symbol has a negative connotation, but in India the use of the swastika is commonplace. In India the swastika has religious connotations and is widely used in both religious and business context.

In addition, it is important to use local or ethnically compatible human models, pictures, and images on international websites. For example, the international websites of IKEA, MTV, 7-Eleven, and Sony have incorporated local models and celebrities from specific local cultures.

Graphics to avoid

Yves Lang (2005) provides some guidelines on using symbols and icons when creating localized products for global markets:

- avoid single-letter concepts, as confusion will be introduced through translation;
- avoid religious symbols and icons;
- avoid graphic elements with text;
- avoid graphics depicting human body elements and body language;
- avoid graphics depicting humor, puns, and slang;
- avoid graphics depicting physical environments;
- avoid graphics depicting ethnic, racial, political, and religious environments;
- avoid graphics depicting gender-specific elements;
- avoid graphics depicting images of animals;
- avoid graphics depicting sexual and violent elements; and
- avoid graphics depicting regional conventions, such as reading direction, date/time, and monetary elements.

Cross-cultural use of colors

Different colors mean different things to people in different cultures. This is because colors have a high symbolic value among different cultures. For example, Ricks, Arpan, and Fu (1974) give an example of a product with a green label that was not well received by some Malaysians, because to them green symbolized the jungle, with its dangers and diseases. Green represents fertility in Egypt, safety in the United States, and criminality in France (Barber and Badre, 1998). Similarly, in Western cultures white is the color for a bride's gown, while in India widows traditionally wear white. White is also seen as a color of mourning in various other Asian cultures.

Different color combinations also carry different meanings in different cultures. For example, in China black on red is a symbol of happiness and is widely used on wedding invitations, while in Japan red over white signifies celebration and the life force (Madden, Hewett, and Roth, 2000). The use of specific colors and color combinations on websites therefore has to be congruent with the needs and expectations of a specific country.

Various studies have investigated which colors are more appropriate in which countries/cultures. The following paragraphs provide some more insights, on the basis of various academic research studies. The insights presented relate to the colors that should be used in a cross-cultural context – something that is important for anyone creating international websites.

- An early study by Adams and Osgood (1973), conducted in nineteen countries, finds that blue is one of the most preferred colors, followed by green and white. They also find that red is the most active color, and that black and grey are the most passive colors.
- Another academic research study, by Jacobs *et al.* (1991), in China, Japan, South Korea, and the United States, finds that, among all four countries, blue is associated with high quality and red is associated with love. Among Japanese, Chinese, and Koreans, purple is associated with expensiveness; in the United States, purple is associated with inexpensiveness.
- A study by Madden, Hewett, and Roth (2000) finds some very interesting color associations and meanings across countries, including the following.

Most liked colors by country:

(1) Austria: blue, green, and white (least liked: purple and gold);
(2) Brazil: white, blue, and green (least liked: orange and gold);
(3) Canada: black, blue, and white (least liked: gold and brown);
(4) Colombia: blue, white, and green (least liked: orange and brown);
(5) Hong Kong: white, blue, and black (least liked: orange and brown);
(6) Taiwan: blue, white, and purple (least liked: red and gold); and
(7) United States: blue, green, and black (least liked: orange and yellow).

Overall, they find blue to be the most liked color in their country sample. Blue, green, and white are seen in Austria, Brazil, Canada, Colombia, Hong Kong, Taiwan, the United States, and China as colors symbolizing peace and calm. Black and brown are seen across the cultures to symbolize sadness or staleness.

- Edwards (2007) elaborates on the color red. In North America, red is associated with love and passion; it is also the color of warning and safety. In western Europe, red is seen as a color of power, strength, and optimism. In eastern Europe and Russia, the color red is associated with communism and revolution. In the Middle East, the meaning of red varies from the color of love and sacrifice to anger and hatred. In some African locales, red is associated with blood and death. In India, it is seen as a sign of fertility and birth. In east Asia, the meaning of red varies from communism to good fortune to celebration. Edwards outlines three basic rules for color use.
  (1) Keep it functional. The meaning of the color being used should be clear for its intended use. Using colors for the sake of design without cross-cultural considerations could be dangerous.
  (2) Keep it context-dependent. Since color usage is context-dependent, designers must understand the context and its cultural significance. For example, using a lot of white on an Indian wedding website might not be appropriate, as white in India symbolizes mourning.

(3) Research potential conflicts. Ensure that color choice will not contrast sharply with nearby locales or intended context. Doing country-specific research is recommended.

Color preferences also vary by subculture within a country. Examples include the frequent use of the color black by the Goth subculture in the United States, or clothing colors associated with specific youth gangs. Because of the gang–color association, some schools have gone so far as to ban certain colored clothing at school. This could be an important consideration for companies planning to market clothing to young teens within specific locales and ethnic subgroups.

Color categories

Cross-cultural differences in categorizing color and color combinations arise because the cultural vocabulary limits the color discriminations people can make. For example, the Japanese identify the color *"aoi,"* a color that is not easily translated in English. *Aoi* is best described as a shade of green, or green may be a shade of *aoi* (Singh and Pereira, 2005). Eskimos have a long list of words to describe snow and its colors; similarly, in India, the color brown can be broken down into several categories. Indians distinguish between various shades of brown, particularly when it comes to skin tone: matrimonial advertisements characterize the complexion of individuals as wheatish-brown, wheatish, wheatish-medium, wheatish-dark, dusky, light-almond, slightly fair, fair, etc.

Japanese and blue

A Caucasian foreigner is said to be a blue-eyed outsider (*aoi me no gaijin*).
A vegetable shop is called a blue-things shop (*aomonoya*).
Green moss is called blue moss (*aogoke*).
An anxious sigh is called a blue breath (*ao-iki*).
A brothel is called a blue tower (*seiryoo*).

Source: Professor Randy A. Oldaker, West Virginia University.

Furthermore, color is used to express moods and emotions. In some cultures yellow is associated with envy, and in others envy is associated with green. Color is also used to express types of people, situations, and things, and, generally, each language has its accepted color associations. For example, in Japanese, being stark naked is referred to as being "red naked" (*sekirara*), a perfect stranger is called a "red stranger" (*aka no tanin*), and a sincere heart is called a "red heart" (*akai kokoro*).

Culturally customizing websites: importance of cultural values

According to Pollay (1983), values determine virtually all types of behaviors, from simple purchasing to religious ideologies. In the marketing and advertising fields, cultural values are recognized as having influence on consumer motivations and product choices (Tse, Wong, and Tan, 1988). Emerging evidence also suggests that cultural values have a significant impact on consumers' disposition toward websites (Singh and Matsuo, 2004; Shareef *et al.*, 2009).

A study by Singh and Matsuo (2004) compared American and Japanese websites on five cultural dimensions, namely individualism versus collectivism, masculinity versus femininity, power distance, uncertainty avoidance, and high- and low-context orientation (definitions of these cultural dimensions are presented in the next section). Their study finds that Japanese websites significantly differ from US websites on several of the cultural category items. For example, Japanese society has been viewed as collectivist and group-oriented (Hofstede, 1980). Japanese people value the feeling of *"amae,"* which means looking out for others in the group. This is reflected in the depiction of features such as online clubs, family themes, and links to local companies. For example, the websites of Fujitsu and Olympus prominently depict features such as camera clubs and news clubs. Japanese culture is also viewed as very masculine, and Japanese websites also show the prominence of clarity in gender roles, as men dominate all the important positions in the company and women hold more customer service positions. The author was hard pressed to find one Japanese site that showed images or mentions of women in powerful company positions.

In comparison to Japanese websites, American websites were less collectivist and were low on power distance, but they were more geared toward low-context orientation. American sites generally were more direct, emphasized rank and the prestige of the company, and had clearly laid out terms and conditions of website use (Singh and Matsuo, 2004; Shareef *et al.*, 2009). In Japan direct comparisons or blatant display of ranks and achievement are considered impolite.

Singh and Pereira (2005) cite several studies and present an extensive discussion on how to depict various cultural values on the web. A general overview of various cultural values is presented, as is the authors' framework for culturally customizing websites based on national cultural values. This cultural value framework can prove beneficial for companies seeking guidance for culturally customizing their international sites.

Definitions of cultural values and their implications[11]

Individualism versus collectivism

This value indicates how closely or loosely a society is knit, as it looks at a belief in the importance of the goals of the individual ("individualism") versus the goals of the group ("collectivism"). In individualistic cultures, the needs, values, and goals of an individual take precedence over group goals; the opposite is true for collectivistic cultures. In individualist societies, ties between individuals are loose, personal freedom is valued, and individual decision making is encouraged. Individualist cultures encourage personal

---

[11] For this section, some excerpts have been taken from the following works: Singh, Zhao, and Hu (2003); Singh and Matsuo (2004); Singh and Pereira (2005); Singh, Zhao, and Hu (2005).

achievement, and the population in general is more self-reliant. Identity in individualist cultures is centered around "I-consciousness"; therefore people in individualist cultures value self-reliance, achievement, independence, and freedom (Hofstede, 1980; Gudykunst, 1998). In collectivist societies, individuals are connected with strong societal bonds; group well-being takes precedence over individual well-being. For example, research indicates that, in collectivist societies such as China, people are willing to sacrifice their individual-level needs for the greater benefit of the social needs (Yau, 1988).

Uncertainty avoidance

This cultural dimension relates to societies that value predictability, structure, and order ("high uncertainty avoidance") versus societies where there is more risk taking and an acceptance of ambiguity and limited structure ("low uncertainty avoidance"). People from countries high on uncertainty avoidance tend to avoid ambiguous situations, view conflict and competition as threatening, and value security over adventure and risk. Individuals from high uncertainty avoidance cultures have a need for clear rules, structure, directions, and codes of conduct. On the other hand individuals from low uncertainty avoidance cultures are comfortable with some degree of ambiguity and risk taking.

Power distance

The power distance value relates to a belief in authority and hierarchy ("high power distance") versus a belief that power should be distributed in an egalitarian fashion ("low power distance"). Societies that rank high on power distance accept a hierarchical and unequal power distribution willingly and are low on egalitarianism. A clear example of a power distribution of such a sort is the existence in India of a large population of lower-class people sometimes called "untouchables," who are generally relegated to menial roles in society and have difficulty interacting in an equal fashion with other, "higher," caste members. People in high-power-distance societies tend to be very sensitive with regard to respect and obedience to the elderly and authority figures. For example, in high-power-distance societies such as China and India, elders are openly respected, and this respect is codified in various cultural practices and language expressions. In India, a more formal language is used when addressing the elderly or people in high positions. It is not uncommon for Indian children to actually bow down and touch the feet of their elders as a sign of respect.

Masculinity versus femininity

Masculine cultures tend to value assertiveness, material possessions, success, clear gender roles, and dominance over nature. On the other hand, feminine cultures place more value on harmony with nature, preserving the environment, the quality of life, blurred gender roles, and nurturance. Countries such as Japan, Austria, Mexico, Germany, India, Australia, the United Kingdom, and the United States are examples of masculine cultures, while most of the Nordic countries, Denmark, and the Netherlands score high on femininity. When developing communications for masculine cultures,

Table 6.1 High- and low-context cultures	
High context	Low context
Japan	Australia
China	Austria
South Korea	Canada
Malaysia	Germany
Indonesia	United States
Thailand	United Kingdom
Taiwan	New Zealand
Philippines	Switzerland
Turkey	Denmark
Greece	Netherlands
France	Scandinavia
Italy	Northern Europe
Spain	
Portugal	
South America	
Africa	
Middle East	

Source: Singh and Pereira (2005).

appeals that relate to success and achievement orientation, realism, and clear gender roles are recommended. Appeals to feminine cultures are more likely to succeed if they include elements of fantasy, imagery, and oneness with nature.

High context versus low context

High-context societies exhibit close connections between group members, and everybody knows what every other person knows to effectively socialize in such societies. Thus, in such societies, most of the information to function in a group is intrinsically known, and there is little information that is explicit. High-context cultures use more symbols and nonverbal cues to communicate, with meanings embedded in the situational context. Advertisements in high-context cultures are characterized by indirect verbal expressions and are implicit, indirect, polite, modest, and even ambiguous (Mueller, 1987; de Mooij, 1998). Direct comparisons are not viewed favorably (Mueller, 1987). Low-context cultures are logical, linear, and action-oriented, and most information is explicit, and formalized (Singh and Pereira, 2005). Most communication in such cultures takes place in a rational, verbal, and explicit way to convey concrete meanings through rationality and language. Some countries that are deemed to be high-context societies include most Asian, African, and South American countries; Mexico; Italy; and a few other southern European countries. Countries categorized as low-context societies include the United States, Scandinavian countries, the United Kingdom, Germany, and Australia. See Table 6.1.

Framework for culturally customizing websites

The previous section outlined various cultural values that can be used to categorize countries around the world. Well-known cultural expert and researcher Geert Hofstede has gathered a great deal of information on how countries rank on some of these cultural values. To access these country rankings, refer to Hofstede's website (www.geert hofstede.com) or his book (Hofstede, 1980). After getting this information for a specific country, refer to Table 6.2. The table shows ways to successfully work with various cultural values on a website. It is important to note that it is not enough just to have certain web features to emphasize a particular cultural value; how well developed or prominent these elements are on the website is also important.

Culturally customizing writing styles

This chapter has explored how cultural values and symbols can be incorporated into the design of a website to make it more culturally congruent. A website's writing style can also be culturally customized.

As individuals, we act and communicate within a context. This context is provided to an extent by the meanings we attach to words, symbols, values, acts, and other elements of the contextual environment. Culture provides the context, which is rich

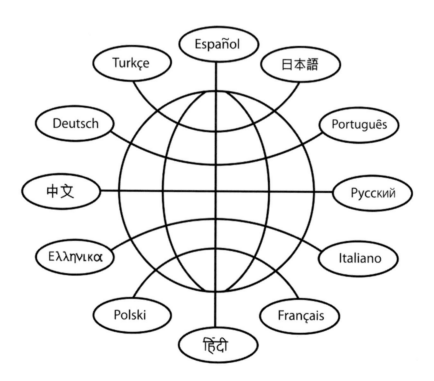

Table 6.2 Framework for culturally customizing websites

Value: collectivism
- Community relations: community policy, giving back to the community, and social responsibility policy.
- Clubs/chat rooms: members' club, product-based clubs, chat with company people, chat with interest groups, message boards, discussion groups, and live talks.
- Newsletter: online subscriptions, magazines, and newsletters.
- Family theme: pictures of family, pictures of teams of employees, mention of employee teams, emphasis on team and collective work responsibility in vision statement or elsewhere on the website, and emphasis on customers as a family.
- Symbols and pictures of national identity: flags, pictures of historic monuments, pictures reflecting uniqueness of the country, country-specific symbols in the form of icons, and indexes. (Reminder: exercise caution with flags/maps of disputed regions.)
- Loyalty programs: customer loyalty programs, company credit cards for specific country, and special membership programs.
- Links to local websites: links to local partners, related country-specific companies, and other local websites from a particular country.

Value: individualism
- Good privacy statement: privacy policy and how personal information will be protected or used.
- Independence theme: images and themes depicting self-reliance, self-recognition, and achievement.
- Product uniqueness: unique selling points of the product and product differentiation features.
- Personalization: gift recommendations, individual acknowledgements or greetings, and web page personalization.

Value: uncertainty avoidance
- Customer service: FAQs, customer service options, customer help, and customer contact or customer service e-mails.
- Guided navigation: site maps, well-displayed links, links in the form of pictures or buttons, and forward, backward, up, and down navigation buttons.
- Tradition theme: emphasis on history and ties of a particular company with a nation, emphasis on respect, veneration of the elderly and respect for the culture, and use of phrases such as "most respected company," "keeping the tradition alive," "for generations," and "company legacy."
- Local stores: mention of contact information for local offices, dealers, and shops.
- Local terminology: use of country-specific metaphors, names of festivals, puns, and a general local touch in the vocabulary of the web page, not just mere translation.
- Free trials or downloads: free stuff, free downloads, free screen savers, free product trails, free coupons to try the products or services, free memberships, or free service information.
- Toll-free numbers: telephone access round the clock.
- Transaction security and testimonials: testimonials from customers and trust-enhancing features, such as reliability seals, seals of trust, and ethical business practices from third parties.

Value: power distance
- Company hierarchy information: information about the ranks of company personnel, information about the organizational chart, and information about country managers.
- Pictures of CEOs: pictures of executives, important people in the industry, or celebrities.

Table 6.2 *(cont.)*

- Quality assurance and awards: mention of awards won, mention of quality assurance information, and quality certification by international and local agencies.
- Vision statement: the vision for the company, as stated by the CEO or top management.
- Pride of ownership appeal: depiction of satisfied customers, fashion statement for the use of product, and the use of reference groups to portray pride.
- Proper titles: titles of the important people in the company, titles of the people in the contact information, and titles of people on the organizational charts.

Value: masculinity

- Quizzes and games: games, quizzes, fun stuff to do on the website, tips and tricks, recipes, and other such information.
- Realism theme: less fantasy and imagery on the website; to-the-point information.
- Product effectiveness: durability information, quality information, product attribute information, and product robustness information.
- Clear gender roles: separate pages for men and women, depiction of women in nurturing roles, depiction of women in "traditional" positions of telephone operators, models, wives, and mothers, depiction of men as macho, strong, and in positions of power.

Value: high context

- Politeness and indirectness: greeting from the company, images and pictures reflecting politeness, flowery language, use of indirect expressions such as "perhaps," "probably," and "somewhat," overall humility in company philosophy and corporate information.
- Soft-sell approach: use of affective and subjective impressions of intangible aspects of a product or service, and more entertainment theme to promote the product.
- Aesthetics: attention to aesthetic details, liberal use of colors, bold colors, emphasis on images and context, and the use of love and harmony.

Value: low context

- Hard-sell approach: aggressive promotions, discounts, coupons, and emphasis on product advantages using explicit comparison.
- Use of superlatives: use of superlative words and phrases such as "We are the number one," "the top company," "the leader," "world's largest."
- Rank or prestige of the company: features such as company rank in the industry, listing or ranking in important media (e.g., *Forbes* or *Fortune*), and numbers showing the growth and importance of the company.
- Terms and conditions of purchase: product return policy, warranty, and other conditions associated with the purchase.

Source: Adapted from Singh and Pereira (2005).

in meaning, values, symbols, and nonverbal elements that are difficult to decipher holistically for a person not belonging to that culture.

Hall (1976) provides us with a cultural dimension that can help companies understand how people in different cultures communicate in their daily lives. To communicate effectively across cultures, companies must consider the context of the communication and how individuals will decipher the information on the basis of their own cultural programming. This context can be labeled as high or low, on a sliding scale. As mentioned in the previous section, in high-context cultures most of the transmitted information is embedded in the context or internalized among the members of the society. In low-context cultures messages are straightforward, detailed, and explicitly coded in unambiguous terms. Now let us see how the ideas of high- and low-context cultures apply to culturally customizing writing styles.

Writing for high-context cultures

As mentioned before, high-context societies have close connections between group members, and therefore, in a cultural context, everybody knows what every other person knows to effectively socialize in the society. Thus, in high-context cultures or societies, much of the information related through communications is embedded in the context. The contextual aspects of the communication or message include things such as nonverbal cues (e.g., body language), signs, colors, the tone of the voice, the use of idioms and metaphors, and the variation between formal or informal communication styles.

The following suggestions may help shape effective text for high-context cultures.

- Depending on the kind of communication, the writing style should be personable and should try to establish a personal connection with the reader.
- The writing style should emphasize a general sense of politeness. For example, Japanese websites depict politeness in the form of customary notes of thanks to the customers, greetings to the customers, and notes of best wishes for good health – which are not commonly seen in the websites of low-context cultures, such as the United States and Germany.
- In a culturally appropriate way, the tone and style should be relatively flowery, colorful, and elaborate.
- In formal communications with customers, a more formal writing style and tone should be used. For example, in Spanish the formal way of addressing another is *"usted"* and the informal way is *"tu."* Similarly, in Hindi, formal usage is *"aap"* and informal usage is *"tu."* Advertising in India tends to use the more formal *"aap"* when communicating with customers. Moreover, in formal communications, it is better to address people by their titles and last name rather than their first names.
- If the high-context culture is also high on power distance, special attention must be paid to the tone and style of writing. The tone and style should be very formal and respectful, with appropriate salutations, when communicating with people in authority positions.

- When communicating with a high-context culture that is also collectivist, special attention should also be paid to the words "we" and "us." The writing style should communicate the group orientation and general sense of collectiveness by using "we" and "us" and deemphasizing "I" and "me."
- In high-context cultures that are also masculine, special attention should be paid to creating gender-specific communication. Communication addressed to female audiences should show extra respect, politeness, and caring.
- Lengthy contracts, documentation, and technical notes should be avoided, or be supplemented with graphics and images to make them more readable. Long contracts are not a norm in several high-context cultures, including Arab cultures, India, and China.
- The sales pitch should be subdued, and can use the subtle linking of the company product to a place, person, event, or symbol to convey the idea of its superiority. Writers for high-context cultures should strive to be less verbally aggressive and maintain a modest tone, even in a pitch.

Writing for low-context cultures

As stated above, low-context cultures are logical, linear, and action-oriented, and most information is explicit and formalized. People in such cultures use precise words to convey meanings, and the message is often received literally, with less reliance on nonverbal cues. Thus the use of direct, explicit, and confrontational appeals in the form of advertising and promotions, as well as aggressive selling, is common in such cultures (Cutler and Javalgi, 1992). Mueller (1987) finds that low-context cultures such as the United States make explicit mention of competitor products and emphasize a hard-sell orientation. Low-context cultures emphasize clear communication and rely less on the unspoken context.

The following suggestions will help when writing for low-context cultures.

- The message should be direct, clear, and succinct.
- Exaggerations, hyperbole, and colorful expressions can be used, but cautiously.
- While the tone of the communication can be respectful, pandering or over-politeness (which is more desirable in high-context cultures than low-context ones) should be avoided.
- A passive, impersonal style is more appropriate when communicating in low-context cultures than in high-context ones.
- The tone can be direct and rhetorical. Statements such as "the number one company," "the leader of the industry," "the best," or "the number one" are common.

- Facts should be explicitly communicated with the customer. In the United States, it is common to see products advertised with reams of fine print detailing various aspects of legal and product information, so as to explicitly communicate with the customers and to protect the company against lawsuits.
- Rational arguments should be emphasized with appeals that are more verbose than symbolic.
- Direct and confrontational appeals should be used in advertising, as is common in low-context cultures such as the United States. Aggressive sales promotions and hard selling are also acceptable to an extent.
- Superlatives should be used. Words such as "best," "highest," and "greatest" are examples of superlatives common in American advertising.

Translation insights

Table 6.3 captures some of the insights relating to translating into various European languages. The translation insights cover various issues relating to grammar, sentence structure, vocabulary, formatting, etc. These translation insights come directly from a localization company (Conversis Global) that is involved in translating documents into various languages. The goal of this industry perspective into translation is to show the complexities that are involved in translation and how even languages within Europe have vastly different structures.

Chapter summary

- Website localization entails various issues, such as the localization of user interface elements, translation, cultural customization, global navigation, global SEO, and the localization of policies, procedures, customer support, online branding, shipping, and transaction processing.
- To help global online users easily find international sites, companies need to implement global SEO and also use global landing pages, geolocation, language negotiation, or some combination thereof.
- The cultural customization of websites entails customizing the web content on the basis of unique cultural signs, colors, and cultural values.
- Websites need to emphasize website elements based on a country's cultural orientation on values such as individualism versus collectivism, power distance, uncertainty avoidance, masculinity versus femininity, and high versus low context.
- The translation of the content should achieve proper translation equivalence and should also be culturally customized on the basis of whether the country uses a high- or low-context communication style.

Table 6.3 Examples of considerations for translating into other languages

Languages	Unique points
Czech	(1) Czech and English do not translate word for word. In some cases, Czech takes more words to communicate the meaning of its English equivalent; at other times, it can take fewer. To play it safe, design materials with the idea that either language might require 15 to 20 percent more type space than the other. (2) Some Czech words do not have what English speakers would consider to be vowels. (3) Czech can actually be written in two different styles: a standard, grammatically correct version or a colloquial one that reflects the everyday language more directly. In most instances, companies should use the standard language; but when a more personalized approach is merited, the colloquial tongue might actually be better.
Dutch	(1) Dutch routinely requires more words – sometimes considerably more – to express the same meaning than its English equivalent. As a good practice, plan for Dutch translations to require 20 to 25 percent more printed space than English materials. (2) Dutch is closer grammatically to German, but, like English, it does not have as many verb conjugations or the complex noun declensions that German does. (3) To communicate effectively in Dutch-speaking markets, communications should be direct and straightforward. Fluffy or indirect language tends to translate poorly into Dutch.
French	(1) French normally requires either more or longer words than English to convey the same message. Plan for the translated French copy to require 20 to 25 percent more space than English. (2) Although French letters are identical to English, French has five accents that are often required in addition to the base letters themselves: • the acute accent, which is placed above the letter "e": "é"; • the grave accent, which is often used with three different vowels: "à," "è," and "ù"; • the circumflex, an accent that looks like an inverted "v," which can be used on all five vowels: "â," "ê," "î," "ô," and "û." (3) French does not use commas to designate thousand-level quantities but spaces. For example, 1,000 is written as 1 000, and one million is written as 1 000 000. (4) Match the right translator with the right geography. Canadian French, for example, often differs from that spoken in France itself.
German	(1) Keep in mind German's longer word length when designing documents in English if they are to be translated into German later. As a rule of thumb, plan for a German translation to require about 10 percent more space than the original English version. (2) German uses periods instead of commas to designate thousands. As a result, 1,000 in English is written as 1.000 in German; one million is written as 1.000.000. On the other hand, when a decimal point is required in English, German uses a comma. For example, 1.5 in English translates to 1,5 in German.

Table 6.3 (*cont.*)

Languages	Unique points
	(3) When "a," "o," and "u" are written with an umlaut – as in "ä," "ö," and "ü" – they represent sounds that are pronounced differently from the same vowels without the diacritics. (4) German has a special letter known as the "sharp s," which the Germans call the "ess-zett." It is written as ß. (5) German also relies on countless verbs with prefixes that separate and, like conjugated verbs in relative clauses, appear only in the sentence's final position.
Hungarian	(1) Since Hungarian and English are entirely unrelated, there is no word-for-word correlation between the two languages. Although it often takes fewer words in Hungarian than it does in English to express the same meaning, Hungarian sentences are usually longer in printed form than English sentences are, simply because Hungarian words can be astronomically longer than their English counterparts. As a general practice, plan for Hungarian materials to require about 15 percent more text than English versions. (2) English speakers use commas to designate thousands, while Hungarians do not. For 9,000 or below, Hungarians write thousands without a space or comma, such as 1000, 2000, 3000, and so on. For 10,000 or more, the Hungarian method is to leave a space where there would be a comma in English, such as 10 000, 11 000, and 12 000. Conversely, when English uses a period to designate decimals, Hungarian employs commas so, for example, 0.5 becomes 0,5. (3) Unlike English, in Hungarian a person's family name comes first and the given name comes second. (4) Hungarians know their language is one of the hardest in the world to learn, and many view its difficulty as a source of national pride. (5) In Hungarian, primary stress is always placed on the first syllable of a word, and, because of its highly predictable stress pattern, the sound of Hungarian sometimes takes on a waltz-like cadence.
Italian	(1) Words and phrases are often longer in Italian than they are in English. As a general guideline, plan for Italian translations to be about 10 percent longer than the equivalent English wording. (2) Italian does not capitalize nearly as many words as English does. Days of the week, months of the year, and seasons are not capitalized. (3) Italian uses periods instead of commas to indicate thousands, whereas it uses commas instead of periods to indicate decimals. For example 1,000 becomes 1.000, while 0.50 becomes 0,50. (4) The Italian alphabet consists of twenty-one letters. It is the same Latin alphabet used in English, but standard Italian does not include the letters "j," "k," "w," "x," or "y." These letters are found only in foreign words. (5) Italian frequently relies on two different accents, which are called the "acute" and the "grave" accents. The acute accent is an angular dash pointing upward to the right that is sometimes used over the "e" vowel, as in the word *perché* (because).

Table 6.3 (*cont.*)

Languages	Unique points
	The grave accent is a dash pointing downward to the right, as in the word "*tè*" (tea), and it can appear above all five vowels – "à," "è," "ì," "ò," and "ù."
Polish	(1) English and Polish do not translate word for word. In fact, in most cases, a Polish translation will require considerably more words to communicate the same meaning conveyed by the English version. If a translation project involves printed materials, plan for the Polish-language versions to require 20 percent more printed text than the original English drafts.
	(2) With seven cases, five grammatical genders, complex verb conjugations, and multi-consonant constructions, Polish is one of the hardest European languages for English speakers to master.
	(3) For the most part, the Polish alphabet is identical to English, except that Polish orthography does not make use of the letters "q," "v," and "x." However, some Polish letters do use diacritical marks that are not found in English, such as "Ł."
	(4) Poles believe strongly in the concept of "correct Polish," and they typically regard slang expressions as improper and uneducated use of the language.
	(5) Whereas English uses commas to designate thousands, Polish relies on periods. Conversely, although English uses periods to designate decimal points, Polish uses commas: for example, 1,000 becomes 1.000 and 0.50 becomes 0,50.
Portuguese	(1) Since English is a member of the Germanic language family and Portuguese is a Romance language, their underlying grammars and modes of expression are fundamentally different. In most cases, Portuguese will require more words to convey the same meaning than English does. As a general guideline, plan for any materials printed in Portuguese to require 15 percent more space than the English draft.
	(2) Portuguese is the seventh most common language globally. As an official language of both the European Union and the African Union, Portuguese is gaining popularity in Africa and Asia as a second language for study. With Portuguese-speaking African countries predicted to reach a population of 83 million by 2050, the language is expected to become an increasingly important trans-African tongue in the future.
	(3) Brazilian Portuguese and the Portuguese spoken in Europe are one and the same language, but they are two very different dialects. Substituting one dialect for another sends a clear message to the target audience that the company is not, in fact, familiar with its local market and customs. The company will certainly come across as an outsider, and, even worse, could offend the very people it is trying to impress.
	(4) Whereas English uses commas to represent thousands, Portuguese relies on periods. Conversely, while English uses periods to designate decimal points, commas are common in Portuguese, so 1,000 is rendered as 1.000 and 0.50 as 0,50.

Table 6.3 (*cont.*)	
Languages	Unique points
Romanian	(1) When it comes to translating between English and Romanian the difference in word count is minimal. Romanian translation will be slightly longer than the English version. (2) Pay special attention to Romanian vowels with diacritical marks that do not exist in English. Omitting or using the wrong accent mark is by far the most common mistake translators make when converting English to Romanian. (3) The Romanians tend to keep foreign place names in their original language rather than adapting them to their own spelling. Unlike in English, the German city Munich, for example, maintains its original German name and spelling – München – in Romanian. (4) Whereas commas are used to designate thousands in English, Romanian requires periods. Conversely, there is no such thing as a Romanian "decimal point": for example, 1,000 becomes 1.000, 0.50 becomes 0,50.
Spanish	(1) As a general guideline, expect Spanish translations to require 20 to 25 percent more space than the English versions. (2) Hundreds of millions of Spanish speakers communicate with each other via dozens of regional variations, some of which differ significantly. Using the wrong Spanish at the wrong time will not only ruin the quality of the work, it will insult the audience as well. (3) Spanish is one of the few languages in the world that can truly be said to be global. Today, Spanish is the official language of twenty-one countries. It is one of the world's top ten spoken languages. An estimated 400 million people speak it as a first or second language, and it is believed that the number will continue to increase in the foreseeable future. (4) The Spanish constitution declares Castilian to be the nation's primary tongue. However, when working in the Spanish market, it is critical to demonstrate cultural respect for Spain's three "non-official" languages. (5) In Spanish, the article changes along with the noun. As an example, the plural form of the Spanish word for "book," *"el libro,"* becomes *"los libros."* (6) Spanish uses periods instead of commas to designated thousands, and, where periods are used to indicate decimal points in English, Spanish relies on commas instead: thus 1,000 is rendered as 1.000 and 0.50 is rendered as 0,50.

Source: Adapted from language primers by permission of Conversis Global; http://conversisglobal.com/language_primers.

REFERENCES

Adams, Francis M., and Osgood, Charles E. 1973. "A cross-cultural study of the affective meanings of color," *Journal of Cross Cultural Psychology* 4: 135–56.

Baack, Daniel W., and Singh, Nitish 2007. "Culture and web communications," *Journal of Business Research* 60: 181–8.

Barber, Wendy, and Badre, Albert 1998. "Culturability: the merging of culture and usability," paper presented at the 4th conference on "Human factors and the web," Barking Ridge, NJ, June 5; available at zing.ncsl.nist.gov/hfweb/att4/proceedings/barber (accessed April 5, 2009).

Barthes, Roland 1977. *Image-Music-Text*. Fontana.

Bourdieu, Pierre 1977. *Outline of a Theory of Practice* (Nice, R., trans.). Cambridge University Press.

Cutler, Bob D., and Javalgi, Rajshekar G. 1992. "A cross-cultural analysis of the visual components of print advertising: the United States and the European Community," *Journal of Advertising Research* 32: 71–80.

Cyr, D., and Trevor-Smith, H. 2004. "Localization of web design: an empirical comparison of German, Japanese and United States web site characteristics," *Journal of the American Society for Information Science and Technology* 55: 1199–208.

D'Andrade, Roy G. 1987. "A folk model of the mind," in Holland, Dorothy, and Quinn, Naomi (eds.), *Cultural Models in Language and Thought*. Cambridge University Press: 112–48.

   1992. "Schemas and motivation," in D'Andrade, Roy G., and Strauss, Claudia (eds.), *Human Motives and Cultural Models*. Cambridge University Press: 23–44.

de Mooij, Marieke 1998. *Global Marketing and Advertising: Understanding Cultural Paradox*. Sage.

DePalma, Donald A., Sargent, Benjamin B., and Beninatto, Renato S. 2006. *Can't Read, Won't Buy: Why Language Matters on Global Websites*. Common Sense Advisory.

Edwards, Tom 2007. "The culture behind colors," *MultiLingual* December: 27–9.

Fiske, John 1990. *Introduction to Communication Studies*, 2nd edn. Routledge.

Fiske, John, and Hartley, J. 1978. *Reading Television*. Methuen.

Geertz, Clifford 1973. *The Interpretation of Cultures*. Basic Books.

Gudykunst, W. B. 1998. *Bridging Differences: Effective Intergroup Communication*, 3rd edn. Sage.

Hall, Edward T. 1976. *Beyond Culture*. Doubleday.

Han, Guang, and Liu, Jingxin 2006. "Cultural symbols or taboos: the cultural conflicts reflected in the cultural image in international advertising," *China Media Research* 2: article 4; www.chinamediaresearch.net/vol2no2/4_Han_Guang_Liu_Jingxin.pdf.

Hartshorne, Charles, and Weiss, Paul (eds.) 1932. *Collected Pages of Charles Sanders Peirce*, vol. II, *Elements of Logic*. Harvard University Press.

Hermeking, M. 2005. "Culture and internet consumption: contributions from cross-cultural marketing and advertising research," *Journal of Computer Mediated Communication* 11: 192–216; available at jcmc.indiana.edu/vol11/issue1/hermeking.html (accessed July 28, 2008).

Hofstede, Geert 1980. *Culture's Consequences: International Differences in Work-Related Values*. Sage.

Jacobs, Lawrence, Keown, Charles, Worthley, Reginald, and Ghymn, Kyung-Il 1991. "Cross-cultural colour comparisons: global marketers beware!" *International Marketing Review* 8: 21–30.

Lang, Yves 2005. "White Papers," ENLASO Corporation, www.translate.com/Language _Tech_Center/White_Papers.aspx.

Leach, Edmund 1976. *Culture and Communication: The Logic by which Symbols Are Connected.* Cambridge University Press.

Luna, David, Peracchio, Laura A., and de Juan, Maria D. 2002. "Cross-cultural and cognitive aspects of web site navigation," *Journal of the Academy of Marketing Science* 30: 397–410.

Madden, Thomas, Hewett, Kelly, and Roth, Martin S. 2000. "Managing images in different cultures: a cross-national study of color meanings and preferences," *Journal of International Marketing* 8: 90–107.

Mueller, Barbara 1987. "Reflections of culture: an analysis of Japanese and American advertising appeals," *Journal of Advertising Research* 27: 51–9.

Pollay, Richard W. 1983. "Measuring the cultural values manifest in advertising," in Leigh, J. H., and Martin, C. R. (eds.), *Current Issues and Research in Advertising.* University of Michigan Press: 72–92.

Quinn, Naomi, and Holland, Dorothy 1987. "Culture and cognition," in Holland, Dorothy, and Quinn, Naomi (eds.), *Cultural Models in Language and Thought.* Cambridge University Press: 3–40.

Ricks, David. R., Arpan, Jeffery S., and Fu, Marilyn Y. 1974. "Pitfalls in advertising overseas," *Journal of Advertising Research* 14: 47–51.

Shareef, Mahmud Akhter, Dwivedi, Yogesh K., Williams, Michael D., and Singh, Nitish 2009. *Proliferation of the Internet Economy: E-Commerce for Global Adoption, Resistance, and Cultural Evolution.* IGI Global.

Singh, Nitish 2004. "From cultural models to cultural categories: a framework for cultural analysis," *Journal of American Academy of Business* 5: 95–102.

Singh, Nitish, and Matsuo, Hisako 2004. "Measuring cultural adaptation on the web: a content analytic study of US and Japanese web sites," *Journal of Business Research* 57: 864–72.

Singh, Nitish, and Pereira, Arun 2005. *The Culturally Customized Web Site: Customizing Web Sites for the Global Marketplace.* Elsevier Butterworth-Heinemann.

Singh, Nitish, Zhao, Hongzin, and Hu, Xiaorui 2003. "Cultural adaptation on the web: a study of American companies' domestic and Chinese websites," *Journal of Global Information Management* 11: 63–81.

　2005. "Analyzing cultural information on web sites: a cross-national study of web sites from China, India, Japan, and the US," *International Marketing Review* 22: 129–46.

Skinner, Jesse 2008. "Parse Accept-Language to detect a user's language," The Future of the Web, May 4, www.thefutureoftheweb.com/blog/use-accept-language-header.

Strauss, Claudia, and Quinn, Naomi 1997. *A Cognitive Theory of Cultural Meaning.* Cambridge University Press.

Tse, David K., Wong, John K., and Tan, Chin Tiong 1988. "Towards some standardized cross-cultural consumption values," in Houston, Michael J. (ed.), *Advances in Consumer Research*, vol. XV. Association for Consumer Research: 387–95.

Yau, Oliver H. M. 1988. "Chinese cultural values: their dimensions and marketing implications," *European Journal of Marketing* 22: 44–57.

Yergeav, François 2004. "When to use language negotiation," W3C, February 26, www
.w3.org/International/questions/qa-when-lang-neg.

2010. *The Art of the Global Gateway: Strategies for Successful Multilingual Navigation*. Byte
Level Books; available at www.bytelevel.com/books/gateway.

Yunker, John 2008. *Going Global with Geolocation: Using Geolocation to Improve Navigation for
Users around the World*. Quova.

7 Managing a web globalization value chain

The value chain concept

A critical part of the development, deployment, and maintenance of international websites is ensuring that web globalization is managed effectively. Previous chapters delved into concepts related to both the back-end and the front-end management of international websites. This chapter takes a look at the processes involved in integrating and managing all web globalization activities in a coherent and efficient manner.

The concept of a value chain can help companies evaluate how various web globalization processes complement and integrate with each other. The basic idea of the value chain concept, which was first introduced by well-known management guru Michael Porter (1985), is that raw material comes into the company and passes through various value-adding steps that transform it into a final product that is delivered to satisfy customer needs. Value chain analysis involves first charting then analyzing the various value-creating activities in the web globalization process. Organizations use this process to identify value-creating activities and then to prioritize them within the organizational workflow.

In Porter's description of a value chain, the "primary activities" in the value chain include inbound logistics, production/operations, outbound logistics, marketing and sales, and services (see Figure 7.1); the "support activities" include administrative infrastructure management, human resource management, information technology, and procurement. However, in the context of web globalization, I would not classify IT as a support activity. On the web, information is not a by-product of the strategic

183

Figure 7.1 Generic value chain: primary activities

activities performed around the physical value chain; instead, information is an integral part of strategic activities in the web-space (Rayport and Sviokla, 1995; Bhatt and Emdad, 2001). According to Rayport and Sviokla, five activities help generate value in the virtual value chain: gathering, organizing, selecting, synthesizing, and distributing information. These five activities help companies use information and value-added resources to gain a competitive advantage.

Value chain analysis can help companies outline the core steps of web globalization. The raw material that enters the web globalization value chain is content; it passes through a series of value-adding steps until it is finally ready for global deployment via the website or other distribution channels. Through value chain analysis, the core value-creating steps of web globalization and the associated processes and people involved with each of them are carefully and systematically identified. When the core steps and linkages between them are identified, processes that lead to waste can also be identified, isolated, and eliminated. When the web globalization value chain is analyzed thoroughly, companies can not only better plan for the activities involved in the process but also make the entire process more efficient by better coordinating those activities.

Web globalization value chain components

The previous section has outlined the basics of value chain analysis; the following sections lay out the components of value chain analysis that are relevant to web globalization efforts.

As mentioned, the raw material that enters the web globalization value chain is content. Content then passes through four primary value-adding activities:

(1) internationalization (i18n);
(2) localization (l10n);
(3) testing; and
(4) global content management.

In the value chain concept, these primary activities are supported and sustained by support activities. In the web globalization value chain, there are three main support levels.

(1) *Support functions* include such departments as human resources; procurement; international business; information technology; marketing; and external vendors

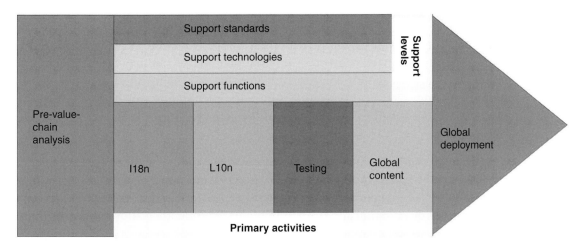

Figure 7.2 Web globalization value chain

(e.g., localization service providers) that provide the human resources, skills, and knowledge to support web globalization activities.

(2) *Support technologies* include tools for specific web globalization tasks, such as translation memory tools, internationalization tools, testing tools, terminology tools, machine translation technologies, authoring tools, project management tools, search engine optimization tools, geolocation tools, workflow automation tools, and other computer-assisted translation (CAT) tools.

(3) *Support standards, formats, and guidelines* include TBX, TMX (a Unicode-based encoding system), the Unicode Common Locale Data Repository, International Components for Unicode, W3C, GMX, Universal Terminology eXchange (UTX), SRX, XML, XLIFF, XHTML, xml:tm, SOAP, DITA, ebXML, the TDA platform for the exchange of language data, ISO 639–2 language codes, and ISO 3166 country/region codes.

    Before content enters the web globalization value chain, it has to be first conceived in a raw form. What is the reason for the content creation, for whom is the content creation taking place, and how will the content be consumed? These core issues need to be resolved before creating global web content, which is an important part of the "pre-value-chain analysis." Figure 7.2 shows the web globalization value chain.

Pre-value-chain analysis

As mentioned earlier, three primary questions are addressed in the pre-value-chain analysis.

What are the reasons for the content creation?

Global content is created for several reasons. A company may be taking its business global and creating localized content for international markets, it may be creating multilingual web pages or mobile content, or it may be creating technical documentation in different languages. At this stage, it is important to analyze why and for whom the localized content is being created. Some of the activities at this level may include the following.

- *Market analysis* An international market assessment can help a company understand market needs, market potential, market growth, and opportunities for diversification. Such an assessment using appropriate business tools will help companies clearly understand the potential and the requirements for content creation to support international expansion efforts.[1]
- *Competitor analysis* Analyzing the competition in terms of its goals, strengths, weaknesses, opportunities, and threats is also important. At this stage it would make sense to analyze competitive websites, search engine efforts, and other platforms where competition content can be accessed. Analyzing competitors' content can help companies understand the market landscape and develop benchmarks for content creation and content localization.
- *Search engine analysis* Search engine optimization must be considered before global content is written and localized. People in different countries use different words and phrases to search for products and services. It is important to analyze the search terms used in the context of your product in the area you are targeting and then strategically include those terms for SEO. For example, Germans searching for mobile phones online would likely not type "mobile" or "cellphone" but instead the German word for cellphone, "*Handy.*"
- *Resource allocation* The availability of resources can be a major issue in determining the extent of localization a company can reasonably hope to achieve. It may also help a company to assess what parts of localization it can accomplish in-house and what parts may need to be outsourced. Thus resource allocation should be considered prior to content development, so that the content can be effectively managed and kept under a budget.

For whom is the content creation taking place?

Companies must determine their target market(s) before any content is created. To communicate effectively, companies have to understand customer needs and expectations.

---

[1] It is beyond the scope of this book to outline the various business and strategy tools related to market assessment, competitor analysis, and other concepts. I would advise readers to take advantage of texts in business strategy and international business.

Who will be the end user of the global content? End users can be internal employees requiring localized multilingual content at various country locations, international suppliers, international customers, or even governmental agencies. In Chapter 3 I discussed various segmentation approaches that could be used to better understand customers. This step will also help companies determine the extent of the localization they may need to develop content for a specific locale. The ultimate end user(s) should always be clearly defined before any content is sent through the web globalization value chain.

How will the content be consumed?

Companies should determine how their content will be deployed and consumed after being churned out from the value chain. Different user interfaces demand different content formats. For example, a company may need to provide content via wireless mobile applications, websites, and video games. In such cases they may need different formats, protocols, and programming languages (such as XHTML). They must also consider that, in some countries, the connection speed is slow and broadband is not universal. Companies must therefore pay attention to the weight of the web content so that the website can load speedily. It may also be helpful to understand how the end users access and consume the content. People access the web content at different places, such as at home, educational institutions, the office, kiosks, etc.

Support layer of the web globalization value chain

The support layer consists of three elements, as mentioned above: support functions, support technologies, and support standards/formats. The primary activities in the web globalization value chain require this support layer. Companies and industries need industry-wide collaboration to develop vendor-neutral standards that allow technologies to be integrated and data to be exchanged in a non-proprietary, or open, environment. Such support infrastructure not only makes processes more efficient for companies but also benefits the whole industry, by creating an open format to exchange various assets among buyers, suppliers, and customers within an industry-wide value chain. In the IT and localization industries, various professional associations and large companies such as IBM, HP, and Microsoft are actively cooperating to further enhance this support layer for the whole industry. Some broad industry-wide efforts with the aim of furthering web globalization management have been led by organizations such as the World Wide Web Consortium, the Localization Industry Standards Association (LISA), the Unicode consortium, the Translation Automation User Society (TAUS), the Organization for the Advancement of Structured Information Standards (OASIS), and the Globalization and Localization Industry Association (GALA).

> ### W3C
>
> The primary activity of the World Wide Web Consortium is to develop protocols and guidelines that ensure long-term growth for the web. The W3C's standards define key parts of what makes the internet work. The W3C Internationalization (I18n) Activity coordinates with W3C working groups and liaises with other organizations to make it possible to use web technologies with different languages, scripts, and cultures.
>
> *Source*: Adapted from www.w3.org/International.

Support functions

The various units within an organization need to collaborate in order to effectively support web globalization efforts. Most companies have not yet created a specialized web globalization department, making collaboration across the company in web globalization efforts even more crucial. Web globalization is an interdisciplinary endeavor, as it requires skills and knowledge from various fields, such as translation and linguistics, IT and computing, communications, international business, marketing, project management, and strategy. The interdisciplinary nature of web globalization is one of the reasons that universities have been slow to create educational programs in the field.

Today, the value-enhancing knowledge and skills that go into the web globalization value chain come from a variety of departments within an organization. Stakeholders from these various departments need to be consulted so that their resources and knowledge can be leveraged effectively. Some examples of departmental contributions of resources and knowledge to the web globalization value chain are as follows.

- *Information technology* Provides technical skills and knowledge in areas such as website design and development, programming, graphic design, internationalization issues, website and software testing, and the management and deployment of web globalization automation technologies.
- *Marketing* Provides skills in areas such as market assessment, customer need identification, market segmentation, new product development and launch, brand management, logistics and distribution, and online marketing techniques such as search engine marketing and optimization.
- *International business* Provides skills and knowledge in areas such as international market environment analysis, market entry mode methodology, international strategic alliance development, cross-cultural insights for web content development, access to local expertise from foreign subsidiaries, and international documentation and shipping.

Besides engaging internal stakeholders, it is also important to collaborate with external stakeholders such as localization service providers, translators, consultants, academics, industry associations, industry consortiums, and other collaborative networks in order to tap into their knowledge and technological resources.

Having a well-staffed web globalization department may not be feasible for most companies, regardless of size, on account of the following reasons.

(1) Companies go through content lifecycles, and the workload increases at certain times (e.g., during a product, software, or website release) and decreases at other times. Making good use of all localization resources (e.g., translators, linguists, and testers) may be a challenge at times when content localization demand is low.

(2) It is sometimes more efficient and cost-effective to seek external expertise than have a person on the payroll. For example, it is generally more cost-effective to seek thousands of translators from around the world than have all of them on the payroll.

(3) For companies, it is sometimes difficult to find professionals who are experienced in certain web globalization tasks. Thus companies generally seek expertise from specialized vendors or external consultants. For example, the cultural customization of websites needs extensive knowledge of various cultures and technology, and such expertise is not always readily available.

As a result, even large companies such as Microsoft, HP, and others seek expertise from external vendors and consultants to facilitate their web globalization activities. Companies have to assess what web globalization competencies they can nurture in-house and which tasks it is better to outsource. The case of Compuware–Changepoint, which is highlighted later in this chapter, shows how balancing in-house and outsourced skills to accomplish localization tasks is possible.

Translation memory (TM) basics

Segmentation This is the process of creating text strings based on certain segmentation rules. TM software automatically processes the segmentation on the basis of segmentation rules in order to start building the initial TM database.

Alignment Once the text segments have been created, the TM software matches or aligns the source text and its corresponding translated text. This process eventually helps to build the TM database.

Fuzzy matching TM software generally uses algorithms to identify exact and fuzzy matches between the source and the target sentence. When a new translation target segment comes into the TM software, a match value is calculated on the basis of character-to-character correspondence with existing source text. If the match value is 100 percent, then it is an exact match, and the match is inserted in the translation document. TM tools also have fuzzy matching algorithms that retrieve similar segments based on a predefined cut-off or match value (a 75 percent match or an 80 percent match) and present the fuzzy matches for further review by the translators.

Support technologies

Several tools have been created to develop and manage the language assets required by web globalization. Some of the support technologies are discussed below.

(1) *Translation memory technology* Translation memory tools store previously translated sentences for reuse in future translation tasks. In other words, TM (also known as sentence memory) consists of a database that stores source and target language pairs of text segments that can be retrieved for use when processing text for new translation. This reuse of translations saves companies money and time. For example, the company Voith Turbo was able to translate 80 percent of its text automatically using the translation memory tools of a well-known localization service provider.[2] Several TM tools also check for translation and formatting errors, enhancing the quality of translations. Companies trying to create and deploy multilingual content for multiple countries can greatly benefit from the use of TM tools, which can enable them to achieve simultaneous shipment or release of the product and minimize turnaround time. Some major TM providers include SDL Trados, STAR Transit, Déjà Vu X, Lingotek, and MultiCorpora. Some TM tools are stand-alone applications while others are part of larger translation management systems. Some companies offering TM functionality as part of a larger translation management system include Across, MultiCorpora, SDL, and Lionbridge. TM tools are widely accepted by the translator and localization professional community.

TextBase approach for translation memory[3]

Some translation memory tools present challenges.

(1) *Dependence on whole-sentence repetition* Several TM systems tend to exploit whole-sentence repetition in previous translations. However, except for highly structured technical documents, whole sentences rarely repeat during translation, and the full potential of TM is not fully harnessed.

(2) *Loss of context* Since TM systems maintain a database of isolated sentences, they lose the surrounding context of the original sentence. The lack of style and usage context results in additional time-consuming translation review and editorial rework because translations built from isolated sentences are more likely to contain inconsistencies or errors.

(3) *Labor requirements* Building a TM database can be prohibitively labor-intensive. With the best alignment tools available, the process of creating a TM of roughly 3,000 words takes one hour of translator time. Some alignment tools take up to twice that time. At these rates, building a sufficiently large TM database takes weeks or months of effort.

---

[2] The example here is from Across Systems: www.across.net/us/form-casestudies-request-voith.aspx.

[3] The box is based on excerpts from MultiCorpora (2005). It is reused with permission from MultiCorpora. The author is showcasing a new functionality in evolving TM systems and not endorsing, favoring, or intending to promote any product.

The TextBase

A searchable, full-text, multilingual TextBase provides a simple, effective solution to these challenges. Rather than tediously building a database that contains isolated whole sentences and their previous translations, the TextBase approach takes a vast collection of legacy documents and their previously translated sister documents and, using advanced search engine techniques, rapidly indexes all the text. It also uses algorithms similar to those used by TM tools to align the translated text with the source text. A very large searchable TextBase of previous translations can be built extremely rapidly, at a rate of approximately 50,000 words per minute on a low-end computer. A TextBase user can perform a search of the entire TextBase for an expression of any length, in any of the languages contained in the TextBase. In barely a few seconds all the instances of that expression in the entire TextBase (in fact, multiple TextBases can be searched simultaneously) are automatically found and retrieved, along with the aligned translation texts. MultiCorpora was one of the first companies to introduce the TextBase approach. Its latest CAT tool is MultiTrans 4.

(2) *Terminology management tools* These tools have a core searchable database called the "termbase," which stores linguistic assets in the form of approved terms and rules regarding the usage of these terms. The use of terminology management tools can help companies manage their linguistic assets so as to increase consistency in the use of terms and phrases. These tools can help companies to avoid the confusion and translation errors that might occur when terms are interpreted differently in different contexts, departments, languages, and foreign subsidiaries. Some of the terminology tools available include SDL MultiTerm, MultiTrans Expert, and Lingo 4.0. Terminology tools also come as part of centralized translation management systems from companies such as MultiCorpora, Across, Lionbridge, SDL, and others. To create content, brand, and presentation consistency, companies need not only terminology management tools but also structured authoring tools. The structured authoring tools allow companies to create and arrange content based on certain structural standards (e.g., style guides) to consistently organize and format information in online and offline documents. Some structured authoring tools include Framemaker, Author-it, XMetal, and RoboHelp.

(3) *Internationalization testing tools* Internationalization testing tools help companies prepare the source code for the future implementation of localization and test for any errors introduced at the internationalization stage. These tools also help companies identify any embedded strings; externalize embedded text; check for any unsafe methods and functions; look for any issues related to data enabling, encoding, concatenation, and locale-specific formatting; and test localizability by performing visual localization (visual localization was discussed in Chapter 5). The author is aware of Globalyzer by Lingoport, which is an internationalization tool that helps with code review and overall internationalization assessment. There are some other internationalization testing tools included in the web globalization resources section of the book. The W3C Internationalization Checker is a free

service by W3C that provides information about the internationalization features of a web page and advice on how to improve its use of internationalization mark-up.[4] Some tools to help with visual localization, including pseudo-localization, include SDL Passolo, Alchemy Catalyst, and Lingobit Localizer.

(4) *Project management tools* Many project management tools are available to help auto-mate the tasks of planning, scheduling, tracking, and communicating project activ-ities. Microsoft Project is one of the most commonly used software tools for project management; it provides powerful planning, scheduling, and reporting features. To provide support for the localization and translation industry, some localization vendors have developed custom project management tools specifically designed to meet localization workflow needs. Two examples are Plunet Business Manager and LTC Worx; LTC Worx is discussed in greater detail later in the chapter.

Beyond the tool categories and tools mentioned above, there are also tools to help automate the whole web globalization value chain. In this book, the integrated tech-nology solutions for connecting the entire web globalization value chain are described later in the chapter, in the global content management section. There is also a cat-egory of emerging tools to facilitate machine translation, and these technologies are described in Chapter 10. More details on various tools and companies providing web globalization expertise are included in the Web globalization resources section.

Support standards/formats and guidelines

In analyzing the web globalization value chain, it is important to outline not only the various value-creating activities but also the various guidelines, rules, formats, check-lists, standards, and best practices associated with each activity. Standards, formats, and guidelines provide several benefits, including:

- the development of open protocols;
- process clarity;
- measurability;
- quality control;
- transparency;
- the documenting of best practices;
- the interoperability or easy interchange of information among various technologies and components of the value chain; and, most importantly,
- increased efficiency.

In the localization industry, such standards have been instrumental in allowing vendors to use a variety of tools and still be able to share data. One of the broadest

---

[4] Excerpt from http://qa-dev.w3.org/i18n-checker/about.html.

standards applicable to various industries is the ISO 900 series, which includes about 18,000 international standards on a variety of subjects. Some 1,100 new ISO standards are published every year (www.iso.org). The ISO/IEC 10646 and the Unicode are important standards relevant to web globalization activities, as they form the basis of the multilingual web by providing several encoding forms. ISO 639-1 and 2 provide several language codes, and ISO 3166 provides country/region codes.

Beyond these, some standards specific to the web globalization value chain include the following (see also Table 7.1).

- *TMX* Translation Memory eXchange was conceived as a vendor-neutral, open-XML-compliant standard for the exchange of TM data created by CAT and localization tools. The purpose of TMX is to allow easier exchange of translation memory data between tools and/or translation vendors with little or no loss of critical data during the process, thus enhancing interoperability (www.lisa.org). TMX was developed by OSCAR (Open Standards for Container/Content Allowing Reuse), which is a LISA Special Interest Group.
- *Terminology standards* Beyond translation memory data there is also terminology data, which needs to be exchanged in the web globalization value chain. Thus standards have been developed to facilitate the exchange of terminology data. The Open Lexicon Interchange Format (OLIF) is an open standard for lexical/terminological data encoding and distribution (www.olif.net). A common terminology standard used in the localization industry includes the TBX or TermBase eXchange TBXLISA/ OSCAR. TBX is an ISO-16642-compliant, open-XML-based standard format for exchanging terminological data while retaining complex embedding structures. It helps in optimizing information assets, enhancing the quality of translation, and reducing localization costs, and it allows for the exchange of terminology data between various tools.[5]
- *Sharing of segmentation rules* SRX, or the Segmentation Rules eXchange, was created by the OSCAR Committee at LISA. It is an XML-based and vendor-neutral standard for describing how to segment text for translation and other language processes. It allows TM and other linguistic tools to describe the language-specific processes by which text is broken into segments (usually sentences or paragraphs) for further processing. It is generally used to complement the TMX and allows for the interoperability of segmentation rules (lisa.org).
- *XLIFF* The XML Localization Interchange File Format is a format for exchanging localization data. According to OASIS, the purpose of XLIFF is to "define, through extensible XML vocabularies, and promote the adoption of, a specification for the interchange of localizable software and document based objects and related metadata" (www.oasis-open.org). Since the diversity of localization tools and technologies

---

[5] www.lisa.org/Term-Base-eXchange.32.0.html.

Table 7.1 Select standards for exchanging localization data[6]

xml:tm (XML-based Text Memory)	XLIFF (XML Localization Interchange File Format)	SRX (Segmentation Rules eXchange)
This is based on the XML standard and is vendor-neutral. XML-based Text Memory is used for embedding text memory directly within an XML document using XML namespace syntax. xml:tm simplifies XML-based globalization workflows. • The integration of linguistic assets with content means TM is always up to date. • It is compatible with DITA. • It integrates seamlessly with other standards.	XLIFF enables the exchange of localizable data across various incompatible software platforms and technologies that support localization. • It removes the complexities of localizing different types of source files. • It provides a common platform for localization tool vendors to write to, thus increasing the number of tools available. • It highlights the parts of a file that are important to the localization process.	This is also an XML-based and vendor-neutral standard for describing how translation and other language-processing tools segment text for processing. • SRX allows translation memory and other linguistic tools to describe the language-specific processes by which text is broken into segments. • It is generally used to complement TMX.

may impede interoperability, XLIFF makes localized text available in a format-neutral manner for easy manipulation.

- *GMX* The Global Information Management Metrics eXchange was developed by LISA OSCAR for defining word and character counts for localization documents (lisa.org).

Primary activity 1: internationalization

Many organizations are either unaware of or lack a full understanding of when and where internationalization is required. According to internationalization expert Bill Hall, internationalization should not be considered an add-on but as an architectural foundation that must be considered from the inception of program design and development. For this reason, I have included internationalization as the first step in the web globalization value chain.

If internationalization is undertaken at later stages, such as inserting an internationalized code in an existing program, major changes in the rest of the software functionality could result and the entire process would likely be less efficient. Thus internationalization is not a feature that can be added later, or at a time that seems more convenient.

---

[6] Reference and credit to lisa.org.

Since this step involves programming and coding, and therefore a certain level of technical proficiency, most non-technical managers may not fully understand the technical details. However, they should still understand the basic value-creating steps at this stage in order to help the technical team accomplish them. Managers therefore need to work closely with their globalization architects, engineers, or internationalization teams to successfully implement the critical steps at this stage. Some important value-creating activities at this stage are listed below.

(1) *Organize the internationalization team.* This may include developers, internationalization engineers, globalization architects, and software and user-interface-testing professionals.

(2) *Ensure that the internationalization team is well trained in emerging technologies and standards.* Few university programs specialize in internationalization training, but resources-related internationalization can be found in the web globalization resources section of this book.

(3) *Create channels of communication between the internationalization team (e.g., designers and developers) and the team members involved with localization (e.g., translators and testers).* This will ensure that problems uncovered at localization or in testing are brought to the developers' attention.

(4) *Clearly delineate all requirements for the website or software,* so that it can be easily adapted to different locale-specific requirements.

(5) *Implement a multilingual database,* in order to enable multi-tier applications and client/server applications to support languages for which the database is configured. During database development, make sure that Unicode is used as the encoding standard.

(6) *Ensure that the end user receives locale-specific information.* Retrieving the right locale in terms of user locale, browser language settings, and other cultural conventions is important. Products should be enabled to display locale-specific information seamlessly on the basis of cultural conventions.

(7) *Remember locale-specific requirements,* such as date and calendar formatting, time formatting, currency formatting, casing, collating methods, sorting and string comparison, number formatting, address formatting, paper size issues, telephone numbers, and measurement units.

(8) *Keep in mind that "localizability" is the final as well as one of the most important steps in the primary value activity of internationalization.*

    (a) *Consider isolating localizable resources into a separate file.* Localizable resources include all the text and elements of the UI that need translation and modification for specific geographic locales.

    (b) *After separate resource files for localizable elements have been created, consider how strings are created and displayed.* At this stage, convey to the internationalization team the need to avoid run-time composite strings, to minimize the use of variables, to use unique variable names, and not to concatenate several variables together (Dr. International, 2002).

(c) *Enhance UI localizability by creating default dialog boxes with sufficient room for future text expansion during translation.* Avoid using UI controls as part of sentences, avoid embedding text in graphics, and use culturally neutral images and icons in your global user interface (Dr. International, 2002).

(d) *Ask developers to consider UI mirroring* if you plan to localize into right-to-left languages such as Arabic, Urdu, or Hebrew.

(e) *Finally, create a terminology glossary, style sheets, and a naming system for localized files.* Most importantly, follow guidelines for international technical writing.

These basic internationalization steps will ensure that the product/website is enabled for the next step, which is the localization of the text, user interface, and other web elements.

Primary activity 2: localization

People often confuse "localizability" with localization; localizability is actually a part of internationalization that prepares the product for future localization. At the localization stage of the web globalization value chain, companies should create a communication interface between the internationalization team and the localization team. The internationalization team should provide the localization team with applications that have been designed to be adapted to locale-specific requirements. The internationalization and localization teams must also communicate to identify all localizable elements that are stored in the resource files. Ideally, if an agile development process is used (to be discussed later in the chapter), then internationalization, localization, and testing will go hand in hand. At the localization stage, the localization team will work on localizing various localizable elements stored in the resource files. Some important value-creating activities at this stage are detailed below.

(1) *Create a localization team.* Members of the localization team may include translators, linguists, graphic designers, e-commerce professionals, cultural consultants, international business professionals, and legal advisors to ensure compliance with global e-commerce regulations. The team should include the project manager and project coordinators responsible for the coordination of tasks between the internationalization team and the localization team, or even with various other departments or country units. The team should work closely with internationalization engineers to ensure the proper handling and localization of databases and tools, the proper implementation of localization guidelines, and adequate testing. In addition, depending on the size of the company, the team may have in-house editors

and in-country reviewers. Usually, companies with less extensive localization needs may rely solely or partially on localization vendors who provide a range of web globalization services.

(2) *Create and implement a localization kit.* A localization kit is a compilation of instructions, standards, notes from developers, localizable resources, and other files that help the localization team or localization vendor to organize and manage localization efforts. It saves a considerable amount of time in project evaluation and preparation by helping the project managers, translators, and engineering team members to quickly understand the scope of work. Furthermore, it reduces the number of queries that managers need to answer during the evaluation and the project itself (www.conversisglobal.com). The localization kit should be developed on the basis of a standard set of guidelines that delineate what kind of information is to be included in the kit, the details and the extent of the information presented in the kit, and how the material in the kit is to be presented (see Table 7.2). Broadly speaking, the four main components of the localization kit are (Zerfaß, 2005) as follows.

(a) *The localization plan* It provides a general overview of the project and includes details about the project team (names, responsibilities, and contact information), a project description, the project scope, milestones, the delivery schedule, the release date, previous localized versions of the website, source and target languages, and locales under consideration.

(b) *Project structure and file list* At this step, a detailed list is created of all files to be used in the project (file versions to be localized), the file content (e.g., word count), and file-handling instructions. Things to consider include the flow of files among different project constituents, the file-naming standard to be followed, instructions on handling various file formats and conversions, and instructions for the localization of various resources (e.g., files, translatable text, UI elements, and editable graphic files). Moreover, it is important to include all developer notes for the localization team (e.g., the handling of UI strings, programs, and the databases used for back-end architecture).

(c) *List of tools* These include the tools and hardware needed to manipulate and/or localize various files and elements of the website/product. This exercise helps not only the internal localization team but also the localization vendor to be prepared for the project. The tool inventory list should include not just the tools required at various localization workflow steps but also things such as the versions and settings of the tools; the tool licenses and their location (details of the person responsible for each tool); details of the manufacturers of the tools; and, if a proprietary tool is used, then instructions on its procurement, installation, and implementation.

(d) *Quality assurance and reference material* At this step, lay out clear instructions about quality expectations, project metrics, and the tests needed for ongoing quality assurance. Specify the tools and criteria for testing and validation.

Table 7.2 Elements of a localization kit

Section	Detail
Project information	• Include client name, product name/project name, names of components (UI, help, docs, web, etc.), contact information.
Scope of work	• Describe the product, what it does, who the end users are, etc. • Identify languages and be as specific as possible. For example, Spanish should be distinguished between Latin American Spanish, European Spanish, or mid-Atlantic Spanish. • Provide component details, such as what portions should be left in English, and whether deliverables are mono- or multilingual.
List of source files and file format	• List estimated word counts, page counts, dialog counts, topic counts, and graphic counts per deliverable.
Leverage	• Do any components have common content? • Do TMs exist? What format are they in? Where are they?
Graphics	• Indicate all graphics requiring localization. Source files should be available for localization; text must be separate from the graphic. • List localized screenshots to be taken or placed.
Assets/references	• Identify TMs. • Give glossary, style, or branding guidelines. • List font information, directory structure/file naming, handoff protocols (FTP [File Transfer Protocol] or CD?), and certification requirements for sites where production will happen (e.g., ISO CMM [Capability Maturity Model]).
Schedule requirements	• Name any languages required earlier than others for release dates. • Identify components required earlier than others for testing. • Provide information on whether a linguistic review will be conducted by the client, etc.
Build/compiling requirements	• Provide these for the software or the web. • Include a note if the build is to be handled by the customer.
Testing requirements	• Functionality testing or linguistic testing? • Test script; provide platform/browser information.
Hardware/ software/ tools required	• Provide any tools, software, or hardware required for working with the files, and the version; also provide any specific localization tools the client wants the localization service provider (LSP) to use.
Locale-specific requirements	• Describe, for example, whether a license agreement is to be in English and French in the French manual, or that paragraph X should be deleted in the warranty statement for Japanese. • Specify requirements for the work to stay in one particular country.
Contacts of client reviewers	• Provide this to help the localization service provider facilitate the in-country review process.

Source: Adopted from Lionbridge, with permission: http://blog.lionbridge.com/translation-and-localization/bid/42760/avoiding-the-Chaos-With-a-Localization-Kit.

Sometimes, during the localization process, tags are accidentally overwritten. The validation process ensures that translators do not introduce errors into the web pages they are working on. In terms of reference material, a detailed terminology glossary that outlines all the terms and notations being used should be available. Other reference material that is useful at the localization stage includes the company style sheets and translation memories.

(3) *Selection of localization service provider.* It is good practice to outline the corporate guidelines for the selection of translators and LSPs. A centralized process that adheres to certain vendor selection guidelines helps create client–vendor partnerships that are based on clear expectations and work requirements. Even in a decentralized environment, having clear vendor selection guidelines helps lead to partnering with vendors that meet company-wide work expectations. When creating multilingual documents and products, companies can choose from translators, single-language vendors, or multiple-language localization vendors. The scope of the project, a company's internal organization support, and the extent of the job will determine whether a dedicated set of localization vendors is required or whether a few translators or an ad hoc team of vendors is all that is needed. Some of the steps at the vendor selection stage are as follows.

(a) *Creating a clear set of criteria against which to evaluate potential vendors.*

(b) *Establishing the metrics for measuring vendor success*, depending on a company's business priorities (e.g., cost, speed, availability of subject matter experts, etc.).

(c) *Determining key factors in the LSP's workflow.* Does the localization service provider use proprietary or public technology? What translation and workflow management tools does the LSP use? Does the vendor follow industry standards in terms of the exchange of translation memory, terminology, and other data?

(d) *Following a disciplined, competitive bidding process* to fairly and thoroughly assess potential vendors.

(e) *Deciding the policy on vendor selection for headquarters and subsidiaries.* Such a policy is crucial for creating standard guidelines for the localization process. It also enables all parts of the localization process to be seamlessly connected in the automated localization workflow process.

(f) *Carefully reviewing quotes* and asking questions about any parts of the quote that are not clear.

(g) *Contracting for a pilot project* to assess the vendor's capability in a client–vendor relationship.

(h) *Determining how the LSP calculates the word count for translations.* This is important, because the translation of the content will be the major cost. Localization service providers have different ways of counting and use different word-counting tools.

At the vendor selection stage, it is also important to determine if the LSP has expertise in using translation memory. The use of TM tools can have an impact on the overall localization cost, as TM allows the reuse of words and reduces translation costs. If the LSP uses TM, determine who will own the memory content, and whether it is to be provided at the end of the project. Companies may need to change localization service providers, and if so they should have easy access to their TM in a standard interchange (TMX) format to deliver to the new LSP. This TM could also be used for future projects.

When selecting a translator or using a vendor for translation, ensure that the translators meet some basic criteria. Here are some suggestions for this process.

- Determine the translator's native language. Ideally, the translator should be a native speaker of the target language, as he or she is better able to account for language nuances and other linguistic issues.
- Clearly convey all translation requirements and associated terminology glossaries and style sheets.
- Consider whether the translator has enough background in the company's industry to easily comprehend industry-specific terminology. It is also advisable to actually train the translator in the terminology if it is extensive and translation is technical and quality-sensitive.
- Ensure that the translator has sufficient translation training and is well trained in various translation technology tools. For high-quality translations, a native speaker lacking translation training will not suffice. Various universities and professional bodies provide translation training and certifications; the translator should have some of these credentials.
- Always ask for references and sample translations.

Primary activity 3: testing

Testing is an important activity for ensuring that the internationalized and localized product meets all quality control criteria. Testing creates substantial value by implementing a layer of quality control, which merits treating testing as a unique step in the web globalization value chain. Here are some of the value-creating activities included in testing.

(1) *The first step is to verify that the website functionality is globalized*, making sure that the internationalization step was properly enforced. Ensuring the proper globalization of key functions saves work, time, and money, since now testers will need only to check how well the website/content is localized for the given locale. Adhering to a stringent internationalization process reduces the need for repeated internationalization testing; in addition, fewer or no resources will be needed to reengineer the product at the end of the development cycle.

(2) *Localizability testing is the next step*, and, according to Dr. International (2002), it should be performed in parallel with the globalized functionality test. The purpose

of localizability testing is to verify that the user interface of the program being tested can be easily translated to any target language without reengineering or making code modifications. Since localizability bugs have to be fixed in the code of the application, they must be looked for at the earliest stage of development possible (Dr. International, 2002: 347).

(a) Pseudo-localization using visual localization tools is a good way to achieve localizability testing. Before localization can take place, localizability should be tested either by inserting fake translation or by simulating the localization. This can help determine problems that may arise from text expansion and contraction, character corruption, hard-coded strings, and other localizability issues.

(b) Code reviews should be performed to ensure resources are separated from the code.

(c) Documentation and UI reviews should also be conducted.

(3) *Localization testing[7] is the next stage, in which localized elements are checked to ensure that they have been properly localized – especially all translated content*. Some general items to be tested at this stage include UI usability testing and content files; operating system compatibility (i.e., verify that the website works well on different operating systems, different web browsers, and with different web browser settings); linguistic accuracy; translation equivalence; sorting rules; upper- and lower-case conversions; website usability; and cultural correctness. It is also important to check from the marketing perspective that local search terms are being properly used in the local search engine optimization process.

The members of the localization team who are to be involved in the testing stage should be carefully selected. Based on the testing requirements outlined above, it is clear that this testing requires a diverse skill set that includes both technical and linguistic skills.

Primary activity 4: global content management

This is the final stage in the web globalization value chain. The global content management stage primarily deals with systematically storing, documenting, leveraging, and maintaining the global content. According to LISA (Toon *et al.*, 2007: 3), global content management refers "to the systems and processes used to create, manage, publish, and archive information as text, images, prices, statistics, measurements, articles, documents, descriptions, sound bites, video clips, etc., in multiple languages and for use in multiple countries, regions and/or markets. A truly global content

---

[7] Content referenced from Dr. International (2002) and http://msdn.microsoft.com/en-us/goglobal/bb688150.aspx. These two sources provide a good in-depth understanding of localizability and testing techniques.

management solution provides the necessary infrastructure to enable an organization to ensure that its content is ready for publishing when and where it is needed, in the right format, language and form. In addition, it should do so efficiently and cost-effectively, and be well integrated with the organization's other systems and processes."

The management of global content is made easier by automating various facets of content creation, management, and deployment. To efficiently manage the web globalization workflow and the reams of localized data and content that are generated, companies are switching to tools and technologies that can help them achieve process automation. Two primary tools that can help to achieve this are (a) content management systems and (b) global management systems, or as they are more commonly known in the localization industry, translation management systems (TMSs). Together, content management systems and translation management systems create an ideal environment for developing, managing, and deploying international websites in an efficient and cost-effective manner.

Basically, CMS software helps with creating, managing, storing, publishing, and deploying content enterprise-wide in a collaborative environment. While a CMS primarily deals with source content, a TMS is geared toward managing and automating the web globalization workflow (localization, translation, language assets) and synchronizing it with the source CMS. Primarily, a TMS system centralizes core language assets in a translation memory (TM) database and terminology database and helps companies integrate the whole web globalization workflow into a single system. Thus all actors in the web globalization value chain can be connected through the TMS. For example, an external translator or localization service provider can easily connect to the company TMS and retrieve, complete, and submit localization/ translation jobs; an internal company linguist or editor can easily check the linguistic quality of the translation job from the vendor; and the project manager can at the same time monitor the whole project and specific tasks as they go through different actors in the web globalization value chain. Translation management systems are therefore proving to be efficient tools for automating the web globalization workflow and achieving transparency, efficiency, quicker turnaround times, and cost savings. In the next chapter, I look at how CMSs and TMSs are being used by companies to optimize their web globalization efforts. The chapter also provides some case studies – real-life examples of workflow automation made possible by emerging translation management tools.

Coordinating the web globalization value chain: localization project management

Now that the elements of the web globalization value chain have been discussed, it is important to note that companies need to develop coordinative routines and capabilities

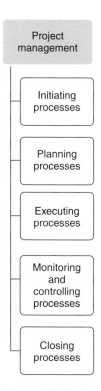

Figure 7.3 Project management steps

in order to synchronize their various value-creating activities in the web globalization value chain. Organizations need to have comprehensive plans and clear processes for managing localization projects. This can be accomplished by instituting localization project management within the organization. According to the Project Management Institute (PMI), project management is the application of knowledge, skills, tools, and techniques to a broad range of activities in order to meet the requirements of a particular project. Project management is comprised of five primary process groups: initiating processes, planning processes, executing processes, monitoring and controlling processes, and closing processes (see Figure 7.3) (www.pmi.org). Project management helps companies link their value-creating activities on the basis of organization strategy so as to achieve organization-specific goals.

Localization project management is the application of project management principles to ensure the efficient management of all value-creating activities in the web globalization value chain. The management of localization projects involves coordinating the workflow of a project from its conception, all the way along its journey through the translation management system. This includes managing various processes and people, such as translators, editors, quality assurance, and testing, and managing linguistic assets (terminology, TM, machine translation, etc.).

Localization project management poses unique challenges, which arise from the involvement of multiple parties, a diversity of tools, the prevalence of various file formats, the incorporation of several language assets, and a plethora of localization requirements. For example, localizing a website in multiple languages may involve translators for multiple languages, linguists, editors, terminology specialists, localization service providers, cultural consultants, graphic designers, localization engineers, multilingual search engine optimization and marketing professionals, and project managers. Many components of the localization project are dispersed not only across various parties but also across geographic regions, and thus pose communication and scheduling challenges. Project managers at both the client and vendor sides have to closely work with each other and with their respective localization teams to create effective channels of communication, to clarify project objectives and guidelines, to regularly monitor the project's progress, and to create iterative steps to control any quality issues or problems. Thus translation and localization project management tools come in handy for simplifying and automating several of the coordination and communication tasks involved in localization project management.

The next chapter addresses the topic of how TMSs can help automate various localization tasks; for now, the several specialized localization project management tools that are available to help with localization projects are discussed. Although several localization project management tools are on the market, to showcase the functionality of localization project management tools the example of LTC Worx tools is used here.[8]

LTC Worx manages various aspects of the localization workflow and includes modules for project management, financial management, and client–vendor management. It helps customize workflows from the initial quotation through the final invoicing. Some of the tasks that can be automated are as follows.

- Creating, calculating, sending, and tracking quotes.
- Creating projects, tracking the project tasks, and allocating resources.
- Invoicing (viewing, printing, saving, and exporting invoices) on the basis of pre-created price lists and the instant checking of balances and outstanding payments.
- Creating management and financial summaries, as well as statistical and graphical reports.
- Monitoring the progress of each work stage or each project phase and identifying potential problem areas. It also allows for the adjustment of deadlines and the rescheduling of allocated tasks.

LTC Worx includes tools for collaboration and document management. It can interface with other applications, such as finance systems and various translation

---

[8] The information on LTC Worx is adapted from www.langtech.co.uk, which is the site for the company that sells this product. The choice of LTC Worx is guided by the motivation to showcase a localization project management tool and implies no endorsement of the product.

Table 7.3 Project management techniques	
Gantt chart	Linear responsibility chart
The Gantt chart is named after its designer, Henry Gantt, and is a commonly used project-planning tool. It is a form of a horizontal bar chart used as a project scheduler for charting the overall duration of project activities from start to finish. The chart also shows the dependencies between project tasks and the associated timeline. It is a good tool for scheduling and tracking the entire project from planning to implementation.	The linear responsibility chart is commonly used in project management to clarify roles, responsibilities, and deliverables. This chart is like a matrix wherein the rows show the project deliverables in a logical sequence and the adjacent column lists the stakeholders with their titles. The LRC helps to clarify stakeholders' roles and responsibilities and is a good tool for delegating authority and enhancing accountability.

applications. LTC Worx can also manage different currencies, time zones, and invoicing requirements. Resources and projects can be moved and shared between sites. In addition, managers can retrieve detailed reports for each individual site as well as for the whole operation, as all the data for all the sites is held in one place.

Agile development for localization efficiencies

Traditionally, localization project management has relied on a predictable list of steps and stages that a project goes through.

- A statement of work outlining project objectives and requirements sets a localization project in motion.
- The project initiation stage outlines the sequence of activities in the project, along with their start and end dates, and delineates the resources, personnel, responsibilities, and milestones.
- The project execution stage involves the sequencing of the all-important web globalization primary activities, including internationalization, localization, global content development, and deployment.
- The project control stage deals primarily with testing and quality control steps prior to the release of the website or applications.
- Finally, the project is closed and lessons from the project are assessed.

This traditional method of project management follows a linear and predictable route. It uses techniques and tools such as Gantt charts or linear responsibility charts (LRCs) (see Table 7.3)[9] to organize, sequence, and assign various project management tasks in a well-defined yet rather inflexible way.

---

[9] The use of Gantt charts and linear responsibility charts in traditional project management does not preclude their use in agile development methodologies.

Scrum

"Scrum" is a generalized set of guidelines or a framework based on the agile development approach, and it is particularly popular for software development projects. In the traditional or "waterfall"-style project management approach, team members are asked to estimate the duration of project sequences and, basically, make an educated guess as to when the project will be completed. This traditional approach leads to less flexibility, a rush to meet deadlines, the missing of deadlines, and even the compromising of quality control and product adaptability. Scrum actually divides the project management around a series of iterative and adaptive "sprints," which can range from a few days to two to three weeks. Each sprint is accomplished by a self-organizing, cross-functional team that refers to a master list of prioritized items (also called a product backlog) and selects the items to be completed during the sprint. The work of the cross-functional team during the sprint is facilitated by a "scrum master," who helps remove any impediments that the team might face during the sprint. The team refers to the "sprint backlog," or items from the product backlog that need to be accomplished during the sprint. The sprint progress is assessed regularly to remove any bottlenecks and adequately review, adjust, test, and implement the product increments to be accomplished in the sprint backlog. At the end of the sprint a comprehensive and retrospective review is undertaken, and the product functionality achieved during the sprint is demonstrated. Thus this adaptive-iterative style of project management helps teams adjust product functionalities without disrupting the workflow, make better estimates by scheduling the project in short iterative steps, seek constant feedback to keep the whole project management process responsive to any changes or bugs, and enhance member involvement and empowerment in the whole process. For more information, see http://scrummethodology.com.

In contrast to this traditional approach to project management, the new concept of "agile development" takes a less linear and more adaptive approach to managing application development projects. The focus of agile development is to emphasize people, communication, collaboration, and customer solutions over processes and tools in order to make the project management more adaptive and dynamic with respect to the external environment (see Figure 7.4). Traditional project management approaches follow an assembly-line perspective in which each step fits neatly into the next step. Thus, in the web globalization value chain, internationalization has to be finished before any localization starts, and so forth. Localizers therefore have to wait till the coding and other aspects of internationalization have been completed. This can lead to long lag times, and in worst-case scenarios, if problems occur at later stages, the project team has to retrace all the steps back to the code development stage – "What a waterfall!"

Previous chapters have emphasized the fact that internationalization leads to the generalization of the product and should always be completed before any localization efforts – but this does not mean that internationalization teams should work in isolation from localization teams. From an agile perspective, it is important to develop

Figure 7.4 Agile development process

several small, cross-functional teams of internationalization engineers, translators, linguists, graphic designers, etc. and have them take on a localization project not in long, predefined stages but in abbreviated steps. Thus localization project management using agile methodology is based on several flexible steps or "sprints" leveraging cross-functional teams so as to enhance the adaptability and flexibility of the project. Each cross-functional team in a sense works on the full website/software development cycle from code development to testing. This allows the changes to be made as the bugs are caught during the web globalization value-creating activities. In essence, such an approach brings people from different functional areas together to work in teams to solve problems in a quick and efficient manner.

Localization project manager

A well-managed web globalization value chain can help companies streamline their processes, achieve system-wide efficiencies, and effectively deploy multilingual content via several international websites. To effectively coordinate all the web globalization value chain activities, companies need to have localization project managers who are well trained in the basics of all web globalization value chain issues and also have advanced project management skills. A localization project manager does not necessarily have to be a software engineer or an expert linguist, but he or she must have a good knowledge of the basic issues involved with various facets of the web globalization value chain. For example, even a non-technical localization project manager should know the problems that can arise from hard-coded strings or the basic issues involved with internationalizing a website or software. Most companies are now moving to using the agile development approach to software development and management, and thus it is important that project managers are also familiar with this methodology. Since project managers serve as an interface between the various parties involved in the web globalization value chain, it is important that these professionals have good people management skills and be good communicators. Some of the desired skills for a localization project manager are outlined in Table 7.4.

Case study: localization management at Compuware–Changepoint[10]

In 2000 Changepoint (today the Changepoint division of Compuware) made the decision to enter the global market, and carefully evaluated different localization models that would fit the company's localization objectives and requirements. The decision to create an in-house localization team was supported by several decisive factors:

- the company's commitment to continuously localize the application and add languages in the process;
- the necessity of integrating the localization early in the product development process, and not considering localization as an afterthought;
- the ability to maintain control over the work process, the project timeline, and the required resources; and
- the importance of optimizing product quality by owning technology and keeping the knowledge and skills in-house.

With the idea of integrating localization early in the product development process, the localization team was put in charge of the linguistic quality of the user interface. The reason behind this assignment was that the UI suffered from a serious case of "technobabble," which made it difficult for end users and translators to understand. The team started defining writing guidelines and created a glossary of preferred terms (a terminology glossary). The team reviewed (and corrected, if necessary) every string written by developers to ensure that the UI complied with the terminology and standards developed for the application, and that the text was coherent and easily translatable.

---

[10] This case was developed by Ariane Duddey, the manager of Technical Communications and Localization at the Changepoint division of Compuware. The companies highlighted in the case are relevant to this case and do not imply any endorsement of any specific company.

Table 7.4 Desirable qualities in a localization project manager
General qualities
(1) Overall people management skills
(2) A proactive orientation
(3) Good communication skills
(4) Leadership qualities to lead the project team
(5) Organization skills
(6) A general sense of empathy
(7) A goal-driven personality
(8) Ability to negotiate and manage effectively
(9) Attention to detail
(10) Ability to anticipate client needs
(11) A creative mindset
(12) Ability to be flexible and resourceful
(13) Problem solver
Qualities specific to localization project management
(14) Basic cross-cultural understanding
(15) Knowledge of project management processes and tools relevant to localization
(16) General knowledge of web globalization issues
(17) Some exposure to foreign languages
(18) Desktop publishing or technical skills
(19) Educational qualifications or certifications to substantiate project management skills
(20) Localization-related experience or specific educational background/certification in localization project management

The team also at first assisted the technical writers in the development of localization-friendly documentation. When the company started planning the localization of the product documentation, it became necessary to redefine the target audience, to devise new writing rules for creating internationalized documents, and to design language-specific layouts and templates. The company currently performs quality reviews on every document before it is sent out for translation, and after the translation is completed. It also makes sure that feedback and error notifications from its translators are worked into the source documentation.

The Changepoint localization team has always consisted of only three localization specialists. The team's initial task was focused on internationalizing the application, defining localization guidelines and standards, and implementing an efficient translation workflow. Once the localization process was up and running, the team regrouped to form a localization project management team, wherein each team member was placed in charge of a specific set of languages and projects.

However, with only three people and eight target languages to manage, the company lacked the linguistic resources and skills required to translate the complete user interface and documentation in all languages. The volume of the components, like the documentation, also made it impossible for just the three people to complete the work on schedule for the product release.

The company therefore decided to share the localization work with external vendors, who generally perform either the translation or the linguistic review, which cannot be done in-house. According to Ariane Duddey, the manager of Technical Communications and Localization, "To decide what will be outsourced and what will be done in-house, we simply answer a few questions. Do we have the skills to do the work in-house? Do we have the time to complete the work in-house? Can we do it faster in-house? Do we have the budget to outsource?"

Most of the linguistic work was outsourced, while the in-house localization team managed the entire localization process:

- setting up projects with the vendors (quotation, timelines and delivery dates, translation instructions, access to the web-based application);
- preparing files for translation (quality reviews of the source content prior to translation, setting up translation projects on the translation management system);
- managing and maintaining translation memories and terminology databases;
- performing desktop publishing and capturing screenshots for translated documentation; and
- generating, reviewing, and testing online help files.

Such a blend of in-house and outsourced models allowed the company to keep control over its localization workflow, the project timeline, and the tools used to complete the work.

According to Duddey, "No two projects are the same, and we continuously adapt and enhance our process to meet new requirements and directives. We currently localize the Changepoint application user interface in eight languages, which are simultaneously shipped with the English version on the release date. We also manage in-between service packs."

The company is still striving to achieve simultaneous shipment for its voluminous documentation (translated in only two languages), which, unfortunately, still lags behind by a few weeks after the release date. However, about two years ago the company moved from a waterfall development methodology to agile development, which reinforced localization as an integral part of the application development and significantly reduced the lag time for the release of the localized documentation.

As part of the agile methodology, the development team at Compuware–Changepoint developed a set number of features within a sprint (following requirements set by the product management team): the finalized features go to quality assurance (QA), the technical writers document the features, and localization personnel start the translation of the user interface and the documentation. The development sprints generally start on a Monday and end on a Friday four weeks later. Most of the time, QA and documentation start during the sprint, as soon as some features are finalized, but it is not feasible to finish all QA and documentation within the sprint. Unfinished tasks are then postponed to the next sprint.

In the waterfall method used previously, the localization team had a large volume of words to translate and review very late in the release, and it usually had to scramble to get everything done on schedule. With the agile development method, this big volume was evenly distributed over ten to twelve sprints of the release, and the team had ample time to translate and perform QA checks for all languages. Moreover, in the last sprints of the release, the volume of translation steadily decreased, and the team had time to work more on the documentation translation.

Compuware's Changepoint division has made significant efficiency gains by balancing its in-house and outsourced workloads and adopting the agile development methodology. According to Duddey, her team is constantly seeking to improve upon existing processes. The next step for her team is to further enhance documentation translation efficiency by moving to XML-based Darwin Information Typing Architecture, utilizing topic-based authoring or a modular approach to content development.

Chapter summary

- This chapter has introduced the concept of value chain analysis and how it can be used to break down web globalization activities into primary and support activities.
- Before content enters the web globalization value chain, several questions should be answered as part of the pre-value-chain analysis. What is the reason for the content creation? For whom is the content creation taking place? How will the content be consumed?
- Three support activities critical to the implementation of the web globalization value chain are:
  - the support functions that help provide organizational infrastructure for managing web globalization;
  - the support technologies used to automate various web globalization value-creating activities; and
  - the support standards used to enhance interoperability and to establish industry guidelines for various web globalization activities.
- Primary activities identified in the web globalization value chain include:
  - internationalization, when a generalized platform is created that can then be localized easily for future use;
  - localization, when an organizational infrastructure and a localization kit are developed to support localization activities;
  - testing, when the product is tested for globalization functionality, localizability, and localization; and
  - global content management, when a way of systematically storing, documenting, leveraging, and maintaining the global content in a centralized system is developed.
- Localization project management is outlined as an organizational process that is crucial for the overall coordination of all web globalization tasks; it ensures that projects are efficiently executed.
- Finally, the concept of agile development is introduced; the methodology makes localization project management adaptive, flexible, and efficient.

REFERENCES

Bhatt, Ganesh D., and Emdad, Ali F. 2001. "An analysis of the virtual value chain in electronic commerce," *Logistics Information Management* 14: 78–84.

Dr. International 2002. *Developing International Software*, 2nd edn. Microsoft Press.

MultiCorpora 2005. *MultiTrans 4th: Taking the Multilingual TextBase Approach to New Heights.* MultiCorpora.

Porter, Michael E. 1985. *Competitive Advantage: Creating and Sustaining Superior Performance.* Free Press.

Rayport, Jeffrey, and Sviokla, John J. 1995. "Exploiting the virtual value chain," *Harvard Business Review* 73: 75–85.

Toon, A., Drahaim, A., Lommel, A., and Cadieux, P. 2007. *Managing Global Content: Best Practices Guide.* LISA.

Zerfaß, Angelika 2005. "Assembling a localization kit," in *Localization: Getting Started Guide.* MultiLingual Computing: 8–13.

8 Optimizing international websites

Introduction

The optimization of international websites is the direct result of the proper management and implementation of the web globalization value chain. The required people, processes, capabilities, documents, and technologies must be managed in a way to allow the four primary activities of the web globalization value chain (see Chapter 7) to be undertaken in a collaborative and effective manner. A well-optimized international website is one that achieves the following:

(1) international sites and pages are easy to find and navigate;
(2) the site is easy to understand and loads quickly;
(3) the site has a desirable user experience and flow;[1]
(4) Unicode is enabled to depict various languages seamlessly;
(5) the site is locale-sensitive and culturally customized;

---

[1] "Flow" is a state wherein the individual is completely engrossed in the task at hand and experiences a sense of complete identification with the task as well as intrinsic enjoyment. On the web, it is ideal if users experience flow, as that provides them with optimal experience and helps them engage with the website. This concept of flow was initially investigated by Mihály Csíkszentmihályi, and his work provides more information: see Csíkszentmihályi (1975).

(6) the site is well internationalized, allowing for adjustments to the user interface for language and locale requirements;

(7) the site is well tested, in order to enhance its navigation, content, and functional quality;

(8) the site achieves content synchronization, currency (i.e., it is up to date), and relevancy across multilingual websites for various countries;

(9) the turnaround for deploying multilingual content is fast; and

(10) multilingual search engine optimization is enabled by proper global content management.

The four primary web globalization activities are crucial in the development of well-optimized international sites, yet it is the support layer of the web globalization value chain that actually enables the optimized outcomes. The following support ingredients, also depicted in Figure 8.1, are critical in international website optimization efforts.

(1) *People* People from various organizational units must bring their cross-functional skill sets together to successfully optimize international sites.

(2) *Processes* These coordinative routines effectively connect, manage, and implement various web globalization activities.

(3) *Capabilities* These inimitable resources, which an organization accumulates over time, include unique ways of leveraging technology, capturing and leveraging the tacit knowledge of its people, and making important decisions. These capabilities result in resource and technology configurations that enable successful web globalization efforts.

(4) *Documentation* This involves the proper management of organizational memory by codifying processes, tacit knowledge, and other localization resources. Documents such as the localization kit, status reports, Gantt charts, and linear responsibility charts are crucial for optimizing international web development efforts.

(5) *Technologies* These are the tools used to automate various web globalization processes. Examples are translation management systems, content management systems, translation memory tools, terminology management tools, project management tools, etc.

The remainder of this chapter focuses on how automating processes, leveraging capabilities and technologies, and enabling multilingual search engine capabilities lead to optimized international websites. The following sections outline the technologies and processes involved in global content management and multilingual search engine optimization.

Optimizing via content management systems

Content management system software helps with creating, managing, storing, publishing, and deploying enterprise-wide content in a collaborative environment. Content

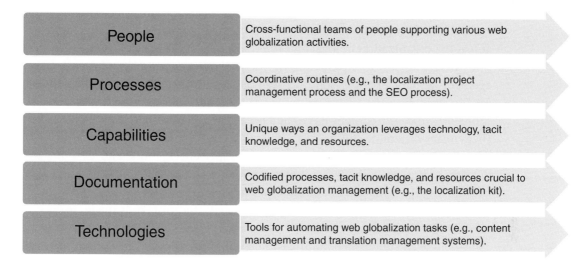

People	Cross-functional teams of people supporting various web globalization activities.
Processes	Coordinative routines (e.g., the localization project management process and the SEO process).
Capabilities	Unique ways an organization leverages technology, tacit knowledge, and resources.
Documentation	Codified processes, tacit knowledge, and resources crucial to web globalization management (e.g., the localization kit).
Technologies	Tools for automating web globalization tasks (e.g., content management and translation management systems).

Figure 8.1 Support ingredients for optimizing international sites

management systems began as simple tools for creating, managing, and distributing content; they are now evolving into more sophisticated enterprise-wide content management (ECM) systems and "single-source" systems that connect various departments, workflows, interfaces, and file formats. Single-source CMSs can be interfaced with various localization tools and are able to exchange data. They help companies manage their content in the most granular form so that content can be reused in a wide variety of formats and outputs (Trotter, 2006). Content management systems can be useful tools for international website development, optimization, and deployment; with them, companies can manage a number of international sites effectively through one core system. More specifically, the CMS can help companies leverage, share, separate, and localize various website building blocks such as content, templates, layout, and pages for developing multiple international sites.

Content management systems have many benefits.

(1) They help automate content management activities along the entire timeline, from content creation to content deployment; they also help to eliminate potential errors and to deploy the content quickly.

(2) They enable the reuse of content throughout multiple websites and in multiple output formats, and easy updating.

(3) They establish a design philosophy and ensure that it is consistently applied throughout the site to maintain corporate identity and branding (www.immediacy.net), providing users with a consistent user interface and web navigation experience.

(4) They enable people with no programming or coding knowledge to author, edit, and work in a WYSIWYG environment, saving precious training and retraining time and allowing non-technical professionals to be engaged in web content development.

(5) They provide a centralized database that can be leveraged and accessed (with prior authorization; access to content can be protected through a CMS) by employees across the organization in local and international offices alike.

(6) They help to instill discipline among the individuals responsible for each management activity of the system, as well as among the departments responsible for disseminating the necessary information required for content management. Moreover, since the content has to fit a predefined website structure, the CMS further creates system discipline.

(7) They automate website management with proper checkpoints, and expedite the delivery of the newly created or edited content to the website, intranet, and extranet, making the management of such sites more effective and efficient (Sen, 2007).

(8) They store several versions of each page, so that, if a mistake is made, users can revert to previous versions of stored pages/data.

(9) They help with content scheduling by keeping track of when the content is ready for deployment, when the content needs updates, and when the content needs to be removed. CMSs therefore become important tools for achieving the simultaneous release of new websites or software.

(10) They generate user-friendly and spider-friendly URLs for SEO. Search engines also require a website to maintain consistency so that relevant content in it can be found rapidly and effectively. A content management system manages the required consistency for all the site's web pages (Sen, 2007). A CMS makes it easy to create title page names, meta tags, keywords, keyword and description tags, and alt tags.

Buying a content management system

Several CMSs are available in the marketplace, and finding them is not difficult. The key consideration when choosing a CMS is that it not only fulfills the need of overall enterprise management but also factors in web globalization functions and multilingual support (e.g., Unicode is enabled). CMSs tend to give web globalization and support for international products a secondary priority. As a consequence, it is important to ensure that the CMS selected supports multilingual and multichannel publishing and can be easily interfaced with the localization tools and standards (e.g., XLIFF) that are part of the web globalization value chain, and also supports the various file formats and versions of tools for various web globalization tasks. Furthermore, a CMS may need to support multiple sites and users from various units and, perhaps, countries, so the CMS should allow users to share files, templates, etc. across multiple sites. The CMS should also have proper security and validation routines, allowing for the granting of access rights to designated people and facilitating corporate governance. Nowadays content is often delivered via mobile devices, so the CMS should be able to format the site for easy delivery via such devices. See Figure 8.2.

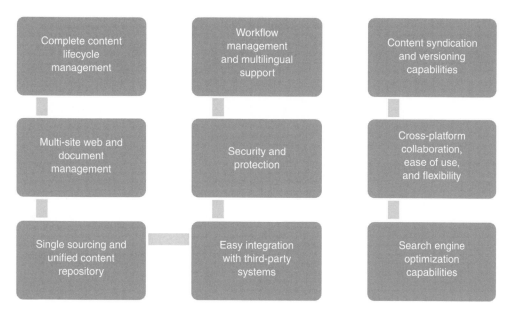

Figure 8.2 Important capabilities of content management systems

Included below are some CMS solutions available in the marketplace that can support international website efforts. This is a subjective evaluation, not based on any objective criteria, and it is not to be read as implying a recommendation. All companies should do their own research prior to selecting the right CMS for their unique needs.

- SDL Tridion seems to specifically support website globalization for multi-site management, balancing central and local messaging, translation management, and a centralized collaborative environment for international organizations (www.tridion .com).
- Sitecore CMS provides good functionality, scalability, and flexibility. Sitecore allows editors to work with the CMS in their native languages by supporting all major languages; websites can be built in several languages. The coordination of various language versions of a website, as well as the translation processes, can be managed through Sitecore (www.sitecore.net).
- Other CMSs with varying levels of support for web globalization activities include documentum/EMC, Ektron, Vasont, Vignette, Interwoven, Fatwire, and EPiSERVER.

Optimizing through a translation management system

While the CMS primarily deals with the source content, the translation management system manages and automates the web globalization workflow (localization, translation, and language assets) and synchronizes it with the source CMS. Several CMSs

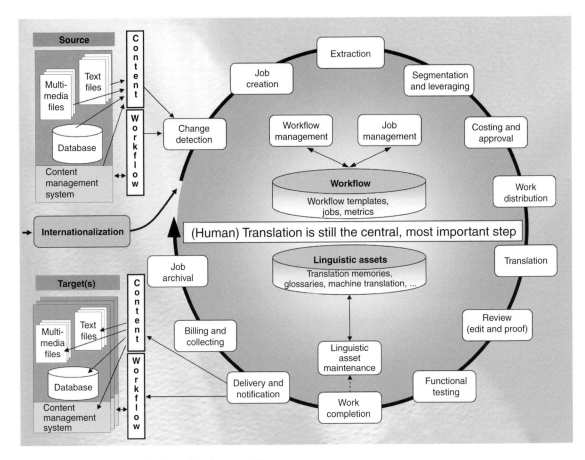

Figure 8.3 The localization workflow

Source: Industry expert Pierre Cadieux; © 2011 Pierre Cadieux, pcadieux@i18n.ca.

boast that they can handle localization, which they do by keeping multiple language versions of content linked, so that all language versions are synchronized. Although a CMS is good at linking various language versions of the content, it does not provide special tools for managing localization-specific tasks and various language assets; this requires additional translation-technology-related plug-ins to the CMS (Toon *et al.*, 2007). As a result, tasks related to managing the localization workflow, such as managing translation resources, sending jobs to translators or localization service providers, tracking the status of localization jobs, leveraging translation memory, or utilizing terminology assets, may not be best done via a CMS. Translation management systems, on the other hand, are designed specifically to effectively automate the localization workflow and manage language assets – and, in the best cases, interface seamlessly with the existing CMS. Figure 8.3 shows the localization workflow that is automated via a TMS. The CMS and TMS together can link, update, interface, and synchronize content efficiently, resulting in significant cost savings. The TMS should be flexible enough to be easily interfaced with a variety of CMS offerings. Furthermore, the TMS should be able to centralize all localization automation within a single system.

Ideally, a TMS should:

(1) be web-enabled and allow for real-time collaboration;
(2) include a centralized translation memory, so that the TM can be seamlessly integrated and leveraged in the web globalization value chain;
(3) enable the centralization of terminology management;
(4) help in automating content creation guidelines, to ensure that the content is stylistically sound and consistent;
(5) enable the automation of all repetitive localization workflow tasks and have modules for localization, project management, finance, and reporting;
(6) have an open architecture, so as to enable integration with the CMS in addition to external collaboration with the LSP and other parties involved; it should be scalable, and allow for the direct transfer of content to be translated between the content system and the translation environment;
(7) support various industry standards (e.g., XML, Unicode, XLIFF, and TMX) and be able to handle various file formats, in order to avoid excessive reformatting and data corruption, thus leading to enhanced interoperability;
(8) allow, when appropriate, for leveraging language data processed using emerging machine translation technologies;
(9) provide transparency or visibility in terms of the localization process;
(10) support a user-friendly interface/editor that can be easily used by non-technical personnel; having WYSIWYG functionality is important for content editors and translators;
(11) have built-in quality control functionality, in order to track corrections/releases and reviewing; the TMS should support metadata to send comments to translators and other actors; and
(12) support the flexible partitioning of documents, so as to allow every translator or proofreader to see the overall context while being permitted to edit only an assigned portion.

Benefits of integrating TMSs and CMSs

Once a company starts on the road toward automating the web globalization value chain, integrating it with a CMS is the next logical step. However, most organizations find the integration of TMSs and CMSs challenging, because they lack the necessary technical and organizational infrastructure. To overcome these challenges, organizations must ensure that the global content management framework that is being built is scalable, facilitates contribution from and expansion into multiple regions, and

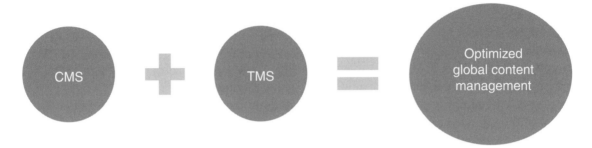

Figure 8.4 Optimizing global content management

addresses localization requirements. By integrating globalization into the content life-cycle as early as possible, companies can ensure that their CMS infrastructure is fully leveraged (Rosenlund, 2006). At a more tactical level, it is also important to have XML support in both the CMS and the TMS, because it allows multichannel publishing, reuse, and automation, which can make globalization more efficient and effective.

Some products act as connectors between the CMS and TMS to enable their seamless integration (see Figure 8.4). For example, Clay Tablet Technologies provides integration software that connects several of the available CMSs and TMSs to make the global content management process more efficient.

Some important benefits of integrating a TMS with a CMS are outlined below.

(1) At an organizational level, the TMS–CMS integration can help integrate web globalization activities throughout the global content development lifecycle.

(2) One of the main advantages of CMS and TMS integration is that various processes in the web globalization value chain, all the way from content creation to deployment, can then be automated and optimized.

(3) A TMS also enhances the visibility of the web globalization value chain. It allows the overall translation workflow to be managed easily by tracking changes to documents and sending alerts to translators, editors, and the project manager when the job is pending and when the job is done. Project managers can easily track the job online, and translators can edit and work in a user-friendly environment. This streamlines the workflow, avoids excessive file sharing, and reduces the time required to extract text for translation and validation. This reduces the overall cost and leads to other efficiencies, such as shortened turnaround time, efficient job tracking, and enhanced workflow management.

(4) CMS–TMS integration also facilitates the sharing of translation/language assets across the entire enterprise. If language assets (such as translation and terminology memories) are to be used across the enterprise rather than maintained in local "silos," a TMS can ensure that all areas of the enterprise and any external partners have access to them on demand (Toon *et al.*, 2007).

(5) With integrated content and translation management systems, a centralized system can be created to connect localization service providers and translators with the in-house web globalization team. The selection of LSPs can also be centralized.

(6) The incorporation of TM tools and fuzzy matching makes it possible to reduce the amount of translation. More CMSs today are using XML, and XML files do not contain formatting. This helps increase the matches in the translation memory and also keeps the TM clean of various formatting standards (Trotter, 2006).

(7) Enabling XML, the interchange of files using XLIFF, and DITA use through an integrated system can create a more structured environment for the sharing, reuse, and multichannel publishing of content.

(8) Since content is created in small blocks in a single-source CMS, the content can be simultaneously created and translated.

(9) The time to (local) market delivery is improved. If content or products that depend on content must be quickly delivered to local markets, TMS–CMS integration provides a way to drastically reduce time to delivery (and thus time to value) of the localized information (Toon *et al.*, 2007).

(10) Integration with TMS helps to leverage terminology resources to create consistent documents and to help create a consistent brand image.

(11) Because of higher levels of reuse and fewer validation steps, it decreases testing efforts.

(12) Other benefits include versioning (keeping past versions of the content for future use and scheduling), the efficient handling of vast global content, and rapid deployment, which improve the ability of local offices to contribute and modify content and lead to improved productivity and a higher return on investment (ROI).

TMS tools

Based on my own industry interactions and meeting TMS vendors at conferences (again, this is a subjective evaluation and does not constitute a recommendation of companies), a selection of companies that offer TMSs includes Across, MultiCorpora, Lionbridge, SDL, Sajan, and Translations.com. An open-source TMS is available through GlobalSight.

In order to show two typical approaches to implementing TMS, I am providing a brief review of the following TMSs: Across, which can be bought as software, and Lionbridge: Freeway™, which is part of Lionbridge's language service.

Across

The Across Language Server can organize, delegate, and efficiently process translation projects. It serves as a central platform for all corporate language resources and translation processes. It provides a uniform workspace in which all involved internal and external actors meet – from editors and project managers to service providers and freelance translators. It makes it possible to recycle content, control processes, and integrate corresponding systems. As a result, qualitative foreign-language content is available more quickly and translation costs are significantly reduced. Some of the components it supports include TM, terminology systems, quality control utilities, multiple format editors, and collaboration tools.[2]

Freeway

Freeway is Lionbridge's online service delivery platform. Access to Freeway's collaboration features and language technology is free for Lionbridge clients and translators. Using Freeway, clients can initiate and track translation projects, collaborate with their project teams, manage linguistic assets, and generate enterprise budget and status reports.[3]

- *Portal and collaboration* An online environment to submit projects, track status, obtain reports, and share knowledge among team members. The client's Lionbridge project manager is available in the same system, ensuring smooth file transfers and real-time access to production information, queries, terminology, and quality review portal.
- *Language asset management (Logoport™)* A centralized, internet-enabled language asset management system with TM, glossary, and machine translation capabilities. Logoport stores translation memories and glossaries in a secure, central repository and supports thousands of concurrent users. Logoport enables the efficient management and sharing of translation memories and glossaries across the products, divisions, and functional groups of a client company.
- *Web services connectivity* Connecting the CMS to Freeway via web services eliminates the manual steps associated with initiating a project and provides the fastest possible turnaround time from creation to translation to global publishing.
- *Workflow and repository* With the Logoport foundation, Freeway serves as a hosted language asset repository. Because the content stays within the Lionbridge architecture and is not physically downloaded to translator desktops, there is greater security than with traditional systems. In addition, Freeway provides workflow capabilities for project management and translator teams.

Case study: 1&1 Internet AG implementing a translation management system for efficiency gains[4]

Company background

With more than 9 million customer contracts, 1&1 Internet AG is one of the world's leading internet providers, offering services via its market presence in Germany, the United

---

[2] Excerpts from www.across.net.
[3] Excerpts from https://freeway.lionbridge.com.
[4] This case was contributed by Across Systems Inc. The companies highlighted in the case are relevant to this case and do not imply any endorsement of a specific company.

Kingdom, France, Spain, and the United States. The day-to-day business operations at 1&1 frequently require texts and documents to be created promptly in various languages. Thus the product offering, which ranges from hosting (websites, servers, domains, and online shops), digital subscriber line (DSL) network connections, telephony, video on demand, and mobile communications to personal information management via the internet, is adapted to the environment of the respective target market. This means that many of the software user interfaces, online help tools, frequently asked questions (FAQs), product documentation, and user manuals need to be localized and translated. A volume of 80,000 or more words is not unusual for such localization projects.

Selecting a translation management system

"We want to significantly improve our response capabilities and thus achieve a rapid time-to-market for our solutions," says Sebastian Zientek, director of Technical Documentation in the area of web hosting product development at 1&1. "It quickly became clear to us that there was significant room for improvement, especially in conjunction with our translation management. The implementation of a suitable language technology was to ensure greater efficiency in the generation of texts, faster response options, and, ultimately, a rapid localization of our product portfolios and the customized e-commerce solutions." Thus, after a careful review of various TMSs available on the market, 1&1 chose the Language Server of Across Systems, a centralized TMS solution for all language resources and translation processes within a company. The open-interface design of the Across Language Server made it very easy to integrate the content management system, which the company implemented simultaneously.

Managing terminology using the TMS

With the implementation of the TMS from Across Systems, 1&1 also wanted to improve the quality of the content and achieve a central data pool to deliver uniform results in German, English, French, and Spanish. The main focus was cleaning up the terminology. "Consistent terminology is essential in order to fully utilize the translation technologies," Zientek says. The existing terminology lists based on HyperText Markup Language (HTML) were completely transferred to the Across Language Server and consolidated there. The in-house staff member responsible for the respective language coordinated the terminology with the product managers and all other involved staff members. The nomenclature was standardized, defined, and stored in the Across Systems terminology database along with the corresponding context information and relations. All special terms were categorized in the new system by a separate distinctive classification into standard, synonym, and disallowed words. More than 800 terms have been classified as "disallowed words," meaning words that are not to be used anymore. Transferring all the terminology data into the system means that a user is also able to see terminology that is not to be used. If a staff member attempts to use a disallowed term, the system points this out and he or she can substitute the term defined as the standard, or a suitable, permitted synonym.

Managing localization workflow using the TMS

The translation processes and workflows vary greatly at 1&1 depending on the project and scope. Smaller translation projects are handled directly by the in-house team. For the large, more extensive projects, 1&1 works with external language service providers. At the start of the project, these language service providers are given either the comprehensive text material to be translated or subsequently completed source texts. The editing of the translations also varies greatly: the review is partly conducted by in-house staff members, and partly by the external language service providers. 1&1 leveraged the TMS to directly incorporate all involved parties into the localization process. The TMS helped the company manage the workflows and establish continuity of the processes, and also enabled the company to centralize all language data. According to Zientek, "Today, the external colleagues are just as immediately involved in the translation processes as our internal staff members who sit in the office next door."

CMS–TMS integration

The Across Systems TMS, like some of its competitors, has an open architecture that includes standard interfaces as well as application program interfaces that enable companies to smoothly integrate any third-party systems. At 1&1, because of the direct connection of the CMS to the TMS, translation purchase orders can be initiated directly from the CMS. All data and information relevant for the translation, which also means the relevant context and the metadata, are exchanged across the system level. Such integration has enabled 1&1 to significantly reduce its workload. Six thousand or more individual HTML files may need to be translated for just one project at 1&1. Today, Across TMS's collaboration tool, CrossGrid, facilitates the transmission of all project-relevant data to the language servers at other 1&1 sites or to external language service providers with a simple click of a button. Phone or e-mail inquiries have significantly declined since then. "That became noticeable during the recently implemented e-shop project, which called for the localization of nearly 80,000 words," says the project leader. "The e-mail correspondence was limited to just two e-mails between the language service provider and us. For a similarly sized localization project that took place three years ago, we exchanged almost a thousand e-mails with the service providers and translators."

Efficiency gains via implementing the TMS

Through the optimized translation management, 1&1 has also been able to achieve a significantly shorter time to market with the localization of a recent e-commerce solution. "For the adaptation of the e-shop to the English-speaking market two years ago, we needed about eight months," Zientek remembers. "The complete localization of the application into Spanish that we just finished was ready to be provided to our customers within only seven weeks. That represents a time saving of over 75 percent."

Connecting the CMS and Across Systems TMS also allows 1&1 to fully utilize single-source publishing for multilingual content. Now the company can use one and the same multilingual content for different target media, for online as well as print publications. According to Zientek, "The potential savings are tremendous, and they are leading to extraordinary efficiency gains within my team."

Overall, by automating its localization workflow, 1&1 has been able to simplify its localization process and achieve structured handling of data, and has accelerated the processing of data and tasks, reducing the time to market.

International search engine optimization

International search engine optimization is a process of optimizing an organization's websites and associated processes so that country-specific search engines can assign them higher ranks and make them more accessible to their target customers. SEO for international markets is not the same as local-country-market SEO. When targeting international markets, several issues complicate search engine optimization efforts, including the following

(1) The diversity of languages for which the site must be optimized. Multilingual content and strategic keywords will be needed to optimize the international site. Local search engines generally give preference to local sites in local languages.

(2) A variety of search engines and directories exist globally, and their popularity varies by country. For example, although Google may be the most popular search engine in the United States, in China the local search engine Baidu holds the top spot. Thus a company may have to consider local or country-specific search engine rules when optimizing sites for a specific country.

(3) Country-specific search engines tend to weigh host identity (ID) or IP address and top-level domains (e.g., ".de" for Germany and ".fr" for France) when searching for sites. It may therefore be important to optimize the site via local hosting and country-specific top-level domains, also called country-code top-level domains.

(4) As discussed later in the chapter, the number and quality of links to a site is crucial to its search engine rankings, and an added challenge in international SEO is being able to strategically link the site to country-specific content, local URLs, and local partners.

(5) Search engines look for duplicate content, and, if an organization's international sites are all in the same language showing similar content, this may negatively impact the rankings of such pages. To overcome this issue it is important to trans-

late the content, as pages in different languages are not generally seen as duplicates by various search engines.

(6) Important technical issues related to geolocation, site maps, tags (e.g., title tags, alt tags, language meta tags), the URL address, internationalized domains, file names, etc. also need to be considered. Various tags need to be translated into the local language to ensure that local search engines effectively leverage them for ranking the international site. More details on various tags are discussed in later sections.

(7) International SEO demands specialized skills and people to help companies effectively research and localize the web content and relevant keywords to optimize the site for international markets.

In the following pages these issues are addressed, as well as strategies to handle various international search engine optimization issues.

Search engine optimization definition

SEO is the process of optimizing the design and content of a website and its "link factor" in the hope that it will lead to a higher ranking for some searches carried out by various search engines, increasing the number of visitors to the website and, ultimately, paying customers.

A common understanding in the business world is that 80 percent of business generally comes from 20 percent of the customers. Thus companies can gain strategic advantage by optimizing their efforts to better target and service the 20 percent of their customers responsible for this 80 percent of their business. A similar story plays out on the web, in that a small number of sites that have a high ranking and generally are visible on the first page of search results tend to get the highest traffic and thus a higher ROI. In fact, studies have shown that the structure of the web is actually like a bow tie, with the best-connected sites being located near the "knot" of the tie and getting the highest search rankings. Various search engine optimization strategies can help companies place their sites more centrally on the web so that they can be better noticed by search engines, directories, and potential customers.

Key factors to consider when attempting to improve higher search engine rankings include the proper use of strategic customer-centric and localized keywords; embedding these keywords in strategic locations on the website; following practices of good website design and navigation; using rich, relevant, and updated web content; and, most importantly, linking the site to attain a central position in the bow-tie structure of the web. Notice that there is no one set of tricks to get a site to rank more highly on search engines. Search engine optimization is a mix of techniques and practices that need to be implemented in order to meet the varied criteria of global search engines.

The rest of this chapter provides additional details on a select number of these key factors and practical insights on how to implement them.

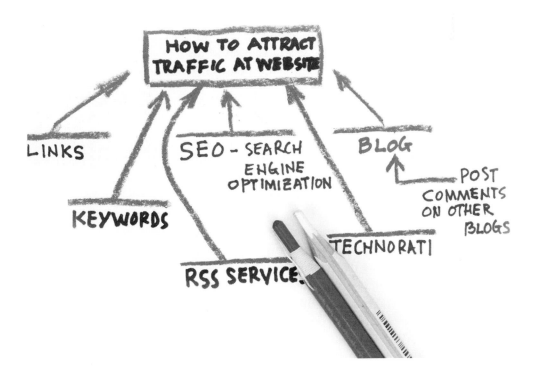

Keywords for local and multilingual sites

"Keywords" are words and phrases that customers type into search engines in order to find the product or service they are seeking. Search engines scan the web for sites that match the customers' search criteria. One of the important tricks to achieve higher search engine rankings, therefore, is to use customer-centric keywords that have been locally researched and are linguistically compliant with search patterns in a specific country. It is not good enough just to have customer-centric and localized keywords; they must also be inserted strategically in the right places (e.g., meta tags and title tags) on the websites. It is also important that the keywords be translated into the local language. Inserting keywords in English for a Russian site will not be very helpful. In fact, local search engines may identify keywords translated into the local language much more readily than if the keywords were not translated. Later in the chapter I discuss strategic keyword placement in greater depth.

However, there are some caveats to this. For example, using *only* the same keywords being used by other established high-ranking sites will lead to minimal results. This is because, when a customer searches using keywords used by top-ranking sites, the probability of the top-ranking sites coming up higher than a less highly ranked site on search is very likely. Thus, beyond creating customer-centric keywords and placing them strategically, companies also need to research the competition for keywords and then decide their keyword selection strategy. This is why SEO is not as simple as it may at first appear.

The following sections offer advice on how to populate a site with the most popular keywords and how to choose strategic keywords to get higher rankings. Here are some techniques and tools to find the most customer-centric keywords.

Head terms and tail terms

Search terms that are short, popular, and generally show higher search volume are called the "head terms." For example, for most localization companies a head term could be "localization" or "translation"; since these terms have high search volumes, most companies tend to use them for SEO.

"Tail terms" are search terms that are very specific; they are generally long phrases and include one or more modifiers – for example, "web globalization certificate from St Louis University." These terms have low search volumes because they are more specific, but if used strategically they can help get high rankings because not many competitors will be using them.

Using a blend of head terms and tail terms can therefore be a good strategy: for home pages, more head terms could be used, while tail terms could be used for specific web pages on the site. Finding tail terms that will resonate with customers is critical. It is always a good idea to have a few focus groups with end users to come up with keyword suggestions.

In addition to talking to customers, there are several other ways to get keyword suggestions on the web.

Keyword suggestion tools

Several automated tools on the market can be used to generate keywords. These tools track search engine volume or have their own search tool bar that generates high-volume keywords. Some of these tools include Google AdWords keyword suggestion tool, http://freekeywords.wordtracker.com, http://compete.com, and Trellian's www .keyworddiscovery.com. Another way of finding various keywords is to look at the source code of competitor sites or sites that rank highly within the industry for a particular search engine. The source code page of the website can be easily viewed by clicking on the "View source" option from the drop-down menu of the tool bar. Several free and paid websites also carry out keyword searches.

Keyword generation does get complicated when optimizing multilingual sites. For keyword search by country, the easiest approach is to look at country-specific engines for their local language keyword recommendation tools. For example, Chinese keywords can be researched at Baidu's keyword tool, http://is.baidu.com/keyword_tool .html, and Russian keywords can be researched at http://wordstat.yandex.ru. Google's keyword tool can also help to select keywords by countries and languages. Another way to supplement the multilingual keyword search is to analyze search term trends by taking advantage of Google Trends, which compares popular search terms by country. Now Baidu also offers search trends in Chinese via its service, Baidu Index. Another technique is looking up keywords in the source pages of country-specific competitor websites and relevant high-ranking sites.

All these methods for searching multilingual keywords are only part of the overall multilingual SEO effort. It is also important to carry out proper research and analysis to ensure the overall relevance of the keywords and translation equivalence of the selected keywords. To generate high-quality multilingual keywords, companies may implement focus groups and other research techniques to come up with the most relevant keywords for a specific country. The aid of translators, localization service providers, and even academics can be sought to generate high-quality and well-researched multilingual keywords. The most important thing at the multilingual keyword research stage is to make sure that the keyword research team has experts or linguists who are native speakers of the language in question and are familiar with the local culture and conventions. It is even necessary to be careful when using English keywords in other English-speaking countries. For example, in the United States people use the word "sweater," but in the United Kingdom people tend to use the term "jumper" instead. A number of such keyword equivalence issues exist, and companies should give serious consideration to them.

Strategic keyword placement

As mentioned earlier, keywords should be customer-centric, well researched, and translated appropriately to reflect local language preference. Keywords can be placed in multiple tags in the source code of a web page. This section describes ways that keywords can be placed in strategic areas.

Meta tags

Meta-elements have significantly less impact on search engine results today than they did in the 1990s, and their utility has declined as search engine robots have become more sophisticated. Meta tags are included in the <HEAD> of an HTML document (see above image). When developing meta tags, the focus should ideally be on the description and the keywords. The description tag will describe what the page is about. Engines that use the meta-description tag will supply the content of this tag when displaying a list of links. The keyword tags help the search engine indexing software categorize the site appropriately, and allow people to find its pages more quickly. Various tools can also automatically generate meta tags – such as that of www.submitexpress.com.

Title tags

The title tag is located on the header of the HTML code and will appear at the very top of the browser. It is good practice to create a succinct statement to capture the customer-centric value proposition to be placed in the title tag. It also helps to punctuate the keywords in title tags with the keywords used in the links, other tags, and web content. Search engines do pay attention to title tags to create a description of the website that will be displayed in their results, and they are an important factor for SEO. Another benefit of having a powerful title tag is that it will be visible to consumers in their bookmarked favorites list if they save the link to their PC, or if they mail a short-cut link to their friends. A memorable title with a positive message will reinforce customer perception of the site, particularly if the title is in the language that the consumer expects to see.

File names and URLs

Generic file names are often used for web pages (e.g., product.html or xyz.html). Using relevant keywords for file names is also proposed as a way to enhance SEO. It is also a good idea to use a URL that reflects customer-centric keywords. However, it is better to keep the URL short and simple, so that customers can remember it and easily type it. Some experts also propose using hyphenated words in the URL and web page file names, as search engines see hyphens as spaces, but using too many hyphens can be construed as spamming. Be very cautious when using hyphens, therefore. The best advice: ensure that the file name and URL are customer-centric.

Header tags

Content in the header tag (a header tag will make the text appear larger and/or bolder than other text on the page) is generally meant to catch attention. In fact, it also catches the attention of the search engines, so it may be a good idea to use keywords in the header tags.

Image tags

Search engines cannot properly read images, thus providing a description of the image using an "Alt" image tag is very useful. Appropriate keywords can be used in the alt tags to describe the image, and this also helps with SEO. In a similar manner to what was discussed above regarding title tags, alt tags are often seen by the consumer as they move the cursor over the page or if images do not display properly. Alt tags should use the language and format that the target consumer expects to see.

Links

When creating hyperlinks on web pages, strategic keywords can be used to further optimize the site. It is also helpful when incoming links to the site have appropriate keywords. Thus, when seeking incoming links, request the external parties to use keywords provided by you. Using keywords in such anchor text can increase the potency of a link exchange program (links are to be discussed later). Finally, check the HTML source code for any errors and validate the source code. A free tool for doing this check is provided by W3C: http://validator.w3.org.

Keyword relevancy and density

Generally, keywords in the title page, the headings, and the first paragraphs are seen more by the search engines and are important for SEO efforts. Keyword relevancy (i.e., choosing keywords that match web page content) is important for successful SEO. If a search engine sees no relevancy between keywords and the web content, then it might discount the content of the site, and sometimes even flag the site for potentially practicing keyword spamming. Some practices that can be flagged as unethical include stuffing the meta tags with several keywords, stuffing the site with keywords, and populating the site with keywords that are not visible to web users. Be very careful to avoid keyword spamming, or unnecessarily adding keywords that do not match the web page content. Moreover, do not create several duplicate landing pages, or fill tags with tons of keywords. Checking the webmaster guidelines of search engines is also a good idea. For example, the Google Webmaster guidelines provide web design and content guidelines, technical guidelines, and quality guidelines on how Google indexes and ranks various sites.

> ### BMW German site blacklisted by Google, 2006
>
> Google noticed that the BMW.de page was using blocks of text with repeated key search words such as "Neuwagen," which means "new car" in German. When a user visited this keyword-rich page he or she would be automatically redirected to another page with less text and more pictures, which was more attractive than the page the crawler saw, but would have scored less in Google's PageRank system.

Robot text file

If it is necessary to create duplicate pages for other countries or create landing sites with similar content, a robot text file can be useful. It can keep the page from being penalized for spamming a search engine with a series of overly similar pages. A robots.txt file provides restrictions to search engine robots that crawl the web. Even if a site does not have any duplicate content or any other such content to be blocked, it is still good to have a robots.txt file, since it can act as an invitation into the site. However, some search engines might penalize a site if the robots.txt file is set up to block too much. Information on creating a robot text file can be found under the Google Webmaster guidelines. Various SEO software packages (e.g., WebCEO) can create robot.txt files.

Keyword density

This is a combination of the number of times a keyword or a keyword phrase, in proportion with other words, appears on a web page. Various keyword density analyzer tools are available free of charge, including keyworddensity.com, webuildpages.com, and googlerankings.com. These keyword tools can analyze the words and phrases that are used most on the website and can also provide a detailed report on the numbers and density of the words. This tool can also check a website's position on Google for each of these keywords.

For international sites

Finally, for international and multilingual websites, translated web pages and country-code top-level domains, such as ".de" for Germany and ".fr" for France, will work better for SEO, as will the use of multilingual or internationalized domain names (see box). "One common misconception is that ccTLDs can only be assigned to web sites physically located in the suffix country. This is not necessarily true. While most countries have specific rules surrounding exactly who can register domains using their suffix and for what purpose, regulations in some countries are more stringent than others. While it is true that in certain cases, the registrant must be an individual/company located within the country of the country suffix they wish to register, there are no restrictions in other cases" (www.brainpulse.com).

Internationalized domain names

Imagine if, each time a British internet user entered an e-mail or website address, he or she was required to include a Chinese or Cyrillic character. For millions of non-English speakers around the world, this is precisely what they experience when they use the internet, as the domain name system is unable to fully accommodate their local language (Michael Geist, www.minc.org). An internationalized domain name (IDN) or multilingual domain is an internet domain name that contains one or more non-ASCII characters. Such domain names could contain letters with diacritics, such as accent marks or characters from non-Latin scripts such as Arabic, Hebrew, Chinese, or Hindi. The sites www.icann.org and www.minc .org also include information related to internationalized domain names.

Domain names are managed by domain name registry organizations. The Internet Corporation for Assigned Names and Numbers is a private, non-profit technical coordination body for the internet's naming and numbering systems (www.icann.org). The Internet Network Information Center website is operated by ICANN to provide the public information regarding internet domain name registration services (www .internic.net). Global domain names are managed under a hierarchy headed by the Internet Assigned Numbers Authority (IANA) (www.iana.org). Country-code top-level domains are delegated by IANA to national registries such as DENIC in Germany, or Nominet in the United Kingdom. Rules governing the acquisition of ccTLDs can be found at InterNIC or the national registries of various countries.

Companies with too few resources to create several translated pages and buy ccTLDs, but that still want to get listed on international search engines, should at least create one translated page and have all the relevant keywords translated and strategically placed. It can then submit this translated page to country-specific search engines and the country-specific sites similar to Google and Yahoo! A company must also thoroughly understand the webmaster guidelines of the major international search engines it is targeting. For instance, if the company is targeting China, where Baidu is a major search engine, it should make sure its Chinese site is optimized in accordance with the best practices outlined by Baidu. Baidu uses simplified Chinese characters,[5] for example, so if the site also uses simplified Chinese it may be listed more highly on Baidu. A company also should research processes for submitting its page to international sites. For example, here is the link to submit sites to Baidu: www.baidu.com/search/url_submit.html.

[5] There are two forms of Chinese characters: simplified and traditional. Simplified characters are standard in mainland China, and traditional characters are used primarily in Taiwan and Hong Kong.

Companies can purchase various SEO software products for keyword generation, analysis, and placement; two of them are trellian.com and WebCEO.com.[6]

Linking strategies for local and international sites

Linking is another important strategy for SEO. Once a site has been built with customer-centric keywords and content and has been optimized for search engines, it is time to start looking for quality links. Linking from one site to another is, in essence, why the internet was created. The "link factor" is the number and quality of links coming to a particular site. Search engines, especially Google, take the link factor very seriously, so links are really a cost-effective way to achieve SEO. A successful linking strategy has the potential to place a website right into the center of the bow-tie structure of the web.

Here are some tips to help companies plan and execute successful linking strategies.

(1) Make a list of the most successful sites in the company's business category or of the company's competitors. Investigate how these sites are reached from other sites, to understand how they have achieved their high ranking in search engines such as Google and Yahoo! To find which websites are linking to these successful sites, search for corresponding "linked from" sites in Google and Yahoo! as follows:
- *in Google search box, type*: link: website address;
- *in Yahoo! search box, type*: linkdomain: website address.

See below the screenshots of searches for incoming links to CNN on Google and Yahoo! Then check if the websites to be approached for links are listed on Yahoo! and Open Directory, to ensure that the sites are relevant to the company's site and may be approached for a link.

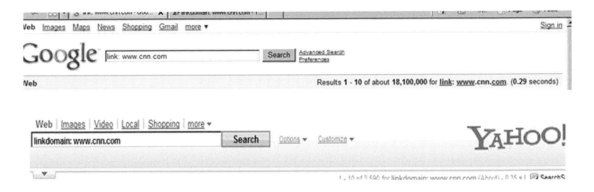

(2) Companies can also look at www.alexa.com, which uses its tool bar to rank sites, etc. It also provides detailed linkage information on the site. The Google "PageRank"

---

[6] This is not to be taken as an endorsement of these companies.

tool bar is another good way to determine if a web page to request a link from has high ranking. Google's "PageRank Checker" tool (www.prchecker.info) is another option.

(3) There are several ways to find the contact person for a website, which will be a necessary step when requesting links. Generally, websites have webmaster information available. Alexa.com also has contact information. Information on the owner of the website and contact details can also be found via the WHOIS database; www.networksolutions.com has a tool that can do it, or check at www.whois.net.

(4) Links coming from ".edu" and ".gov" domain-named pages are considered high-quality links by search engines, and are likely weighted more heavily than links from other sites.

(5) The anchor text is sometimes called "link text," as it is the text that a user clicks on to go to a link; it may be the URL or something else. For inbound links, this is one of the most important factors in SEO, as anchor text is usually used to indicate the subject matter of the page that it links to. Suggesting the best, most relevant keywords to include in anchor text to anyone linking to the target site can be useful.

(6) What will encourage other sites to link to the site? Sites with a high link factor have relevant content for the target market, are content-rich, and provide valuable information to users. Sites that have low relevant content and rely too much on Flash and databases tend to have a low link factor. Database-driven sites constantly change, and there are no static pages to link to.

(7) Industry media, associations, and trade shows can be helpful to find relevant resources to link to and get links from.

(8) Join newsgroups and chats related to your industry and promote the site there, if it is relevant. Companies can get links from various industry blogs or community pages, or they can get links from Facebook, MySpace, YouTube, LinkedIn, etc. Social bookmarking sites such as dig.com, Yahoo! Buzz, Delicious, etc. can also be helpful.

(9) Publishing an article or articles can also help generate visibility in the industry and increase the number of links.

(10) Creating a special link page so that people can easily find it and offering reciprocal links to webmasters from this page will encourage them to add a link to their own site.

Getting international links

The procedure above also works to find high-quality links in different countries of interest. For example, to find good-quality links on French search engines, the best way is to check the top French engine and Google.fr and Yahoo! France. It is also worth checking Alexa.com for top French websites. Mseo.com has a list of various search engines and directories in different countries ("Foreign search engine directory"), which can be used to find the search engines in a particular country.

Webcertain.com publishes a global search and social report in which it lists prominent search engines and social media tools by countries; it is available for free download at www.webcertain.com/WebCertain_Search_and_Social_Report_2010.pdf. Local blogs can be a useful source of links too. It is also worth looking into getting links from various international social media sites (www.internationalindustrialseo.com/international-social-marketing):

(1) Bebo (primarily in the United Kingdom, but with US and Canada audiences as well);
(2) Orkut (Google's social marketing site, extremely popular in Brazil);
(3) Xiaonei (China's very popular Facebook-like site);
(4) Kaixin001 (China's most popular social marketing and media website);
(5) Odnoklassniki (a Russian social network similar to Facebook);
(6) SkyRock (more popular in France than Facebook and MySpace combined; it targets francophone areas, but is also available in English, German, and Spanish);
(7) StudiVZ (a German social network so similar to Facebook that it has been sued for copying key Facebook design and features);
(8) Sonico (this site was only a year old as of early 2011, but was already one of the biggest websites of all in Latin America, and intends to launch a new Portuguese version soon); and
(9) Wamba (this Spanish website targets all of Europe, and it is hoping to reach Latin America as well).

A local IP address can also improve search engine rankings. Search engines and visitors will be able to see the IP address of a website's domain, and will use it in their ranking algorithm. Although it may be more expensive to have a site hosted in the target region, a local IP address will increase its relevancy in foreign searches. They will consider a site hosted in Germany, for example, more relevant to a German user than one hosted in Canada. Companies should ask their web hosts what they do in terms of foreign hosting and whether they have hosting ability in the target region (www.internationalindustrialseo.com/international-seo-a-quick-start). However, note that, when considering website or database hosting in another country, it is advisable to thoroughly investigate the legal, security, data privacy, and tax impact of collecting and storing data in that country.

As m-commerce (mobile commerce) is expanding far more rapidly in Europe and Asia than in the United States, companies should ensure that their sites are mobile compatible and can be easily viewed on mobile browsers.

Several companies can help with both local and international SEO. Here are a few examples (again, this is not to be taken implying a recommendation for any of the companies):

• www.mcanerin.com;
• www.webcertain.com;

- www.mseo.com; and
- www.ecreativeworks.com/international_seo.htm.

Various localization companies, such as Lionbridge, Acclaro, Conversis, and Globalization Partners International (GPI), can help with translation and multilingual keyword generation.

Some questions that Google Webmaster tools recommend when selecting an SEO company include the following.

(1) Can you show me examples of your previous work and share some success stories?
(2) Do you follow the Google Webmaster guidelines?
(3) Do you offer any online marketing services or advice to complement your organic search business?
(4) What kind of results do you expect to see and in what time frame? How do you measure your success?
(5) What's your experience in my industry?
(6) What's your experience in my country/city?
(7) What's your experience developing international sites?
(8) What are your most important SEO techniques?
(9) How long have you been in business?
(10) How can I expect to communicate with you? Will you share with me all the changes that you make to my site and provide detailed information about your recommendations and the reasoning behind them?

Case study: Marina Bay Sands, Singapore, developing a multilingual web presence[7]

Marina Bay Sands (MBS) opened in April 2010, with an official opening celebration in June. It was developed to become a premier entertainment destination in Singapore, with its vibrant diversity of attractions and facilities. The vision was to build an integrated development that is timeless, a landmark that possesses a distinct identity that will distinguish Singapore from other cities. The property's web presence needed to be just as distinct and inspiring. The site needed to be available in seven relevant languages and to be easily found in search engines by potential customers around the world.

Specific project objectives included:

- to assess MBS's existing website, its effective product display, and its existing reusable assets and architecture;

---

[7] This case material was contributed by Globalization Partners International, Sid Lee, and Marina Bay Sands. The companies highlighted in the case are relevant to this case and do not imply any endorsement of a specific company.

- to consider website design best practices, requirements, and essentials, and to form a guide for the redesign of the MBS website;
- to evaluate the leading websites of direct competitors and the hotel industry in general, and to identify assets that MBS requires, and areas to avoid;
- to devise a timeline of phases for the development and deployment of the MBS multilingual websites to best suit the needs of the various areas of the property and the interests of the consumer; and
- to ensure that the technology and navigation tools selected comply with supporting multiple languages and maximizing search optimization in order to drive traffic to the new sites.

With these objectives, Marina Bay Sands sought out a multilingual web development team comprising internal members and external vendors:

- *Marina Bay Sands' internal team (strategy and planning)* The internal team provided the overall strategic planning and coordination with all external vendors. The team initially undertook an extensive assessment of the technical, architectural, and creative execution aspects and laid out parameters for project requirements and the selection of external vendors. Thereafter, the team worked closely with the vendors to ensure that project requirements were met and that web design met positioning, branding, and localization objectives. The team was also involved in content development and overall project management.
- *Sid Lee (design)* This creative agency provided the creative team for the design, artistic direction, ideation, and creative quality assurance aspects, and for electronic production (video and sound).
- *Globalization Partners International (localization, CMS implementation, and global SEO)* This globalization services provider managed the development of the multilingual content, including the initial website globalization strategy, glossary development, translation and copywriting, country-specific search engine optimization, website localization quality assurance and testing, and the integration of a content management system and the associated localization workflows. GPI provided project management via the translation services portal of its Globalization Project Management Suite (GPMS).

This multidisciplinary team of external vendors was brought together to design, develop, and deploy a new multilingual web presence driven by a CMS for the Marina Bay Sands complex in Singapore. The team was responsible for developing content in English, Indonesian, Korean, Japanese, simplified Chinese, traditional Chinese, and Thai. In the following paragraphs, the case study outlines how various project requirements were met and how they facilitated the development and deployment of multilingual web content for MBS.

Development of user-centric design

Most users do not really read web pages. Instead, they scan text for specific pieces of information in a process called information retrieval. With user-centered design (UCD), the usefulness (relevance) and usability (ease of use) of websites is improved by considering information retrieval and other factors. Accordingly, the design team asked the following questions.

- Who are the users of this website?
- What are the tasks and goals of these users?
- What experience levels do the users have with computers, the web, and interfaces like the one on this site?
- What hardware, software, and browsers do the users have?
- How can the design of this interface facilitate users' cognitive processes? How do the users discover and correct errors?
- What functions do the users need from this interface? How do they currently perform these tasks? Why do the users currently perform these tasks the way they do?
- What information might the users need, and in what form do they need it?
- What do users expect from this website? How do users expect this interface to work?

The guidelines for user-centric web page design that the team strived to follow included these.

Visibility Making important elements such as navigational aids highly visible, so that users can determine at a glance what they can and cannot do. Visibility helps users predict the effects of their actions. The aesthetics of the interface play an important role in communicating information and tone to users.

Memory load Making screen elements meaningful and consistent across the site so as to reduce memory load. In this way, users do not have to remember what elements mean from one page to another. It is important to relate new items and functions to ones the user already knows.

Feedback Providing immediate feedback when a user performs an action. For example, when the user clicks a button, something on the screen should change so that the user knows the system has registered the action.

Accessibility Users need to find information quickly and easily; therefore, it is important to offer users a few ways to find information, such as navigational elements, search functions, or a site map. However, it is best to offer only a few options at a time, in order to avoid confusion. Information should be organized in small, digestible pieces using a schema or hierarchy that is meaningful to the user. Finally, it should be easy for users to skim, so it is important to provide clues that allow users to find the information by scanning rather than reading.

Orientation/navigation Helping users orient themselves by providing navigational clues, such as descriptive links, a site map, obvious ways to exit every page, and clearly visible elements on each page that inform users where they are in relation to other pages and how to navigate to other pages.

Errors Minimizing user errors by avoiding situations in which users are likely to make mistakes.

Satisfaction Making the site pleasant to use and view. Users' satisfaction with the interface influences their perception of the site's ease of use, their motivation for learning how to use the site, and their confidence in the reliability of the information it contains.

Legibility Making the text easy to read.

Language Making the site easier to use and understand by using concise language and simple sentence structure, everyday words instead of jargon or technical terms, active voice and active verbs, and verbs instead of noun strings.

Web globalization strategy

The overall web globalization strategy for Marina Bay Sands included other requirements to ensure:

(1) that target market users in the Asia-Pacific region as well as globally were served country-specific, search-engine-optimized content in seven languages with the ability to add additional languages;

(2) 24/7, optimized hosting from a locally hosted infrastructure;

(3) that the web content management platform utilized fully supported storing, authoring, and publishing multilingual/localized content; and

(4) that workflows and teams were established to support daily updates in all languages to the dynamic site.

Specifically, this included the following.

- *Internationalization and localization support* The selection of the Ektron web content management system addressed most web localization requirements, as the platform supports multilingual websites, character sets, and site management and uses the Microsoft .NET platform. The CMS provides support for the XLIFF file format, allowing the exchange of localization data and enabling translators to concentrate on the text to be translated without worrying about text layout. Many CMSs today offer varying degrees of multi-language site support.

- *Managing multilingual content workflow* With daily updates for events and attractions, the MBS website needed to be able to publish new content every day in English and six other languages. To enable localization workflow, an experienced provider of website globalization was selected as a partner, and the provider's suite of globalization tools was utilized to enhance global collaboration, project management, and service delivery. Globalization Partners International's global teams of in-country translators, copywriters, web localization specialists, and SEO specialists collaborated globally via their GPMS translation services portal. GPMS provided project scheduling and budget reporting, management for all localizable resources, project archiving, quality control functions, status reporting, and translation memory management.

- *Integrating the web CMS* GPI provided the implementation for all the design from Sid Lee into the CMS. This included working from original Photoshop files to use as base templates for the creation of the html/aspx templates for the site.
- *MBS and GPI developed the translation workflow, leveraging a connector for the CMS.* Every time a user modifies a page/content, or new content is created, the connector notifies the translation resources about this new content. The content is stored on a translation queue. A quote is created, and, after the quote has been approved by MBS or once MBS confirms the translation of the new/modified content, the content is sent to translators for translation. When the content is back, it is pushed from GPI's translation project management tool (GPMS) into the CMS using the same connector. The connector also lets translation resources pick individual pages for rush translations and put them back, outside the normal translation workflow.

Multilingual search engine optimization

The multilingual search engine optimization of the Marina Bay Sands' websites was addressed by the client and partner teams. Sid Lee and MBS completed the English-language SEO, and GPI and MBS performed the country-specific (multilingual) SEO. Global websites need to make sure that the English and new target language websites are well received and well visited by the intended audiences around the globe. It is highly recommended that as part of any new website design and development project, and/or as part of a website globalization project, the company performs some initial and ongoing search engine marketing (SEM). This could include both organic search engine optimization and search engine advertising (SEA), such as pay per click (PPC), paid inclusions, or contextual advertising. Whether a company has an SEM agency or in-house team providing English and/or multilingual SEM services, these tasks will help the company achieve better visibility in both its home-market search engines and in country-specific search engines. This will lead to increased traffic and ROI with its target-language-version websites. Marina Bay Sands addressed global SEM requirements by including both organic SEO and SEA. Some specific activities included:

- comprehensive website translation and localization;
- English and multilingual keyword phrase research, refinement, and localization;
- English and multilingual search engine optimization and copywriting of the main site content;

- English and multilingual SEO of meta tags, titles, alt tags, header tags, HTML, etc.;
- submissions to major locale (in-country) and international search engines;
- website traffic and keywords ranking reporting;
- PPC campaign content localization; and
- PPC country-specific campaign management.

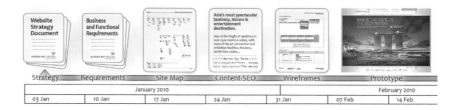

Conclusion

Marina Bay Sands was able to meet its time frame of about nine weeks to develop and then launch its multilingual websites. The project started on January 3, 2010, and was finished on April 3, 2010. The site were launched on April 11, 2010.

Chapter summary

- International website optimization involves the collaborative management of people, processes, capabilities, documents, and technologies in order to effectively synergize the four primary activities in the web globalization value chain.
- The content management system can help companies gain significant efficiencies, as CMS can help leverage, share, separate, and localize various website building blocks such as content, templates, layout, and pages for developing multiple international sites.
- When selecting a CMS for international website management, it is important to make sure that the CMS not only fulfills the needs of overall enterprise management but also takes into consideration the web globalization function and multilingual support.
- A translation management system is important for automating the localization workflow. The TMS can handle tasks related to managing the localization workflow, such as

managing translation resources, sending jobs to translators or localization service providers, tracking the status of localization jobs, leveraging translation memory, utilizing terminology assets, etc.

- The integration of content and translation management systems allows the various processes in the web globalization value chain, starting from content creation and going to content deployment, to be automated and optimized.
- International search engine optimization is a process of optimizing websites and associated processes so that country-specific search engines can assign them higher ranks and make them prominently accessible to target customers.
- When performing international SEO, important processes to consider include using an effective strategy for implementing multilingual keywords, increasing the link factor of international sites, and listing the sites on country-specific search engines.

REFERENCES

Csíkszentmihályi, Mihály 1975. *Beyond Boredom and Anxiety.* Jossey-Bass.

Rosenlund, Dave 2006. "Integrating globalization into content life cycle," in *Content Management: Getting Started Guide.* Multilingual Computing: 8–10.

Sen, Prabir 2007. "Key benefits of content management," Ezine Articles, March 5, http://ezinearticles.com/?Key-Benefits-of-Content-ManagementRid=472424.

Toon, A., Drahaim, A., Lommel, A., and Cadieux, P. 2007. *Managing Global Content: Best Practices Guide.* LISA.

Trotter, Paul 2006. "Single-source content management," *MultiLingual* October/November: 61–4.

9 Assessing web globalization efforts

Chapter objectives

- Provide a broad overview of various web usability issues.
- Present challenges associated with enhancing website usability for different countries/locales.
- Provide a general outline of web usability guidelines.
- Outline the importance of using web analytics to constantly improve international website usability.
- Present the technology acceptance model as a basis for measuring international website acceptance.
- Provide empirical research highlights into how cultural customization impacts website acceptance and usage.
- Offer a localization score card to help companies measure their website localization efforts.
- Outline twenty-five ways to reduce web globalization costs.

Global website usability issues

Before addressing specific ways to assess web globalization efforts, it is important to outline some basic measures of web usability. After all, no matter what goals a website's creators may have set for it, the website must allow consumers to interact with the site before those goals can be achieved. Web usability analysis is important for any website development effort, and should be a part of overall website assessment.

In simple terms, website usability can be defined as the ease with which users can find, understand, and use information that is displayed on the website (Keevil, 1998). A generally accepted usability definition is presented by ISO 9241:[1] "The effectiveness, efficiency, and satisfaction with which specified users achieve specified goals in particular environments." In tactical terms, web usability is a rating of how easy it is for the user to manipulate website features to accomplish desired goals, such as shopping, finding information, filling out forms, completing order forms, interacting on discussion board or forums, etc. Thus website usability measures the performance of the website in terms of its ability to engage users and allow them to accomplish specified goals.

[1] www.w3.org/2002/Talks/0104-usabilityprocess/slide3–0.html.

Website usability

A website's usability is a measure of the performance of the site in terms of its ability to engage users and allow them to accomplish specified goals. In tactical terms, web usability is a rating of how easy it is for the user to manipulate website features to accomplish such desired goals as shopping, finding information, filling out forms, completing order forms, interacting on discussion board or forums, etc.

However, usability perceptions tend to vary from culture to culture. A US website may receive a high ranking on usability from US customers, but Arabic-speaking customers from Saudi Arabia may find the same site extremely difficult to use. Differing perceptions of usability between cultures have many causes, and some of them were discussed in previous chapters; to reiterate, some usability challenges attributed to differing cross-cultural perceptions include the following (see also Figure 9.1).

(1) Spatial orientation and navigation varies across languages. For example, since Arabic is read from right to left, an Arabic user may find an American-English language site difficult to use.

(2) Studies have shown that people's web page viewing patterns are related to their cognitive style or their approach to organizing and representing information. For example, a study by Dong and Lee (2008) finds that Chinese and Korean online users tend to scan the whole web page and show nonlinear scanning patterns, whereas American web users tend to focus on information groups and categories and tend to follow a sequential reading pattern.

(3) Icons, symbols, indexes, and other signs tend to be culturally determined, and thus may not be interpreted the same way, which could decrease website usability.

(4) Colors are interpreted differently. Carlson and McLoughlin (2010) show that a green arrow is used to depict an upward financial market trend in the United States, while in Taiwan and Hong Kong a red arrow shows an upward financial market trend.

(5) Web design characteristics also differ between countries and may pose usability challenges. For example, some common characteristics of Japanese web design include big product images, the use of smiling faces, the extensive use of interactive graphics and 3D images, and the use of colors to express emotions.[2]

(6) The way that postal codes, dates, times, and other measurements are used is another topic that varies by country and can pose usability challenges.

(7) Differences in consumer behavior may also pose usability challenges. For example, consumers from high-uncertainty-avoidance cultures need extensive navigational guidelines, and research has shown that websites from such cultures use site maps, navigational simulations, graphics, and other methods more extensively to enhance navigation.

---

[2] www.jay-han.com/2010/04/02/the-common-characteristics-of-japan-web-design.

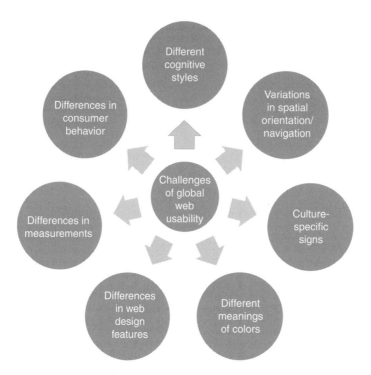

Figure 9.1 Global usability challenges

Besides these broader usability challenges for international websites, several culture-specific issues can also complicate global usability. Cultural issues can be investigated in greater depth in relation to content type, content presentation, content structure, content flow, and content processing and interpretation. For example, when designing sites for high-power-distance cultures, it is important to highlight the titles of important people in the company. In high-power-distance cultures such as China and India, users like to see detailed organizational charts to help them navigate and find information on organization hierarchy. Website usability therefore becomes a much broader challenge when a company plans to meet diverse global consumer expectations. Thus there is all the more reason to create well-localized international websites that pay special attention to culturally customizing the user interface and the content. In the next sections I provide some generic measures of web usability, and then proceed to assessing web localization efforts.

Web usability guidelines

A vast body of research exists on website usability. Various website usability checklists have been developed, and various frameworks have been proposed. For example, Jakob Nielsen's book *Designing Web Usability* (2000) is standard reading for those working on web usability. It is beyond the scope of this book to go into detail on the various aspects of web usability assessment, but an overview of important web usability parameters is presented.

The International Organization for Standardization has created detailed principles of website usability under ISO 9241 (part 151) standards. These principles include factors that impact website usability, such as:

- the objectives and goals of the website, and the target audience;
- the organization of the website relating to its structure, page layout, navigation, and search functions;
- the presentation of information to enhance user interaction;
- the speed and accessibility of the website; and
- the international readiness of the website.

Another set of web usability guidelines, elaborated in a study by Agarwal and Venkatesh (2002), includes the Microsoft Usability Guidelines, or MUG. The MUG prescribes guidelines around five broad areas.

- *Content* This criterion deals with the issue of how pertinent, current, and detailed the content depicted on the website is to the end user.
- *Ease of use* This criterion deals with how well the website is organized around the needs of its end user and the extent to which the website interacts with the user.
- *Promotion* This criterion is not directly related to website design but assesses how well the site is advertised and search engine optimization is used to drive traffic.
- *Made for the medium* This criterion deals with the extent to which the website is personalized to meet end user expectations.
- *Emotion* This criterion relates to how the site emotionally interacts with the end user to create user interest, challenge, trust, and a state of flow.

Some common parameters based on various web usability guidelines include navigational ease; the accessibility of the content; the download speed of the website; the website's layout and organization; the appearance and presentation of the content; the currency, usefulness, and relevance of the content to the end user; website interactivity and responsiveness; website security and credibility; purchase facilitation features on the website; customer feedback mechanisms; and website personalization features.[3]

Beyond these web usability parameters, companies also need to be aware of issues that can be detrimental to web usability. Cappel and Huang (2007) outline several common web design choices that should, ideally, be minimized or avoided.

---

[3] Studies consulted for this section include those by Agarwal and Venkatesh (2002), Palmer (2002), Tarafdar and Zhang (2005), Cappel and Huang (2007), and ISO (2008).

- *Splash screens* These are sometimes elaborate and take time to load, causing the user to have to wait for the content. If the website is heavy and the internet connection is slow, the user may lose interest rapidly.
- *Horizontal scrolling* Sometimes the use of frames or a lack of proper testing result in a site that needs horizontal scrolling to fully view the content. This can be cumbersome and confusing.
- *Self-link on home page* This is a common error, in which a web page includes an active link to itself; as a result, clicking on this link merely reloads the same page.
- *Text links not underlined or in blue* Users cannot recognize this text as a hyperlink, which creates confusion. Sometimes links are also placed on pictures and graphics, and users may not realize that they are links. Such "mystery meat"[4] navigation techniques are not recommended.
- *Text link color does not change* If this happens, the user will not know if the link has already been clicked on or not. This can, again, lead to confusion and browsing discomfort.
- *Hyperlinked company logo missing* If the company logo with the homepage hyperlink is missing from internal pages, users have to find other ways to go back to the homepage. This leads to cognitive stress and is not a good practice.
- *Lack of a breadcrumb trail* A good way to enhance navigational ease, a breadcrumb trail allows the user to see the succession of links or pages he or she has browsed. Including a breadcrumb trail enhances navigation; not having one can cause frustration.
- *Missing site search function or FAQ/help section* If these are missing, users find navigating and searching for content more difficult.

Following established web usability guidelines can help companies create better end user experiences, which leads to enhanced website performance and effectiveness.

While designing the website and testing its usability, companies should also keep users with disabilities in mind. W3C's Web Accessibility Initiative (WAI) provides Web Content Accessibility Guidelines (WCAG) (www.w3.org/TR/WCAG20) to help web designers create content that is accessible to people with disabilities.

Web analytics for international web assessment

Web analytics is an important assessment activity that complements usability testing by measuring, collecting, analyzing, storing, and reporting clickstream data on an ongoing basis. Clickstream data is the electronic footprint of an online user's web activity. In other words, the clickstream is the succession of clicks that the user made during

---

[4] Vincent Flanders coined the term "mystery meat," which generally refers to navigational hyperlinks that are hidden or difficult to discern. More web usability information can be found in his book *Web Pages that Suck* (Flanders, 1998).

a web-browsing session. Web analytics serves as a feedback loop to the web usability process by providing valuable clickstream data for analyzing web usage patterns and rectifying any navigational blocks. Clickstream data collection can start as soon as users start browsing a company's web pages. The clickstream analysis can help people investigate the web pages that users access and browse, how much time they spend on each web page, what items and links they click during their visit, and the sequence of click activities that leads to the final exit from the website. Clickstream data can therefore provide useful insights into how site visitors browse a website and what pages and links they click most often, or what links and pages are posing navigational challenges. Improving the web browsing experience for end users is an ongoing task, and clickstream data measurement and assessment is a crucial part of that process.

From an international perspective, web analytics is crucial to understanding international online user behavior. By analyzing clickstream data along with other web analytics, the following insights can be gathered in terms of a company's international website efforts.

- The data provides an understanding of which local search engines, websites, social media, and even mobile interfaces send the most web traffic to the country-specific sites. Such information can be useful for search engine optimization and marketing efforts.
- Clickstream data can also show how web visitors find country-specific sites from the main company website. For example, do they take advantage of a global gateway page, or do they type the URL of the country site or country-code top-level domain directly, or do they click on an international sites link or another global navigation feature that the main site may have, such as language links, maps, and flags? Such analysis of global navigation behavior can help companies understand what aspects of their global navigation web structure are working and what aspects are presenting navigational challenges.

- Web analytics can prove a useful technique for understanding which products, services, promotions, and other marketing offers do well in certain countries. Such customer feedback, via web analytics, can prove useful to further localizing the product and service selection and customizing marketing offers for various countries.

- Clickstream data can also show aspects of a site that are more popular in various countries. For example, web analytics can show which pages are most visited by country. Web analytics can also reveal country-specific usage of web navigational features such as site maps, search boxes, back and forward buttons, breadcrumb trails, icon-based hyperlinks, navigational tabs, simulations, FAQs, and other features. Information can also be gathered on the popularity of community features, e-shopping, user-generated content, types of customer support, and other content.

- As mentioned in previous chapters, culture plays an important role in how consumers perceive content, communicate, and behave. Web analytics can provide valuable insights into how web navigation behavior differs between countries. For example, in high-context cultures, individuals respond better to graphics and images with implied meaning; in low-context cultures, individuals respond better to clear and explicit communication. Thus web analytics can be useful for discovering if consumers from high-context cultures are using more graphic-oriented navigational features than consumers from low-context countries. In fact, web analytics can provide useful insights in relation to how international customers are responding to different navigational schemes, colors, icons, symbols, spatial orientations, etc. A research study of 229 North American and 139 European online users on B2B websites found that user preferences differed geographically. According to this study, the quality of information is ranked as more important to European users than to North American users, and usability is more important to North American users than to European users (Chakraborty, Srivastava, and Warren, 2005). Web analytics can prove beneficial for understanding such cross-national differences in online behavior and fine-tuning web localization efforts.

- Clickstream data can also provide unique insights in terms of optimizing country-specific investments. Clickstream data in conjunction with other sources of information can be used to further justify increased localization investment, or perhaps even divestment if the returns on investment do not look promising. For example, clickstream data may show that a certain country sends a high amount of traffic onto a particular site but that the eventual conversion rate (e.g., the number of visitors who eventually purchase products) is low. In light of this information, a company may further investigate the reasons for low conversion, such as low consumer purchasing power, competition in the market, or lack of browsing comfort.

- Clickstream data may be complemented by geo-demographic data, transaction history, and other customer data to fine-tune international online targeting and segmentation efforts.

- Finally, web analytics can prove very useful in terms of assessing the impact of incremental localization and cultural customization efforts. For example, longitudinal clickstream data can be collected prior to and after certain web localization enhancements and can help measure the effectiveness of such efforts.

The two common techniques for capturing web analytics data are web server log analysis and page tagging. The log files on the servers keep a record of every time a visitor requests a file from the website. These log files can be analyzed via various log file analyzers on the market. Another technique is page tagging, which involves the insertion of a tracking code into web pages by placing a small invisible image using a Java script. When a visitor's browser successfully loads a tagged page, the software records the page tag on the site's server, and this action can be read from the server files (Wilson, 2010). Some of the companies providing web analytics solutions are Coremetrics, Google, Lyris, Omniture, and Webtrends. Companies with several international sites should ensure that the web analytics solution they use is capable of centralizing all efforts across multiple sites. For example, according to a case study by Webtrends, its web analytics solutions helped Nestlé achieve centralization so as to "uniformly measure and evaluate the performance of its websites and the success of its campaigns, as well as compare performance in different countries based on global benchmarks and standards."[5]

Measuring international website acceptance

Web usability testing is different from usability guidelines, which were described above. Web usability testing in the context of this chapter is the measurement of users' perceptions of a website's effectiveness and efficiency, and their overall satisfaction with the website. It should be noted that internationalization and localization testing, which were discussed in previous chapters, are separate testing activities that need to be performed before doing website usability testing. In an international context, companies need a web usability testing framework that is not context dependent and can measure international online user perceptions of website effectiveness. Such a framework should also be flexible enough to incorporate the measurement of cultural adaptation to determine whether the website meets end user cultural expectations. See also Table 9.1.

The technology acceptance model (TAM)

One of the most tested and widely used models for measuring technology acceptance is the technology acceptance model, which was first proposed by Davis (1989). This

---

[5] www.webtrends.com/upload/cs_Nestle.pdf.

Table 9.1 Constructs used to measure international website acceptance

- *Perceived ease of use (PEOU)* measures the degree to which an individual finds the task of using the website effortless. It relates to clear organization, logical flow, and navigational ease.
- *Perceived usefulness (PU)* measures the degree to which an individual perceives that the website provides useful information to accomplish the task at hand. It relates to quality, usefulness, presentation, and relevancy of content.
- *Attitude toward the site* measures the general sense of favorability when interacting with the website. It relates to satisfaction with the content and willingness to engage with the website.
- *Behavioral intention on the site* is a broad measure that assesses a consumer's willingness to engage in the behavior intended by the marketer. A consumer's intention to make a purchase on the site can be measured, which could be a proxy for eventual purchase behavior.
- *Perception of cultural adaptation* measures how congruent to the local culture and subjective norms the website is perceived to be by local users.

---

model has been tested in international contexts and found to be a useful way of measuring international online user acceptance of websites, as well as of assessing the effect of cultural adaptation on website acceptance (Singh, Fassott, Chao, and Hoffmann, 2006) (see Figure 9.2). TAM provides one of the closest ways to measure whether the technology user will take the action that the marketer wants the user to take. For example, if a company wants to measure whether a Brazilian user will purchase from its newly localized Brazilian site, TAM can help the company test that in a lab setting, and provides a proxy for actual purchase behavior.

Basically, the model posits that, if the user finds a website or technology easy to use and also finds it useful, then he or she will have a more favorable attitude toward it and a higher likelihood of accepting or using it. Along with my co-researchers I have tested TAM to predict purchase intentions on international websites, and found the model to be reliable and valid across experiments in various countries. TAM was tested for international website acceptance by eighty Brazilian, 130 German, and 140 Taiwanese online consumers (Singh, Fassott, Chao, and Hoffmann 2006). Each respondent browsed nine different websites belonging to American and Japanese B2C multinational enterprises. On average, each respondent took eight to ten minutes to browse each website; respondents then filled out questionnaires about their perception of the website's ease of use and its perceived usefulness, their attitude toward the site, their perception of cultural adaptation on the website, and their purchase intention on the website. This study shows that cultural adaptation is an important explanatory variable when determining international website usage. The study provides empirical evidence showing that cultural adaptation not only enhances ease of use on the website but also leads to a more favorable attitude toward the website, which in turn affects intentions to transact online.

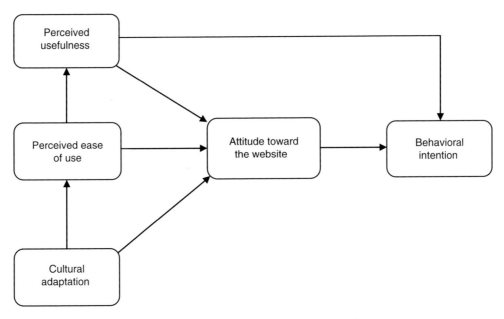

Figure 9.2 Technology acceptance model for international website acceptance
Source: Adapted from Singh, Fassott, Chao, and Hoffmann (2006).

Using eye tracking in usability experiments

Web usability data can be collected in a variety of ways. Asking users to accomplish certain online tasks and then fill out a questionnaire on the basis of their usability perceptions, as described above, is one method. Eye tracking is a way to capture usability data without the user explicitly stating his or her preferences via a survey or questionnaire. The eye-tracking software directly monitors a user's eye movements and captures the unique cognitive strategies employed by the user while interacting with the web interface. Some of the commonly used eye-tracking metrics used in such experiments include the following.[6]

- *Fixation* This measures the focusing of the eye on certain web objects. The fixation measures depend on the context; some of these measures include the fixation duration, fixations per area of interest, and the number of fixations.
- *Gaze duration* This is the "cumulative duration and average spatial location of a series of consecutive fixations within an area of interest" (Jacob and Karn, 2003: 581). Some measures of gaze duration include the gaze duration mean and the gaze rate on each area of interest.

---

[6] The measures for eye movements are referenced from Poole and Ball (2006) and Dong and Lee (2008).

- *Saccades* These are eye movements that happen between the fixations. Some measures of saccades include the number of saccades, the saccade amplitudes, and saccades revealing marked directional shifts.
- *Scan path* This is the sum total or the sequence of interconnected saccades and fixations. Measures of scan path include the scan path duration, the scan path length, and the scan path direction.

A variety of eye-tracking software can be found in the market, and there are also companies that can run usability experiments using eye-tracking methods. Various universities and research institutions have their own usability labs. Some examples of eye-tracking software include NYAN 2.0XT Eye Tracking Data Analysis Suite, by Interactive Minds GmbH; Eye Tracker, by Tobii Technology; EyeTrackers, by Cambridge Research Systems; and Eyetracking, Inc. (ETI) at the Cognitive Ergonomics Research Facility at San Diego State University.

Experimental design

When conducting experiments on international website acceptance, the design of the experiments and the instruments being used require careful attention. The results of the usability testing will be as good only as the methods used for collecting data and the procedures used for data analysis and interpretation. A qualified person with experience in usability testing and knowledge of scientific research methods and techniques should be in charge of these experiments. A non-trained person may not even be aware of some of the issues that need to be addressed when setting up usability experiments to ensure that the results are valid – issues such as sample selection, pre-testing, controlling for various variables, the use of a control group, internal and external validity, and experimental designs. Furthermore, the right research methods must be used to analyze the data to get the complete and the most accurate picture. Assessing international sites on the five constructs (PEOU, PU, cultural adaptation, attitude toward the site, and purchase intention on the site) outlined in this section can help companies better understand whether an e-commerce website will be well accepted by international audiences. This step can help companies make the changes needed to enhance international website acceptance.

Beyond this usability assessment and localization and internationalization testing, companies can take other supplementary steps to assess their overall web localization efforts. The next sections discuss ways to assess an organization's website localization efforts.

Assessing web localization efforts: the localization score card

The localization score card proposed in this section (see Table 9.2) is a way to assess a website's localization efforts on four primary dimensions (Singh, Toy, and Wright, 2009):

(1) content localization;
(2) cultural customization;
(3) links to international websites; and
(4) translation quality.

These four dimensions can be used to measure web localization efforts targeted to any country or locale.

Content localization

This construct addresses the equivalency, relevancy, navigation, support, and currency of the website's local content. The variables that measure content localization provide a general understanding of how the company has localized the basic web content to the local audience. Some of the measures used to analyze content localization are as follows.

- *Percentage of translated pages* The amount of translation conducted for localizing a site for a specific country. This can be calculated by checking the number of translated pages as a percentage of pages in the local/home-country language. A cursory approach is just to count the number of translated pages, but for a more detailed analysis it is important to count the number of translated words versus the words in the home-country site. A word count program can be used for calculating the amount of translated content as a percentage of the original non-translated content on the home site.
- *Content depth* The extent of the content made available in the localized websites in terms of contact information, product information, services, company information, shipping, and handling (1 = basic store and contact information; 5 = all sections from English pages are translated and have all the information needed for local customers). Thus, on a scale of one to five the website will get only "1" if just the basic contact information is localized, versus "5" if all the sections from the home-country site are localized. For example, HP is a company known for its emphasis on creating localized pages. Its Canadian site has localized pages in both English and French (due, in part, to laws regarding language usage in Canada), but the US site is in English only. Spanish content is not available for the Spanish-speaking US population; a telephone number is all that is provided. Similarly, Amazon has an extensive US English site, but the Spanish content for US Hispanics is limited to a help section. HP and Amazon therefore both get a score of "1" for their content depth relating to establishing site content for the US Spanish-speaking population.
- *Content synchronization* The currency of the content or how up to date or fresh the content is on localized pages. It is measured by comparing the currency of the localized site content to the home-country site content (1 = content is out of sync with home-country content; 5 = most localized content is in sync with home-country website content). An example of good content synchronization can

Figure 9.3 Sections in Yahoo! en Español

be found at Yahoo! The Yahoo! en Español site is well localized in Spanish for US Hispanic users, and many of its English content categories are also available on the Spanish site (see Figure 9.3).

- *Navigation* The quality of the navigational features provided by the localized site in comparison to the home-country site. This includes navigational elements such as an adequate site map, hyperlinks, forward and backward buttons, directories, navigational bars, breadcrumb trails, FAQs, and online search help (1 = very poor navigation attributes; 5 = very good navigation attributes). For example, the international sites of Amazon.com are well translated and have excellent navigation features, including the ability to track a shopping path via a breadcrumb trail.

- *Website service and support* The extent to which the available localized customer support is equivalent to that offered on the home-country web pages (1 = no online support for localized web pages; 5 = website support that is equivalent to or better than what is provided on the home-country site). Online support includes features such as basic contact information, frequently asked questions, product support information, customer support phone numbers, customer support documents, e-mail options, chat options, simulations, etc. The support page on the Dell China site covers very detailed information on Dell Support Services for Chinese customers. Dell Support Services start from the company's customer segments (family customers, small and medium-sized businesses, large businesses, the public sector, and governments) and provide different types of services to each customer segment. Compared with the the Dell global site, the Dell China support site is comparable and extensive. As an example, the Dell China support site provides support services based on specific Chinese customer needs. Recently, more Chinese consumers have acquired printers for their homes. Dell China provides a "Printer Support" service online to help these newer users with issues such as printer installation and troubleshooting.

Cultural customization

The cultural customization dimension helps measure the extent to which the company is culturally customizing its content and offerings via the international website. This construct examines the use of appropriate colors, graphics, and web page design that are unique to the country market segment. This topic is covered in more depth in the cultural customization framework provided in Chapter 6. Using that framework's thirty-six cultural website categories, a company can do an in-depth cultural customization assessment.

During the early 2000s I undertook an extensive analysis of the extent of website localization practiced by Forbes 900 companies. Of the 900 companies, only 598 were found to target international customers (Singh and Boughton, 2005). The sample included 307 US companies, 164 European companies, and 127 companies from the Asia-Pacific region. Fewer than half the websites (255) fell into the "Localized" and "Highly localized" categories under the classification scheme, with none qualifying as having achieved comprehensive cultural customization. Now I am seeing more companies taking cultural customization seriously, and there are a few emerging examples of companies creating sites that may have consciously incorporated local cultural values and symbols. One such example is the company Lush, which manufactures handmade cosmetic products. Lush has 650 stores and several factories in more than forty countries. It also has several international sites that have been customized to unique local and cultural requirements (see the box for a description of Lush's website cultural customization efforts). MTV is a good example of a company that not only localizes its content for international sites but also localizes products and services. MTV's international sites generally tend to maintain brand consistency but use different colors, images, symbols, and graphics, and they also promote country-specific media content such as local bands, music, VJs, and DJs.

Cultural customization of international sites: case of Lush.com

Lush (trademarked as "LUSH") is a handmade cosmetics company headquartered in Poole, Dorset, in the United Kingdom. It produces and markets various handmade and natural cosmetic products ranging from bath soap to facial masks. It prides itself on being environmentally sustainable and has several green initiatives. It also has an extensive online presence, with some thirty-eight international sites. For some of its country-specific sites, it leverages its global web template but still customizes the graphics, colors, etc. For other country-specific sites, such as those in Norway, Japan, Saudi Arabia, India, France, and the Philippines, it has created country-specific templates. The colors, images, and symbols tend to reflect local culture. For example, its Indian site features local children, local charities, and the use of the colors yellow and red, which are viewed favorably in India. Similarly, its website in Saudi Arabia is culturally sensitive in that it does not display images of female or male models and primarily uses product images and graphics to create a visually appealing site. (However, I was surprised to see that the scroll bar was on the left-hand side on its Saudi page.) Overall, Lush has kept its core brand identity consistent across various international sites, and still depicts localized visuals and content.

Source: Lush.com (accessed December, 2010).

Links to international websites

This dimension measures the ease of finding the international websites or web pages. For example, Yunker (2006) recommends placing global gateways on a company's main web page, where they can be easily located so that global consumers can quickly find country- or language-specific sites. Having a global gateway page is generally a good practice, but some companies have not adopted them, because they are using geo-targeting, or for some other reason. Without a global gateway page, the next best approach is to have a clear section or link for selecting international sites in the upper right-hand corner. Having a relevant country-specific URL or ccTLD (such as ".de" or ".fr") is also good practice.

Translation quality

This parameter measures how well the English website pages are translated into the local language. This measures conceptual, vocabulary, and idiomatic translation equivalence, as proposed by Singh and Pereira (2005). Product names and concepts are precisely translated with appropriate words and are easy to understand on Clinique's website for China. Here is an example: Clinique China is launching the new product "Clinique repair wear laser focus wrinkle & UV damage corrector." On the Chinese site, the product name is translated into "倩碧焕妍活力精华露." The translation "焕妍活力" fully expresses the product concepts not only from a functional perspective but also from an emotional perspective. Chinese consumers sometimes do not quite understand a new technology concept, so the Chinese translation does not include the word "laser" and avoids talking about this. On the other hand, the translated words on the Chinese site are read with fluency and no awkwardness. For example, "Gentle, versatile makeup removal" is translated into "温和,全面的卸妆体验." Here the word "体验" is added in the translation, while there is no word for "体验" in the English name of this product. The Chinese translation has made the Chinese product name sound comprehensible and fluid. The site also has examples of the appropriate use of idiomatic equivalence. For instance, "expert tips" is translated into Chinese words that are idiomatically unique to Chinese users. In general, the translation uses appropriate conceptual equivalence, idiomatic equivalence, and vocabulary equivalence. The translation quality is therefore good.

E-commerce enablement

Since not all companies conduct e-commerce, I include this as an optional variable for localization assessment. Companies that do engage in e-commerce should evaluate if their localized sites have comparable e-commerce features such as transactional

Table 9.2 The localization score card

Translation quality

Very poor translation quality	1	2	3	4	5	Very good translation quality

Links to international websites

No link on home page	1	2	3	4	5	Upper-right corner of home page
Relevant URLs not supported	1	2	3	4	5	Relevant URLs fully supported

Content localization

0 to 20 percent of web pages translated	1	2	3	4	5	80 to 100 percent of web pages translated
Basic store and contact information provided	1	2	3	4	5	All sections of English website appropriately translated
Local content is out of sync with home-site content	1	2	3	4	5	Most/all of local content is in sync with home-site content
Very poor navigation attributes	1	2	3	4	5	Very good navigation attributes
No online support for local web pages	1	2	3	4	5	Online web support that is equal to/better than for home-site pages

Cultural customization

Standardized web design based on English web pages	1	2	3	4	5	Unique web design based on local cultural norms
Standardized graphics	1	2	3	4	5	Unique graphics based on local cultural norms
Standardized colors	1	2	3	4	5	Unique colors based on local cultural norms
Standardized product/service promotions	1	2	3	4	5	Unique product/service based on local cultural norms

Source: Adapted from Singh, Toy, and Wright (2009).

capability, local currency conversion, local shipping and returns, localized ordering forms, local terms and conditions, and other local compliance details.

Research highlight: assessing the impact of cultural adaptation on international website acceptance[7]

Research goals

A study was carried out to measure German, Chinese, and Indian consumer perception of cultural adaptation on international websites. Specifically, the aim of the study was

---

[7] This research highlight is adapted from my co-authored study: Singh, Fassott, Zhao, and Boughton (2006).

to provide empirical evidence as to whether local consumers prefer culturally adapted websites or standardized (home-country) websites. The study had two main research objectives. The first was to measure the degree of cultural adaptation as reflected on US companies' websites for Germany, China, and India. The study then ranks the websites on the basis of the degree of cultural adaptation, from a high degree of cultural adaptation to little or no cultural adaptation. The second objective was to explore whether German, Chinese, and Indian consumers would find highly culturally adapted websites designed for their country to be more effective (in terms of website acceptance measures: presentation, navigation, purchase intention, and the consumer attitudes toward the site) than websites that are not highly adapted to their respective cultures or standardized (home-country) websites of American multinationals.

Measuring cultural adaptation on websites

To see the impact of culture on user perceptions of adapted versus standardized websites, it was necessary to first measure the cultural adaptation of the websites, and then classify them based on the degree of cultural adaptation they exhibited. The study uses content analysis to analyze the cultural content. Content analysis technique is widely used for measuring the frequency of a certain item of interest in the published content. It is beyond the scope of this book to describe the content analysis technique but the interested reader is referred to Krippendorff (2004).

To measure the depiction of culture on the websites, the framework for cultural customization proposed by Singh and Pereira (2005) was used. Chapter 6 on localization presented this framework and its thirty-six category items used to measure cultural content on the websites. In total, twelve German websites, twelve Chinese websites, and ten Indian websites of American companies were content-analyzed. The unit of analysis was the whole website. To perform content analysis, two bilingual German, Chinese, and Indian coders were used. The inter-coder reliability for American companies' German websites was 86 percent, for Chinese websites it was 86 percent, and for Indian websites it was 88 percent. The intra-judge reliability was calculated after a month interval and was 87 percent, 88 percent, and 90 percent, respectively, for Germany, China, and India. Based on this analysis, the websites were given an overall cultural adaptation score and classified as high, medium, or low on cultural adaptation.

Sample

There were two primary samples selected for the survey of consumer perceptions of adapted versus standardized websites. The first was a set of international websites for Germany, China, and India from American companies, and the second was a group of local German, Chinese, and Indian online consumers. "Adapted websites" are international websites of American companies specifically designed for each of the countries.

The adapted websites have three characteristics. (1) They have country-specific URLs, such as ".de" (Germany), ".in" (India), and ".cn" (China). (2) Websites falling into this category exhibit localization in the form of country-specific, culturally congruent web content. (3) Adapted websites are displayed in local country-specific language (in the case of India, English).

The "standardized websites" selected for the study were home-country websites of American companies designed for an American audience. These standardized websites are in English and are not targeted specifically to the local German, Chinese, or Indian consumers. Only business-to-consumer shopping websites were selected for the study, to provide some control.

The sample of online consumers was comprised of German, Chinese, and Indian bilingual university students. At the screening stage, the students were asked if they were regular internet users and had had an online shopping experience. In total, a sample of sixteen German respondents, ten Chinese respondents, and ten Indian respondents was used. The respondents browsed each website for eight to ten minutes, and then filled out a questionnaire about their perceptions of presentation, navigation, attitude toward the site, cultural adaptation, and purchase intention.

Analysis

Based on the parameters specified above, experiments were developed in which the respondent browsed the sites in a lab and recorded his or her preference of websites depicting various levels of cultural adaptation (this is just a brief overview of the research methods used).

Partial least squares (PLS) were used for measurement analysis. The quality of the measurement efforts were assessed by investigating reliability, convergent validity, and discriminant validity. The path coefficient analysis revealed that, across the three countries, the attitude toward the site and the perception of cultural adaptation both have a significant impact on purchase intentions.

Using the "cultural score" variable, the websites for each country were divided, using a median split, into those that were high, medium, or low on adaptation. Next, consumer perceptions of various variables of site effectiveness were measured for the three categories of websites (high, medium, or low adaptation), plus standardized websites, to test the basic proposition "Websites that are highly adapted to local culture are perceived to be more effective on the five variables used in this research compared to websites low on adaptation and standardized websites." Multivariate analysis of variance (MANOVA) followed by post hoc tests were used to determine how user perceptions differed from website to website on the basis of their level of cultural adaptation.

The results (shown in Table 9.3) show that websites ranked higher on cultural adaptation are perceived to be more effective by local consumers in terms of their perception of navigation, presentation, attitude toward the site, and purchase intention on the

Table 9.3 MANOVA results and post hoc group comparisons by degree of cultural adaptation measured by cultural score, calculated using cultural dimensions proposed in the framework

| Measures | Adaptation level[a] | | | | F[c] | Tukey tests[b] |
	High	Medium	Low	Standard		Group comparisons[d]
Germany						
Presentation	3.94	3.54	3.79	3.44	8.51	H > M & S; L > S
Navigation	3.78	3.54	3.68	3.31	6.08	S < H & L
Attitude toward site	3.70	3.30	3.34	2.90	11.58	S < H, M & L; H > M
Purchase intention	3.21	2.67	2.71	2.19	13.81	S < H, M & L; H > M & L
Cultural adaptation	3.32	3.10	3.09	1.96	75.10	S < H, M & L
India						
Presentation	3.69	3.64	3.46	3.57	n.s.[e]	
Navigation	3.78	3.58	3.38	3.52	4.45	H > L
Attitude toward site	3.87	3.64	3.45	3.41	8.63	H > L & S
Purchase intention	3.92	3.75	3.49	3.36	13.04	H > L & S; M > S
Cultural adaptation	4.00	3.86	3.56	3.19	30.32	H > L & S; M > L & S
China						
Presentation	3.47	3.59	3.43	3.58	n.s.	
Navigation	3.58	3.42	3.49	3.66	n.s.	
Attitude toward site	3.45	3.38	3.14	3.00	4.98	S < H & M
Purchase intention	3.26	3.25	2.91	2.57	9.99	S < H & M
Cultural adaptation	3.60	3.15	2.86	2.39	14.64	H > L & S; M > L & S

Notes: [a] Mean values are reported. [b] Comparisons that are significant at the < 0.05 level are reported. [c] "F" = F-value; p-value < 0.00. [d] H = high adaptation, M = medium adaptation, L = low adaptation, S = standardized. [e] "n.s." = not significant.

site. For those not familiar with this research analysis technique, the key numbers are the mean values listed in Table 9.3. These mean values tend to be higher for websites classified as high on cultural adaptation. The mean values for different categories differ by only a few points, but in statistical terms most are deemed as highly significant.

Assessing web globalization costs

Companies need to assess all the costs associated with the various web globalization primary and support activities. This analysis can help them see which activities cost the most and how to create efficiencies to reduce such costs. Some of the important cost drivers in web globalization are the costs for the processes, people, and tools associated with internationalization and localization activities. Major cost elements include:

- translation costs, which tend to be the bulk of localization costs for many companies;
- project management costs;
- internationalization costs;
- testing and quality assurance costs;
- costs associated with the use of various automation tools (TMS, CMS, TM, etc.); and
- content creation and publishing costs.

Other costs result from maintaining international website hosting and servers, acquiring international domains, conducting multilingual search engine optimization and marketing, facilitating international shipping and international transactions, complying with legal and privacy issues, and international documentation and duties. The direct and indirect costs of web globalization efforts are significant, and, unless a company assesses these costs, it may not be able to effectively create efficiencies to control them. However, it should also be noted that, as with any organizational function, web globalization fulfills a crucial role and thus has associated costs and benefits. In fact, web globalization is a cost-effective way to tap several international markets without the need for the various fixed expenses that could be involved if the company set up local subsidiaries or marketing arms in various countries. In determining a business case for web globalization, the anticipated revenue should, of course, be compared to the costs of a project, but the question "How many more units will we sell if we localize than if we don't localize?" should also be asked and satisfactorily answered.[8]

Web globalization has to compete with other business functions to receive top management attention; be considered a strategic priority; get a share of corporate resource allocation (funds, human resources, tools, training, etc.); and, most importantly, be recognized as an important business function. Currently, web globalization is a fluid concept in many companies. Web globalization tends to revolve around IT, marketing, or international business. In many companies it does not even figure as a separate line item in the corporate budget.

The onus of elevating web globalization to a strategic position lies in the hands of those who recognize its importance and see its potential. The status of web globalization can be elevated by clearly demonstrating:

- the impact on overall company revenues;
- how it fits into the overall global business strategy of the company;
- how it positively affects customer satisfaction and retention;
- how it enhances the productivity of other value-creating activities in the organization;
- how it is a cost-effective way to reach international customers; and
- its importance as a global branding tool.

---

[8] The quote is from industry expert Richard Sikes at MultiCorpora.

Twenty-five ways to reduce web globalization costs

Companies can reduce the costs related to web globalization efforts if they are able to recognize how to perform various web globalization activities efficiently and effectively. Based on the knowledge shared in the previous chapters, here is a summary of some important ways to reduce web globalization costs.

(1) Internationalize, internationalize, internationalize. This is a crucial step that must be carried out before any localization is undertaken. Internationalization ensures that the back end can properly support future localization efforts. It enables companies to leverage a global web template across multiple country/locale sites. Refer to the internationalization checklist provided in Chapter 5. Proper internationalization can prevent many headaches and significantly reduce costs.

(2) Use a web globalization model that centralizes the core activities involved in supporting various web globalization activities, but that also allows local subsidiaries enough control for them to leverage their local knowledge. This can help reduce the duplication of effort by various subsidiaries, ultimately reducing costs.

(3) Use a global web template for international sites. This will reduce web design and development costs and at the same time provide global brand consistency. However, localize the content, graphics, and other elements as necessary for unique locales.

(4) Do not embed text in graphics, as creating new graphics for new locales can be expensive.

(5) Implement a localization workflow process as well as best practices in project management to maximize gains in productivity and efficiency.

(6) Automate as many steps as possible in the localization workflow process. Several localization workflow tools and other localization/translation technology products can help with this process. Automation can reduce repeatable tasks, increase process efficiency, and reduce the overall cost associated with the process.

(7) Content management systems can streamline the development, storage, dispersal, retrieval, and updating related to the production of multilingual content. This can lead to substantial cost savings by creating workflow and automation efficiencies.

(8) Pay special attention to the quality assurance and testing of the localized versions of your sites/content/software, etc. In addition, have all content reviewed prior to publishing. Development errors in connection with the coding, the translation of tags, text expansion, content errors, lack of translation equivalence, etc. result in costs that could have been avoided.

(9) Using agile development methods allows companies to make their project processes flexible and adaptive, and accelerates the release time of new localized versions. The quality gains, flexibility, and earlier release time achieved via agile methods can have a significant impact on overall costs.

(10) Culturally customize the website to the needs of the locale in question. A lack of cultural customization can lead to cultural blunders, translation blunders, users finding the website unfamiliar and strange, a lack of "stickiness" (the amount of time a user spends on the site per visit), a lower propensity to make a purchase, a lack of repeat visits, bad word of mouth, and many other attitudinal and behavioral actions from customers that can undermine web globalization efforts.

(11) Implement a style guide to establish standards for design and language. This will ensure consistency and reduce the translation time, and thus the costs, related to translations.

(12) Create a terminology glossary that can define all the main terms being used. This will greatly improve the quality of translation and also reduce the translation time and translation costs.

(13) Implement a translation memory system or ensure that the localization vendor uses a TM system. This will help companies reuse past translations and reduce the number of words that need translation, thus reducing overall translation costs.

(14) Implement the best practices and guidelines for international writing. This can lead to the creation of clear and simple text that can be easily translated and easily understood by end users. Also advocate the in-country review of documents, to reduce review costs and increase translation equivalence.

(15) The use of controlled languages and DITA during content creation can help create content that is succinct and needs less translation and thus reduces translation costs.

(16) Migrating to an XML-based solution to avoid duplicity in data formats, platforms, fonts, and conflicting feature sets can also help reduce overall costs.

(17) Use exchange standards such as XLIFF (this could be used to exchange data between companies, such as a software publisher and a localization vendor, or between localization tools), TMX, and TBX (TermBase eXchange). These exchange formats can help create process efficiencies and save time and money.

(18) Constantly update the content and archive or get rid of the content that is outdated (such as old press releases). Also reconsider keeping content pages that show low user traffic and time spent. This can help achieve global costs savings because of efficiencies gained via enhanced search engine optimization.

(19) Keep tabs on the localization of PDF (Portable Document Format) Files, brochures, white papers, etc., as they can easily add to the cost of localization.

(20) Carefully assess localization vendors and negotiate the best prices. It is good to have a centralized localization vendor selection process to enhance the bargaining power of the company; but also allow local subsidiaries to seek local vendors for specific jobs at the subsidiary level.

(21) Prioritize content for international markets. Some markets will be more important (higher growth potential/higher revenues) than others, and having clear priorities helps companies to efficiently allocate limited resources (people, budget, tools, etc.).

(22) Companies may explore machine translation tools (statistical machine translation, etc.) to reduce translation costs. However, I would advocate their use only in cases in which translation quality is not paramount. Machine translation software has not yet reached the same level of quality as translations done by people, and often results in errors related to idiomatic and conceptual equivalency.

(23) Perform an extensive international e-environment review to ensure that websites are in compliance with various geopolitical, cultural, economic, and legal issues.

(24) Judiciously leverage the concept of virtual teams and community localization to reduce overall web globalization costs.

(25) To create long-term efficiencies and reduce costs, do not recruit web globalization staff members on the basis of a single criterion, such as because a person is fluent in multiple languages or is tech-savvy. Ensure that web globalization staff have had proper web globalization training.

Chapter summary

- The chapter presents various global web usability challenges in terms of cross-cultural variations in cognitive styles, web usage, colors, signs, measurements, and consumer behavior.
- Some well-known web usability guidelines in ISO 9241–151 and the Microsoft Usability Guidelines, which can help web designers create better international websites, are presented.
- Web analytics as an important web usability tool is elaborated in the chapter. Using clickstream data, companies can assess the usability of their international sites. This clickstream data for web analytics can serve as a way to constantly monitor international website usage and use the feedback to make progressive improvements.
- It is emphasized in the chapter that, to accurately measure international website usage, a reliable and cross-culturally valid framework is needed. The technology acceptance model is presented as a good way to measure international website usage on parameters such as the perceived ease of use, perceived usefulness, the perception of cultural adaptation, attitudes toward the site, and purchase intentions on the site.
- The localization score card presented in the chapter can help companies assess their website localization efforts on levels of content localization, cultural customization, links to international sites, and translation quality.
- Finally, the chapter presents various web globalization costs and twenty-five ways to reduce web globalization costs related to internationalization, translation, project management, process automation, etc.

REFERENCES

Agarwal, Ritu, and Venkatesh, Viswanath 2002. "Assessing a firm's web presence: a heuristic evaluation procedure for the measurement of usability," *Information Systems Research* 13: 168–86.

Cappel, J., and Huang, Z. 2007. "A usability analysis of company websites," *Journal of Computer Information Systems* 48: 117–23.

Carlson, Michele, and McLoughlin, Robert 2010. "Localization strategies and best practices: why design really matters," paper presented at Localization World conference, Seattle, October 6.

Chakraborty, G., Srivastava, P., and Warren, D. L. 2005. "Understanding corporate B2B websites' effectiveness from North America and European perspectives," *Industrial Marketing Management* 34: 420–9.

Davis, F. D. 1989. "Perceived usefulness, perceived ease of use, and user acceptance of information technology," *Quarterly* 13: 319–40.

Dong, Y., and Lee, K. P. 2008. "A cross-cultural comparative study of users' perceptions of a webpage: with a focus on the cognitive styles of Chinese, Koreans and Americans," *International Journal of Design* 2: 19–30.

Flanders, Vincent 1998. *Web Pages that Suck: Learn Good Design by Looking at Bad Design.* Sybex.

ISO 2008. *Ergonomics of Human-System Interaction – Part 151: Guidance on World Wide Web User Interfaces,* ISO 9241–151: 2008(E). ISO; available at www.iso.org/iso/catalogue _detail.htm?csnumber=37031.

Jacob, R. J. K., and Karn, K. S. 2003. "Eye tracking in human–computer interaction and usability research: ready to deliver the promises," in Hyona, J., Radach, R., and Deubel, H. (eds.), *The Mind's Eye: Cognitive and Applied Aspects of Eye Movement Research.* Elsevier Science: 573–605.

Keevil, B. 1998. "Measuring the usability index of your web site," in *Proceedings of the 16th Annual International Conference on Computer Documentation.* Association for Computing Machinery: 271–7.

Krippendorff, Klaus 2004. *Content Analysis: An Introduction to Its Methodology,* 2nd edn. Sage.

Nielsen, Jakob 2000. *Designing Web Usability.* Peachpit Press.

Palmer, J. 2002. "Website usability, design, and performance metrics," *Information Systems Research* 13: 151–67.

Poole, Alex, and Ball, Linden J. 2006. "Eye tracking in human–computer interaction and usability research: current status and future prospects," in Ghaoui, C. (ed.), *Encyclopedia of Human Computer Interaction.* IGI Global: 211–19; available at http:// citeseerx.ist.psu.edu/viewdoc/download?doi=10.1.1.95.5691&rep=rep1&type=pdf (accessed December 24, 2010).

Singh, Nitish, and Boughton, Paul D. 2005., "Measuring website globalization: a cross-sectional country and industry level analysis," *Journal of Website Promotion* 1: 3–20.

Singh, Nitish, Fassott, Georg, Chao, Mike C. H., and Hoffmann, Jonas A. 2006. "Understanding international web site usage: a cross-national study of German, Brazilian, and Taiwanese online consumers," *International Marketing Review* 23: 83–97.

Singh, Nitish, Fassott, Georg, Zhao, Hongxin, and Boughton, Paul D. 2006. "A cross-cultural analysis of German, Chinese and Indian consumers' perception of website adaptation," *Journal of Consumer Behaviour* 5: 56–68.

Singh, Nitish, and Matsuo, Hisako 2004. "Measuring cultural adaptation on the web: a content analytic study of US and Japanese web sites," *Journal of Business Research* 57: 864–72.

Singh, Nitish, and Pereira, Arun 2005. *The Culturally Customized Web Site: Customizing Web Sites for the Global Marketplace.* Elsevier Butterworth-Heinemann.

Singh, Nitish, Toy, Daniel, and Wright, Lauren 2009. "A diagnostic framework for measuring web-site localization," *Thunderbird International Business Review* 51: 281–95.

Tarafdar, Monideepa, and Zhang, Jie 2005. "Analyzing the influence of website design parameters on website usability," *Information Resources Management Journal* 18: 62–80.

Wilson, R. Dale 2010. "Using clickstream data to enhance business-to-business website performance," *Journal of Business and Industrial Marketing* 25: 177–87.

Yunker, John 2006. "The web globalization report card 2006." Byte Level Research; available at www.bytelevel.com/reports/global2006 (accessed January 2, 2007).

10 Strategic industry insights and emerging localization trends

Chapter objectives

- Discuss emerging trends that have the potential to change the scope of localization.
- Explore the importance and challenge of increasing mobile web usage for localization.
- Present tips to help companies adapt their web content for mobile delivery.
- Introduce the concept of crowdsourcing, as well as key opportunities and challenges associated with it.
- Share strategic insights from industry experts on community localization, machine translation, and game localization.

Introduction

The goal of this final chapter is to present emerging trends, opportunities, and challenges that may affect the localization strategies of companies worldwide. Global e-commerce grew immensely in the past decade, and this trend is expected to accelerate. The growth of technologies such as the mobile web, machine translation, and crowdsourcing applications will further enhance global economic activity on the web. In addition, new opportunities in areas of video game localization and global social media localization have yet to be fully leveraged. For example, the social media are spreading rapidly among consumers worldwide, and their commercialization is also on the rise. Marketers now have a better understanding of how to use the social media to both reach global audiences and engage them in a targeted way.

Leveraging social media commercially allows companies to create brand communities and crowdsourcing models, gain consumer insights, enhance product and brand awareness, improve search engine optimization efforts, reduce customer acquisition and service costs, and optimize overall marketing and communication efforts (Scott, 2009; Weinberg, 2009; Stelzner, 2010). Recent social media usage data shows that there are significant differences between countries and regions in the ways that social media are used, content is created, and "crowd wisdom" is shared. Furthermore, 60 percent of the online population is now non-English-speaking; Chinese is the second most popular language used over the internet, with 407 million online users, compared to the 495 million users who speak English (internetworldstats.com). The multilingual and cultural diversity on the web is creating a multilingual social media landscape, with unique global usage and consumption patterns (King, 2010).

Global social media content – indeed, web content in general – is increasingly accessed via a host of mobile devices in lieu of computers. In fact, the mobile web and mobile commerce are emerging as new opportunities to expand economic activity that was previously conducted via traditional websites accessed through computers.

In this chapter, these emerging trends that are shaping global commercial activities are discussed. The following sections address how to adapt content and websites for delivery via the mobile web and how to effectively leverage global social web communities to take advantage of crowdsourcing opportunities. The chapter also presents insights from localization industry experts into emerging trends such as community translation, machine translation, and video game localization.

The mobile web

In 2010 technology experts Chris Anderson and Michael Wolff predicted that the web is "dead" and that a new era of mobile web and applications (apps) is on the way. Mobile usage is certainly surging, and more people are accessing the web via mobile devices. The term "m-commerce" is commonly used to describe commercial activity that is enabled by mobile devices. The proliferation of mobile devices and the web has led to enhanced accessibility and convenience; it has made it possible to browse the web from nearly anywhere, so that users are no longer bound by their PC's location for web access.

M-commerce

Mobile commerce or m-commerce is defined as any activity that is related to a commercial transaction (or a potential one) – an exchange of services or goods for money – and is conducted via wireless and mobile communication networks and uses wireless and mobile devices as user interfaces.

Source: Benou and Bitos (2008: 63).

According to the International Telecommunication Union (ITU) (2010), mobile subscriptions reached some 5.3 billion by the end of 2010. Today the United States is among the leading nations in terms of mobile usage, but China will likely have more mobile users by the end of 2011 than there are people in the United States. The China Internet Network Information Center (CNNIC, 2010) estimates that China had 277 million mobile web users as of 2010.

Mobile usage is expanding worldwide, which means that a significant percentage of the world's population will soon be using the "mobile web," or using a wireless network to access internet-based applications and web content via mobile devices. In fact, according to Morgan Stanley (2009), in the coming five years it is possible that more users will connect to the internet via mobile devices than via desktop PCs. The report also predicts that the mobile internet market will be at least twice the size of the desktop internet market by the end of these five years. The ITU study has made similar estimates of mobile web access in the near future.

The Nielsen Company (2010b) estimates that 28 percent of US mobile users are now using smartphones. This trend toward accessing the internet via mobile devices is strong not only in developed countries but also in developing countries. The Nielsen Company (2010a) finds that mobile phone penetration increases with a rise in per capita GDP, and mobile penetration happens earlier and more rapidly than internet adoption. According to this study, "Over the next 5–10 years, mobile penetration will rise to roughly 140 phones per 100 inhabitants, even in very low per capita GDP countries, and then rise gradually with income." Thus we will see an acceleration in mobile adoption rates in developed and developing countries alike.

To tap this vast mobile web user market, companies are creating sites and applications that can be easily accessed by the internet via mobile devices. DotMobi's "Mobile web progress" study analyzes trends relating to the development of the mobile web. The 2008 study found only 150,000 mobile-ready sites; in comparison, the 2010 study found approximately 3.01 million (dotMobi, 2010). Most companies are finding that mobile devices are a great way to reach users on the go and are reaping the rewards of mobile commerce. A survey by FitForCommerce in 2010 found that almost 41 percent of merchants have seen a positive return on investment in mobile commerce (Butcher, 2010). Top mobile trends that companies are trying to leverage include mobile coupons, social media, customer service, location, and iAd[1] (Tsirulnik, 2010). Beyond these trends in mobile web usage, the use of several other m-commerce applications is increasing: mobile banking, mobile advertising, mobile retailing, mobile ticketing, mobile reservations, mobile auctions, mobile entertainment (games, social media), mobile inventory management, and mobile CRM (Benou and Bitos, 2008).

[1] iAd is the mobile advertising platform launched by Apple. For more information, refer to http://advertising.apple.com.

Companies can reach mobile web users in several ways, including through their existing sites, through sites optimized for the mobile interface, and through sites created specifically for the mobile interface and mobile apps. If companies are really serious about tapping the mobile web market, developing sites adapted for mobile devices is highly recommended. A nicely designed site for mobile devices will be significantly easier for the user to access, download, read, browse, and interact with.

Challenges presented by the mobile interface

As the use of mobile devices and the mobile web increases, web content needs to be delivered seamlessly and presented in a format customized for mobile interfaces. Several problems can arise if companies do not adapt traditional websites for mobile access and presentation. Some of the issues that may affect how web content is delivered and seen on mobile interfaces include the following.

(1) *Screen sizes* Traditionally, websites have been designed to be viewed via desktop and laptop computers. Most mobile devices today have small screen sizes, which pose a challenge for web usability, as lengthy or image-laden web pages may not depict properly via the mobile interface.

(2) *Varying characteristics of mobile devices* Different mobile devices use varying resolutions, screen sizes, screen rotation, browsers, key pads, and multimedia support. Thus a one-size-fits-all strategy may not work well in the context of mobile interfaces. Content that adjusts dynamically to these varying requirements is needed for better accessibility and presentation.

(3) *Lack of standard desktop features* Mobile devices lack several features that PCs have, including mouse usage, elaborate keyboards, large screens, long battery life or continuous access to power, available memory and storage space, the ability to open multiple windows, and support for multimedia applications such as Flash.

(4) *Navigation issues* Mobile devices emphasize touching the screen for browsing and generally use "one-handed interaction." They also have limited input capabilities compared with desktop PCs. People tend to access the mobile web in a non-location-bound manner, such as while shopping, traveling, or at meetings or social gatherings. As a result, a standard website for desktop applications with a complex navigation system, a lack of touch screen icons and clear buttons, and long blocks of text may pose a challenge when accessed via mobile devices. Minimizing text input and maximizing information input via buttons and icons can help mobile web navigation.

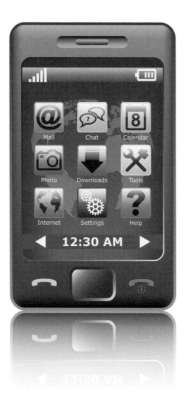

(5) *Top-down interaction* Due to small screen sizes and limited space, the mobile user interface is oriented for top-down interaction; side scrolling is limited.

(6) *Context* The web is accessed differently via mobile devices from how it is via desktop devices. When accessing the mobile web, people generally are on the move, have limited time, and are looking for quick answers. Their session lengths are generally shorter than desktop web browsing sessions. These differences need to be considered when adapting web content for mobile delivery. Mobile web content should be accessible quickly and easily, and it should achieve its purpose in a few clicks. Therefore limiting the number of clicks or operations needed to accomplish a particular task – a good idea in general – is a particularly important consideration when developing content for the mobile web.

(7) *Mobile browsers* Mobile web browsers are not the same as traditional web browsers. Mobile browsers optimize the site to conform to size and screen restrictions and to the lower memory and bandwidth capacities of mobile devices. Thus a website optimized for desktop web browsers may not display in the same way on mobile web browsers.

(8) *Target audience* Mobile web users are a more diverse and heterogeneous group than people who access the web via desktop computers. People around the world who

have never accessed the web at all are now gaining access to the internet via mobile devices. Mobile penetration is effectively closing the digital divide, and the new users coming online en masse have varying levels of education and technical expertise. In developing countries, mobile use has even leapfrogged telephone use. There are villages in south Asia that never had telephone lines and transitioned straight to using mobile phones and accessing the mobile web. As a consquence, when designing content for the mobile web, it is important to keep it simple, easy to use, and task-focused. Some good examples of sites with simple mobile web applications include Facebook, Twitter, and Gmail.

(9) *Download speed* Finally, compared to desktop PCs, mobile devices have limited bandwidth, and thus download speeds are slower. The speed also varies by the network and the mobile browser. Although download speeds are getting better, companies still need to develop lighter web content that can be downloaded more quickly.

These are just some of the issues that affect mobile web access. The following section offers some tips to help companies adapt their web content for mobile devices.

Tips for adapting content for the mobile web

(1) *Understand mobile devices* When adapting sites or applications for mobile devices, remember the unique properties of the mobile devices. A mobile device does not have a mouse, an elaborate keyboard, a wide screen, etc.

(2) *Use of XHTML-MP* The eXtensible HyperText Markup Language Mobile Profile (XHTML-MP) is now the most widely supported markup language, used by various mobile web browsers. XHTML-MP is the markup language defined in WAP (Wireless Application Protocol) 2.0 and brings together technologies for mobile internet browsing and for the web.[2] Additionally, Unicode UTF8 should be used as the encoding standard.

(3) *Simplify* The mobile web is accessed under constraints imposed by bandwidth, processing time, screen size, mobile browsers, etc. To optimize a site for mobile devices, the structure of the website should be simplified, long forms for users to fill out should be avoided, navigation should be as clear and simple as possible, and extensive formatting should be reduced or removed (mobile devices have limited support for font sizes and effects). A very basic free online tool for optimizing sites for the mobile web is Instant Mobilizer, which automatically resizes images, reformats text, and inserts other mobile-friendly features to ensure that a website will work well on mobile devices (http://instantmobilizer.com).

---

[2] www.developershome.com/wap/xhtmlmp/xhtml_mp_tutorial.asp?page=introduction   and   www .passani.it/gap.

(4) *Understand the mobile user* Carefully reviewing site metrics and conducting basic user research such as online surveys can provide important information such as how, why, where, and when a site's users access a website from mobile devices. Questions to investigate include the following. What value does this mobile web content provide the users? Where do mobile users access the web content? How do they interact with the content?

(5) *Prioritize content* Based on the results of this research, content should be prioritized, and only information that is critical for mobile users to complete common tasks should be presented to them.

(6) *Keep content "light"* Keeping site images and graphics to a minimum will improve site performance in situations with limited bandwidth. Images should be optimized for faster download on mobile browsers and defined via textual descriptions or alt tags. Considering the constraints imposed by mobile networks and devices, companies should provide scaled-down versions of their full websites for mobile web use.

(7) *Pay extra attention to navigation* Navigation should be kept simple so that the user does not have to click more than three to five times to reach whatever he or she is looking for or attempting to accomplish. The typical interface on mobile devices has the header on the top, then content, navigation, and footer; all these elements fit in a vertical format. It is better to break down the content into simple vertical blocks to avoid lengthy pages and scrolling. Having a navigational link such as a back button or a link to the home page at the bottom of each page is a good practice for the mobile web.

(8) *Content presentation* Although the technical features of the actual phone to facilitate content display are beyond the scope of content developers, mobile web content should be presented in a manner that enhances visibility and readability. The use of appropriate font sizes, colors, color contrasts, graphic elements, and page layout can help enhance readability. Mobile devices are accessed outdoors, indoors, in cars, and (to the chagrin of many educators) in classrooms. Mobile manufacturers are now even coming up with models customized for an outdoor lifestyle. For example, Samsung Xplorer includes outdoor-friendly features, such as loud external speakers, noise cancellation, and a flashlight.

(9) *Minimal use of external resources* Each linked resource (such as an image, style sheet, or other object) requires a separate request across the network. This may add significantly to the page's load time in the mobile context. Thus the number of externally linked resources should be kept to a minimum.[3]

(10) *Consider input limitations* Because of the small screen, limited key pad, and typing capabilities, input methods for mobile interfaces should be user-friendly. Input via

---

[3] www.w3.org/TR/mobile-bp.

typing and long forms should be minimized; information should be entered as much as possible with radio buttons, selection lists, and other controls.

(11) *Limit the use of tables* For mobile devices, tabular representation should be limited unless developers know that their users are primarily using devices that can support tables. Nested tables, frames, pop-ups, and Flash should also be avoided.[4] Not all mobile devices support Flash or JavaScript.

(12) *Flexibility* Content should be made as flexible as possible so that it can be easily displayed across various mobile browsers and devices. Avoiding the use of fixed measurements such as pixels can help content to fit the mobile device display.

(13) *Website link* As smartphones improve and technology allows for better and faster multimedia and content display, some users may want to access standard full-fledged websites via their mobile devices. Companies should provide mobile web users with the option to visit their standard websites as well.

(14) *Testing* Mobile sites should be tested on several mobile web browsers, such as Opera Mini and Opera Mobile, Safari (iPhone), Google Android, and Skyfire. One of the freely available tools for quick basic testing for the mobile web is the mobiReady testing tool, which evaluates mobile readiness using industry best practices and standards. This tool can be found at http://ready.mobi.

(15) *DotMobi* A site's URL should be simple and short for easy entry into mobile devices. The ".mobi" top-level domain has been developed to ensure that the internet can be accessed via mobile phones. More information on how to register and use this top-level domain can be found at http://mtld.mobi. Companies are also using subdomains for their mobile sites in order to keep all web content under one primary domain.

The growing crowdsourcing trend

Another important development, with the potential to impact global e-commerce and localization, is the growing trend toward crowdsourcing. Crowdsourcing in simple terms refers to outsourcing organizational tasks to the community at large. In this section I explore the concepts, issues, challenges, and benefits pertinent to crowdsourcing.

According to Rumelhart (1992), knowledge resides in the pattern of connections built in and around systems. However, harnessing this intelligence is a challenge. Companies can use various crowdsourcing models to gather this knowledge; before they try to do so, they should fully understand what this knowledge is and how it is created.

The knowledge that resides in networks of people connected by technology is a valuable resource, and a company that can adequately identify and strategically leverage this knowledge can gain competitive advantage. Amazon has achieved this by pioneering

---

[4] www.w3.org/TR/mobile-bp/#d0e1374.

affiliate marketing programs, YouTube has harnessed the power of viral marketing, and Facebook has redefined social networking during the past decade.

The emerging trend of crowdsourcing may also help companies leverage network resources in unique ways. Companies are using crowdsourcing models to enhance their global e-commerce capabilities. The following sections first review the concepts underlying the emerging crowdsourcing trend and then look into ways that crowdsourcing is enabling various aspects of global e-commerce.

Collective intelligence

Individuals are the source of intelligence; networks are the vectors that connect individuals; cultural norms are the informal structures that facilitate human interaction; and organizations are the formal structures around which knowledge is created. All these elements work together to give rise to what is known as "collective intelligence." Collective intelligence arises when several individuals are connected via networks, guided by informal or formal structures, to work on a specific problem.

The rise of the internet and Web 2.0 technologies has facilitated the process of the rise of collective intelligence. Web 2.0 technologies provide opportunities for large-scale interactions via e-mail, instant messaging, news groups, chat rooms, forums, blogs, wikis, podcasts, and the like. "Using such 'collective intelligence' technologies, it is now feasible to draw together knowledgeable individuals, analytic tools, and information sources on a scale that was impossible a few short years ago" (Iandoli, Klein, and Zollo, 2008). Today individuals can access collective intelligence via popular blogs, users' groups, social networking sites, and wikis.

User-generated content (UGC)

The result of the harnessing of collective intelligence via emerging web technologies is user-generated content. Intelligent web services and tools such as interactive applications, blogs, wikis, chat rooms, etc. are creating a new participative web that allows users to develop, rate, collaborate, customize, and distribute content via the internet (Organisation for Economic Co-operation and Development [OECD], 2007).

The OECD outlines three main characteristics of UGC.

- *Its public nature* User-generated content should be public in nature and widely available. Thus, content generated for private or internal company use does not qualify as user-generated content; e-mail, instant messaging, and internal protected company forums can be excluded from this broad category of UGC. In essence, UGC should lead to content that can be seen publicly via platforms such as blogs, wikis, etc.
- *Its creative nature* For the content to truly be classified as UGC, it should have a creative component. Some examples are creating new knowledge, configuring existing

knowledge for new use, or combining knowledge from various fields to solve a problem. Some examples showing the creative nature of UGC include product reviews posted by users on sites such as TripAdvisor, photo-sharing and reviews on sites such as Flickr, or videos and reviews posted on YouTube.

- *Its nonprofessional nature* Since UGC started as a grass-roots movement with amateur content, one of its original characteristics was that it was not created by organizations but, instead, was produced by nonprofessionals without the expectation of profit or remuneration. Nonprofessionals are motivated to create UGC to connect with their peers; to achieve a certain level of fame, notoriety, or prestige; and to express themselves. As more organizations see the value and economic potential of UGC, this third characteristic of it is evolving to have both a professional and nonprofessional nature and a non-economic and economic nature.

Crowdsourcing

Crowdsourcing is the next step in the evolution of UGC from being a nonprofessional/amateur product to a product that is actively leveraged by organizations for economic activity. The word "crowdsourcing" was coined by industry expert Jeff Howe to describe the way amateurs and businesses were connected in a value-generating process.

Using crowdsourcing, organizations take a task traditionally performed by employees or contractors, and outsource it to an undefined, generally large, group of people in the form of an open call (Howe, 2008). This way, organizations can put more brains to work on a task or solving a problem, which usually achieves faster results at a lower price. The crowdsourcing model enables companies to access vast human and knowledge resources without hiring them and committing significant organizational resources to manage and develop them.

In the broadest sense, companies can use crowdsourcing to spread the workload to a broader base at a lower overhead cost. It may also be used by companies:

- to seek new and numerous ideas and insights from the wisdom of the crowds worldwide;
- to solve technical problems or to work on developing new technology;
- to analyze reams of data and to identify patterns;
- to conduct usability and product testing and to seek consumer feedback;
- to develop products;
- to build brands;
- to conduct market research; and
- to translate websites for international markets.

Many companies, governmental institutions, and non-profit organizations are leveraging the crowdsourcing model. For example, threadless.com gives designers and artists an opportunity to unleash their creativity and submit their designs for T-shirts, posters, etc. Threadless.com customers vote on the designs, and winning designers receive $1,000 in cash and prizes, in addition to having their design printed and sold on a T-shirt.

Understanding how Web 2.0 technologies are used to leverage collective intelligence and create business value can help companies find innovative uses for the crowdsourcing model in their web globalization efforts. Examples of crowdsourcing online include epinions.com, YouTube, NASA clickworker, Netflix, Innovation Exchange, HumanGrid, Elance, Spreadshirt, CafePress, IStockPhoto, Lego Factory, and MensaProcess.

InnoCentive: crowdsourcing model

InnoCentive is a good example of crowdsourcing to facilitate open innovation. InnoCentive connects companies, academic institutions, and public sector and non-profit organizations with a global network of more than 200,000 scientists and skilled labor from 200 countries via its online Open Innovation Marketplace™. The pool of talent at the InnoCentive marketplace includes engineers, scientists, inventors, and businesspeople with expertise in life sciences, engineering, chemistry, math, computer science, and entrepreneurship. These individuals join the InnoCentive Solver™ community to help solve some of the world's toughest challenges. The seeker or the organization posting the challenge offers a cash prize, which can reach hundreds or thousands of dollars. Companies such as Procter & Gamble regularly use this unique online marketplace to their advantage. Using the InnoCentive marketplace offers companies several advantages.

- It can put thousands of minds to work on its problem and get the solutions more speedily in this fast-growing knowledge economy.
- The diversity of inputs engenders creativity.
- It helps take research and development (R&D) costs off the balance sheet; the company pays only for the solution that works.
- It gives the company access to a worldwide pool of human talent.

As of July 2010 1,044 challenges had been posted on InnoCentive; total solutions submitted were 19,346 and total amounts awarded stood at $5.3 million.

Source: www2.innocentive.com.

Benefits of crowdsourcing

Crowdsourcing can provide a company with a variety of benefits

(1) *Monetization* Online communities and UGC are not just for fun anymore; they can also yield significant profits. Companies can monetize the wisdom of the crowds in several ways (OECD, 2007).
  - Voluntary donations: examples are those used by Wikipedia and several blog sites.
  - Pay-per-item: for example, royalty-free photos can be bought by users at IStockPhoto and Dreamstime for nominal fees.

- Subscription-based model: companies such as LinkedIn and Flickr derive their revenues from advertising and subscriptions. A person can purchase an upgraded account to subscribe to unlimited storage, upload, bandwidth, permanent archiving, and an ad-free service.
- Advertising-based model: using this popular model, sites can attract large traffic on account of their UGC. Advertisers and services such as Google Adsense put ads on their sites for their viewers. Facebook and LinkedIn, for example, use this model.
- Selling goods and services to the user community: sites relying on user-generated content, such as Second Life and Cyworld, actually sell virtual products to their users to enhance their online avatars, etc. Virtual land, virtual pets, virtual shoes, etc. can be bought.

(2) *Human capital* Access to a vast global network of human capital can be gained. The example of InnoCentive shows how companies can tap worldwide collective intelligence. Another example is MensaProcess, through which Mensa members can participate in live brainstorming panels to solve problems.

(3) *Complementary offerings* Crowdsourcing can help companies boost demand for their complementary offerings. For example, according to Tapscott and Williams (2006), open-source communities generate returns from selling complementary services, support, hardware, etc. – such as Second Life selling its users virtual products.

(4) *Cost reductions* Companies may enjoy significant cost savings from crowdsourcing efforts. The example in the box shows how the use of InnoCentive can help move R&D off company balance sheets, so that companies pay only when the desired solution is achieved. Through the open-source approach, IBM were able to save almost $900 million on operating systems (Tapscott and Williams, 2006).

(5) *Enhanced innovative capability* By having a large and diverse set of talent working on a problem, the likelihood that innovative solutions will be generated increases.

(6) *Benefit to the crowd* Crowdsourcing models allow people around the world to participate in economic activity and reap both monetary and non-monetary rewards. Non-monetary rewards could include being positioned as a knowledge expert, status, fame, and publicity. Other non-monetary rewards include self-expression, peer recognition, networking with other people, fun, the acquisition of new skills, establishing credibility, belonging to a group, access to exclusive content, etc.

(7) *SEO* Social media sites and other community sites can help companies optimize their sites for higher search engine rankings. For example, Delicious is a social bookmarking website; this may help users let their friends know about their favorite sites. Another example is Aboutus.org: it is a wiki for, and about, businesses, organizations, blogs, forums – and, really, anything or anyone that has a website.

(8) *Web globalization* Using crowdsourcing models to translate content is now becoming common. Companies such as Facebook and Google are already using this model to generate translation for their global web expansion efforts. I explore this in more detail in the section on community translation.

Crowdsourcing concerns

Concerns about crowdsourcing are also growing, and they may affect how the business and consumer world evolves.

(1) *Crowdsourcing = outsourcing* Tasks that would otherwise be performed by a salaried position are being completed by freelancers or even unpaid contributors. For example, instead of hiring someone to carry out R&D, and paying them benefits as well as a salary, the work may go to random individuals who are paid (or not) for individual pieces of work (www.LawFont.com).

(2) *Quality* Another big concern is the quality of the work. For example, several professors discourage their students from using Wikipedia as the content on it can be altered and created by anybody. It takes just a few "bad apples," and a lack of proper monitoring can compromise the content. What, therefore, can companies do to enhance the quality control of UGC?

  • Implement recommendation systems through which users can critique the work, such as those of Amazon, Netflix, eBay, etc. Peer review (voluntary and mostly unpaid) is extensively used in academia to control the quality of academic research.
  • Have a voluntary editorial team or even paid employees check for poor quality and offensive content.
  • Develop standards and rules around which contributions can be made.
  • Put someone in charge. This helps establish authority and responsibility.

(3) *Attracting contributors* Without proper "language," companies may find it difficult to locate the best talent to work on their crowdsourcing models. Companies need to understand what their diverse contributors find valuable about interacting with and contributing to the community. It could be a combination of monetary and non-monetary incentives. Thus companies need to carefully phrase their recruitment statements so as to attract the best and most relevant talent.

(4) *Intellectual property issues* The ideas and solutions generated from crowdsourcing models may pose challenges relating to IPR protection. For example, a person submitting an idea to an advertised competition may have submitted the same idea to other competitions. Moreover, it is difficult to monitor if the ideas and content are original or plagiarized.

(5) *Strategic concerns* These relate to whether using a crowdsourcing model will compromise the security, privacy, and strategy of a company's efforts. If the company uses crowdsourcing models to solve its strategic problems or conduct market research or other business activities, then its competitors can easily know company strategy relating to such moves.

(6) *Happy slapping, crowd slapping* This is when someone attacks an unsuspecting victim while an accomplice records the assault (commonly with a camera phone or a smartphone) and users share these via community sites. Crowd slapping took place

when Chevy Tahoe wanted its users to post their videos about Tahoe and received several satirical videos (crowdsourcing.typepad.com).

(7) *Digital divide* Crowdsourcing further exacerbates the problem of the digital divide, by providing an opportunity for people with web access to be part of the productive collective intelligence effort, while those without access may not have the same opportunity.

These are just some of the concerns that crowdsourcing may create. It is imperative to develop a crowdsourcing model that addresses such concerns and enhances a meaningful collaborative environment.

Strategic industry insight 1: community translation[5]

Various companies, such as Google, Wikipedia, Facebook, and Microsoft are now leveraging crowdsourcing models for translation and localization work. In this strategic industry insight, longtime localization industry expert Willem Stoeller provides unique insights into the growing trend toward community translation.

Core concepts

Community translation is the act of taking a job traditionally performed by professional translators and outsourcing it to a preexisting community of partners, end users, and volunteers.

To avoid confusion, a clear distinction should be made between community translation and collaborative translation. Collaborative translation is the act of assigning translation to a team of translators (professionals or community members, as in community translation) using an online translation platform with centralized and shared translation memory. The process speeds up translation by using internet-based translation technology.

The role of translation marketplaces

Translation marketplaces bring together buyers and sellers of translation. They often provide some form of reputation management.[6] Translation marketplaces eliminate the need for a middleman in the form of a translation services provider. Most buyers of translation using a translation marketplace are small businesses, professionals, and individuals. Most sellers of translation using a translation marketplace are professional

---

[5] This strategic insight on community localization has been provided by Willem Stoeller, PMP, a director at Lingotek, Inc., who has worked in the translation industry since the early 1990s.

[6] Reputation management is the process of tracking an entity's actions and other entities' opinions about those actions; reporting on those actions and opinions; and reacting to that report, creating a feedback loop. All entities involved are generally people, but that need not always be the case (Wikipedia).

translators or semi-professional translators (doing translation as a second job and often not formally trained as translators).

Translation marketplaces fall into two categories:

(1) *those dedicated to translation only*, such as ProZ.com, language123, translationjob .com, Language Marketplace, Google Translation Center, Bewords, LanguageScape, and aquarius.net; and
(2) *general marketplaces*, such as Mechanical Turk, oDesk, and even Craig's List and Kijiji.

Translation marketplaces do not provide community translation or collaborative translation; in fact, most do not provide any translation management tools at all. However, translation marketplaces can be, and are, used to crowdsource translation to a largely undefined group of professional and semi-professional translators. Usually payment is made, unless the translation is for a charity or non-governmental organization (NGO) with a perceived strong social benefit. For example, the Cambodian charity Krousar Thmey recently used ProZ to find professional translators who could translate its website using a collaborative translation platform.

Community translation: success stories

Microsoft
Microsoft has been using community translation successfully for six years and for fourteen languages. It addresses the needs of the long tail of smaller markets. In many cases only the software is translated, while the full product is translated for other languages.

Open-source software communities
Open-source software communities have been using community translation successfully for more than six years with success.

Charities and NGOs
Charities and not-for-profit organizations have embraced the concept of community translation fully, with many success stories, such as Kiva, the crowd-funding site, and the TED Open Translation Project for the translation of TED Talks videos (already translated into eighty languages). Religious not-for-profit organizations, such as the Church of Jesus Christ of Latter-day Saints, are also embracing community translation. Even professional translators regularly contribute to community translation projects for charities and other sites with perceived substantial social benefit.

Facebook
In 2008 Facebook started community translation using its enormous user base as a source of translators. It was able to launch versions in sixteen different languages in six months.

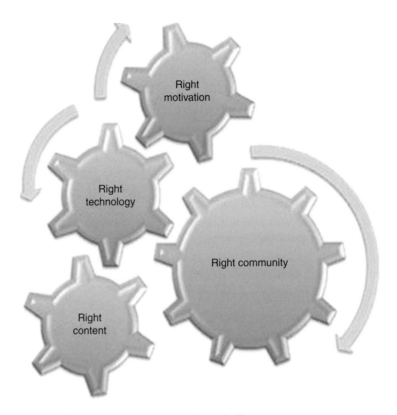

Figure 10.1 Community translation challenges

Community translation challenges

Community translation has four major challenges: finding communities, matching the content with the communities, aligning community objectives and organization objectives, and identifying project management controls. See also Figure 10.1.

(1) Finding communities

Most examples of community translation involve communities that were already involved with the organization in ways other than translation: end users (Adobe, Facebook, Second Life, Novell, Symantec), partners (EMC) or even in-house personnel (Cisco), or volunteer members (charities, religious organizations, etc.). Creating end user or partner communities from scratch requires substantial work and support from experienced consultants. It is also possible to enlist help through an open call to translator marketplaces such as ProZ, LanguageScape, Translationjob, or even to general marketplaces such as Mechanical Turk, Craig's List, or oDesk. When using such an open call to translation marketplaces, it will be necessary to pay the translators (per word or hour) unless the translation is for a charity or other non-profit organization with a perceived substantial social benefit.

(2) Matching the content and communities

Community members are most often not linguists; instead, they are bilinguals with specific domain knowledge (e.g., bilingual Facebook users). The selected community needs to have both the capacity and the ability (domain knowledge) to translate the content. For some content (e.g., sales and marketing materials for a commercial enterprise) it will be very hard to find communities with the ability to translate the content and the motivation to do so. This leads to the next point.

(3) Aligning objectives

Most of the community management effort will go toward motivating the communities. Aligning the goals of the community with those of the organization seeking to use community translation is critical to the success of community translation. If there is no alignment, communities will falter or, worse, the effort will be perceived as exploitation by the organization. Community translation is not a means to get free translation for the organization's content. Attempts by an organization to replace its translation service providers and professional translators with free community translation may have quality problems, and in some cases may fail and be criticized. Often when using semi-professional translators through one of the translation marketplaces it becomes a trade-off between linguistic quality and cost.

(4) Identifying project management controls

Any project manager involved with community translation will wonder how to control deadlines, confidentiality, and quality. Control over deadlines requires a community translation platform that provides a means to set up deadlines and to report progress on a granular level. If missing a deadline becomes likely, the organization can then switch to professional translators.

If confidentiality is essential (e.g., a new product release), community translation is not a good solution. It is not possible and reasonable to expect community members to adhere to a non-disclosure agreement. In this case, professional translation or, if possible, in-house translation is the way to go.

The linguistic quality of community translated content will not equal that of content translated by professionals, although meaning typically will be translated correctly if the community is well matched with the content.

Quality can be increased by:

- using glossaries developed in-house or by professional translators;
- using peer review and a mechanism to flag totally inappropriate translation; and
- implementing a separate review phase in the workflow carried out by in-house specialists, professional translators, or a very experienced subset of the community.

Community translation infrastructure needs

Any translation management system supporting community translation should meet the following requirements.

(1) The software needs to be browser-based (preferably without downloading any software). In order to avoid any IT workload, a cloud-based system is preferable. It is also remembering that community members are not always computer-savvy and may not have the same software platform.

(2) Registration as a community member, setting up projects, and managing communities all require simple browser-based functionality.

(3) Translation memories need to be centralized and sharable in order to maximize their use and to allow sharing across projects and communities.

(4) The software needs to support terminology enforcement with a warning/audit system if a different translation is used.

(5) Community translation will often be combined with machine translation and post-editing work. Therefore any software for community translation needs to allow integration with multiple machine translation systems and to support the post-editing of MT output.

(6) Work packets for translators and reviewers need to be small and variable in order to support community members with different levels of commitment and capacity.

(7) Especially for larger communities, a system of peer review (usually implemented through voting) is recommended.

(8) A separate quality review, often performed by in-house specialists or professional translators, is also recommended.

(9) Smartphone support should be in place for countries with limited broadband.

(10) Some recognition/motivation tools, such as leader boards, should be used.

Community translation: is there a role for professional translators?

Is there still a role for professional translators within the community translation model?

Yes, because organizations using community translation are in need of linguistic consultancy, glossary development, final review, and standby resources when communities threaten to miss their deadlines – all tasks usually requiring experienced professional translators. In addition, professional translators will often participate in community translation if they perceive a substantial social benefit, such as translation for charities, disaster relief, etc.

Community translation will be mainly used to address the needs of the long tail of small markets and the translation of corporate and end user materials currently left untranslated. Traditional professional translation is usually cost-prohibitive for these two types of translation needs.

Although the bulk of product documentation, software strings, training materials, and marketing materials for existing, larger markets will likely continue to be translated by professional translators, other factors such as machine translation and collaborative translation platforms will continue to impact the "traditional" translation process.

Strategic industry insight 2: emerging machine translation technologies[7]

The combination of new language automation technologies and business models that leverage the wisdom of crowds is redefining how content is created for global use. The role of a translator has been evolving throughout this history.

Will the role of the translator be challenged as new automated translation tools emerge and companies leverage their community of users for voluntary translation jobs? In this section, Kirti Vashee, an industry expert and statistical machine translation (SMT) evangelist, shares his insights into emerging machine translation technologies and their future.

Machine translation

Amazingly, after more than fifty years of empty promises and repeated failures, interest in machine translation continues to grow. It is still something that almost everybody hopes will work someday. Is MT finally ready to deliver on its promise? What are the issues with this technology, what will it take to make it work – and why do we continue to try after a half-century of minimal success? This overview attempts to provide a lay perspective on the ongoing discussion in the evolution of the two main approaches to "machine translation" that are in use today, and attempts to answer these questions. Although other technical approaches to MT do exist, this overview focuses only on rule-based MT (RbMT) and statistical machine translation, as these approaches underlie virtually all the MT systems in use today.

Stories of MT mishaps and mistranslations abound (it is easy to make MT look bad), but many companies are seeing that it is important to learn how to use and extend the capabilities of this technology successfully. Although MT is unlikely to replace human beings in any application in which high quality is really important, a growing number of cases show that MT is suitable for:

- highly repetitive content, for which productivity gains with MT can dramatically exceed what is possible just by using TM alone;
- content that would not get translated otherwise;
- content that is not worth an investment in human translation;
- content that changes frequently;
- content that facilitates and enhances the global spread of critical knowledge;
- content that is created to enhance and accelerate communication with global customers who prefer a self-service model; and
- content that does not need to be perfect but just understandable.

---

[7] This strategic insight on emerging machine translation technologies has been provided by Kirti Vashee, vice-president of Enterprise Translation Sales for Asia Online.

How machine translation works

As with all engineering problems, automated translation starts with a basic goal: to take a text in a given language (the source language) and convert it into a second text in another language (the target language), in such a way as to preserve the meaning and information. Although several approaches have been tried, to date, two approaches stand out: rule-based machine translation and statistical machine translation. Table 10.1 summarizes the key characteristics of each.

Rule-based machine translation

The foundation for rule-based systems is relatively easy to understand intuitively. Languages can be considered to have two foundational elements:

(1) the meaning of the words – the semantics; and
(2) the structure of how the words are put together – the grammar, syntax, and morphology, etc.

An RbMT system attempts to map these two elements of the source language to the target language. While this may sound simple on the surface, it quickly gets complicated. Developers of RbMT solutions combine the theories of traditional grammarians and linguists and attempt to convert this linguistic knowledge into systematic, encyclopedic sets of rules encompassing grammar, morphology, syntax, and meaning across a language pair. Programmers encode this information into rule sets and dictionaries and try to get as much linguistic knowledge as possible into these rule sets. Linguistic knowledge refers to information about word structure (singulars and plurals, first-, second-, and third-person endings, etc.), word meanings (dictionary definitions), grammar (word order, part of speech, typical phrasing), and homonyms (e.g., ambiguous terms that can have different meanings in different contexts). Very simply put, an RbMT system comprises of a dictionary and a set of rules for the language combinations that the system can process.

Statistical machine translation

SMT approaches have been gaining considerable momentum since 2004. The premise of these new approaches is that purely linguistic knowledge is far less important than having large volumes of human-translated data to analyze and process. By analyzing large bodies of texts instead of just one sentence, the new systems attempt to simulate the way human translators work. Human translators have general knowledge of the everyday world, and they quickly grasp the context and the domain in which they operate. As computer storage and processing capacity increased exponentially, and as large digital bilingual corpora became available, researchers began to suggest that computers could "learn" and extract the systematic patterns and knowledge that humans have embedded into historical translations.

Table 10.1 Characteristics of rule-based and statistical machine translation

	RbMT	SMT
Background	In development since the early 1960s, many systems have been around for over thirty years.	First systems began to emerge from 2004 onward, based on IBM patents.
Language coverage	Fifty to sixty language combinations after more than fifty years of efforts. New language pairs take at least six months to years to develop to reach any kind of useful level of usability.	Over 1,200 language combinations developed in less than five years. The European Union alone has 462 engines built out of Euromatrix project data. Development is possible wherever bilingual data is available.
Customizability	Based on complex dictionary and rule set modifications.	Easily carried out when domain specific data is available.
Effort to customize	Complex, long, and expensive, but recent versions allow dictionary-based customization.	Easy if adequate data and computing resources are available.
Quality trends	Has essentially reached a plateau and remained fundamentally the same for many years. Some recent improvements have come about as a result of statistical post-processing efforts.	Most systems, especially Google systems, have been improving rapidly and are expected to continue to improve over the coming years. The best quality approaches human draft quality.
Community collaboration	Very little ability to incorporate community feedback except for dictionary contributions.	Microsoft, Google, and Asia Online actively seek and incorporate massive "crowd" collaboration to correct raw MT and enable rapid improvements in quality. This practice may set SMT quality apart from all previous MT.
Resource requirements	Relatively low and desktop installation is also possible. A single server can run more than ten language pairs.	Significant computing resources are required to both build and run SMT engines, and it is not really suitable for single-user desktop installation. Better suited to be a server, cloud-based solution.

SMT systems have in a few short years overtaken the RbMT systems in quality in virtually all the baseline systems available on the web today. These second-generation SMT solutions adopt a data- and probability-based approach to translation, and are also often called "data-driven" approaches. Simply put, SMT systems are developed by computationally analyzing large bodies of parallel bilingual text, which they treat as strings of characters; determining patterns; and exploiting these regularities by matching these patterns in new material that is presented for translation.

The current status quo

Today both rule-based and statistical machine translation approaches can claim success in many different kinds of applications. RbMT systems are in use at EU government bodies, Symantec, Cisco Systems, Fortis Bank, and many other places to enhance translation productivity and accelerate translation work. The system used by the Pan American Health Organization is one of the most respected and actively used MT systems in the world, and it includes integrated post-editing capabilities.

Several vendors offer RbMT solutions that can run on the desktop and are sometimes used by translators as a productivity tool. These vendor companies include Systran, ProMT, and the two large localization service providers: SDL and Lionbridge. Other vendors focus on regional languages; they include Apptek and Sakhr (Arabic, Middle Eastern) and Open Logos, BrainTribe, and Linguatec (German). Japanese companies have developed a whole suite of RbMT systems, to their credit, with Toshiba and Fujitsu enjoying the best reputations in this respect.

Many RbMT companies have started and failed along the way. Systran is probably the best-known name in the RbMT world, and it has the broadest range of languages available. However, the reputation of MT in general has been based on these systems, and several of the RbMT systems we see today are the result of over thirty years of effort and refinement. Many say now that RbMT systems have reached the limit of their possibilities, and that we should not expect much more evolution in the future.

The SMT world is where most of the excitement in MT exists today. Perhaps the most successful MT application in the world today is the Microsoft Knowledge Base, a customer service system that is used by hundreds of millions of users across the globe and is mostly an SMT-based effort. Google, the Microsoft Live free translation portals, and the Lionbridge RTTS portal (using IBM technology) are powered by SMT. In just a few years SMT systems have caught up in quality with RbMT systems that have decades of development efforts behind them. Given that we are just at the start of the SMT systems technology, which today consists mostly of phrase-based SMT (PBSMT) applications, and really no more than simple direct transfer systems, there is real reason for optimism as these systems start to incorporate linguistics, add more data, and get access to more computing power. SMT systems are also much better suited to massive online collaboration. Commercially, several alternatives are now available from vendors such as Asia Online, Pangeanic, ESTeam, ALS, Languagelens, and SDL Language Weaver; many others will likely be launched in the coming years. A growing open-source movement around the technology (Moses) is already outperforming the systems produced by SMT pioneers such as ISI. Several automotive companies, Intel, and others have implemented SMT-based translation productivity or technical knowledge base systems.

The future

MT technology has experienced decades of failures; SMT appears to be the increasingly dominant way of the future, but there is still some distance to go. Raw MT technology still falls short of any widely understood and accepted standard of quality.

The path to higher quality has to involve humans. Language is too complex, too varied, and too filled with irregularities to be resolved just by algorithms and computers with lots of data. One of the most promising new trends is a movement toward more intensive man–machine collaboration in large-scale translation projects. The combination of SMT with massive online collaboration could bring the industry to a tipping point that really does help MT technology to become more pervasive.

Microsoft has led the way in showing how much value domain-focused MT can provide to a global customer base. The company is now adding crowdsourcing into the mix and having its best resellers manage crowdsourced editing to improve the raw MT that is in the bulk of the Microsoft Knowledge Base.

Asia Online has embarked on a project to translate the English Wikipedia into several south Asian languages in an attempt to reduce information poverty in these regions. Initially, internal staff linguists post-edit and help raise the quality of raw MT to a level at which 100 percent comprehensibility is reached. This still imperfect content is then released, and people who use the content, or roaming bands of bilingual surfers, help to put the finishing touches to the output. Some do it because they want to help, and others take part because they might win prizes. These edit changes flow back into the learning systems, and the systems continue to improve. Based on early results, it is conceivable that the translation quality will gradually improve. Even Google invites the casual user to suggest a better translation. These efforts will steadily drive SMT quality higher.

Should companies therefore expect that MT is their future? The best MT systems will need to earn the respect of real translators, professional and amateur alike, and these translators will be interested in using these systems only if they have evidence that they can work more quickly, more efficiently, and more effectively using the technology.

In addition, translators are among the most competent people to judge what is good and what is not on issues related to translation. Until MT vendors are willing to submit to their judgment and earn their approval, or even an endorsement from them, the MT market will stumble along in the doldrums as it has for the last fifty years, making empty promises.

The combination of massive computing power, ever-increasing volumes of clean bilingual text, and a growing band of motivated bilingual humans (not always professional translators) will be the key forces that drive this technology forward. The scientists may also produce better algorithms along the way, but their contributions will be relatively small. The most important driving force will be the human need to know and understand what other humans across the globe are saying – the need to share and the urge to learn. The breakthrough that will end (or at least reduce) the language barrier will be social, not technical.

Strategic industry insight 3: game localization's challenges and opportunities[8]

The final strategic insight presented in this chapter is about the growing need for video game localization. Video game localization has emerged as a new and growing field ripe with possibilities for content localization. In fact, the young field of game localization is already a complex mesh of technology, culture, entertainment, global user base, and geopolitical controversies. In this section, geocultural expert and game localization expert Kate Edwards presents some insights into the challenges and opportunities of game localization.

Game localization

According to a recent study by PricewaterhouseCoopers (2010), the projected global revenue of the video game industry is expected to reach around $84 billion by 2014; this represents an incredible 100 percent increase from the $41.9 billion in 2007. Without question, the gaming industry is one of the fastest-growing media segments, and it is forging the way as one of the frontiers of global "transmedia" (i.e., content that is served to consumers across a wide range of locales and platforms, including movies, books, games, mobile apps, etc.).

What is ever more telling in these numbers is the forecast that sales in the United States will lag behind the rest of the world during the next several years, averaging around a still admirable 6 percent annual growth, while Asia and the Europe/Middle East/Africa region will average over 10 percent. What does this mean for the game developers and publishers? Quite simply put, the ongoing desire to increase revenue will require companies to increase their global distribution. As games are distributed and consumed globally, their localization to different locale-specific requirements (translation, cultural adaptation, content adaptation, etc.) is becoming more important. Game localization already accounts for roughly 50 percent of the global game industry's revenue, but, as the industry continues to grow, game content will be developed for many new cultures, languages, and locales. Creating content that appeals to a more global gamer will be increasingly critical for companies, which in turn requires new market strategies, new localization challenges, and the introduction of culturalization as an increasingly critical success factor.

---

[8] This strategic insight on game localization has been contributed by Kate Edwards, geographer and principal consultant, Englobe Inc.

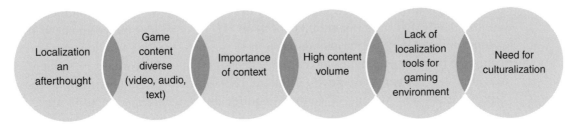

Figure 10.2 Game localization challenges

Game localization challenges

Games represent a unique challenge to localization companies, for a number of reasons (see Figure 10.2). First and foremost, the game development community has a persistent perception that localization is something that always should occur late in the development cycle. To many developers, localization is seen as something of a nuisance, and even burdensome to their creative process and vision for the content, while, for localization personnel, the task of localizing staggering amounts of game content in a very limited time window before release is daunting at best. This is especially challenging as AAA game titles become larger in scope. Just as an example, the game title *Fable II* (2008) had more than 400,000 words to translate and 48,000 audio files per language to record, among other types of content that required localization.

Moreover, it is not just the perception of localization as an afterthought that is a problem, but the lack of knowledge on the part of developers as to what localization actually entails. Many of the common problems relate to internationalization practices, such as the very common problem in which developers create code to accommodate the English language, while not accounting for the vast linguistic differences between languages. Related issues include aspects such as language length (e.g., English versus German), grammar, and the notions of both gender and tense in choosing an appropriate word in another language. With the advent of online translation resources, developers sometimes imagine that translation is a fairly straightforward exercise, as easy as going to Google's translation site or using Babelfish. Although more sophisticated machine translation alternatives, as discussed in the previous section, are emerging, high-quality translation is attainable only with expert, experienced translators – particularly when dealing with creative content. Game players are not naïve; if they see a poorly localized game, many will stop playing it and then tell their friends. In fact, players in regions such as Scandinavia tend to prefer the original English version, not just because of their good English skills but because the quality of localized games in Scandinavian languages has often been subpar.

Another major localization challenge is that games are an aggregation of many different types of content – from text to audio to video to animations, and so forth – which are applied in a wide variety of game types, such as role-playing games, first-person shooter, and real-time strategy. The diversity in content coupled with the volume essentially demands that the game developer has an excellent content management system or some efficient method for managing content versions, tracking locations, and overseeing the non-sequential development of a product that will eventually be sequential in nature (i.e., the game will have a coherent, consistent flow from beginning to end).

This variety and volume of content requires atypical localization tools that are unique to the gaming environment, in which context is critical. To achieve higher-quality localization, tools such as those that allow in-game editing and localization are essential (i.e., the WYSIWYG approach). However, because localization still has a "secondary" role in game development, many game developers will not invest in such localization tools, and they still deliver dialog and text to be translated in the form of a spreadsheet with no images and no clues as to the context during game play. This is very likely the reason why, when translating the game *Modern Warfare 2* (2009) from English to Japanese, the translators accidentally translated the line "Remember, no Russian" to "Kill them, they are Russians." This made a lot of Japanese gamers confused, as they started shooting the wrong targets in the game! However, if the translators had seen the line spoken by the character in the context of the actual scene, the meaning would have been much more obvious.

One issue that is becoming increasingly more challenging for game localization is the need for content "culturalization," namely accounting for the potential geopolitical and cultural sensitivities in game content that can cause a severe backlash from local governments and consumers. Many games typically touch upon fictitious and actual socio-historical scenarios, feature new cultures (including religions, languages, and ethnicities) derived from actual ones, and employ a very generous use of symbols, flags, maps, and other content known to have higher propensity for sensitivity. There has been little question that game developers often intentionally incorporate themes and scenarios that are more "edgy" and potentially volatile. This is to be expected in any expressive art form, and games are no different. One example of this type of issue is a scenario from the original PC game *Age of Empires*, in which the Yamato armies of Japan invade the Korean peninsula and overwhelm the Chosen Empire. Historians tell us that this is what occurred, and so the game designers diligently replicated history. However, the government of South Korea saw things differently, and disputed the historical accuracy of the game scenario. To appease government concerns, a downloadable patch was developed that changed the scenario so that it was more in favor of the Chosen Empire armies.

What needs to happen to change the perception and process of game localization?

The biggest change that needs to occur among game professionals is realizing that the model of developing a game for a single market and then passing it over to localization is antiquated. We all live and work within an interconnected, dynamic, global content market. Any content that is released in one market, particularly the United States and Europe, will be distributed worldwide literally overnight. Whether companies desire it or not, their content will be swiftly viewed by diverse cultures and judged on its initial merit. If the version they view is intended only for a US audience, the local perception of the game may be radically different from what was intended.

The goal, then, must be to embrace the reality that content development is global; a game should be designed and developed from the outset as a global-facing piece of content. When even that one assumption is changed, the game development process matures on all levels: designers can create beyond a single market, and programmers will account for all the linguistic challenges in code. The end result is a game that will have a greater potential for universal appeal, will have a greater global reach, and will thus maximize global revenue.

Once this realization is in place, localization becomes an integral aspect of the game design and development team. Tools will be developed on a par with the quality of tools available for designers and developers, allowing localization to be part of the creative process from day one. When you think about it, it is almost a "no brainer" proposition: as artists, writers, and designers create from their specific cultural context, the local-ization personnel should work alongside them to help guide their choices to be more inclusive of various languages and cultures. This would also help to alleviate the stress of making fundamental changes late in the process; early tweaks are always far cheaper than late revisions. Fortunately, this notion of localization as an afterthought is slowly changing through various awareness efforts, including those of the Game Localization Special Interest Group within the International Game Developers Association.

The culturalization of game content will become an increasingly important aspect of game development as developers and publishers push further into new markets. Many areas of the world remain untapped, and much of the "usual" fare of game titles is becoming tiresome to the saturated markets in the United States and Europe. If the industry is to continue to expand both creatively and geographically, it must account for these cultural risks in order to maintain open markets for its games as well as to improve government relations and its public image among local gamers. Usually such problems are very limited in nature, such as a single audio file containing chanting from the Qur'an, or a misused symbol, or the use of a sensitive word. They can often be extracted "surgically" very easily, but only if identified and addressed as early as pos-sible in the development cycle.

Well-executed localization and culturalization within a game development cycle do not happen overnight, nor without some commitment of resources, but the benefits to a company's content quality will prove to be an invaluable long-term return on invest-ment. Game developers should create the games they want to create, but they should not forget the global, multicultural audience who will be participating in their vision and, hopefully, enjoying it without any linguistic or cultural disruption. Although localization and culturalization may seem likely to dampen the creative forces behind game development, they are actually a path to ensuring that the creative vision can be enjoyed by as many cultures as possible. Thus the real key to successful localization is to simply act respectfully and proactively to the local market's expectations, taking a moment to view the game content from the local context.

Chapter summary

- A number of emerging trends enhance the scope of localization; companies can take advantage of opportunities for leveraging emerging localization technologies.
- The growth of the mobile web highlights the importance of creating web content that is optimized for mobile devices.
- For mobile devices, websites need to be optimized in terms of size, presentation, navigation, coding, encoding, content, etc.
- The benefits of crowdsourcing include monetization opportunities, cost reductions, innovation, access to worldwide communities, search engine optimization, and web globalization.
- Some challenges associated with crowdsourcing include ensuring the quality of the content, recruiting community users, meeting timelines, implementing reward structures, protecting intellectual property, and bridging the digital divide.
- Some challenges to community translation are finding communities, matching the content with the communities, aligning community objectives and organization objectives, and identifying project management controls.
- RbMT systems comprise a dictionary and a set of rules for the language combinations that the system can process.
- SMT systems are developed by computationally analyzing large bodies of parallel bilingual text, which they treat as strings of characters; determining patterns; and exploiting these regularities by matching these patterns in new material that is presented for translation.
- Challenges associated with game localization include these factors: localization is not seen as a critical process in game development; there is a lack of localization tools and skills; games are highly context-dependent and have diverse content; and the importance of culturalization is not fully appreciated.

REFERENCES

Benou, Poulcheriam, and Bitos, Vaios 2008. "Developing mobile commerce applications," *Journal of Electronic Commerce in Organizations* 6: 63–78.

Butcher, Dan 2010. "41pc of merchants have seen positive ROI from mobile commerce: study," Mobile Commerce Daily, November 17, www.mobilecommercedaily.com/2010/11/17/41pc-of-merchants-have-seen-positive-roi-from-mobile-commerce-study.

CNNIC 2010. *Statistical Report on Internet Development in China: July 2010.* CNNIC; available at www.cnnic.cn/uploadfiles/pdf/2010/8/24/93145.pdf.

dotMobi 2010. "2010 study of mobile web trends shows continued explosion of mobile-friendly content," dotMobi, October 20, mtld.mobi/node/1857.

Howe, Jeff 2008. *Why the Power of the Crowd Is Driving the Future of Business*. Crown Business.

Iandoli, Luca, Klein, Mark, and Zollo, Giuseppe 2008. "Can we exploit collective intelligence for collaborative deliberation? The case of the climate change collaboratorium," Research paper no. 4675–08 Sloan School of Management, Massachusetts Institute of Technology.

ITU 2010. "The world in 2010: the rise of 3G," ITU; available at www.itu.int/ITU-D/ict/material/FactsFigures2010.pdf.

King, Cindy 2010. "Do you need social media localization?" Cindy King, April 28, cindyking.biz/localization-of-social-media.

Morgan Stanley 2009. *The Mobile Internet Report: Ramping Faster than Desktop Internet, the Mobile Internet Will Be Bigger than Most Think*. Morgan Stanley; available at www.morganstanley.com/institutional/techresearch/pdfs/mobile_internet_report.pdf.

Nielsen Company 2010a. "Going global means going mobile in emerging markets," Nielsen Wire, August 17, blog.nielsen.com/nielsenwire/global/going-global-means-going-mobile-in-emerging-markets.

2010b. "Mobile snapshot: smartphones now 28% of U.S. cellphone market," Nielsen Wire, November 1, blog.nielsen.com/nielsenwire/online_mobile/mobile-snapshot-smartphones-now-28-of-u-s-cellphone-market.

OECD 2007. *Participative Web and User-Created Content: Web 2.0, Wikis and Social Networking*. OECD; available at www.oecd.org/dataoecd/57/14/38393115.pdf.

PricewaterhouseCoopers 2010. *Global Entertainment and Media Outlook 2010–2014*. PricewaterhouseCoopers.

Rumelhart, David E. 1992. "Towards a microstructural account of human reasoning," in Davis, S. (ed.), *Connectionism: Theory and Practice*. Oxford University Press: 69–83.

Scott, David M. 2009. *The New Rules of Marketing and PR: How to Use News Releases, Blogs, Podcasting, Viral Marketing and Online Media to Reach Buyers Directly*. John Wiley.

Stelzner, Michael A. 2010. *2010 Social Media Marketing Industry Report: How Marketers Are Using Social Media to Grow Their Businesses*. Social Media Examiner; available at www.socialmediaexaminer.com/social-media-marketing-industry-report-2010.

Tapscott, Don, and Williams, Anthony D. 2006. *Wikinomics: How Mass Collaboration Changes Everything*. Portfolio.

Tsirulnik, Giselle 2010. "Top mcommerce trends for 2010: what's hot and what's not," Mobile Commerce Daily, August 3, www.mobilecommercedaily.com/2010/08/03top-mcommerce-trends-for-2010-%E2%80%93-what%E2%80%99s-hot-and-what%E2%80%99s-not.

Weinberg, Tamar 2009. *The New Community Rules: Marketing on the Social Web*. O'Reilly Media.

WEB GLOBALIZATION RESOURCES

Included is a compilation of various resources that you may find useful in your web globalization efforts. This list is by no means exhaustive, and it represents some resources I know of or have come across during my research. The mention of the companies and their products does not imply any endorsement, and readers should carry out their own research.

Global e-commerce resources

- **ECT News Network** is one of the largest e-business and technology news publishers in the United States. The network includes several e-business and technology news sites: the E-Commerce Times®, TechNewsWorld™, LinuxInsider™, CRM Buyer™, and Mac News World. www.ectnews.com.
- **Internet Retailer** includes the website and the magazine, which together cover the latest trends and developments in e-tailing worldwide. www.internetretailer.com.
- **Internet World Stats** is an international website that features up-to-date world internet usage, population statistics, and internet market research data for some 233 individual countries and world regions. www.internetworldstats.com.
- **The Internet.com** is a comprehensive source for the latest global news and information about information technology and the internet. The site has five content channels: Developer, Internet News, IT, Personal Technology, and Small Business. www.internet .com.
- **ZDNET** carries news, reviews, articles and resources related to IT and e-commerce. ZDNET has news editions for the United States, China, Australia, the United Kingdom, France, Germany, and Japan. www.zdnet.com.
- **Forrester Research** is an independent research company that produces research reports and also consults in the technology and business area. The company has in the past published several reports related to global e-commerce issues. www.forrester.com.
- **eMarketer** is a business information service. It provides trend analysis on digital marketing and media by aggregating, filtering, and organizing data from over 4,000 global sources. www.emarketer.com.
- **Byte Level Research**, headed by industry expert John Yunker, provides cutting-edge research related to various issues in web globalization, such as global navigation, international domains, translation resources, etc. www.bytelevel.com.
- **Common Sense Advisory** is a market research company involved in assisting clients to operationalize, benchmark, optimize, and innovate industry best practices in translation, localization, interpreting, globalization, and internationalization. www.commonsenseadvisory .com.

- **Wilson Web** is a website that contains a repository of articles, books, and resources related to various issues in web marketing and e-commerce in general. www.wilsonweb.com.

Universities and institutes for localization training

- **Saint Louis University** offers the Executive Online Certificate in Web Globalization Management (**John Cook School of Business**). This is an online program for both non-technical and technical students. It provides one of the most comprehensive educations concerning a range of issues related to web globalization. www.globalizationexecutive .com or www.slu.edu/x25816.xml.
- **California State University (CSU) at Chico, Center for Regional and Continuing Education**, offers localization and localization project management certificates. http:// rce.csuchico.edu/localize/certification.asp.
- **The Localization Institute** offers various collaborative programs with other universities and also offers seminars in various localization and internationalization topics. www .localizationinstitute.com.
- **Austin Community College** offers certificate programs in connection with localization. www.austincc.edu/techcert/localization.php.
- **Monterey Institute of International Studies, California**, has a couple of courses in localization that are a part of the broader degree program: IMGT 8601, Globalization/ Localization in Management, and IMGT 8672, IT Localization. It also offers a Master's program in Translation. www.miis.edu/academics/courses/node/1351.
- **Kent State University** offers a Master of Arts in Translation (French, German, Japanese, Russian, or Spanish) and Ph.D. in Translation Studies. www.kent.edu/mcls/graduate/phd _translation.cfm.
- **The Institute of Localisation Professionals** offers onsite workshops in localization. www.tilponline.net/about.shtml.
- **Professional and Continuing Education University of Washington** offers a certificate program in the area of software localization. www.pce.uw.edu/certificates/localization -software.html.
- **The University of Limerick** offers an M.Sc. in Global Computing and Localization. www .csis.ul.ie/course/LM632.

Internationalization (I18n) resources

- **I18n Guy** is a resource site run by industry expert Tex Texin. The site compiles various checklists, standards, and resources relating to internationalization, and also provides other web globalization resources. www.i18nguy.com.
- **W3C Internationalization Activity** is part of the W3C group, and its mission is to ensure that W3C's formats and protocols are usable worldwide in all languages. The site provides various internationalization resources. www.w3.org/International.
- **Go Global Developer Center** is a resource by Microsoft that provides a good overview for creating internationalized or world-ready applications. http://msdn.microsoft.com/ en-us/goglobal.
- **Sun Developer Network** has source material, sample codes, testing tools, and useful links to help you learn more about software internationalization and localization. http:// developers.sun.com/global.

- **ICU – International Components for Unicode** is a mature, widely used set of C/C++ and Java libraries providing Unicode and globalization support for software applications. http://site.icu-project.org/docs.
- **The Unicode Consortium** is a non-profit organization devoted to developing, maintaining, and promoting software internationalization standards and data, particularly the Unicode standard. http://unicode.org.
- **The Unicode CLDR** provides key building blocks for software to support the world's languages, with the largest and most extensive standard repository of locale data. http://cldr.unicode.org.
- *Globalization Handbook for the Microsoft .NET platform,* parts I to IV, by industry internationalization expert Bill Hall. www.multilingual.com/books.
- **Multilingual Computing's** *Internationalization: Getting Started Guide.* April/May 2007. www.multilingual.com/downloads/printSupp87.pdf.
- **Dr. International's** *Developing International Software*, 2nd edition, 2002. Microsoft Press.

Website cultural customization resources

- **Cultural resources and country cultural rankings** The website of Geert Hofstede provides country rankings on various cultural values. The website also has information on the Culture GPS iPhone tool. www.geert-hofstede.com.
- **Cultural IQ test and more** On the CulturallyCustomized website you can find a quick and fun cultural IQ test, as well as resources and books related to the cultural customization of websites. www.theculturallycustomizedwebsite.com.
- **Interesting article on global gateway pages** http://uxmag.com/strategy/select-country-select-language.
- **Web globalization report card** Byte Level Research annually publishes its rankings of top global sites in the "Web globalization report card." The report card analyzes websites on global gateway design and other localization parameters. http://bytelevel.com/reportcard2011.
- **American Registry for Internet Numbers (ARIN)** is a regional internet registry (RIR). www.arin.net.
- **Geolocation services providers** These are some companies that provide IP address geolocation services:
  - Quova: www.quova.com;
  - IP2Location: www.ip2location.com; and
  - Ipligence: www.ipligence.com.
- **When to use language negotiation** A document published by W3C. www.w3.org/International/questions/qa-when-lang-neg.
- **A color chart** showing the meaning of colors in different countries can be found at www.globalization-group.com/edge/resources/color-meanings-by-culture.
- **Cultural Interface Design Advisor Tool** (CIDAT) A tool developed at the National Research Council, Canada. www.nrc-cnrc.gc.ca/obj/iit-iti/doc/cidat_e.pdf.
- **Country etiquette guides** Intercultural communication resources can be found on the website of Kwintessential. www.kwintessential.co.uk.
- **Insights related to working with high- and low-context cultures** www.culture-at-work.com/highlow.html.

Automation tools for the web globalization value chain

Internationalization tools

- **Globalyzer 3.0** by Lingoport helps entire enterprises and development teams effectively internationalize existing code and automatically scans, tracks, and reports on internationalization progress and status. www.lingoport.com/software-internationalization -products/globalyzer-3.
- **World Wide Navi** (wwnavi) is a software internationalization tool that helps in the following ways: detecting problems in source codes, summarizing them, suggesting solutions, indicating missing codes, automatically externalizing embedded strings, etc. www.kokusaika.jp.
- **The globalization kit**, by Globalization Partners International, helps scan source code in any languages (ASP, JSP, PHP, c#, VB, HTML, JavaScript, Java, etc.) and on the basis of a predefined set of rules, and helps in the detection of i18n issues and their management. www.globalizationpartners.com.
- **Alchemy Catalyst** is one of the available visual localization tools in the market. www .alchemysoftware.ie.
- **SDL Passolo 2011** is another software visual localization tool, which facilitates the translation of graphical user interfaces. www.sdl.com/en/language-technology/products/ software-localization/sdl-passolo.asp.
- **Visual Localize** is also a CAT tool for translating software and adapting the GUI. www .visloc.com.
- **RC-WinTrans 7** is a software localization environment for localizing the GUI of Microsoft Windows Win32 and .NET 1.1 and .NET 2.0 Windows. www.schaudin.com.
- **Rainbow**, by Enlaso technologies, is a Java application that helps with preparing files in various formats (XML, SVG, etc.) and converting files from one encoding to another. www.translate.com.

Authoring tools

- **The Enterprise Authoring Platform**, by Author-it, is a collaborative authoring environment that promotes content reuse and repurposing. www.author-it.com.
- **Sajan Authoring Coach™** is an authoring memory tool. It is not an editor but, rather, works along with editors to enhance the authoring process and reuse existing content. www.sajan.com.
- **MadCap** produces the Authoring and Translation Product Suite and other content authoring and publishing applications. www.madcapsoftware.com.
- **crossAuthor Linguistic** by Congree provides rule-based authoring assistance, with authoring memory, and a terminology system. www.congree.com.

Translation memory and terminology management tools

The following companies provide TM tools as part of their localization solutions.

- **Across Language Server** includes both translation memory and terminology management applications in its overall localization solution. www.across.net.
- **MultiCorpora's MultiTrans** global management system includes TM and terminology application. www.multicorpora.com.

- **SDL Trados and SDL Multiterm** are the translation memory and terminology management applications by SDL. www.sdl.com.
- **STAR Transit and TermStar** provide both TM and terminology management functions and also testing. www.star-group.ne.
- **OmegaT** is a free translation memory application written in Java. www.omegat.org.

Translation management systems

- **Freeway** is Lionbridge's online service delivery platform for overall localization workflow management. https://freeway.lionbridge.com.
- **SDL Translation Management System** is the TMS by SDL that centralizes translation process automation for control and collaboration. www.sdl.com.
- **MultiTrans** by MultiCorpora is another TMS for automating localization workflow. www.multicorpora.com.
- **The Across Language Server** by Across Systems is the central platform for managing corporate language resources and translation processes. www.across.net.
- **GCMS™** is an enterprise-class translation management system by Sajan. www.sajan.com.
- **Lingotek's Collaborative Translation Platform** is another TMS with translation technologies, workflow management, and community collaboration. www.lingotek.com.

Localization project management tools

- **LTC Worx** is a business management solution that handles project management tasks and other business-related functions for facilitating localization workflow. www.langtech.co.uk.
- **Plunet Business Manager**, by Plunet GmbH, is a localization project management tool for optimizing localization workflow. www.plunet.de.
- **The Globalization Project Management Suite**, by Globalization Partners International, contains all the standard project management features to facilitate localization workflow. www.globalizationpartners.com.
- **Project Open** is an open-source-based project management application. www.project-open.com.

Machine translation tools

- **Lionbridge GeoFluent** is a real-time automated translation solution by Lionbridge. It combines translation workspace, cloud-based translation memory capability, real-time translation services, and IBM's machine translation engine. http://en-us.lionbridge.com.
- **SDL Language Weaver** is a real-time automated translation tool. www.sdl.com.
- **Asia Online** provides a machine translation tool based on a statistical machine translation platform for handling real-time translation needs. www.asiaonline.net.
- **Systran Translation** provides a hybrid machine translation solution that combines rule-based and statistical machine translation methods. www.systransoft.com.

Search engine optimization resources

Keyword suggestions, metadata, relevancy, and density tools and guidelines

- **Google Webmaster guidelines** will help Google find, index, and rank your site.
- **Google AdWords** keyword suggestion tool helps find various keywords based on selected words or phrases.

- **Word Tracker** provides a free keyword tracking tool. http://freekeywords.wordtracker.com.
- **Compete** provides free site traffic information and lists of the most popular sites across the internet, ranked by any metric available on Compete.com. http://compete.com.
- **Trellian's Keyword Discovery** tool compiles keyword search statistics from major search engines of the world. www.keyworddiscovery.com.
- **SubmitExpress** provides various free tools for generating and checking keywords. It also has various other search analytic tools. www.submitexpress.com.
- **Keyword Density Analyzer** is a free tool for analyzing keyword density on your web page. www.keyworddensity.com.
- **WeBuildPages** provides SEO and internet marketing services, including keyword suggestions. www.webuildpages.com.
- **Google Rankings** is a free search engine optimization tool for checking the ranking of the web page on Google. www.googlerankings.com.
- www.mseo.com has a foreign search engine directory for various countries.

Internationalized domain name resources

- **The Internet Corporation for Assigned Names and Numbers** coordinates the global internet's systems of unique identifiers, in particular to ensure the stable and secure operation of the internet's unique identifier systems. www.icann.org.
- **The Multilingual Internet Names Consortium** is a non-profit organization that focuses on developing and promoting multilingual internet domain names and keywords. www.minc.org.
- **InterNIC** is the organization that provides public information about internet domain name registration services. www.internic.net.
- **The Internet Assigned Numbers Authority** (IANA) deals with the global coordination of domain names, IP addressing, and other Internet Protocol resources. www.iana.org.
- **DENIC** is the central registry for all domains under the top-level domain ".de" (Germany). www.denic.de.
- **Nominet** is the internet registry for ".uk" domain names. www.nominet.org.uk.

Link ranking analysis resources

- **Alexa** provides site traffic and link information for sites from various countries. www.alexa.com.
- **PRChecker** is a free tool to check Google's page rank of websites. www.prchecker.info.
- **Whois** can help you find registration data on domains. www.whois.net.

Social networking sites

- www.internationalindustrialseo.com/international-social-marketing.
- Facebook, MySpace, YouTube, LinkedIn, dig.com, Yahoo! Buzz, del.icio.us.
- Bebo, Orkut, Xiaonei, Kaixin001, Odnoklassniki, SkyRock, StudiVZ, Sonico, Wamba.

SEO products and services

- **Localization companies** providing multilingual SEO services: Acclaro, Conversis, Lionbridge, and Globalization Partners International.
- **International SEO blog** has various resources on international SEO. www.internationalindustrialseo.com.

- **Trellian** provides a complete SEO toolkit. www.trellian.com.
- **Web CEO** provides search engine marketing and optimization software. www.webceo.com.
- **Mcanerin** provides multinational, multilingual SEO and SEM services. www.mcanerin.com.
- **WebCertain** provides multilingual search engine optimization services. www.webcertain.com.

Global website usability

- **ISO 9241–151: 2008** Ergonomics of human–system interaction – part 151: guidance on World Wide Web user interfaces. www.iso.org.
- **W3C Web Accessibility Initiative** Resources for developing a web accessibility business case for your organization. www.w3.org/WAI/bcase/resources.html.
- **The Massachusetts Institute of Technology's Information Services and Technology** website has a usability guideline reference chart. http://ist.mit.edu/services/consulting/usability/guidelines#lang-content.
- **Best Practices in Web Globalization** This white paper provides some interesting user experience guidelines. http://globe.miis.edu/LB_Web_Globalization_Best_Practices.pdf.
- **The Usability Professionals' Association** supports people who research, design, and evaluate the user experience of products and services. www.upassoc.org.

Usability testing and web analytics companies

- **Google Analytics** is the enterprise-class web analytics solution. www.google.com/intl/en/analytics.
- **Webtrends** is one of the leading web analytics companies. It also specializes in social media measurement and paid-search optimization. www.webtrends.com.
- **Coremetrics** positions itself as a marketing optimization company specializing in web analytics and integrated marketing optimization applications. www.coremetrics.com.
- **Usercentric** provides various usability services, including usability testing, usability evaluations, user-centered design, user research, and eye tracking. www.usercentric.com.
- **Omniture** has now been acquired by Adobe. It provides various web usability services, such as online analytics, social media analytics, multichannel analytics, etc. www.omniture.com.
- **TandemSeven** provides various web usability and testing services and it also designs and builds applications and portals. www.tandemseven.com.
- **Human Factors International, Inc.** provides various user-centered design services. The website also has several resources for usability issues, including a usability quiz. www.humanfactors.com/downloads/webquiz.asp.

Eye-tracking software

- **Eyetracking, Inc.**, founded by Dr. Sandra Marshall and several colleagues from the Cognitive Ergonomics Research Facility at San Diego State University. www.eyetracking.com.
- **Cambridge Research Systems'** eye trackers. www.crsltd.com/catalog/eyetracker-toolbox.
- **Interactive Minds GmbH** NYAN 2.0XT Eye Tracking Data Analysis Suite. www.interactive-minds.com.
- **Tobii Technology's** eye-tracking and eye control software. www.tobii.com.

Localization magazines, books, and trade publications

- *Multilingual Computing* is a publication that serves as an information source for the localization, internationalization, translation, and language technology industry. Its website and print supplement carry an extensive resource section on localization issues. www.multilingual.com.
- **Singh, Nitish, and Pereira, Arun (2005).** *The Culturally Customized Web Site: Customizing Web Sites for the Global Marketplace.* Elsevier Butterworth-Heinemann.
- **Esselink, Bert (2000).** *Practical Guide to Localization:* John Benjamins.
- **Yunker, John (2002).** *Beyond Borders: Web Globalization Strategies.* New Riders Press.
- **DePalma, Donald A. (2002).** *Business without Borders: A Strategie Guide to Global Marketing.* Global Vista Press.
- **Dr. International (2002).** *Developing International Software,* 2nd edition. Microsoft Press.
- **Chandler, H. M. (2004).** *The Game Localization Handbook.* Charles River Media.
- **tcworld magazine** is tekom's e-magazine for international information management. tcworld focuses on how companies face the challenges of communicating with customers, partners, and associates in an increasing number of international markets. www.tcworld.info.
- **GALAxy Newsletter** is a localization-industry-focused newsletter published by the Globalization and Localization Association (GALA). www.gala-global.org/GALAxy.

Professional associations

- **W3C** is an international community that develops standards to ensure the long-term growth of the web. www.w3.org.
- **GALA** promotes collaboration between all companies working in the translation, localization, internationalization, and globalization industry. www.gala-global.org.
- **TAUS** is a think tank for the translation industry, undertaking research for buyers and providers of translation services and technologies. www.translationautomation.com.
- **The American Translators Association** provides resources related to translation and a translator directory. www.atanet.org.
- **The Unicode Consortium** is a non-profit organization devoted to developing, maintaining, and promoting software internationalization standards and data, particularly the Unicode standard, which specifies the representation of text in all modern software products and standards. www.unicode.org/consortium.
- **ACL** (the Association for Computational Linguistics) is *the* international scientific and professional society for people working on problems involving natural language and computation. www.alcus.org.
- **ELIA** is a non-profit organization, aiming to represent and promote the interests of the language industry in Europe. www.elia-association.org.
- **LISA** has been involved with the development of standards, but its website has recently been closed down.
- **The STC** is an individual membership organization dedicated to advancing the arts and sciences of technical communication. www.stc.org.
- **tekom** is one of Europe's largest professional associations for technical communication. www.tekom.de.

Conferences and workshops in the web globalization area

- **Localization World** conferences are dedicated to the language and localization industries. They include educational and networking opportunities. This is one of the largest localization events held annually in North America and Europe. www.localizationworld.com.
- **The WorldWare** conference illuminates the "Why?" and "What?" of internationalization in a two-day conference setting. www.worldwareconference.com.
- **The Language of Business** conference series is a localization industry educational and networking event. www.gala-global.org/language-business-conferences.
- **TC World** conferences cover broad areas of localization, technical writing, and business. www.tcworld.info.
- **The Localization Certification Workshop** is organized annually by CSU Chico, the Localization Institute, and the author of this book to provide three days of educational training in localization. The workshop also includes extensive online resources. http://rce.csuchico.edu/localize/certification.asp.
- **The Localization Project Management** workshop is organized annually by CSU Chico, the Localization Institute, and the author of this book to provide two days of educational training in localization project management. The workshop also includes extensive online resources. http://rce.csuchico.edu/localize/projectmanagement.asp.
- **Project Management Round Tables** are organized annually by the Localization Institute for senior project managers in the localization field. www.localizationinstitute.com.
- **The Internationalization and Unicode** conference is one of the technical conferences focusing on multilingual global software and web internationalization issues. www.unicodeconference.org.

International business resources and databases

- **GMID** Euromonitor International's Global Market Information Database is an integrated online information system providing business intelligence on industries, countries, and consumers. www.euromonitor.com.
- **Export.gov** is the official US government export resource site, and it includes a variety of resources related to export/import documentation, market research, rules and regulations, etc.
- **GlobalEDGE** is one of the most extensive resources related to the international business area, covering research reports, country resources, trade data, international business tools, courses, etc. GlobalEDGE is hosted by the Center for International Business Education and Research at Michigan State University. http://globaledge.msu.edu/resourcedesk.
- **The World Trade Organization** is the global international organization dealing with the rules of trade between nations. The website has various resources relating to world trade, reports, and audio and video material. www.wto.org.
- **The World Bank** has more than 80,000 documents related to global business and economic development. The site features country reports, economic sector reports, global data sets, etc. www.worldbank.org.
- **The OECD** publishes regular economic outlooks, annual overviews, and comparative statistics. www.oecd.org.
- **Plunkett Research**, Ltd. is a leading provider of business, internet, and industry information. It provides industry sector reports and analysis for e-commerce, financial services,

retail trade, internet infrastructure, infotech, energy/utilities, telecommunications, entertainment/media, health care, biotech, and engineering-/R&D-based industries. www.marketresearch.com.

- **Mintel** provides data, market research reports, comprehensive analysis, and timely recommendations relating to various industries for global business. www.mintel.com.
- **The Latin America Data Base** is the University of New Mexico's premier English-language Latin America news service. This service provides an online searchable archive of articles on politics, economics, human rights, the environment, etc. for Mexico, Central America and South America. http://ladb.unm.edu.

Academic journals for global e-commerce research

- The *International Journal of Electronic Commerce* serves the needs of researchers as well as practitioners and executives involved in electronic commerce. Topics published include e-commerce in business globalization, m-commerce and pervasive computing, business value in e-commerce, internet business models, e-tailing and multichannel selling, the social media, and social networks. http://www.gvsu.edu/business/ijec.
- The *International Journal of E-Business Research* publishes on topics such as global e-business, m-commerce, online consumer behavior, emerging e-business theories, architectures, and technologies. www.igi-global.com.
- The *Journal of Global Information Management* is the primary forum for researchers and practitioners to disseminate the evolution of knowledge in the theory and practice related to IT and the management of information resources at the international level. www.igi-global.com.
- The *MIS Quarterly* publishes research relating to the development of IT-based services, the management of IT resources, and the use, impact, and economics of IT with managerial, organizational, and societal implications. www.misq.org.
- *Communications of the ACM* is the leading print and online publication for the computing and information technology fields. http://cacm.acm.org.
- The *Journal of Management Information Systems* publishes on topics such as business globalization and IT, information systems for competitive positioning, business processes and management enabled by IT, the business value of information technology, and electronic commerce. www.jmis-web.org.
- The *Journal of Electronic Commerce Research* focuses on electronic commerce, including its theoretical foundations, infrastructure, and enabling technologies. www.csulb.edu/journals/jecr/a_j.htm.
- The *Journal of Advertising Research* is the research and development vehicle for professionals in all areas of marketing, including media, research, advertising, and communications. www.journalofadvertisingresearch.com.
- The *Journal of Interactive Marketing* publishes in topic areas such as databases, customer segmentation, the strategic use of information technology, customer relationship management, multichannel marketing, social networking, e-business strategy, online advertising, and online branding. www.elsevier.com.

Localization service providers

- **Acclaro** provides a full range of localization services, including quality assurance and testing. www.acclaro.com.

- **Conversis** is a localization service provider offering the full gamut of localization services and also international marketing consulting. www.conversisglobal.com.
- **Enlaso** provides enterprise language solutions, including translation, localization, interpreting services, and multilingual SEO. www.translate.com.
- **Globalization Partners International** is a full localization service provider. In addition, it provides various tools, multilingual SEO, and cultural adaptation services. www.globalizationpartners.com.
- **Jonckers** is another full-service localization service provider. www.jonckers.com.
- **Lionbridge** is one of the largest localization service and tool providers. It also offers authoring, product engineering, and global crowdsourcing services. http://en-us.lionbridge.com.
- **SDL** is another of the largest companies in the localization industry. Beyond localization services and tools, it also provides content management and e-commerce services. www.sdl.com.

INDEX